THE ILLUSTRATED WORLD ENCYCLOPEDIA OF
MARINE FISH
& SEA CREATURES

THE ILLUSTRATED WORLD ENCYCLOPEDIA OF
MARINE FISH
& SEA CREATURES

A natural history and identification guide to the animal life of the deep oceans, open seas, reefs, shallow waters, saltwater estuaries, and shorelines of the world

AMY-JANE BEER AND DEREK HALL

This edition is published by Lorenz Books

Lorenz Books is an imprint of Anness Publishing Ltd
Hermes House, 88–89 Blackfriars Road, London SE1 8HA
tel. 020 7401 2077; fax 020 7633 9499
www.lorenzbooks.com; www.annesspublishing.com

If you like the images in this book and would like to investigate using them for publishing, promotions or
advertising, please visit our website www.practicalpictures.com for more information.

© Anness Publishing Ltd 2007

UK agent: The Manning Partnership Ltd, 6 The Old Dairy,
Melcombe Road, Bath BA2 3LR; tel. 01225 478444; fax 01225 478440; sales@manning-
partnership.co.uk

UK distributor: Grantham Book Services Ltd, Isaac Newton Way,
Alma Park Industrial Estate, Grantham, Lincs NG31 9SD;
tel. 01476 541080; fax 01476 541061; orders@gbs.tbs-ltd.co.uk

North American agent/distributor: National Book Network,
4501 Forbes Boulevard, Suite 200, Lanham, MD 20706;
tel. 301 459 3366; fax 301 429 5746; www.nbnbooks.com

Australian agent/distributor: Pan Macmillan Australia, Level 18,
St Martins Tower, 31 Market St, Sydney, NSW 2000; tel. 1300 135 113; fax 1300 135 103;
customer.service@macmillan.com.au

New Zealand agent/distributor: David Bateman Ltd, 30 Tarndale Grove, Off Bush Road, Albany,
Auckland; tel. (09) 415 7664; fax (09) 415 8892

Because of our ongoing ecological investment programme, you, as our customer, can have the pleasure
and reassurance of knowing that a tree is being cultivated on your behalf to naturally replace the
materials used to make the book you are holding. For further information about this scheme, go to
www.annesspublishing.com/trees

A CIP catalogue record for this book is available from the British Library.
10 9 8 7 6 5 4 3 2

Publisher: Joanna Lorenz
Editorial Director: Helen Sudell
Project Editor: Catherine Stuart
Production Manager: Don Campiniello
Consultant: Geoff Swinney (National Museums of Scotland)
Book and Jacket Design: Nigel Partridge
Artists: Mike Atkinson, Peter Bull, Peter Barrett, Penny Brown, Jim Channell, Felicity Rose Cole,
Julius Csotonyi, Anthony Duke, Stuart Jackson Carter and Denys Ovenden

*Frontispiece: Small coral fish such as basslets (Grammatidae family) and damselfish (Pomacentridae) are drawn
away from the sanctuary of their habitat to feed on plankton.*
Endpaper: A grouper (Epinephelinae) lurks within its reef habitat.

CONTENTS

INTRODUCTION

To land-dwelling humans, the concept of maintaining life within a wholly aquatic world seems complex at best. Yet marine creatures face the same fundamental challenges as animals living in every other type of habitat: to function, grow and mature sufficiently to reproduce, and pass on their genes to future generations.

It seems an obvious statement to make, but water is quite different to air, and the inhabitants of an underwater environment face quite a different set of challenges to those met by plants and animals on dry land. But, in marvelling at the many ways marine organisms find to cope, it is easy to forget that, in fact, an aquatic life is the norm. Life on Earth originated in the seas, and it is perverse to think of this existence as being more difficult or alien than one reliant upon air. And, while the means of carving out an existence may differ dramatically between habitats, the principles of survival remain basically the same for all living organisms.

The principles of life

Life itself is a complex series of chemical reactions, but these reactions do not take place without the necessary chemical ingredients and

Below: Blackbar soldierfish (Myripristis jacobus) belong to a family group known as squirrelfish. As with a large number of creatures, their common name is based on a distinguishing physical characteristic: an oblique black bar behind the head.

expenditure of energy. Obtaining these essentials is the most immediate problem for any living thing. Plants, including most algae, derive their energy requirements directly from the sun – absorbing packets of light energy called photons using special pigments, mainly chlorophyll, in a process known as photosynthesis. They use solar energy to convert water and carbon dioxide (simple chemical compounds available to them in abundance) into more complex ones known as carbohydrates.

Above: Corals and sponges, such as this azure vase sponge (Callyspongia plicifera), may look rather like plants, but their reliance upon the consumption of other organisms to obtain energy means that they are classed as animals.

These carbohydrates can be stored within the plant and broken down later to release the energy required to make other reactions happen – either inside the original plant or within the body of any creature that eats it. For it to occur, this process of energy release requires the presence of another vital ingredient – oxygen. Animals cannot make use of the sun's energy directly – all their fuel ultimately comes from the consumption of other living organisms, such as plants, that act as fuel to be 'burned' in the presence of oxygen.

Throughout its life, the principal aims of any organism are to obtain fuel, obtain the oxygen with which to make use of the fuel, and to dispose of the waste products that result from this process. Of course, if its life is to be a successful one, the organism must live long enough to reproduce, and this means avoiding being eaten or otherwise destroyed. These aims apply to marine, freshwater and terrestrial organisms alike, but the adaptations required of the former depend upon a number of important environmental factors.

The challenges of marine life

Oxygen is 30 times more abundant in air than it is in water. Some areas of the ocean are more oxygen deficient than others – warm water contains less oxygen than does cold water, and some regions of the deep oceans have extremely low levels. Typically, animals living in these habitats compensate by

Above: Although the anatomy of a dolphin (Delphinidae) enables it to swim very fast, for much of the time it is comfortable cruising at a speed of around 6–8kmph/3.75–5mph.

having low-energy lifestyles and enhanced oxygen-gathering abilities – such as enlarged gills.

A further difficulty encountered by aquatic creatures is the relative density of water: moving through it simply requires more energy than moving through air, so marine organisms that need to move quickly are typically streamlined and hydrodynamic in shape. But the viscosity of water also has its

compensations – it offers many times more support than air. Terrestrial organisms, for example, need to invest significant resources in both skeletal and muscular tissues in order just to support the weight of their own body on land. The ocean-dwellers are spared this expense, and many marine organisms invest bodily resources very differently. For example, they may become extremely large, or supremely athletic or well armoured. Where light and food are in short supply, as in some deep-sea habitats, still further adaptations are required.

The aim of this book is to consider some of the major animal groups in the diverse marine community. Read on, and you will encounter the speed of predatory sharks and billfish, the ethereal beauty of corals and glass sponges, and deep sea squid so monstrous that their very existence was once considered a seafaring myth. Sadly, the combined pressures of commercial exploitation, pollution and global climate change are placing marine habitats under immense strain. Marine wildlife is therefore becoming a top priority for conservation groups, educational bodies and governments alike. Investing in the necessary research to understand and protect is vital for the future of all life in this vast, complex and mysterious realm.

Below: Porcupinefish belong to the order Tetradontiformes, which also includes pufferfish. These inhabitants of coral reefs can inflate their body by gradually filling their stomach with water. Once puffed out, spines set deep in the skin also become erect, helping to thwart attacks by predators.

THE CHALLENGE OF LIFE IN THE SEAS

The Earth is about 4,600 million years old. For about 500 million years, the planet was simply a fiery globe of molten rock, but by 4,100 million years ago it had cooled sufficiently for a crust to form. Water arrived on the planet through collisions with comets made up of ice, but for a long time all this moisture existed only as vapour in the atmosphere – the surface was far too hot to allow liquid water to form. Eventually, however, cooling took place and water began to accumulate in the hollows and depressions in the Earth's uneven crust.

Today, the Earth is a spinning blue sphere dominated by water. Observers from another world might puzzle over the fact that many races of its dominant species call it Earth, since dry land occupies such a small proportion of their actual living space. In terms of surface area, seas and oceans make up about 70 per cent of the planet's ecosystems. But if we think of the planet in three dimensions, taking account of depth as well as area, then water comprises a much greater proportion of all the available living space on the planet – about 1,370,000,000 cubic km/ 330,000,000 cubic miles of it. This vast marine realm and its manifestations, and the mind-boggling variety of creatures that live within it, are the subjects of this book.

Above, left to right: Life in the oceans is more varied than anywhere on dry land. Coral reefs, in particular, teem with life, and subaqua divers might find themselves sharing this underwater world with mushroom-like sea nettles (Chrysaora species), graceful turtles (Cheloniidae) or curious, carnivorous fish such as groupers (Serranidae).
Left: These humpback whales (Megaptera novaeangliae) are feeding on schooling fish, probably herring. They work as a team, circling the school and releasing great curtains of bubbles that frighten the fish, driving them into an ever tighter ball close to the surface, where they become trapped. Each whale is then able to engulf vast numbers of the cornered prey in its enormous mouth.

EVOLUTION OF MARINE LIFE

The story of life on Earth began in the sea. These waters were not the vast, often chilly oceans we know today. When the Earth was younger, the seas were mostly shallow and very warm, and they contained a potent blend of the chemicals that were to become the stuff of living organisms.

The warm cocktail of chemicals found in early seawater is popularly known as 'primordial soup'. Within this soup, molecules mixed and mingled and reacted with one another. In time, a new type of molecule appeared, one able to use the chemicals in the soup as the basic materials for creating new copies of itself. These copies went on to form further copies and those copies were copied until, in time, they were reproducing so rapidly that the building materials required to make more copies began to grow scarce.

Random chance

Thus, life on Earth faced its first crisis. It could all have ended there, but for the fact that the copying process was not always 100 per cent perfect. Random glitches in the process introduced an element of variability in the molecules produced. Some varieties were better at replicating than others and so they proliferated faster. A few more random glitches (or mutations as they are

Below: A lot of dry land was once ocean floor, and it is common to find marine fossils far from the shore. At Kings Canyon, in the heart of Australia, erosion has exposed the remains of a sea bed that was once buried and turned to rock. The ripples in the rock were created by water moving across the sand.

Above: Seaweeds have their origins in the very earliest multicellular life on Earth. This brown algae, Fucus vesiculosus, *has been used medicinally by humans for centuries.*

better known) gave some molecule complexes the ability to break down others, so that their basic materials could be extracted, recycled and used to make more copies of themselves.

Simple beginnings

The processes of building and copying molecules requires energy. Some replicating molecules evolved a means of obtaining the energy they required by breaking the chemical bonds of other molecules. Some small molecules have bonds that release relatively large amounts of energy and the larger replicators began converting other materials into these easy-to-use, easy-to-store fuels.

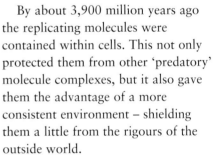

Right: Great chalky deposits formed on the ocean beds during the Cretaceous Period, some 135–65 million years ago, from the remains of shelled marine creatures such as the fossilized animals shown here. Some of these ancient invertebrates, such as ammonoids (shown middle), are now extinct as a group. Others, such as bivalve molluscs (top) and echinoids (bottom), continue to thrive in the seas.

By about 3,900 million years ago the replicating molecules were contained within cells. This not only protected them from other 'predatory' molecule complexes, but it also gave them the advantage of a more consistent environment – shielding them a little from the rigours of the outside world.

These first cells were little more than membrane-bound packets of self-replicating material enclosed along with a soup of useful molecules, including proteins, amino acids and lipids. But their simple and effective means of reproducing meant that inconceivable numbers of their direct descendants have continued copying and diversifying to this day as the simple life forms we know as bacteria and other prokaryotes.

Around 3,000 million years ago, certain bacteria evolved a means of producing energy from the sun (a process called photosynthesis), which produced a new by-product – oxygen gas. Oxygen levels in the oceans and the atmosphere increased dramatically, and proved toxic to many forms of

Above: The surface of a brain coral (Diploria species). Each stony compartment of the coral contains an individual coral polyp, a tiny animal a bit like an anemone.

bacterial life. Other life forms adapted, however, and found ways to burn the oxygen as part of the chemical process they used to obtain energy from their reserves of fuel.

Complexity develops

As successful as the bacteria undeniably are, they have not inherited the Earth or the oceans alone. About 2,100 million years ago, a more complex form of life arose. It seems likely that certain ancient bacteria developed a close, mutually beneficial (symbiotic) relationship, in which one type lived and replicated inside the other, benefiting from the host's protection while performing some other function that served the needs of the host. These symbionts were the precursors of cell organelles, such as mitochondria and plant chloroplasts. The cells in which they lived were the first eukaryotes.

Between 700 and 800 million years ago, eukaryotic cells began living in close-knit colonies, which evolved into the first truly multicellular organisms, in which different groups of cells took on specialist tasks. The first multicelled organisms were plants. Multicellular animal life took rather longer to get started, but by about 600 million years ago, at the end of the period known as the Precambrian, the sponges, flatworms and jellyfish were well established.

Then, at the start of the Cambrian Period, animal life underwent a diversification so sudden that it is now referred to as the Cambrian Explosion. In the space of a few million years, the ancestors of all the major animal

The Devonian: The age of fish

The first fish-like animals were small, jawless creatures known as agnathans. This branch of the tree of life originated in the late Cambrian, diversified dramatically in the Ordovician, but subsequently went into decline. Today, only two small groups of jawless fish, the hagfish and lampreys, remain and the seas are dominated by the other fish groups, which appeared later. Fish with jaws, such as the lungfish, whose dental anatomy is still seen in living lungfish, first appeared and increased hugely in numbers and diversity during the Devonian Period, 416–359 million years ago. Other groups that appeared at the time included primitive sharks called placoderms, now extinct, as well as the ancestors of modern sharks, the lobe-finned sarcopterygians, and the ray-finned bony fish, whose descendants now dominate the seas.

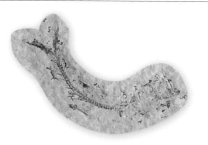

Above: Leptolepis sprattiformis was one of the earliest teleosts, or bony fish. This Late Jurassic fossil has clearly preserved the shape of its vertebral column, or backbone.

Below: The preserved upper jaw of the fish Belonostomus cinctus, lined with tiny, sharp teeth. Belonostomus was a member of the Holostei, ancestral to modern bony fish, and although this particular fossil dates to the Cretaceous, holosteans had been largely replaced by teleosts by this period.

groups (phyla) known made their appearance, though they often differed greatly from those alive today.

Chordates (the group that includes vertebrates) are thought to have evolved from the free-living larval forms of tunicates – animals not unlike modern salps. These larvae were tiny, tadpole-like animals with an elongated body supported by a rod of tissue called the notochord. The ancestor of modern chordates probably looked something like the 510-million-year-old *Pikaia* –

a tiny chordate not dissimilar to today's living lancelet or amphioxus, *Branchiostoma*. The notochord was the precursor of the backbone, and all vertebrates have a notochord at some stage in their life. In higher vertebrates, it appears only in the embryo and forms a kind of template around which the spinal column develops.

Below: In modern fish such as these yellowtail snapper (Ocyurus chrysurus), the notochord is replaced by an articulated vertebral column surrounding a dorsal nerve cord.

THE MARINE TREE OF LIFE

Taxonomy is the science of classification. Without it, biologists would find it impossible to keep track of the 1.7 million or so living species that have already been described. Assigning organisms to a category can also help our understanding of how they evolved from common ancestors.

As well as allowing us to organize our knowledge of living things, taxonomy also helps us to categorize fossils and to work out how they relate to living organisms. Phylogeny is a related area of study concerned with the evolutionary relationships between all organisms – both past and present. Before Charles

Darwin (1809–82) managed to explain his theory of natural selection as the force driving evolution, even those with an inkling that evolution might be the answer used to think of life on Earth as being hierarchical – with simple, 'primitive' species, such as flukes or anemones, at the bottom of a

ladder that climbed, rung by rung, through more 'advanced' forms, culminating with mankind at the top.

Nowadays most people find it helpful to think of phylogeny in terms of an extended family tree, where all living species, however simple, are represented by the tips of the branches.

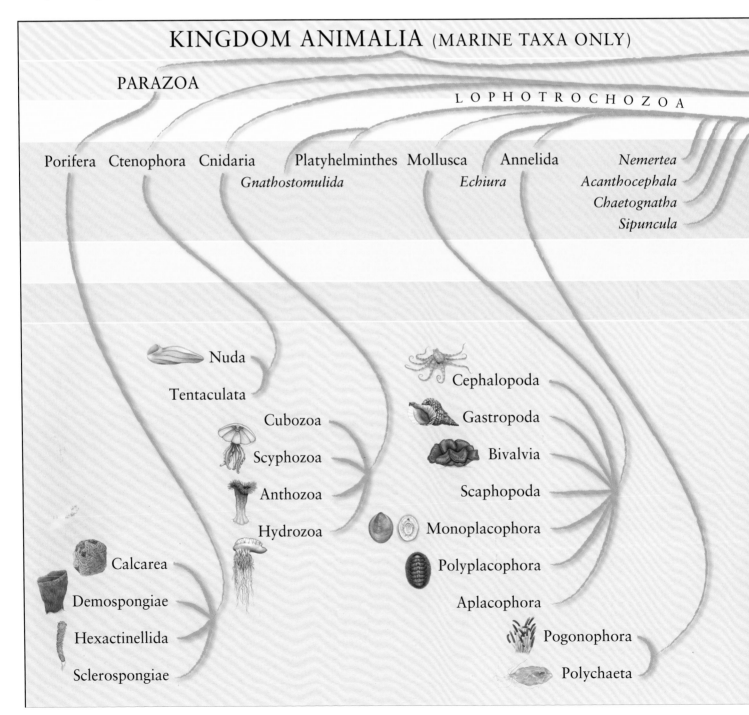

KINGDOM ANIMALIA (MARINE TAXA ONLY)

PARAZOA

LOPHOTROCHOZOA

Porifera   Ctenophora   Cnidaria   Platyhelminthes   Mollusca   Annelida   *Nemertea*
Gnathostomulida   *Echiura*   *Acanthocephala*
Chaetognatha
Sipuncula

Nuda
Tentaculata
Cubozoa
Scyphozoa
Anthozoa
Hydrozoa
Calcarea
Demospongiae
Hexactinellida
Sclerospongiae

Cephalopoda
Gastropoda
Bivalvia
Scaphopoda
Monoplacophora
Polyplacophora
Aplacophora
Pogonophora
Polychaeta

Refining techniques

As life began in the oceans, the marine tree of life includes every major group of animals that has ever lived on Earth. But the complexity of such a tree is enormous and inevitably contains many 'grey areas' in which relationships between species have not yet been fully teased apart.

In producing phylogenetic trees, scientists have traditionally relied on morphological comparisons – comparing the physical attributes of various species and defining groups based on their shared, derived characteristics. However, nature throws up a great many red herrings – animals with quite different ancestries that have evolved misleading similar adaptations.

The marine animal kingdom

The diagram below and accompanying key (right) indicate the major categories, or 'taxa', used by scientists to group marine animals. Exclusively terrestrial or freshwater groups are not present. This tree concludes at class level, below which are the smaller groupings order, family, genus and species. The majority of the taxa shown on this tree are discussed in the following pages, and all are defined in the Glossary. Where illustrated, class members feature in the Directory of Marine Species.

Subkingdom Both parazoans and metazoans are multicellular, but the latter are more complex organisms, with, typically, organs, cell tissues, and more advanced digestive and nervous systems.

A loose grouping based on distinct patterns in embryonic growth: in protostomes, the intestine develops first at the mouth; in deuterostomes, it is at the anus. Lophotrochozoa and Ecdysozoa are two of the major protostome groups.

Phylum A distinction is made between the major recognized phyla, and smaller phyla (italic) discussed under Marine Worms and Other Invertebrates.

Subphylum

Superclass

Class

EUMETAZOA

PROTOSTOMIA   E C D Y S O Z O A   DEUTEROSTOMIA

Phoronida   Nematoda   Arthropoda   Echinodermata   Chordata   *Hemichordata*
Bryozoa   *Nematomorpha*
Brachiopoda   *Priapulida*
Rotifera   *Kinorhyncha*

Chelicerata   Crustacea   Urochordata   Vertebrata

Agnatha   Gnathostomata

Pycnogonida

Appendicularia

Malacostraca

Ascidiacea

Maxillopoda

Thaliacea

Branchiopoda

Myxini

Cephalocarida

Cephalaspidomorphi

Cirripedia

Echinoidea

Chondrichthyes

Ostracoda

Holothuroidea

Actinopterygii

Copepoda

Ophiuroidea

Sarcopterygii

Remipedia

Asteroida

Reptilia

Crinoidea

Mammalia

WHAT IS A FISH?

Our fascination with the sea has much to do with the many species of fish that live there. Throughout history we have marvelled at their variety, wondered at the ease with which they exploit an environment that daunts and frightens us and, above all, prized them as a source of food.

The question 'What is a fish?' is not as easily answered as it may at first seem. This is mainly because the animals we generally think of as being 'fish', in fact, belong to several groups, and there are few truly hard and fast rules that apply to all of them.

It is easy to make generalizations about the defining characteristics of fish, but, as with most forms of life, there are exceptions to prove just about every rule. It is amazing just how many 'obvious' truths about the nature of fish begin to wobble when subjected to closer scrutiny.

Are all fish aquatic vertebrates?

There is a common generalization that fish live exclusively in water. But some, such as common eels and mudskippers, have the ability to move about on land, while others even take to the air in a controlled fashion – flying fish can glide up to 200m/660ft, skimming the waves like fast-flying seabirds. Some species of lungfish can survive periods of several months, or even years, cocooned in mud.

Most, but not all fish are vertebrates – meaning that they are animals with a skeleton that includes a cranium, or

Above: Strangely reminiscent of a large moth, the flying gurnard swims by means of huge, modified pectoral fins.

Below: The mako shark is technically 'cold-blooded', but the heat generated by its fast metabolism means that its body temperature is several degrees above that of the chilly waters in which it swims.

Below: Fish is a food source for millions of people, but overexploitation is placing species such as tuna (Thunnus) under terrible strain.

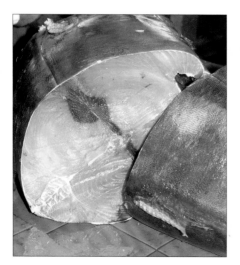

skull and a functional backbone. They also possess paired pectoral and pelvic appendages known as fins.

The exceptions to this particular generalization are the strange, rather primitive-looking hagfish (Myxini). These slimy, eel-like animals have a simple cartilaginous skull but no vertebrae, and instead of a backbone they just have a rod of springy connective tissue – the notochord previously described. This springy rod gives the body of the hagfish some rigidity, yet it is also flexible enough to allow the fish, quite literally, to tie itself in knots. Thus, hagfish as a group are categorized as chordate, but not vertebrate, animals.

Are all fish cold-blooded?

Fish are often described as being 'cold-blooded', but this is another rather misleading generalization. Most fish are 'poikilothermic', which means that they are unable to maintain a steady body temperature in the face of changing environmental temperatures. Thus, their body temperature is similar to that of the water in which they swim – so a fish of the icy polar seas will undoubtedly have cool blood, while one swimming in a shallow tropical lagoon may be almost as 'warm-blooded' as you are.

However, there is more to the story than this. Some fish, while unable to maintain a constant blood

Major groups of fish

The living species of fish are classified as five major groups or classes, as illustrated below and in The Marine Tree of Life. Each class is, in turn, divided into smaller taxa such as orders, families, genera (the plural of genus) and species, based on shared characteristics. For example, within the class Actinopterygii (the ray-finned fish or teleosts), there are 12 superorders at the next level down. The superorder Acanthopterygii is the most numerous of these, with 14 subgroups, or orders. Names of orders end in '-*formes*' (the English versions of these Latin names omit the 'e'); family groupings end in '-*idae*'.

Hagfish (Class Myxini)
These primitive fish lack a backbone. Instead, the body is supported throughout life by a flexible, but non-compressible rod called a notochord. Thus, hagfish do not really qualify as vertebrates – which means that, strictly speaking, they are not fish, but fish-like chordates. Hagfish lack functional eyes and paired fins. The mouth is surrounded by whisker-like barbels, which are sensitive to touch and chemicals.

Lampreys (Class Cephalaspidomorphi)
Like hagfish, lampreys also lack paired fins, but they have eyes and a backbone comprising simple cartilaginous vertebrae. The lack of proper jaws is no problem to these strange, primitive-looking fish. As larvae, they live on organic material filtered from the water. As adults, many turn parasitic and feed on chunks of flesh rasped from the bodies of larger vertebrates using a sucker-like mouth lined with horny teeth.

Cartilaginous fish (Class Chondrichthyes)
The cartilaginous fish include the chimeras or rabbitfish and the more familiar sharks and rays. There are thought to be around 1,000 species living today – the group is also well represented by fossil species. Sharks and their relatives have a skeleton made of cartilage, complete with articulating jaws and paired fins. Most have five sets of gills. They vary

Lobe-finned bony fish (Class Sarcopterygii)
The lobe-finned fish include the living coelacanths and lungfish, characterized by a bony skeleton, heavy-set body and stout, fleshy pectoral and pelvic fins. Only two known marine species from this once great group have survived to present times – the coelacanths *Latimeria chalumnae* and *L. menadoensis*.

Ray-finned bony fish (Class Actinopterygii)
This is the largest class of living fish, with an enormous variety of body forms. The paired and median fins, which are supported by spines or soft rays, are more variable still. The class includes about 24,000 scientifically described species, of which about 60 per cent are marine. There are 12 superorders within this class; many are referred to and defined in the following pages.

---

temperature, are nevertheless able to elevate their body temperature above that of the surrounding water. They do this by conserving metabolic heat. You will be familiar with the fact that, when humans exert themselves physically, the muscles produce heat. In most fish, this heat is rapidly lost from the body surface (mainly via the gills), but in some, mainly fast-swimming fish, such as mackerel and various sharks, it is conserved and body temperature can be raised significantly above ambient.

The difference between fish and mammals or birds (true homeotherms) is that the fish cannot maintain a constant, elevated temperature at rest.

Right: The decorative boxfish belongs to the order Tetradontiformes, which also includes pufferfish and filefish. It lives in the shallow sunlit waters of coral reefs, feeding rather indiscriminately on its neighbours – including sponges and small molluscs. Boxfish are notable for the 'honeycomb' pattern on their skin – a network of platelike scales that form a solid-looking carapace, rather like a box.

Do fish need gills to breathe?

Another standard generalization is that all fish have gills. These are organs with a large surface area of delicate tissue over which respiratory gases (oxygen and carbon dioxide) can be exchanged. Oxygen is taken up by the blood (indeed, all fish have blood), and carbon dioxide, a waste product of respiration, is released into the water.

Some fish, however, are so tiny, at least in their larval stage, that a large percentage of the oxygen that is required by their body tissues is taken up by simple diffusion of gas across other parts of the body surface. Some freshwater fish are even able to supplement their oxygen intake with respiratory organs more akin to lungs than gills.

ANATOMY OF CARTILAGINOUS FISH

The 1,000 or so living species of shark, ray and chimera include some primitive-looking fish, as well as some of the world's most immediately recognized, most admired and most feared animals. The group also includes the world's largest fish – the gargantuan whale shark.

Members of the class Chondrichthyes – the chimeras, sharks and rays – are almost all marine animals. However, some shark species occasionally venture into the brackish waters of river estuaries. A few will swim far upstream and enter fully fresh water for a time, and a handful of ray species spend their entire lives in rivers.

Cartilaginous skeleton
Cartilaginous fish have an extensive skeleton made exclusively of cartilage rather than bone. Cartilage is a tough, flexible tissue that begins to form from tissues deep within the body early in the development of an embryo. The principal constituent of cartilage is a smooth, gel-like material called chrondromucoprotein, which is produced within specialized cells called chrondrocytes, and secreted into the surrounding space. The chrondrocytes remain trapped within tiny bubbles within the cartilage they produce.

As the young fish develops, the cartilage accumulates certain minerals, especially calcium carbonate, which make it heavier, stronger and more

brittle – in large sharks the skeleton can be so heavily calcified that it looks and feels very much like bone. The skeletons of bony fish and higher vertebrates also contain cartilage – it appears earlier than bone during the development of the embryo and persists in its unmineralized, springy 'hyaline' form in parts of the skeleton where some flexibility is required.

*Above: The great white shark (*Carcharodon carcharias*) is perhaps the most infamous of all sharks, thanks to movies such as* Jaws. *Those who have survived or witnessed a great white attack speak of its raw power and startling speed; often enormous amounts of water are displaced during an assault.*

Body form and musculature
Most sharks show some ventral compression, or flattening of the underside. This is more exaggerated in species that live close to the sea floor, such as dogfish, and is taken to an extreme in the pancake-like rays.

The chimeras have a distinctive shape, known as 'chimaeriform', in which the head and body are large, but taper drastically into a long, whip-like tail. A similar shape is seen in unrelated bony fish, such as rattails and spiny eels.

Sharks are amazingly muscular – up to 85 per cent of their body is muscle, arranged for the most part in a series of symmetrical blocks on either side of the body. In most sharks, almost all of this muscle is of the white, fast-twitch, or sprint, variety. This is capable of very rapid contractions, generating great power but for short periods of time. In sharks that swim continuously,

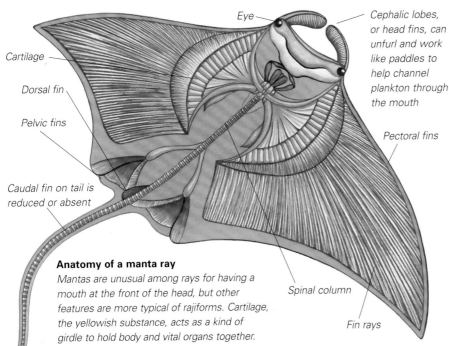

Eye

Cephalic lobes, or head fins, can unfurl and work like paddles to help channel plankton through the mouth

Cartilage

Dorsal fin

Pelvic fins

Pectoral fins

Caudal fin on tail is reduced or absent

Spinal column

Fin rays

Anatomy of a manta ray
Mantas are unusual among rays for having a mouth at the front of the head, but other features are more typical of rajiforms. Cartilage, the yellowish substance, acts as a kind of girdle to hold body and vital organs together.

such as the great white, these swimming muscles are supplemented with bands of dark-red, slow-twitch muscle, which is adapted for stamina rather than speed.

A shark's skin is connected to its muscular system in such a way that it acts as a giant tendon, helping the body to spring back into shape after each flex. This adds considerably to the efficiency of swimming.

Fins

Sharks and rays have two sets of paired fins – the pectorals and the pelvics. In male sharks, the pelvic fins are modified into specialized structures called claspers, used to help transfer sperm directly to the female reproductive tract during mating.

Sharks also have one or two dorsal and anal fins. All fins are supported by internal rods of cartilage, which keep them rigid. The typical triangular first dorsal fin of large sharks has become an iconic symbol, thanks largely to a series of Hollywood blockbusters, but first and foremost it is a fine example of natural marine engineering. The unpaired fins of sharks and other fish (known as median fins because they run along the midline of the body) help enhance stability when swimming, in much the same way as a keel on a boat. It is no coincidence that keels, dagger boards and the fins on windsurf boards are all much the same shape.

The tail fins of cartilaginous fish shows considerable variation. Those of rays and chimeras are very small, while those of sharks can be very large indeed. Shark caudal fins are typically 'heterocercal' – meaning that the top and bottom portions are different in size and shape. Invariably, the upper lobe is larger than the lower. The shape of the pectoral fins is also distinctive. For the most part, these are long and tapering with a rounded leading edge, convex upper surface and tapered trailing edge. Interestingly, both these features are mimicked in aircraft design.

Lift is important for sharks because they lack a swim bladder, the organ that helps other fish to maintain buoyancy. Sharks have a large, oily

*Above: This electric ray (*Narcine *species) is able to produce an electric discharge capable of stunning small prey.*

liver, which provides some lift, but even so, most are still slightly heavier than water and sink if they stop swimming. Many species allow this to happen and spend extended periods resting on the sea floor. Those that have opted for a fully pelagic (open-water) existence, such as the blue shark (*Prionace glauca*), have adapted a body shape of such hydrodynamic perfection that the energetic costs of constant swimming are as low as they can be. The forces of friction or drag are reduced not only by overall body shape, but by the fine structure of the body surface.

Body teeth

Sharks have teeth all over the body. Known as dermal denticles, these have much the same structure as regular teeth, with a central pulp cavity, an intermediate layer of dentine and an outer layer of a special, hard enamel. This material is as resistant to abrasion as steel – no wonder shark hide can be used in place of sandpaper.

*Below: Dermal denticles on the body of a zebra shark (*Stegastoma fasciatum*).*

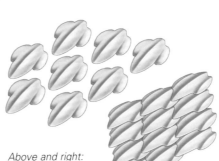

Above and right: Denticles vary in shape and distribution between species. (Top) Dogfish sharks (Squaliformes) tend to have body teeth that are narrow and flat, with a prominent central ridge, giving the skin an extremely rough texture. (Bottom) Those of sevengill sharks (Hexanchiformes) tend to overlap, and are so thin as to be almost transparent.

Adult mako shark   *Juvenile great white shark*

Adult blacktip reef shark

Regular teeth

As well as these characteristic body teeth, sharks also have conventional teeth. Those of the requiem sharks (the great white and its relatives) are truly fearsome – up to 7.5cm/3in long and sharp enough to slice leather. They are triangular in shape and have a serrated edge. Requiem sharks will continually shed and replace teeth throughout their lives.

THE LIVES OF CARTILAGINOUS FISH

The head of a shark or ray is equipped with a battery of highly refined sense organs, granting them powers that can appear to verge on the supernatural. Breeding behaviour is extremely varied in cartilaginous fish, and the embryos of some species even perform uterine cannibalism.

The mouth of all sharks is underslung, though in some the jaws can be protruded so that the shark can bite at large objects without its snout getting in the way. Most rays are bottom feeders, with a mouth that usually opens on the underside of the flattened body ('ventral' position). The mouth of manta rays is at the front of the head ('terminal' position), a distinction which, among other biological factors, is encouraging scientists to consider them a unique species of ray.

Most obvious among the sense organs of sharks and rays are the eyes, which are typically large and provide vision rather better than that of humans. In many species, a reflective layer at the back of the eye, called the *tapetum lucidum*, helps make the most of any available light in gloomy waters, and most groups are able to 'blink' in some way to protect the surface of the eye. In some species, this mechanism takes the form of a movable nictating membrane (transparent 'third eyelid') attached along the bottom of the eye, while in others there is a movable upper or lower eyelid.

The nostrils are located in the snout. In rays, they lie in grooves connected to the mouth. Sharks have a phenomenal sense of smell – large predatory species, such as the oceanic white tip (*Carcharhinus longimanus*), are famed for their ability to detect the scent of blood at concentrations as low as

1:20 million. This acute sensitivity is also helpful in allowing sharks to find one another, especially males tracking down females in breeding condition.

Also located on the snouts of sharks are sense organs that detect electrical activity. Tiny pits, called the ampullae of Lorenzini, are arranged in rows on the underside of the snout (and on the pectoral fins of rays). These pits are lined with hundreds of electro-receptor cells, which allow sharks and rays to sense the tiny electrical fields generated by other animals, and in some cases may also enable them to navigate using the Earth's magnetic field.

Respiration

Gills, located at the head, are the organs of gas exchange. They are typically supported on five cartilaginous arches, and water flows past them and out of five gill slits on either side of the head. A few species of shark have six or

*Above: Although not hunted commercially, many blacktip reef sharks (*Carcharhinus melanopterus*) are victims of bycatch.*

seven sets of gills, and the chimeras have just four, all sharing a single common opening on each side of the body. In large filter-feeding species such as the basking shark (*Cetorhinus maximus*), whale shark (*Rhincodon typus*) and the giant manta ray (*Manta birostris*), the gill arches also bear comb-like gill rakers, which act as filters trapping plankton. Rays and some sharks have a small, round opening just behind the eye known as the spiracle. This is a modified gill opening, but instead of serving as an outflow, like the regular gill slits, it acts as an intake valve – in bottom-dwelling species it would be difficult for a fish to take in water for respiration through the mouth without also taking in sediment that would clog the gills.

Respiration and metabolism in sharks
Sharks' blood is oxygenated at the gills. At the same time, carbon dioxide, a by-product of respiration, is released from the gills into the water.

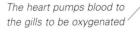

Outflow of oxygen-depleted water

Gills

Stomach

Intake of oxygenated water

The heart pumps blood to the gills to be oxygenated

Pancreas

Intestine

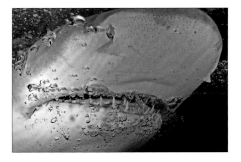

*Above: A lemon shark (*Negaprion brevirostris*) displaying the ampullae of Lorenzini on the surface of its broad snout.*

Feeding

Sharks and rays adopt a diverse range of feeding strategies, from filter feeding, as seen in the manta ray (see right) and basking shark, through scavenging, as in the sleeper shark (*Somniosus pacificus*) to active hunting (most other sharks and rays).

Predatory sharks target prey of all sizes and habits, from relatively sedentary bottom-dwelling invertebrates to schooling fish and large active animals, including fast-swimming fish, such as tuna, smaller whales and seals. These large prey are usually subdued quickly with a savage bite – those that

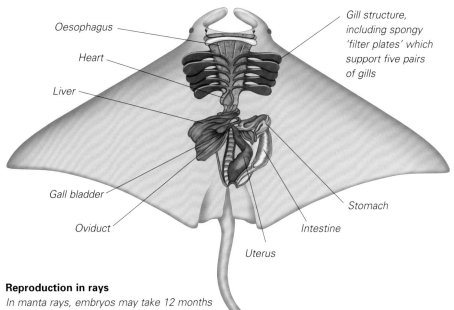

Oesophagus

Heart

Liver

Gall bladder

Oviduct

Uterus

Intestine

Stomach

Gill structure, including spongy 'filter plates' which support five pairs of gills

Reproduction in rays
In manta rays, embryos may take 12 months to reach full term. In other species, there are typically two pups born per litter, but manta rays produce just one.

fight back vigorously may be left alone until they are weakened by blood loss. Rays generally target smaller prey than their relatives the sharks, but they have some dramatic hunting techniques – for example, members of the electric ray family (Narcinidae) are able to stun

their prey with an electric shock before eating it. They have plate-like teeth for crushing food rather than biting it.

Humans have an uneasy relationship with sharks. The large, predatory species of shark are among the most feared animals on Earth. They are among the relatively few animals able to reduce humans to mere prey, but only a handful of more than 500 known species are considered dangerous and overwhelmingly it is man that hunts and kills sharks. Sharks are fished commercially on a grand scale, and the fins are the most valuable part. Deplorably, defined sharks may be thrown back into the sea by some fishermen, where they will drown.

Below: The egg case of a dogfish, containing a developing embryo, attached to some kelp.

Reproduction in cartilaginous fish
Cartilaginous fish exhibit a full range of breeding strategies, from egg laying to the bearing of live young nourished on secretions of the uterus. Fertilization always takes place within the body of the female. Many oviparous (egg-laying) sharks and rays produce distinctive eggs, known informally as 'mermaids' purses'. They have a tough, rubbery or leathery case, often with hooks or long tendrils sprouting from the corners – these help to anchor the egg in the sediment or attach it to seaweed, thus offering the developing embryo some protection.

The young of live-bearing sharks, however, hatch internally and are retained within the body of the female until they have reached a size where they are able to look after themselves. They develop within the expanded oviduct, or uterus.

All young sharks are sustained during their early development by individual yolks, but in some this is supplemented by ingesting a rich secretion called uterine milk, which leaks from the wall of the uterus. In several species, aggressive predatory habits are honed before birth – young tiger sharks (*Galeocerdo cuvier*) feed on their siblings within the uterus – only the largest and strongest will be born.

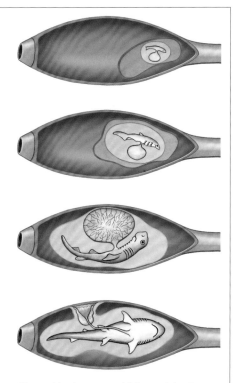

Above: Live-bearers exhibit ovoviviparity (aplacental viviparity). Embryos develop inside the oviduct, attached by a yolk sac. As they near full term, they may ingest the secretions of the oviduct wall.

ANATOMY OF BONY FISH

For all the variety and impressive adaptations shown by the sharks and rays, and by marine invertebrates such as crustaceans and echinoderms, it is the bony fish that have achieved true dominance in the modern oceans, exploiting every niche from rock pool to abyssal depths.

Modern bony fish fall into two categories – the lobe-finned Sarcopterygii and the ray-finned Actinopterygii. Of these, the ray-fins undoubtedly reign supreme in the aquatic world, but the lobe-fins have a significance that far outweighs their apparently limited diversity. They, or fish very like them, are the likely ancestors of all tetrapod vertebrates, including amphibians, reptiles, birds and mammals.

Body shape
The laws of hydrodynamics dictate that the most efficient shape for an object moving through water is torpedo-like – with a blunt or rounded nose, a slender body and a tapering tail. And many marine organisms do look very much like this – herrings and mackerel are good examples.

But fish come in a huge variety of other shapes. Some are greatly elongated, such as eels. Some, like cusks and oarfish, are flattened laterally, while some are flattened ventrally. Others, such as boxfish and pufferfish, can make themselves almost spherical. Many are far from hydrodynamic – seahorses, for example, have sacrificed swimming efficiency for elaborate frills and camouflage and the ability to lurk unseen among weed.

Colouration
Very few fish are colourless in their adult form – and those that are mainly live in dark water. One of the purposes of coloured skin is to protect the internal organs from the effects of ultraviolet (UV) radiation.

But colour and patterning are much more than mere sunscreen, and most species are highly pigmented. Colour can serve as a camouflage, as a beacon to potential mates or as a warning of toxicity. A large proportion of pelagic species are countershaded, with a dark back and flanks and pale underside.

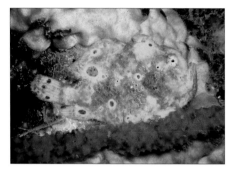

Above: A frogfish (Antennarius *species*) adapts to the colour of its new spongy habitat.

Below: The markings on this scrawled filefish (Aluterus scriptus) *afford some camouflage.*

This helps to cancel out the effect of light shining down from above, making the fish more difficult to see.

Skin pigments are produced and stored in cells called chromatophores, but some of the most dazzling colours are created optically – the result of the reflection and splitting of light by crystalline structures inside specialized skin cells called iridiophores. Colour and pattern are not fixed in all fish – in some skin cells, packages of pigment or reflective crystals can be reorganized to bring about dramatic changes. These may take place gradually, over a period of days or weeks, as with seasonal or breeding colours, or be much quicker, as in species such as frogfish, which can change colour in a matter of minutes to match a new backdrop.

Bioluminescence
A great many fish are able to produce light from specialized cells called photophores. The light can take the

Above: The silvery scales of this soldierfish (Myripristis jacobus) *reflect ambient light.*

Below: Yellowfin tuna (Thunnus albacares) *lack scales on part of the flank.*

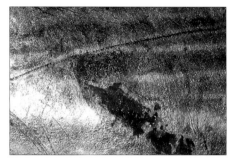

form of sudden flashes or a steady glow of blue, green, red or yellow. The effect is usually achieved in one of two ways: either the fish synthesizes the light by producing the protein luciferin within its own body, or it enlists the help of other bioluminescent organisms. These are usually bacteria stored within the light organ and masked until the fish needs to light up.

Respiration and circulation
Water contains considerably less oxygen than air – at best, about 3 per cent the concentration. Therefore, obtaining enough oxygen to survive is a challenge for all aquatic organisms. The larger and more active the animal is, the greater the demand – and for some fish, respiration alone accounts for up to one-third of the average daily energy expenditure.

The organs of respiration are the gills – delicate tissues with a large surface area and rich blood supply.

The walls of the gills are so thin that gases, such as oxygen and carbon dioxide, can easily diffuse through them, as long as there is what is known as a 'concentration gradient', down which molecules of gas migrate from areas of high concentration to areas of low concentration.

In order to maximize the efficiency of gas exchange, it is important that a fish maintains a steady flow of water over the gills. Water passes in through the mouth, over its gills and out via openings in the sides of the head, which are usually protected by an operculum, or gill cover. The water flow is maintained by a pumping action of the mouth – or throat – forcing water into the gill chambers, and of the opercula, which open and close, thus sucking the water through. In fish that lack buccal (mouth) or opercular pumps, the respiratory current is generated by ram ventilation – continual swimming with the mouth open, forcing a flow of water over the gills.

Blood circulation in fish consists of a single circuit. Oxygen-deficient, carbon dioxide-rich blood is pumped by a simple, three-chambered heart directly to the gills, where gas exchange takes place. Blood passing from the gills is carried off around the body then drains back to the heart once more.

Fins, tails and scales

Bony fish may have one, two or three dorsal fins, which may merge to form a continuous fringe along the back or which may remain distinct. Dorsal fins may be supported by sharp spines or branched rays or a combination of the two. They may function as stabilizers when swimming or be highly modified, forming the fishing lures of anglers, the suctorial disc of remoras or the dramatic frills of lionfish.

Bony fish tails come in a great many shapes and sizes. Some are heterocercal – asymmetrical like those of sharks, with the upper lobe larger than the lower. Homocercal tails are externally symmetrical and can be rounded, squared off, forked or crescent shaped. A few fish have a long, tapering tail with no obvious fin – this style is known as leptocercal. Another rare form is that exhibited by the giant sunfish (*Mola mola*), where the tail stock and caudal fin are absent and the body ends abruptly.

Most, but not all bony fish have scales. These come in three main types: ganoid, cycloid and ctenoid. Ganoid scales are stout and rhomboid in shape, and look a bit like armour plating. They are found on primitive species, such as sturgeons. Cycloid scales, such as those seen on salmon, are thin, flat and almost round, and they are arranged in an overlapping pattern on the fish's body. Ctenoid, or comb scales, are similar in overall shape and arrangement to cycloid scales, but their rearward edge bears tiny teeth that help improve streamlining. Fish with ctenoid scales include gobies and most perciforms.

Below: The following species exhibit a range of some of the most distinctive dorsal fin modifications exhibited by bony fish. (Top) The oarfish (Regalecus glesne), known as the 'king of herrings', has a crown of elongated fin spines and a dorsal fringe running to the tip of the tail. (Middle) Remoras (Remora species) have a remarkable sucker which enables them to attach to much larger fish, and even ocean giants such as whales, to effectively 'hitch a ride' with the host. (Bottom) The spectacular dorsal 'sail' of the aptly-named sailfish (Istiophorus platypterus) may lie almost completely flat when the fish is swimming at speed but is raised when making fast turns, thereby increasing manoeuvrability.

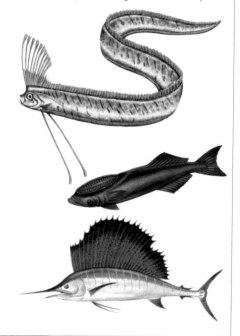

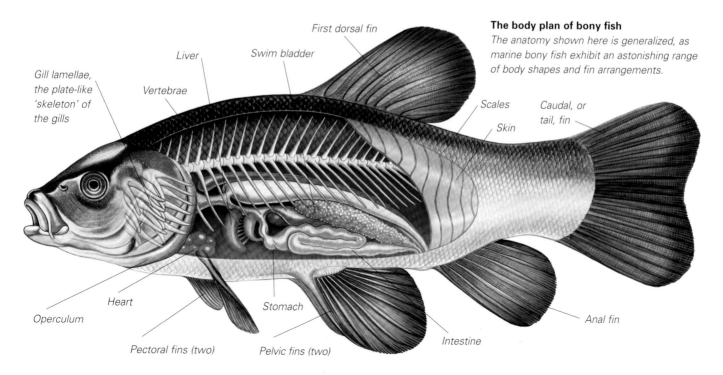

First dorsal fin

Liver

Swim bladder

Gill lamellae, the plate-like 'skeleton' of the gills

Vertebrae

Scales

Skin

Caudal, or tail, fin

Heart

Operculum

Stomach

Intestine

Anal fin

Pectoral fins (two)

Pelvic fins (two)

The body plan of bony fish
The anatomy shown here is generalized, as marine bony fish exhibit an astonishing range of body shapes and fin arrangements.

MOVEMENT OF BONY FISH

When it comes to moving about, the physical properties of water can be a mixed blessing. The density of water is about 800 times that of air, meaning that it offers plenty of support. However, pushing through it requires a lot of energy – swimming is hard work!

Fish swim using symmetrical blocks of muscles arranged in a repeating pattern along either side of the body. This pattern of repetition, known as metamerism, was inherited from the common ancestor of all bony, cartilaginous and jawless fish, and is more obvious in some species than in others. Because a fish's body is supported by the non-compressible backbone, contraction of the muscles on either side causes it to flex. If the muscles on opposite sides of the trunk contract alternately, the body performs a side-to-side wiggle, pushing against the surrounding water and, thus, propelling the fish forward. The addition of median fins (the dorsal caudal and anal fins) increases thrust to the animal's movement and also adds stability.

Types of swimming

In long-bodied fish, such as eels, swimming involves the side-to-side undulations of the whole body, a form of swimming known as anguilliform. The undulations are greatest towards the tail end, which generates considerable turbulence, making this an energetically expensive means of moving from place to place. Turbulence is reduced by a tapering body shape and the addition of a tail fin. The fin also increases the surface area available to generate propulsion.

Modes of swimming

The carangiform mode (shown right) is a powerful method of swimming adopted by many fish, including jacks, salmon and snappers. These fish swim using their trunk muscles, but most of the movement is in the rear half of the body while the head remains steady (1). The tail undulates in one direction, then snaps back (2), propelling the fish forward. The tail then undulates towards the opposite side, to repeat the process.

A modified and less powerful version of carangiform swimming is often described as 'oscillatory'. This is where contractions of the trunk muscle cause the body to flick from side to side (3), passing through an s-shaped wave (4).

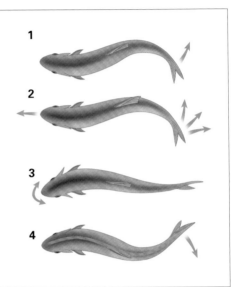

The most energy-efficient mode of swimming is that adopted by members of the family Carangidae, a group that includes jacks, pompanos and the like, With these marine and brackish-water fish, side-to-side movements are restricted to the rear end of the fish only, and a large tail fin serves to reduce turbulence and increase efficiency. When this type of swimming technique is adopted the head remains still, helping to stabilize the fish's vision and maintain a steady direction.

A few fish use just their fins for propulsion. Examples of fish that use this swimming technique include the opah, or moonfish (*Lampris regius*), which sculls with its pectoral fins, or the batfish, which uses its pectoral and pelvic

*Above: The rainbow runner (*Elagatis bipinnulata*), found in warm and tropical seas, swims in the carangiform style.*

fins to pull itself along the sea floor. Seahorses and oarfish swim with the body held vertically in the water, so that the dorsal fin is at the back – wave-like ripples running along the dorsal fringe and fanning movements of the pectoral fins are enough to propel the fish very slowly forward.

Buoyancy

The lifting force exerted by water on an object less dense than itself is known as buoyancy. Objects that are less dense than water are positively buoyant and they float or rise towards

*Above: Mosaic morays (*Enchelycore ramosus*), in common with other eels, tarpons and sea snakes, rely on snakelike movement of the whole body to propel themselves forward.*

the surface. Objects that weigh more than their equivalent volume of water are negatively buoyant. They will sink.

The body of a fish contains several types of dense tissue, such as muscle and bone, that are negatively buoyant. For species that make a living close to the sea floor, this is an advantage – they are able to save energy simply by letting gravity take effect, and many will spend long periods resting on the bottom. They are able to raise themselves up into the water when necessary by expending energy and swimming. For fish that live in very deep water, where food is scarce, the ability to save energy is a crucial survival adaptation.

The swim bladder

However, space is limited on the ocean floor, especially compared with the vastness of the open ocean, and so there can be advantages to life in mid water. Most pelagic bony fish have a specialized buoyancy organ, the swim bladder, that helps reduce the energy required to maintain a constant depth.

The swim bladder is a large, gas-filled chamber whose volume can be adjusted so that the fish achieves neutral buoyancy and so can 'hang' stationary in mid water. Gas can pass in and out of the bladder via a direct connection with the outside (by the oesophagus), or it can be removed by absorption into the bloodstream through a permeable area of the wall lining. Alternatively the bladder can be inflated by secretion of gas from a

*Above: A peacock flounder (*Bothus lunatus*) rests on coral. This flounder favours reefs as a habitat, although it is often difficult to see as it may be partially buried in sand.*

*Below: The batfish (*Ephippidae*) moves from place to place using its pelvic and pectoral fins to effectively 'crawl' along the ocean floor.*

gland, known as the *rete mirabilis*, associated with a specialized network of capillaries in animals.

One of the chief limitations of the system is that the volume of the bladder cannot be adjusted instantaneously. Thus, if the fish is brought suddenly to the surface – for example on the end of a line – the abrupt decrease in

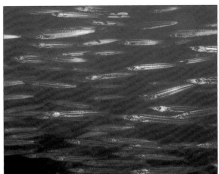

*Above: Fast-swimming schools such as these needlefish (*Platybelone argalus*) may swim in a diamond formation, taking advantage of the slipstream created by other individuals.*

*Below: Seahorses, such as this long-snouted species (*Hippocampus reidi*), use their dorsal fins to propel their body forward through the water. The tail is used to 'moor' when at rest.*

pressure causes the gas in the bladder to expand very rapidly, crushing other organs and sometimes rupturing the bladder itself. Once a swim bladder has over-expanded, the fish is so buoyant it becomes unable to return to its preferred depth.

A few types of bony fish have given up on the swim bladder. For example, mackerel rely on speed and agility to hunt as well as to evade predators, and this means that sudden changes in pressure are part of their daily lives. Their oily muscles are positively buoyant, and this goes some way to compensating for the lack of a swim bladder, but even so they must swim continuously in order to hold their position. They have also dispensed with any kind of pump to deliver water to the gills, relying solely on the flow of water generated by swimming.

*Left: The bulge of the swim bladder can be seen in this map pufferfish (*Arothon mappa*).*

BONY FISH AND THEIR SENSES

Like all animals, bony fish face the routine challenges of finding food, attracting mates to breed and avoiding predators and other adversaries in order to survive. To help them in these daily pursuits, they have at their disposal an array of acute senses with which to scan their surroundings.

Fish are alert, responsive animals and they use their senses to monitor their environment in a variety of ways. Some of these, such as vision, touch and hearing, are familiar to us because we use them ourselves; others, however, including the chemical senses related to smell and taste, are so highly refined as to seem almost supernatural. In addition, fish possess extra senses that are completely alien to us – an electrical sense, for example, and an extraordinary ability to detect and interpret vibrations in the water.

*Above: A flashlight fish (*Photoblepharon palpebratus*) displaying a bioluminescent bluish-green glow around the pectoral area.*

Above: Many fish, like this porcupine fish, have eyes positioned on either side of the head, granting them excellent all-round vision.

Vision

Light is absorbed rapidly by water. At a depth of just a few metres, even bright sunlight is reduced to a gloomy blue-green glow. Thus, the eyes of fish are exceptionally good at gathering light, making the most of whatever illumination is available.

Go deeper than a few hundred metres and there is next to no sunlight. But this does not mean there is nothing to see – far from it, since a great many deep-sea creatures are able to produce light of their own – a phenomenon known as bioluminescence – to advertise themselves to mates, to lure prey or even to confuse and disorientate predators. Thus, while it is true that some deep-sea fish are blind, the majority have functional eyes, but

vision is not necessarily the most important of the senses employed – it is just one in a range.

In most fish, the eyes are located on the side of the head, giving a wide field of vision. But all-round vision is of little use to species that live on the sea floor, and so in many such species the eyes are found on top of the head, looking upwards. More commonly in flatfish, such as turbot and flounder, which lie on one side on the sea floor, both eyes are situated on the same side of the head.

Hearing

Fish have no external ears or eardrums. But because their bodies are of a similar density to the surrounding water, sound waves carry directly to the inner

ear through their ordinary tissues. The ear of a fish consists of a system of chambers and canals within the bones of the head. Deep inside the head, sound waves are detected when they cause tiny hairs to bend or vibrate. The hair cells have a neural

Following the scent of home

The chemical senses of fish are important in navigation and orientation. Many species have been shown to recognize their home waters by scent – for example, migrating salmon can home in on the precise tributary in which they were born six or seven years previously.

Minute quantities of chemicals from local rocks and soil and from other local organisms create a unique scent of home that the fish recognizes even if they are blind or the river itself looks different following flood damage or other changes.

*Below: Pink salmon (*Oncorhynchus gorbuscha*) swimming up the Indian River, Michigan, USA, to spawn.*

Anatomy of a bony fish ear
Generalized example showing the position of the internal ear.

Swim bladder

Ear canals consist of three semi-circular chambers containing otoliths

Ossicles, or tiny bones

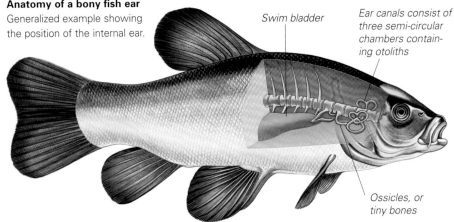

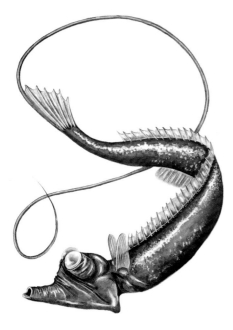

*Above: The telescope-like eyes of the tube-eye (*Stylephorus chordatus*) point upwards to scan for small prey swimming in deep waters.*

Above: A grouper monitors its surroundings for food and potential threats.

connection to the brain. Also present in the inner ear are mineralized structures known as ear stones, or otoliths. These structures develop into characteristic shapes that can be used to identify species, and if they are cut open they also reveal annual growth rings that can be used to age the fish. In certain fish, the swim bladder has a bony connection with the inner ear. This transmits vibrations and allows the taut membrane of the bladder to act as an outsized ear drum.

Chemical sense

Water makes an excellent solvent and it is able to dissolve a vast array of different chemical compounds. As a result, the seas have become a vast, dilute soup of various chemicals, including mineral salts and a huge variety of compounds that originate from biological sources. The ability to detect and differentiate these chemical signatures provides fish and other animals with vital clues to help them find food, detect danger, track down a mate or even navigate a course.

Bony fish have nostrils entirely independent of the mouth and that are lined with a delicate tissue rich in scent receptors. Water is drawn in through the anterior (front) nostril and exits via the posterior (rear) one. In addition,

many species have chemical receptors distributed over the body, and especially on the snout and in the mouth. Some species have sensory barbels (fleshy filaments growing from the mouth or snout), richly endowed with chemical receptors.

Not all fish, however, have a keen sense of smell – seahorses for example have very limited olfactory epithelium.

Sense of taste

Bony fish also have a sense of taste and are able to distinguish the same broad taste groups humans recognize – salt, sweet, bitter and sour. Most species have taste buds in and around the mouth and lips, while some also have them on the tips of their sensitive barbels, so they can feel and taste food items buried in sediment.

Lateral line

The lateral line organ of fish comprises a series of tiny sensors, known as neuromasts, which are arranged in a row along the flanks. In some species, the neuromasts lie at the surface of the body; in others, they lie under the skin in a canal that is linked to the outside

environment via a series of pores. All the neuromasts are connected directly to the nervous system. They are highly sensitive to the vibrations and pressure waves transmitted through the water whenever anything moves – thus, fish will be aware of another animal approaching well before it can be seen. Because fish of different sizes and shapes produce different frequency vibrations, different species may be able to recognize those produced by their own kind. This may explain how schools of fish can merge and separate with such apparent ease.

*Below: In some species, the lateral line can be recognized by a break in colouration, as in this big-eye snapper (*Lutjanus lutjanus*).*

BONY FISH AND FEEDING

Feeding is an essential part of day-to-day life for most fish species. Marine food webs can be enormously complex and feeding strategies vary greatly, with one thing assured – no species is exempt from the possibility of one day becoming food for other predatory or scavenging animals.

The digestive process in fish begins in the mouth, the size and positioning of which is variable. Fish that engulf large prey usually have a mouth that opens at the front, bottom feeders have an underslung mouth, and those that pluck small prey from the surface or lie on the sea bed to attack prey passing above have a mouth directed upwards.

The mouth and jaws of some species are highly modified. The tiny tubular mouth of the butterfly fish family (Chaetodontidae) opens at the tip of a narrow snout, working like a pipette to suck up small items of food from small crevices. At the other end of the spectrum, the huge gape of the gulper eel (*Eurypharynx pelecanoides*) engulfs

Cleaning stations

Several groups of bony fish have become specialized 'cleaners'. They are adapted to feed only on the small external parasites that attach themselves to the bodies of other fish. A heavy load of parasites can place a severe strain on the body of a host, so the ministrations of cleaner fish can be highly beneficial. In fact, many large fish, even voracious predators, will wait in line for this marine valet service. Cleaners and their 'clients' develop an extraordinary level of mutual trust – the cleaners venturing close to jaws than could snap them up in an instant and the client waiting patiently while the cleaner nibbles away at gills and other vulnerable body parts.

*Below: An Argus grouper (*Cephalopholis argus*) being cleaned by a much smaller cleaner wrasse (*Labroides species*).*

Generalized marine food web

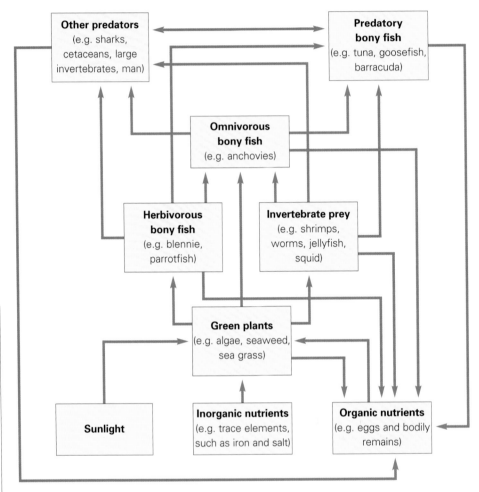

Above: The marine food web follows a loose size hierarchy, with smaller creatures often becoming food for larger predators. However, as shown by the downward arrows, both the eggs, larvae and, ultimately, the remains of the largest creatures supply the organic nutrients that feed the most basic forms of life.

small prey along with large volumes of water. Fish that hunt larger prey have smaller jaws, but they are much more powerful, and typically lined with sharp teeth. These teeth might be excellent for snagging prey and preventing its escape, but they are not much use for cutting it up – thus the scariest-looking fish often swallow their prey whole. Often teeth of this sort flex towards the back of the throat to ease the inward passage of prey.

Teeth used for slicing and dicing, like those of the great barracuda (*Sphyraena barracuda*), which bites large prey into chunks, need to be rather more robust. The parrot fish (*Sparisoma* species) has teeth in the form of a stout beak that can bite off chunks of coral.

Herbivores

Vegetarianism is rare among fish. Virtually all species eat other animals during some part of their lives, and especially during the early stages when a relatively large intake of protein is required. However, some species do become essentially herbivorous later in life – this is more common in the tropics, where warm water and long hours of bright sunlight permit plentiful growth of marine plant material.

The digestive system of a bony fish
The length of the intestine varies among species, but is usually shorter in carnivores. The fingerlike pyloric caecae, attached to the gut, may aid the absorption of food.

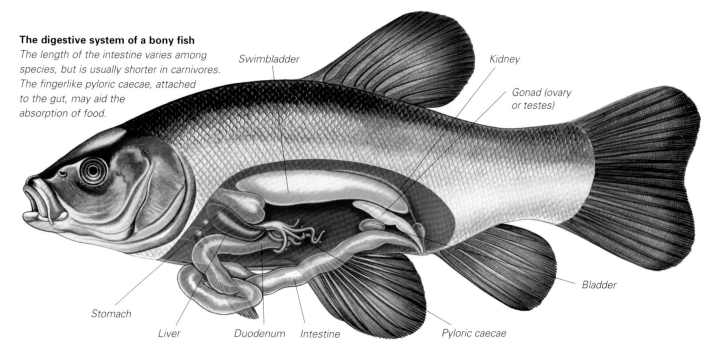

Swimbladder

Kidney

Gonad (ovary or testes)

Bladder

Stomach

Liver

Duodenum

Intestine

Pyloric caecae

Filter feeding

Bony fish have four pairs of gills located within the pharynx, or 'throat'. In filter feeding species, the bony arches that support the gills also bear long, slender rakers – rigid structures that project inwards, forming a sort of sieve through which water passing in via the mouth and out through the gill slits is strained. The size of food taken varies with the species, from algae to baby fish, squid and shrimps.

Predators

Most fish are hunters. Zooplankton and communities of small, bottom-dwelling invertebrates, including worms, molluscs and crustaceans, are an important source of food, as are fish fry. Hunting techniques among predatory fish vary from opportunistic snapping at any small passing animals to lie-in-wait ambush techniques.

Many ambush predators are very well camouflaged – the disguises of stonefish (order Scorpaeniformes) can fool the sharpest eyes. The ambush is taken a step further by species of anglerfish (order Lophiiformes), which not only exhibit perfect camouflage, but also draw prey near with a lure.

Ambush predators often have a large mouth – when this is opened suddenly, the prey is carried in with the inrushing water. Other forms of weaponry, such as stings or electric shocks, may also be used for defence.

Parasites

There are numerous interesting twists on the predatory theme. A number of fish are parasitic – they live in close association with their prey, feeding off them without immediately killing them.

The key to being a successful parasite is to avoid killing the host – once dead, it is of limited use, but kept alive it may provide a source of food for life. Some parasites are better at this than

others. For example, the carapid cucumberfish lives within the body of a sea cucumber, feeding off the tissues of the respiratory and reproductive systems, which continually regenerate.

Not all parasites commit to a single host – many simply swim to their victim, take a bite and swim away. Often they improve their chances of getting close enough by impersonating benign species, especially cleaners (see box).

*Above: A spotted moray eel (*Gymnothorax moringa*) in typical threat position.*

*Below: The 'beak' of the queen parrotfish (*Scarus vetula*) contains chisellike teeth.*

*Above: Caribbean trumpetfish (*Aulostomus maculatus*) with its elongated snout.*

*Below: The aptly-named deep-sea common fangtooth (*Anoplogaster cornuta*).*

BONY FISH: SOCIAL BEHAVIOUR AND REPRODUCTION

Individual fish share their habitats with many others, and all must find a way to maximize their own success among the competitors, predators and potential mates.

Bony fish employ a large variety of breeding strategies. Often zoologists talk of oviparity (egg laying) versus viviparity (live bearing). Female oviparous fish produce eggs, which they release into the water where they are fertilized by sperm from the male. In most cases, the numbers of eggs involved are extremely large. Viviparity is far less common, and only about one in every 30 families of fish have true live-bearing species in which mating occurs and embryos develop inside the female, nourished by way of a connection to the mother.

Between these two apparently distinct strategies there is a large grey area, known as ovoviviparity, that leads to some degree of confusion. Ovoviviparity is where a female fish produces eggs that are fertilized and hatch internally so that the mother gives birth to live young at any stage from early larvae to fully formed, sexually mature offspring.

Parental types

As well as physiological differences in reproductive biology, fish also exhibit a striking variety of behaviours and strategies, designed to maximize their chances of successful breeding. These can be grouped into three main types, based on how the parent fish treat their offspring. These types, or guilds, are non-guarders, guarders and bearers.

Below: The male yellowhead jawfish (Opistognathus aurifrons), an oviparous bearer, broods hundreds of eggs in its mouth.

Above: A false clown anemonefish (Amphiprion ocellaris) guards its eggs in the substratum near to the base of its host anemone.

Non-guarders are oviparous. They produce eggs and sperm, either in a single large spawning or several smaller sessions, and leave nature to take its course. In some cases, the eggs are released in open water as part of a mass spawning, while in others they are shed above a specially selected substratum – for example, gravel or weed. In both cases, the chances of any single fertilized egg developing to adulthood is tiny, so non-guarders tend

Below: Free-swimming larvae mingle with eggs that have not yet hatched in this school of planktonic life.

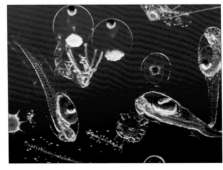

to produce eggs in vast numbers. The eggs of species that show some substratum selectivity may have a slightly improved chance of survival, and may thus be produced in slightly smaller numbers than those that are simply released to the mercy of the prevailing current.

Guarders are also oviparous, but they tend to produce fewer eggs and take rather more care of them, sticking around and defending the eggs, which are typically laid in a nest or adhesive mass, to be guarded externally.

Bearers may be oviparous, viviparous or ovoviviparous, but in all examples the offspring are carried with one of the parents as they develop – either as eggs or as larvae. In oviparous bearers, the female lays eggs, but they are then gathered up into the mouth of one of the parents, who holds them there until they hatch.

Males and females

From a mammalian perspective, the differences between sexes usually seem clear cut. The distinction is often less definitive in fish, and hermaphroditism – where both male and female sex organs develop within the same individual – is common.

In most of these instances, fish are sequential hermaphrodites – meaning they start life as one gender and then at a later stage switch to the other. For example, anemone fish (family Pomacentridae) start out as males and become females. This makes physiological sense because sperm are relatively cheap and easy to produce, even for small fish, whereas eggs require much more investment, something that is more readily afforded by large individuals.

But there can also be a sound ecological advantage to working the other way around – many wrasses and sea basses (families Labridae and

Schooling

A 'school' is the term used for a group of similar-sized fish that move in a coordinated manner, always swimming in the same direction and reacting almost as one. There is no leader. Members of a school use sight and the lateral line sense to stay together.

There are several benefits to be gained from schooling behaviour. First, there is never any difficulty finding a mate. Second, the members of a school may help each other to find food. Finally, and perhaps most important of all is the principle of 'safety in numbers' – the greater the numbers, the better the chance of members surviving an attack from predators, who may find it difficult to target and pick off individuals.

Of course the system is not perfect – larger schools are conspicuous and some hunters specialize in herding fish together into a dense bait ball that can be taken whole. But in general, as long as the school remains larger than the average predator's appetite, the benefits outweigh the risks.

Below: Very large schools may present predators with a formidable moving 'wall'.

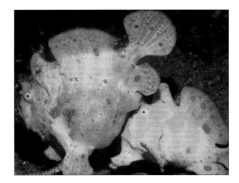

A pair of painted frogfish (Antennarius pictus) courting. The male of the species (shown right) is smaller than the female. Fertilization happens externally, with the female laying eggs held together by a mucus-like substance, known as an 'egg raft'. They are non-guarders.

Serranidae) begin life as females and become males only when they have grown sufficiently large to maintain control of a territory or a harem. Synchronous hermaphrodism, where a fish produces both female and male gametes that can function at the same time, is less common, but in species such as tripodfish this may allow individuals to self-fertilize.

Seasonality

Most fish species of temperate seas are seasonal breeders – in other words, they come into breeding condition at much the same time each year. Seasonality is regulated by hormones – chemicals released into the blood by glands, such as the hypothalamus and pituitary. This allows the fish to respond physiologically to environmental conditions – the temperature, day length and lunar cycles, for example.

Some fish breed at any time of year. These tend to be species of the warm tropics, where sea conditions remain relatively constant year round and so no season is particularly favourable. The same is true of deep-sea habitats, which are beyond the influence of surface temperatures and day length. It is thought that many deep-sea species are year-round breeders, though details of this are rarely understood in full.

Semelparity

For some fish, breeding is a once-in-a-lifetime event. These species are called semelparous, and they include eels, roughies and some salmonids, adults of which invest all their available body resources in producing large numbers of high-quality eggs to ensure a good chance of survival. Spawning leaves the adults drastically weakened and with quite literally nothing more to live for.

Survival strategies

Fish larvae are highly vulnerable to predation, but most have developed at least some adaptations that help reduce the risk of being eaten.

Some larvae, for example, are almost transparent, making them hard to see. Many have large spines or filaments that make them difficult for other small animals to swallow, while others grow exceptionally fast in order to minimize the time they spend at risk from predators of a certain size. Very often, schools of larvae live in different locations or at different depths to adults of their own species, thus reducing the risk of cannibalism when the latter feeds on small organisms.

Below: The characteristic flat, oval shape of this flounder is easy to identify in the advanced larval state.

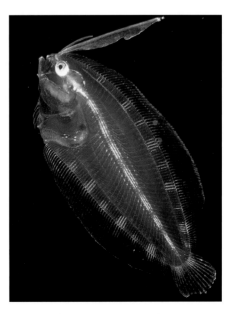

SPONGES, JELLIES AND CORALS

The simplest animals alive in our seas today are also among the oldest and the most beautiful of all marine creatures. Their simple body plan has withstood the test of time and they continue to hold their own among other much more advanced animals.

Sponges and jelly animals are among the most ancient forms of multicellular animal life. They originated 540–550 million years ago, in the period known as the Precambrian. They differ from most other forms of multicelled life in having very simple body organization.

Sponges

These animals exist in many forms, from rock-encrusting sheets to branching, vase-like structures up to 1.2m/4ft tall. Whatever their shape, all sponges grow rooted to the spot, and some are easily mistaken for plants. There are over 5,000 marine species, and a few that live in freshwater.

In sponges, the space between the inner and outer surfaces is packed with supporting material known as mesohyl (a jelly-like substance containing a mesh of protein fibres, mineral spicules and cells called amoebocytes) that makes up the bulk of the animal's mass and gives it rigidity. Amoebocytes are able to develop into any other kind of sponge cell, and will gather where the body is growing or in need of repair.

The bodies of sponges come in three main forms. The simplest are small and tubular and riddled with tiny

Above: A table coral spreads out to maximize the exposure of algae living in its polyps to sunlight. The white area around the perimeter marks the direction of continuing growth.

pores known as ostia, which open on to a central cavity, the atrium. The atrium is lined with feeding cells known as choanocytes. Each choanocyte bears a long, whip-like flagellum (filament), the beating of which draws water in through the ostia and forces it out through a large opening at the top of the atrium, called the osculum. This flow brings fresh, oxygenated water and food within reach of individual choanocyte cells and carries away carbon dioxide and other metabolic wastes.

In sponges of the next level of complexity, the atrium has a folded structure, and thus an increased

*Above: The common name of the boring sponge (*Cliona celata*) originates from its habit of boring into limestone rock and other calcareous matter.*

surface area over which food and respiratory gases can be absorbed. This improved efficiency allows them to grow larger than the tubular sponges. In the most complex forms, the atrium is reduced to a network of narrow channels and minute chambers. The current generated by the choanocytes lining these intricate channels means that a large sponge of this type can filter food and oxygen from tens of thousands of litres of water a day.

Most sponge species belong to the class Demospongia. They come in a huge variety of sizes, shapes and colours, but all have a soft, spongy skeleton – typified by that of the

Below: Aplysina archeri tubular sponges growing among corals. Water taken in through tiny pores on the side is filtered for food.

*Below: These barrel sponges (*Xestospongia* species) may grow several feet tall, indicating the efficiency of this simple body structure.*

*Below: A deep-sea glass sponge (*Hyalonema*). The fibres that form the core of the basal stalk are rather like the strands of a fibre-optic cable.*

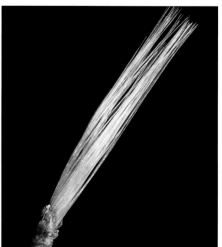

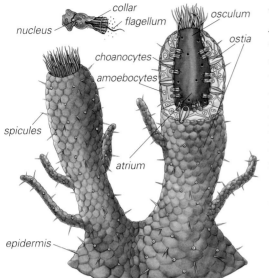

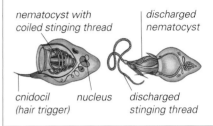

Generalized anatomy of a tube sponge

Inset, top-left, is a cutaway illustration of a choanocyte, or feeding cell. These cells line the inner surface of the sponge (see main artwork), and have a vital role to play in the intake of nutrients and expulsion of waste.

familiar bath-time sponge – made up of the proteins collagen and spongin. But other types of sponge are not at all 'spongy'. Glass sponges, of the class Hexactinella, are so-called because their skeleton is made of silicate. In calcareous sponges, class Calcarea, the skeleton spicules are made of calcium carbonate. Both glass and calcareous sponges are brittle and fragile.

Sponges feed on particles suspended in the water, including bacteria, algae and organic debris, all of which are absorbed by the choanocytes. Some sponge species allow certain algae to live inside their body, where the latter 'pay rent' by releasing small quantities of nutrient into the sponge cells.

Sponges can reproduce asexually by budding or producing a tough little packet of cells called a gemmule. This can drift about for months, or even years, before settling and developing into a new sponge.

Sponges can also reproduce sexually. Most produce both male and female sex cells, or gametes, but not at the same time. Sponge sperm are released into the water and taken in as food by other sponges. But instead of being digested they are used to fertilize eggs; these are released into the water and eventually settle to form new sponges.

Jelly animals and corals

Jelly animals – including jellyfish, corals, anemones and comb jellies – are more complex than sponges in that their cells are arranged into distinct tissues. Their bodies, however, still have just two basic layers – an external layer (ectoderm) and an internal layer lining the gut (endoderm). The jelly that fills the intervening space and gives the animals their distinctive appearance is known as mesoglea.

Cnidarian jelly animals come in two forms. Medusae, commonly known as 'jellyfish', are free-swimming, bell-shaped animals with a fringe of tentacles and a mouth located inside the bell. The second form, the polyps, is tube-shaped with a mouth surrounded by tentacles at the top and a basal disc with which the animal is usually attached to the sea floor or other object.

In some species, organisms alternate between polyp and medusoid forms, while in others, such as many anemones and corals, the medusoid form has been lost. In both medusae and polyps, the mouth opens on to a gastrovascular cavity that serves as both a simple gut and a surface for gas exchange.

Medusae are sexually reproductive, while polyps, which are thought to have evolved later, can reproduce asexually by budding or splitting in two. In groups that have lost the medusoid form, polyps can also produce gametes.

The polyp forms of two classes, the Hydrozoa and Anthozoa, which include the hard and soft corals, may

Stinging cells

All cnidarians are armed with specialized stinging cells called cnidocytes. Each stinging cell contains a small sac, called a nematocyst, in which a toxic, barbed thread lies coiled, ready to be deployed like a tiny harpoon. The potency of the toxin and the quantities in which it can be delivered vary between species. Some toxins, such as those of the box jellyfish, are lethal even to humans.

develop into colonies, some of which become the basis of reefs. These can become habitats for an enormous variety of marine life.

Ctenophores, or comb jellies, are jellyfish-like animals without a polyp form. They lack the stinging cells of cnidarians and, instead, hunt by simply engulfing anything small and weak enough they bump into. In some cases they also snare prey in tentacles that ooze a glue-like secretion.

Both cnidarians and ctenophores have a very simple, noncentralized nervous system, which allows them to process sensory information from organs, such as eyespots, gravity sensors and chemosensory pits, and coordinate activities, such as feeding, swimming and self-defence.

*Below: The upside-down jellyfish (*Cassiopea xamachana*) spends much of its life resting on the bottom of sunlit shallow seas.*

WORMS

'Worm' is a term applied loosely to a wide variety of different animals, and it is often used wrongly to imply a somehow inferior type of animal. In the marine realm, worms are highly significant, and, unlike most of their relatives on land, some have a spectacular appearance to match.

The long, thin marine animals referred to as 'worms' belong to a diverse range of taxonomic groups, as demonstrated by the italicized phyla in The Marine Tree of Life (pages 12–13). All are bilaterally symmetrical, with an elongate body and usually a head at one end. But here the similarity ends. Some groups, such as flatworms, are very simple anatomically, but others are much more complex, with highly evolved organs and complicated life histories. Nematode worms, for example, are distantly related to arthropods; both undergo periodical moults as their bodies develop. Other worm phyla, such as hemichordates, possess some vertebrate anatomy.

Annelids
The phylum Annelida comprises about 9,000 species, known as annelids or segmented worms, varying in size from a few millimetres to more than 1m/3.25ft. The basic annelid body is long, bilaterally symmetrical and made up of many segments called somites. There is usually a head at the front end, an internal system of vessels for carrying blood and metabolites and a segmentally organized nervous system.

The components of each segment are separated by walls of thin tissue. Even structures that run along the length of the animals, such as the gut and major blood vessels, have segmental features, such as digestive glands and branching lateral vessels. External features, such as the bristly 'legs', or paddles, of polychaetes like ragworms, are also arranged segmentally.

There are three major groups of annelid. The leeches occur mainly in freshwater and damp terrestrial habitats. The oligochaetes are also best known as terrestrial animals, in the form of earthworms. The polychaetes, however, are mostly marine, and come in a dazzling variety of forms, including lugworms, ragworms, Christmas tree worms and the creeping sea mice.

Nematodes
Nematode worms, often known as roundworms, live everywhere – in the soil, in rivers and streams, inside animals and plants and in the sea, from shore to abyssal depths, buried in sediment or within the bodies of host organisms. Most are small, like tiny snippets of thread, but some grow very long indeed – more than 4m/13ft.

The body of a nematode is simple, circular in cross section, and sheathed in a flexible cuticle, which is shed periodically as the animal grows.

Platyhelminths
Flatworms, which include the parasitic tapeworms and flukes as well as the free-living planarians, are the simplest of all the worm groups. However, their three body layers – ectoderm, mesoderm and endoderm – place them a level of structural complexity above the corals, anemones and jellyfish.

Tapeworms and flukes live as parasites inside the bodies of most marine animals, or as ectoparasites attached to the outside. Planarians are free-living and feed on microscopic animals and organic detritus collected from the sea floor or the water. Most are rather drably coloured, but there are a few exceptions. They are sensitive to light.

*Above: The reef-dwelling Christmas tree worm (*Spirobranchus *species) is a filter feeder. It retreats into a calcareous tube when disturbed.*

Below: Ribbon worms, such as this specimen of the Cephalothrix *genus, have a cylindrical front end and a flattened body.*

*Above: The slug-like zebra flatworm (*Pseudoceros zebra) *is often found on the surface of sponges and corals.*

*Below: The horseshoe worm (*Phoronis australis) *is seen here in its larval state. Larvae develop as free-swimming plankton.*

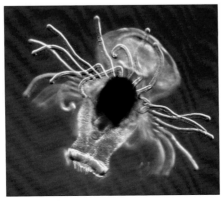

*Right: The sand mason worm (*Lanice conchilega*) spends much of its life within a tube made of sediment and shell fragments. A crown of tentacles emerges when it feeds.*

Other worm-like animals

The acorn worms (Hemichordata) share several important characteristics – such as a dorsal nerve cord and gill slits – with vertebrates. However, they never develop a notochord, the all-important supporting structure present in all chordates, and so are now classed in a separate group. A hemichordate has a trunk (up to 2.4m/7.9ft) long that is linked to the front section – a spear- or acorn-shaped proboscis – by a tiny middle section called the collar.

The unsegmented peanut worms (Sipuncula) occupy varied marine habitats, and usually live within a tube or empty mollusc shell. They feed using a retractable tube, the introvert, which extends to collect food from the surrounding substratum or water.

Priapulid worms (Priapula) live in bottom sediments, anchored in place by a knobbly or spiny tail. Like the peanut worms, they use a tube to reach out and catch food. They bear a superficial similarity to another group of sediment dwellers, the kinorhynch worms; the latter are, however, a distinct group.

Gnathostomulid worms are small flatworms that live in muddy marine deposits. They feed on organic material collected using tiny jaw-like structures.

Beardworms (Pogonophora) live in deep waters, within papery tubes made of secreted chitin. They lack a mouth and a gut, and rely on colonies of symbiotic bacteria living inside the body to provide nourishment. The front of the body bears a 'beard' of tentacles that provides a large surface area for gas exchange. Most are small but species associated with hydrothermal vents grow up to 1.5m/5ft.

Horseshoe worms (Phoronida) are tube-dwellers of warm tropical seas, named for their long, U-shaped gut. Food is gathered by a retractable crown of tentacles – the lophophore.

Arrow worms (Chaetognatha) are small, free-living, predators. Their bodies are long and straight with stabilizing fins along the flanks and tail. These worms have simple eyes and the head is armed with several stiff bristles, used for catching other small plankton-dwelling animals for food.

The parasitic spiny headed worms (Acanthocephala) live within the bodies of vertebrates, especially bony fish. They attach to the lining of the gut using a spiny or barbed proboscis. They have no mouth – they simply absorb predigested material from their surroundings. The horsehair worms (Nematomorpha) are also parasitic, but most infect freshwater or land-dwelling organisms, with just a few specializing in marine hosts.

Spoonworms and innkeeper worms (Echiura) are exclusively marine. They live in tubes in sand or mud, anchored by hooks on the tail. At the front end is a proboscis, used for shovelling up sediment that is swallowed so that the organic contents can be digested.

*Below: The cast of a lugworm (*Arenicola marina*) – an annelid whose burrowing aerates the sand as an earthworm does soil.*

Worm hydraulics

Annelid worms have no hard parts to help support their body, but they still manage to hold a firm shape and move much more actively than other worms by using what physiologists call a 'hydraulic skeleton'.

Each segment of the body contains a sealed fluid-filled space, the coelom.

Because water is not compressible, the worm can change the shape of these compartments by squeezing with muscles, but the overall volume stays the same. Thus, if the muscles on one side of a worm segment contract, the other side is forced to expand and the segment bends to one side. Alternatively, if a worm shortens its body, it also becomes thicker. In this way, the segmented worms are able to make a variety of movements from rapid wiggling modes of crawling or swimming to powerful thrusts through the sediment.

Left: This bristle worm uses simple hydraulics to great effect, propelling itself along with a characteristic s-shaped wiggle.

MOLLUSCS

Molluscs range from humble but tasty cockles and mussels to premium oysters, spectacular sea slugs and giant squid of mythical proportions. With more than 110,000 species in the phylum Mollusca, molluscs are as interesting and varied as they are numerous.

The molluscs are the second most numerous group of living animals after the arthropods. More than 110,000 modern species have been described, and literally tens of thousands more are known from the fossil record. Most molluscs produce some kind of hard shell, and it is because these preserve so well that we have this detailed record.

Of the known species, the vast majority are marine, though it should be borne in mind that certain members of the group have been extremely successful in inhabiting freshwater or terrestrial habitats.

Modern molluscs

Those molluscs living today fall into seven major groups or classes, all of which are best represented in the seas.

Of these, the most obscure are the Aplacophorans – a small group of mostly small, worm-like animals in which the shell is replaced by a flexible cuticle reinforced with calcareous spicules. Aplacophorans live mostly in deep water, so the details of their biology are not well understood.

Much better known is the next group, the Polyplacophora, commonly known as chitons. Chitons are wholly marine, and most live attached to rocks close to the shore by means of a muscular foot, on which they can creep slowly along. The largest species reach up to 40cm/15.75in in length, but most are far smaller – fitting easily into a human hand.

The most distinctive feature of chitons is a series of eight shell-like plates lying along the back and overlapping slightly. These plates are surrounded by a skirt-like girdle, which protects the underside of the creature, where the mouth, gills and reproductive organs are located in a chamber that surrounds the foot. Chitons feed mainly on algae and other encrusting organisms, which they scrape from the rocks using a muscular radula, or tongue.

The other five groups of mollusc all descended from a single, shell-bearing ancestor. The smallest group living today, the Monoplacophora, is represented by only a handful of 'living fossils' – animals such as

Above: The retracted 'foot' of this Queen conch shell (Strombus gigas) is just visible inside the opening, or aperture.

Neopilina galatheae, which was discovered as recently as 1952. *N. galatheae* is thought to resemble the common ancestor of all other shelled, or conchiferan, molluscs. With a little imagination it is possible to see how an animal such as this, with its single conical shell and muscular foot, could have given rise to members of the next group, the Gastropoda.

The gastropods include the limpets and snails. But also included within the gastropods are a number of lineages of

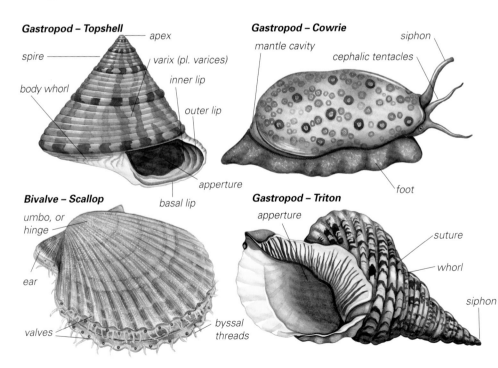

Gastropod – Topshell
apex
spire
varix (pl. varices)
body whorl
inner lip
outer lip
apperture
basal lip

Bivalve – Scallop
umbo, or hinge
ear
valves
byssal threads

Gastropod – Cowrie
mantle cavity
siphon
cephalic tentacles
foot

Gastropod – Triton
apperture
suture
whorl
siphon

The anatomy of molluscan shells

Most gastropod molluscs are univalves, or creatures possessing a shell of only one piece. They exhibit a variety of physical forms, as shown by (clockwise from top-left) the common topshell (Calliostoma zizyphinum), eyed cowrie (Cypraea argus) and giant triton (Charonia tritonis). Bivalve molluscs, like this queen scallop (Aequipecten opercularis), bottom-left, have a shell comprising two hinged parts, usually referred to as the left and right valve.

Where gastropods have a spiral shell, terminating in an apex, the hard anatomy is generally separated into two parts: the body whorl and spire. The latter is made up of numerous individual whorls, or spiral ridges, which are joined together via 'sutures'. The whorls are transversed by longitudinal ridges, called varices, which mark the points of growth.

*Above: The Caribbean reef squid (*Sepioteuthis sepioidea*) is a torpedo-shaped cephalopod with typically large eyes.*

slug-like molluscs that have lost their shells. These are the sea slugs, known as nudibranchs, and they include some of the most spectacular looking animals found in the sea.

But the prize for the most dramatic mollusc has to go to another group, one in which the shell is often greatly reduced. The cephalopods include the octopuses and squids as well as the prehistoric-looking nautilus, which, unlike its other living relatives, retains a substantial shell. Of the 700 or so living species of cephalopod, all are marine, all are carnivorous and most are fast swimming pelagic predators with refined sensory organs and nervous systems. The group includes the largest known invertebrates, the giant and colossal squids, which sometimes exceed 15m/50ft in length.

All adult cephalopods have a cluster of arms and/or tentacles around the mouth area – these appendages bear suckers or hooks that help them manipulate prey and also function in self-defence from the attentions of predators and when mating.

Swimming is achieved by a form of jet propulsion or by rhythmic movements of the arms, which are sometimes webbed. A few species of squid have developed fins, which look rather like giant flapping ears.

In most ancient cephalopods, the shell served as protection and a buoyancy device. In modern species, however, it is much reduced or absent.

The last two groups of molluscs both have distinctive-looking shells. The first, class Bivalvia, includes such familiar two-shelled forms as mussels, scallops and clams. The second, class Scaphopoda, includes the 500 or so deep-water species known as tusk shells.

Members of both groups are typically bottom-dwellers. They live resting on or buried in the substratum or, in the case of some bivalves, attached to hard surfaces. The two shells of the bivalves open to allow a current of water bringing both food and oxygen to the animal inside.

Tusk shells feed on small particles of food and detritus. This is plucked from the water or surrounding sand

Above: The shells of whelks and tritons, often found on the shore, are typically spiral in shape.

*Above: The fingerprint cyphoma (*Cyphoma signatum*) is a very small and rare mollusc.*

and transported to the mouth by unique tentacle-like structures within the shell, called captacula.

Molluscs and man

Mussels, oysters, clams, scallops, abalone, cockles, winkles, whelks, limpets, squid and octopus are all harvested for food throughout the world. Their abundance and slow movement make them easy to collect. The shells of various molluscs also have value as tools, ornaments and jewellery – even as currency in some societies. Pearls, for example, are made when an oyster coats a particle of sand lodged inside its shell with a mix of aragonite and protein. Some species have been dangerously over-exploited.

But not all molluscs are beneficial – in the past, the shipworm bivalve (*Teredo navalis*) caused untold damage to wooden ships by burrowing into their hulls. It undoubtedly cost many lives when the weakened timbers gave way and ships were wrecked.

The role of the shell

Mollusc shells protect the soft tissues of the animal within from damage by other creatures and from the effects of drying out when exposed to the air. Shells also provide a rigid attachment for the muscles in much the same way as a vertebrate skeleton. However, in most molluscs the shell lacks flexibility, so that the animal, such as a snail or limpet, must emerge to some extent from the safe interior in order to move about and feed. Chitons solve the problem by having an articulated shell made of plates which offer the creature some flexibility, if a little less protection.

Below: By day, this chiton is submerged and remains motionless, attached to the reef.

Below: At low tide, the tough girdle around the plates helps seal moisture into the body.

CRUSTACEANS

More than 45,000 species of crustacean are known to science. They are among the most diverse of all invertebrate groups and, while a few taxa including terrestrial crabs and woodlice have adapted to life on land, the vast majority of them are aquatic and marine.

Crustaceans belong to the huge group of jointed-legged invertebrates known as arthropods, which also includes insects, arachnids (spiders and scorpions) and myriapods (millipedes and centipedes). They come in a truly startling variety of sizes and shapes, ranging from microscopic copepods to giant spider crabs with a 4m/13ft leg span. Some species, such as prawns and lobsters, are familiar as food items, while others are considered so bizarre they are used as models for alien movie monsters. Many species have great economic importance and there are global fisheries for shrimps, prawns, lobsters and crabs. Many species are increasingly being taken to be ground into 'fishmeal'.

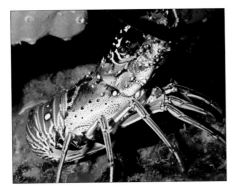

*Above: Spiny lobster (*Panulirus argus*) with exoskeleton intact.*

Below: The freshly moulted exoskeleton includes even the finest appendages.

*Above: Ghost crab (*Ocypode quadrata*) on the shore. Their prodigious burrowing habits contribute to the sandy camouflage.*

Family tree

According to the latest version of the crustacean family tree, the group contains five classes, of which three – the Branchiopoda (brine shrimps and relatives), the parasitic Remipedia and obscure Cephalocarida – contain relatively few species.

The other two are extremely large and diverse. The class Maxillopoda encompasses about 25,000 species, including the barnacles, copepods and ostracods, while the Malacostraca includes all the shrimp and louse-like species as well as the familiar decapods – true shrimps, lobsters and crabs.

Growing a new skin

The word *crustacean* means 'with a crust' – and describes the hard, highly mineralized exoskeleton that encloses the animal's body, offering both support and protection from predators. Unlike the internal skeleton of vertebrates, the exoskeleton does not grow as the animal develops, and so it must be moulted periodically.

In the days leading up to a moult, the animal concerned begins to appear lacklustre, as nutrients are withdrawn from the cuticle. Every part of the body covering is shed, including fine hairs and even the covering of the eyes. Withdrawing from the rigid exoskeleton can be a strenuous ordeal, and occasionally things can go wrong – for example, lobsters that have very large claws can become stuck in their old skin, and the only way to escape is to leave a claw behind. It does not grow back.

Having shed its restrictive suit of armour, the animal can expand slightly before the new exoskeleton begins to harden. During this soft-shelled period, it is very vulnerable to predation.

Below: The decapod arrow crabs, of the family Majidae, have sharply tapered bodies. Their long slender legs have also given them another common name – spider crabs.

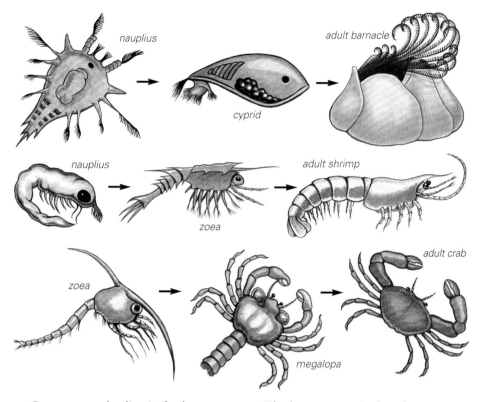

nauplius

cyprid

adult barnacle

nauplius

zoea

adult shrimp

zoea

megalopa

adult crab

Crustacean larval stages

With the exception of isopods such as marine bugs, some of which produce fully-formed young brooded in a pouch, most crustaceans undergo successive larval stages after hatching, defined by the development of various appendages and body segments. This development begins at the head. The naupliar stage (see Crustacean larvae as plankton, page 207) is characterized by an enlarged anterior section bearing a single eye. Intermediary zoea and megalopae, which belong to members of the Malacostraca such as true shrimps and crabs, exhibit marked thoracic and abdominal growth, including swimming appendages and, in zoea, the extension of the carapace to cover the head. In Maxillopods such as barnacles, the planktonic nauplius metamorphoses into a swimming cyprid larva, which, once settled in a suitable place, attaches itself to the substratum, awaiting transformation into a smaller, yet fully formed, version of the adult.

Crustaceans also live in fresh water and on land, but it is in the oceans that the group has been most successful, partly because seawater contains a ready supply of the essential minerals needed for shell building, in particular calcium carbonate. This makes the process of growing a fresh exoskeleton after every moult less of a problem.

Body design

Crustaceans have a segmented body and jointed appendages. Often, the segments are grouped into a distinct head, thorax and abdomen and there is a pair of appendages growing from each segment.

These appendages are specialized to perform a variety of very different functions. Those of the head are antennae (two pairs) and mouthparts (three pairs). But in many groups, the head and front part of the thorax have become fused into a joint structure called the cephalothorax, in which case the next few sets of appendages serve as additional mouthparts called maxillipeds. The regular thoracic appendages, known as thoracopods, are usually modified for walking. The abdomen often goes by the alternative name pleon, and its appendages are generally referred to as pleopods, swimming legs or swimmerets.

The last segment is the telson, or tail, and its appendages, if present, are called uropods or cercopods. In crabs, the abdomen is reduced and tucked away under the front of the body. The head, thorax, cephalothorax or whole body may be protected by a cylindrical or shield-like carapace, or shell, that grows from the animal's back.

Life cycle

Crustaceans develop from eggs to adults through a series of intermediate larval stages, or instars, interspersed by full moults, during which the animal sheds its exoskeleton and emerges as a slightly larger, more complicated version of its previous form.

Early larvae are plankton-dwelling creatures with a shield-shaped body that sprouts antennae and a variable number of other appendages. These simple animals are known as nauplii, and they are the most abundant form of multicellular life on Earth.

With each moult the nauplius gains segments and/or appendages, becoming more like its parent. The older larvae of different types of crustacean have different names: young barnacles are cyprids; young copepods are copepodids; shrimp-like animals pass through a larval stage called a manca; and baby crabs are known as zoea.

Xiphosurans and pycnogonids

In addition to crustaceans, there are two further classes of marine arthropods: the Xiphosura, or horseshoe crabs, and the Pycnognida, or sea spiders. Though both groups contain just a handful of living species, they represent a much larger number that existed in the past.

Horseshoe crabs belong to the same groups as spiders and scorpions, but at up to 75cm/30in in length they grow much larger than any other living member of the group. There are just four living species, all of which live in warm, shallow water on soft sediments.

The pycnogonids are more numerous – more than 1,000 species have been described, but most are inconspicuous members of the bottom fauna. Their slender legs and small bodies mean all but the largest species are easily overlooked.

Below: Horseshoe crabs are curiosities, but rarely harvested for food.

ECHINODERMS AND TUNICATES

A close look at a sea urchin or sea star is a little like examining an alien life form – they do things so differently to other animals. And, surprising as it may seem, they have some important features in common with the tunicates and with vertebrates, including ourselves.

The Echinodermata is an ancient group, and, with about 6,000 living species, it is the largest exclusively marine animal phylum. The living species are classified in five classes: the Asteroidea, or sea stars; the Ophiuroidea, or brittlestars; the Crinoidea, including sea lilies and feather stars; the Holothuroidea, or sea cucumbers; and the Echinoidea, otherwise known as sea urchins and sand dollars.

Echinoderms

The echinoderms are abundant in all the world's oceans, occupying benthic (sea floor) habitats from tidal zones to abyssal plains, where they are often the most conspicuous form of animal life. Adults of a few species of crinoid and holothurian are able to 'swim' short distances, but for the most part, echinoderms move only over the sea floor – creeping on hydraulically operated tube feet (urchins and sea stars), inching forward on waves of muscular contraction (cucumbers), or progressing by means of rapid flailing of the arms (brittlestars).

Adult crinoids are usually sessile, meaning that they spend their lives in one spot, attached to the substratum.

Most adult echinoderms are radially symmetrical – with a central mouth surrounded by body parts in radiating rows or rays, usually in multiples of five. The body is supported by a brittle endoskeleton (internal skeleton) made up of calcite plates. This is most obvious in the urchins, in which the skeleton forms a rigid 'test', which is covered by only a very thin layer of living tissue.

In sea stars, brittlestars and sea lilies the skeletal plates are separated by flexible tissue, allowing the animal to move its arms freely. In the sea cucumbers, the skeleton is greatly reduced and the animals are soft and rather rubbery to the touch.

In all echinoderms, the main organ of locomotion and movement is the water vascular system. This is a system of internal canals arranged on the same radial plan as the rest of the body, with a central ring canal and five radial canals – one running along each arm that manifests as a groove, called an ambulacrum. The canals are connected to tube feet, and when water is forced into a tube foot, it extends out through a pore.

In some species the podia, or tube feet, are used only for gas exchange – their walls are thin enough to allow dissolved gases to pass through. Often they also have a sensory role and are sensitive to touch and to chemicals in the water. In urchins and starfish, in particular, the tube feet are equipped with powerful suckers. These are used for attaching to and creeping over surfaces and for manipulating food or other objects.

In some cases, the tube feet are capable of exerting huge forces – for example, a small common sea star is able to pull open the shell of mussels to get to the animal inside.

Echinoderms eat a variety of plant and animal matter – urchins graze algae and other encrusting organisms and scavenge the remains of dead animals, which they rasp at using five

Above: A sea cucumber deposit feeding as it moves across the ocean floor.

Below: The mobile spines of this sea urchin (Diadema antillarum) *help to deter predators.*

Above: The odd proportions of this sea star suggest it may be regenerating lost body parts.

Below: The short-spined sea urchin (Lytechinus variegatus) *has a round, fat body.*

Above: Colourful crinoids orientate their feathery arms into the direction of the current to trap particles of food.

little teeth mounted on a bony, jaw-like apparatus called Aristotle's lantern. Starfish can ingest small particles of food, but are also capable of taking large items by everting their own stomach out through the mouth to envelop the prey. Brittlestars, crinoids and cucumbers are all filter feeders and omnivorous detritivores – meaning that they will consume any particulate organic material that comes their way.

Tunicates

Tunicates, which are commonly known as sea squirts and salps, are members of the phylum Urochordata. Most adult tunicates are simple, sedentary animals with a bag-like body with two siphons, or openings – one that draws fresh water in and another through which waste water is expelled. Inside the body is a large chamber, where food is filtered from the water as it passes through and gas exchange takes place.

Larval tunicates are free-swimming, tadpole-like animals that exhibit many of the characteristics used to identify chordates – namely a notochord, which stiffens the body, a dorsal nerve cord, gill slits in the pharynx and a tail that extends beyond the position of the anus.

Most significantly from an evolutionary perspective, one group of tunicates, known as larvaceans, retains these larval characteristics throughout their entire lives. It seems likely that animals very much like these may have been the ancestors of modern chordates. Apart from these free-living forms, most modern sea squirts live attached to the sea floor, some in very deep water. Sometimes they are also found attached to pieces of floating debris. There are a large number of colonial forms.

Distant relatives

Although it may seem unlikely, both the echinoderms and tunicates belong to the same evolutionary group as vertebrates – including ourselves. We may not look or feel remotely similar, but we are more closely related to these strange marine animals than we are to other invertebrate groups, including snails, insects or worms.

Evidence for this is to be found in the early stages of embryonic development. In the embryos of most invertebrate groups (arthropods, molluscs and the various worms), the mouth develops before the anus. It forms when the embryo is no more than a hollow ball of cells called a gastrula. The mouth starts off as a little dint in the ball, which enlarges to

Above: Brightly coloured sea squirts of the genus Rhopalaea *are reef-dwellers, and usually found in this opaque blue form.*

form a pocket. Cells from this pocket go on to develop into the mesoderm tissues, which make up most of the internal organs.

In echinoderms and chordates, however, the first dint goes on to form not the mouth, but the anus. The mouth forms later – hence the name for this group of animals, Deuterostomia, meaning 'mouth second'. This seems to suggest that echinoderms and chordates share a common ancestor.

How an echinoderm feeds

The radial symmetry of echinoderms is based on a network of vessels that manage the absorption of water and food.

The arrangement of this internal anatomy is effectively duplicated in each of the five arms. The central body contains the stomach, the cardiac portion of which can be pushed out through the mouth to engulf prey. When the prey is brought back, partially digested, into the body, the food is then transferred to the pyloric portion of the stomach where it is broken down further. Subsequent digestion takes place in radial passages of the gut, called pyloric caecae, and waste is excreted via the anus on the top side of the body.

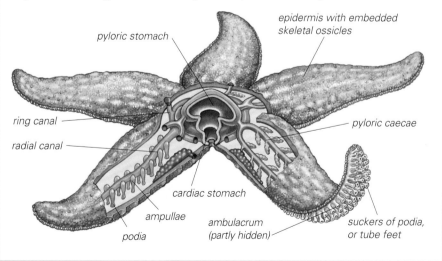

pyloric stomach
epidermis with embedded skeletal ossicles
ring canal
radial canal
pyloric caecae
cardiac stomach
ampullae
podia
ambulacrum (partly hidden)
suckers of podia, or tube feet

OTHER INVERTEBRATES

As well as the relatively well known invertebrate groups described on the previous pages, the seas are home to several other groups of animals, many of which are small and inconspicuous, but which, nevertheless, play important roles in the ecology of the world's oceans.

The smallest marine animals are protozoans. The name means 'first animals' and each individual consists of a single cell, which performs all the functions necessary to sustain life. But not all protozoans are microscopic; some can grow to several centimetres (an inch or so) across. Most feed on single-celled algae and are themselves an important source of food for a host of larger animals. Most protozoan groups live mainly in fresh water, but two large groups, related to amoebas, are predominantly marine.

Foraminiferans

Known as forams for short, these complex protozoans can grow surprisingly large – many are easily visible to the naked eye. Forams secrete a protective shell, called a test, made of calcium carbonate, silica, protein or cellulose. The test is completely enveloped in a thin layer of membrane-bound cytoplasm, which can be extended in all directions.

As the organism begins to outgrow its original shell, it starts to secrete a second test, which remains attached to the first, and the cytoplasm gradually flows into the new living space it has created for itself. Chamber after chamber can be added in this way,

Below: The fossilized remains of orbitolites – foraminiferous organisms that originated during the Eocene Epoch.

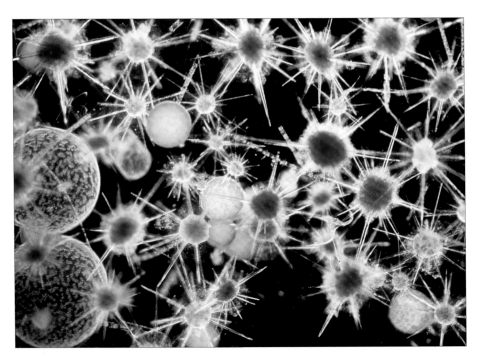

Above: Radiolarians drifting as part of a community of zooplankton.

each larger than the previous one, often creating a spiral structure that looks like a tiny snail shell.

When the foram dies, the test sinks to the bottom of the sea, where it rests in the sediment that collects there until it is eventually incorporated into sedimentary rock. Indeed, when viewed under a microscope, the particles that make up rocks such as chalk can be seen to consist almost completely of the tests of forams and other minuscule small organisms.

Below: Bryozoan colony growing on seaweed fronds. These moss-like animals have ancient origins and are common as fossils (see right).

Radiolarians

The second group of mainly marine, plankton-dwelling protozoa, the radiolarians, are generally spherical cells with a secreted external skeleton of silicate or sulphate, often ornately decorated with barbs and radiating spines. Among the spines are mobile slender, axopods – extensions of the cell membrane containing stiff

Below: Fenestella, often described as 'lace-bryozoan' due to its radiating branches, thrived during the Carboniferous Period, but was extinct by the beginning of the Permian. Fossilized remains are common in quarries.

Above: Laboratory specimen of the flat, jelly-like placozoan Trichoplax adhaerens.

cytoplasm and supported by an internal scaffold of microtubules, which serve as the structural components within cells.

Several species are sufficiently large that individuals can be seen with the naked eye, while others form floating spherical colonies that can grow as large as several centimetres across.

Lampshells

Of the 30,000 or so described species of brachiopods, also known as lampshells, more than 99 per cent are extinct and are known only from fossils. Lampshells were formerly classified as bivalve molluscs because most of the body is enclosed within two articulated shells. The ventral shell, on the bottom, is larger than the dorsal one on the top, and it often has an extended lip or spout, which makes the animal look a little like a Roman oil lamp.

Internally, these animals are nothing like molluscs. Most of the space inside the shell is taken up with a large gut and a tentacled feeding organ, the lophophore – a larger version of the feeding structure seen in bryozoans. Lampshells live attached to hard substrates by a fleshy stalk. They occur at all depths and are eaten by many larger animals.

Below: The extinct brachiopod Terebratula semiglobosa, *which lived during the Cretaceous Period, displaying its stalk.*

Plate animals

The phylum Placozoa contains only two described species of what may be the simplest of all multicellular animals. Certainly they contain less DNA that any other animal ever tested. The best known is *Trichoplax adhaerens*, a flat, jelly-like organism comprising little more than a packet of jelly-like material containing fibrous cells enclosed between two layers of outer cells. The cells on the upper surface are flagellated. It was first discovered clinging to the glass of an aquarium, but it has since turned up in samples collected in tropical and sub-tropical seas around the world.

Moss animals

Known scientifically as bryozoans, moss animals are small, mostly marine invertebrates that live in colonies encrusting rocks, seaweeds and the like, as well as man-made structures such as sea walls, ships' hulls, piers and buoys.

The individual animals (zooids) within a bryozoan colony are tiny – usually less than a millimetre long. They are known as zooids and live inside individual walled compartments, keeping contact with their neighbours via tiny pores.

Bryozooids are anatomically very simple. Each one possesses a large U-shaped gut with a cluster of ciliated tentacles, called the lophophore, around the mouth. When feeding, the lophophore is thrust out into the water under hydrostatic pressure. The tentacles are covered in tiny cilia, which sweep particles of food into the gut.

Colonies grow by asexual budding of individual zooids. In species such as the common kelp sea mats, colonies form flat, encrusting masses that spread gradually to cover an ever-increasing area, a little like terrestrial moss. In other species, the colonies are more elaborate – for example, the branching *Burgula* and the rose or ross 'coral', which form large, brittle structures resembling hard coral.

Most kelp sea mat colonies are short-lived and develop fast, especially in spring, but they die towards the end

*Above: The elaborate structure of a ross 'coral' (*Pentaphora felicia*), a bryozoan colony.*

of the summer, along with the algae on which they grow. In longer-lived colonies, such as the intricate ross coral, individual zooids die and are replaced by new ones, which digest the remains of their predecessors. So very little is wasted.

Bryozoans also reproduce sexually, producing eggs and sperm that combine and develop into free-swimming larvae. These disperse a short distance and settle when they make contact with a suitable substratum. Having attached themselves, they begin budding off new individuals and develop rapidly into a new colony.

Below: One of the few living brachiopods, Neothyris lenticularis, *is found only in deep waters off New Zealand and the Subantarctic.*

MARINE AMPHIBIANS AND REPTILES

The cold-blooded amphibians and reptiles provide an evolutionary link between the wholly aquatic fish and the so-called higher terrestrial vertebrates, such as birds and mammals. While few modern amphibians tolerate life in salty water, the reptiles are well represented in the seas and oceans.

There are no purely marine amphibians, and very few species can even tolerate salt water for more than a few minutes. Their thin, permeable skin allows salt to be absorbed and water to be drawn out of the body by the process of osmosis – leading rapidly to dehydration and death. The handful that can cope with these conditions are all species of frog and toad – most notably the marine toad (also known as the cane toad) and the mangrove-dwelling crab-eating frog of southeast Asia. Reptiles, with their impermeable skin, are air breathers, but they are better equipped to cope with the osmotic rigours of sea water.

Snakes and lizards

Of the four living orders of reptiles, only one consists of wholly marine representatives. In the order Squamata,

*Above: A hawksbill turtle (*Eretmochelys imbricata*) is seen here feeding on salps.*

Above: The hawksbill shell displays the typical cheloniid plates, or 'scutes'.

which includes snakes and lizards, there are about 70 species of sea snake, all hailing from the cobra family, Elapidae. All sea snakes have a salt gland under the tongue that helps them to maintain osmotic balance. Members of the subfamily Laticaudinae, sometimes known as sea kraits, are restricted to near-shore habitats and must come ashore to bury eggs. All the other species are fully aquatic and give birth to live young without ever leaving the water.

Other aquatic adaptations in snakes include a well-developed tail fin or a flattened, ribbon-like body to help generate thrust when swimming and nostrils that can be closed to prevent water from getting in. Most species are associated with reefs or other near-shore habitats, but the yellow-bellied sea snake may be found hundreds of kilometres from any shoreline. In addition to the sea snakes, there are also a few 'marine' lizards, such as the well-known Galapagos iguana (*Amblyrhynchus cristatus*), although none is wholly aquatic. These animals breed on land and forage in the shallows.

Turtles

Marine turtles belong to the order Testudines, along with the terrestrial and freshwater turtles and tortoises. They evolved from land-dwelling ancestors and remain tied to land for purposes of breeding, but in all other respects they are fully marine animals.

*Below: The leatherback turtle (*Dermochelys coriacea*) is the largest living turtle. It can grow to more than 2m/6.6ft in length.*

In their element

Sea turtles are highly efficient swimmers, and positively speedy compared to their land-bound relatives the tortoises. Most species can cruise at about 20kmph/ 12mph but green turtles and leatherbacks have both been recorded fleeing at speeds of up to 32kmph/20mph when alarmed. Sea turtles can dive for up to two hours at a time, and leatherbacks have been recorded at depths as great as 640m/2100ft.

*Below: A green turtle (*Chelonia mydas*) swims to the surface.*

Above: A female leatherback turtle may lay anywhere between 60 and 100 eggs in holes excavated in the sand. When hatched, they will leave the nest in small groups.

Above: These hawksbill hatchlings will race to the sea minutes after hatching. Their chances of survival on land are slim: many fall victim to predators, such as birds.

Marine turtles are anatomically distinct from other turtles in having front limbs modified into wing-like flippers. This makes them clumsy on land, but equips them magnificently for the open sea. Within the flippers, the turtles retain the five-fingered, or pentadactyl, skeleton of their ancestors, although the bones of the digits are bound together by a tight sheath of connective tissue that prevents them moving independently. The hind limbs are paddle-shaped.

The carapace, or shell, of marine turtles is thinner than that of land-living species. To improve streamlining, it is also flatter and typically tapers to a point on the trailing edge. Another characteristic of sea turtles is their size – they include several of the largest turtle species in the world.

The seven species of sea turtle fall into two main groups – the leathery-shelled Dermochelyidae, with one species, and the Cheloniidae with six.

The leatherback turtle lacks scales or bony scutes, but beneath the tough skin is a shell of thin plates made of bone and a layer of fatty blubber. This insulating layer allows the species to survive in much colder water than any other turtle species and it often ventures into high latitudes while other species are restricted to the tropics and warmer temperate zones.

In contrast, the bodies of cheloniid turtles are more tortoise-like, with a bony shell covered with scutes of lustrous tortoiseshell made from the same dermal (skin) protein found in the scales, horns, nails, claws, hair and feathers of mammals and birds. The number and arrangement of scutes, and of scales on the skin, is different for each species.

Turtles lack teeth, but most have beak-like structures, sheathed in the horny substance keratin, on the upper and lower jaw. The shape of the beak varies between species, according to the different dietary specializations of the animals concerned.

Marine turtles are the only reptiles that undertake migrations on the scale of those of terrestrial vertebrates. While the hawksbill (*Eretmochelys imbricata*), Australian flatback turtle (*Natator depressus*) and loggerhead turtle (*Caretta caretta*) spend extended periods associated with reefs and near-shore waters, the other species are highly oceanic, except when the need to breed brings them close to shore.

Apart from at breeding times, turtles will travel widely in search of food – sometimes purposefully crossing whole oceans or simply wandering with no fixed destination in mind. Most retain an impressive loyalty to their roots,

Below: Part of the endangered population of marine iguanas (Amblyrhynchus cristatus), which inhabit the Galapagos islands.

however, and having come of age will journey thousands of kilometres in order to breed in the vicinity of their home beaches.

Adult turtles mate at sea and the females venture on to sandy beaches where they bury batches of rubbery-shelled eggs above the high-tide line. As with other reptiles, the speed of development and the sex of the developing young are dependent on temperature – below a certain threshold incubation temperature, clutches of eggs all hatch as males; above it, they are all female.

Conservationists are now expressing concern that the onset of global warming may deal turtles a double blow – not only will hotter sand temperatures interfere with the normal sex ratios, but also raised sea levels and increasingly stormy weather will threaten their breeding beaches.

Crocodiles

Members of the third order of reptiles, the crocodilians, are occasional visitors to the sea. Crocodiles, alligators and their relatives are principally freshwater animals, and there are no fully marine species. However, several species are tolerant of salty water and it is quite common for certain species to venture into the sea. For example, Australian saltwater crocodiles (*Crocodylus porosus*) spend their early lives in freshwater habitats, close to the parental den, but they are often pushed out as young adults. They may then spend extended periods at sea, hunting on reefs, before returning to the river systems and swamps to claim a territory.

Below: Even juvenile saltwater (estuarine) crocodiles (Crocodylus porosus) may be up to 2m/6.6ft in length.

MARINE MAMMALS

Mammals are warm-blooded vertebrates that evolved on land from reptile-like ancestors. Members of several mammal groups have returned to the sea, but the degree to which they have committed to the marine lifestyle varies considerably.

Early mammals were tiny shrew-like insectivores, but they diverged rapidly following the demise of the dinosaurs approximately 64 million years ago, and in time became enormously successful on land.

The defining characteristics of mammals are warm blood, a body that is covered in hair or fur, a lower jaw that hinges directly from the skull, nucleated red blood cells and the ability of females to nourish their young on milk secreted from specialized glands, or mammae, in the skin.

Semi-aquatic mammals

The return to the sea has been made more than once by animals on very different branches of the mammal family tree. Modern marine mammals vary in the degree to which they have embraced the aquatic lifestyle. Some, such as otters, use the sea merely as a supermarket – visiting when they need to feed, and sometimes spending hours drifting lazily at the surface, but returning to land on a daily basis.

In contrast, polar bears are at least as much at home at sea as they are on land. They breed and hibernate on the

*Above: Sea otters (*Enhydra lutris*) float on their backs when resting on the water's surface.*

*Below: Sireneans, such as dugongs (*Dugong dugon*) have a distinctive bulbous snout.*

sea ice that covers the Arctic Ocean during the winter months, and return to dry land only in summer when the ice melts.

Seals and sealions feed at sea and may spend several months in the open ocean, but they, too, like the otter,

*Above: A colony of female southern elephant seals (*Mirounga leonina*) hauled up on land.*

Below: Sadly, many dugongs, although a protected species, drown in trawler nets.

must return to land to breed, rear young and moult. All semi-aquatic mammals have retained some of the features typical of land-dwelling mammals, including a coat of fur and an ability to move about on land.

Fully aquatic mammals

Two groups of mammals have committed fully to a wholly aquatic lifestyle: sirenians (the dugongs and manatees) and cetaceans (the whales and dolphins).

Returning to the sea brought several advantages to the ancestors of modern marine mammals. For a start, the seas were full of food – fish and invertebrates for the predators and kilometres of green sea grasses at the edges for the grazers. In water, the bodies of marine mammals become virtually weightless, and once relieved of the need to support their own body mass, some have been able to become very large – reaching sizes so great that

There she blows

When a large whale exhales at the surface, it expels not only air, but also moisture from the lungs. In cool air, this condenses as it leaves the warm windpipe and forms a visible cloud of vapour. Differences in the shape and positioning of the blowholes in different species give the vapour cloud, or 'blow', a characteristic appearance that experienced whale watchers can use to identify the species concerned.

For example, the blow of a sperm whale is always directed forwards and to the left, while those from the twin blowholes of right whales form a distinct 'V'. The blow of a fin whale is tall and disperses before the whale's back rolls forward. The blow of a minke whale is much lower and appears simultaneously with the rolling back.

*Below: The distinctive 'blows' emitted by whales vary in height and shape. Here we see the exhalations of (from left to right) the blue whale (*Balaenoptera musculus*), southern right whale (*Eubaleana australis*) and bowhead whale (*Balaena mysticetus*).*

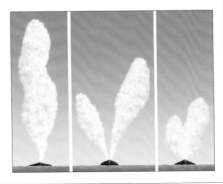

*Above: Striped dolphins (*Stenella coeruleoalba*) 'porpoising' – a high-speed action combining long jumps and swimming*

adults have nothing to fear from any predator, except humans. Size, and a thick layer of blubber, allows great whales to exploit even very cold polar waters, where food is available in great abundance at certain times of year. Having committed fully to an aquatic lifestyle, the ancestors of modern whales and sireneans lost most of their fur – blubber provides more effective insulation in water.

Sireneans now live only in warm, shallow coastal waters of the Indian and Atlantic Oceans. The only known Pacific species, Steller's sea cow (*Hydrodamalis gigas*), was hunted to extinction in 1768. Bycatch continues to pose a threat. The sea cow was a cold-water species – considerably larger than its surviving relatives. The living species of dugong and manatee are gentle grazing animals. They swim slowly using forelimbs modified into flippers and a dorsoventrally flattened tail – rounded in dugongs and concave, like a whale's flukes, in the manatees.

Cetaceans are the ultimate in mammalian marine adaptation. Not only do they spend their entire lives at sea, they exhibit a range of finely tuned adaptations that parallel those of fish. Indeed, historically cetaceans were sometimes regarded as a kind of fish. In Western science it was the Greek naturalist Aristotle who first correctly classed them as mammals due to their breeding biology.

The similarities between, say, a shark and a dolphin are the result of evolutionary convergence – different organisms developing similar adaptations in response to the same set of challenges. But despite their fish-like fins and body streamlining, cetaceans still carry full mammalian credentials: they are warm blooded, give birth to live young and they suckle them for the first months or years of life. And, they breathe air.

When a young whale is born, its mother, sometimes helped by other family members, bears it gently to the surface to take its first breath. Whales breathe through modified nostrils on top of the head.

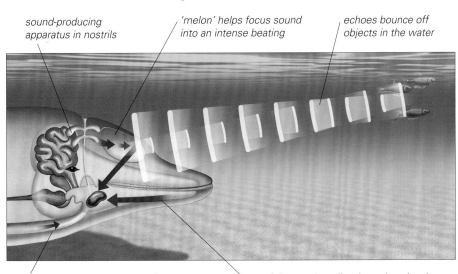

sound-producing apparatus in nostrils

'melon' helps focus sound into an intense beating

echoes bounce off objects in the water

air forced along wind pipes from lungs is used to generate sound

sound detected as vibrations along jaw bone is interpreted by the brain

How dolphins use sound to navigate
Dolphins are able to produce a variety of different sounds, and build a picture of their surroundings using echo-location, or sonar. This enables them to hunt in total darkness.

SEA LIFE AND HUMANS: CONSERVATION AND EXPLOITATION

Humans have always depended on the sea to provide food, as a means of exploration and as a source of scientific insight. But exploitation comes at a price, one that threatens to land us all in very deep water.

Man's insatiable appetite for food and resources has placed enormous stress on marine ecosystems. Many species have been hunted or harvested to the brink of extinction, and some have already disappeared.

One of the most shocking examples of this was the hunting of Steller's sea cow (*Hydrodamalis gigas*) – a relative of the dugongs and manatees that was hunted to extinction just 27 years after its discovery in 1741. Other large marine mammals were almost lost – and some may still disappear despite efforts to conserve them – blue whales, fin whales, right whales and sei whales are all listed as endangered by the IUCN (see panel, opposite).

One of the best documented cases of overfishing concerns cod. Hundreds of years ago, these fish were so common in some parts of the northwest Atlantic that they could be scooped out with a basket. Even 120 years ago, biologists believed it would be impossible for them ever to be fished out. But, improved fishing technology changed all that and allowed trawlers to pursue ever dwindling stocks with greater intensity.

The western Atlantic cod fishery reached crisis point in 1992, when the Canadian government was forced to

Above: The flensing deck of a whaling station where carcasses were stripped or 'flensed' of hide and meat. Happily, this one, in Australia, now only functions as part of a museum.

establish a total moratorium on fishing for cod. The ban remains in place, as stocks have still not returned to levels where cod fishing could be sustained. Recovery remains doubtful.

Pollution

The seas have been used as a dumping ground for waste for centuries. With human civilization now consuming more raw materials than at any time in history, the volume and variety of waste is greater then ever. Wastes that end up in the sea include heavy metals, pesticides and persistent toxic and even radioactive chemicals originating from agriculture and industrial sources.

However, not all pollution involves man-made chemicals. Any substance put into the oceans in inappropriate quantities can be damaging. Silt, for example, is a fine sediment that occurs naturally in rivers and is ultimately washed out to sea. But in areas where deforestation leads to excessive erosion, the silt load can be immense, choking all life close to the river estuary. Oil is another natural substance, but released into the sea can cause severe damage not only to the environment, but to all species that rely on the water.

When oil breaks up, the chemicals it contains can still cause problems – for example, polynuclear aromatic hydrocarbons (PAHs) lead to abnormalities in fish and other marine animals.

Other toxic chemical pollutants include mercury, which accumulates in the bodies of animals that consume contaminated food. In this way, it becomes more concentrated the higher up the food chain it travels. Dioxins from paper-making and agrochemicals cause mutations in living cells and are known carcinogens. Polychlorinated biphenyls (PCBs), which were released in large quantities up until the 1980s, lead to reproductive problems in many animals. Tributyl tin (TBT), widely used in paints designed to prevent barnacles and other fouling organisms settling on ships' hulls, was found to be the cause of deformities in many shellfish, often masculinizing females. Other chemicals that frequently enter the water system have similar gender-bending effects on fish and other aquatic organisms.

Below: These living stromatolites, rock-like organisms, are the oldest form of life on Earth. They are protected within the Shark Bay World Heritage Site, Western Australia.

Above: Cage traps are easily entered but hard to escape. As they do not damage the catch, they may be used by the aquarium trade.

Light and sound are also a form of pollution and both have been shown to disrupt the behaviour of marine animals. Several recent mass strandings of whales have been attributed to military operations involving loud underwater explosions.

Global warming

Climate change and global warming driven by the greenhouse effect are often cited as the most serious problems facing today's world. Rising sea levels and increasingly stormy, unpredictable weather patterns will

undoubtedly cause problems for animals living on land, especially on the coasts. But what about those living in the sea? Climate change is already taking a toll in all our oceans. Even slight increases in average temperatures can lead to sensitive animals, such as corals, dying off across wide areas. The phenomenon known as coral bleaching has already hit parts of all the world's major reef systems.

Other likely effects of warming include changes in some of the major ocean currents, which may mean whole seas changing their temperature or nutrient profile. Local species not able to adapt will then face extinction.

The fossil evidence of millions of years shows that life in the oceans has suffered enormous setbacks before. Life has continued, one way or another. But the environmental decisions being made now may determine how long our oceans retain the assemblages of species we are familiar with today.

Conservation

The story of man's relationship with the sea and the animals that live in it is not all one of exploitation and

Above: These corals died when the seawater became too warm. The process, known as 'bleaching', is an increasing problem.

destruction. In recent years, the conservation movement has made significant advances that go some way to redressing the balance.

In response to international concerns over the state of the world's oceans, the United Nations has designated a number of natural World Heritage Sites with a marine element and various nations around the world have given areas of coast or ocean protected status as marine National Parks or reserves. Several global conservation charities invest heavily in marine projects, and there are literally hundreds of charities and non-governmental organizations devoted exclusively to the protection of the seas and marine animals.

In 1986 the International Whaling Commission established a global ban on commercial whaling, although Japan has exploited a loophole allowing them to kill a certain number of whales 'for scientific purposes', and Norway has resumed hunting minke whales in contravention of the ban.

Another international agreement, the Convention on International Trade in Endangered Species of Wild Flora and Fauna (CITES) was signed in 1973. It now has 169 signatory nations. International agreements are also in place to protect migrating animals (the Convention on Migratory Species), stocks of fish and other marine animals. Even though these systems involve an enormous amount of bureaucracy, their attempts to moderate exploitation must be seen as a step in the right direction.

Marine life in peril

The International Union for Conservation of Nature and Natural Resources (IUCN) Red List profiles species considered to be at risk of extinction. Species on the list have been assessed by experts and are placed into categories that reflect the severity of the threat they face. Species included within the categories Vulnerable, Endangered and Critically Endangered include 429 mostly

marine crustaceans, nearly 1,000 molluscs (marine, freshwater and terrestrial), 66 sharks and rays, 731 bony fish (freshwater and marine) and 14 cetaceans.

Other groups are less represented on the list, but this does not mean they are not at risk. The inaccessible nature of many marine habitats means that many species could dwindle and disappear without recognition.

*Below: The IUCN lists the hawksbill turtle (*Eretmochelys imbricata*) as Critically Endangered. Many drown in fishing nets.*

Below: The shell of a drowned hawksbill is cleaned for display as part of a school campaign addressing threats to local fauna.

SEA WATCHING

An abundance of books, television programmes and Internet websites make it possible to learn an enormous amount about marine wildlife and the oceans without ever leaving the classroom or the comfort of your favourite armchair. But what about exploring the real thing?

For most marine enthusiasts, there is no substitute for experiencing the ocean and its astonishing diversity of life first hand. While most of us will never have the opportunity to descend to the deep ocean floor, there is no reason why we cannot experience more accessible marine habitats – sometimes without even getting our feet wet.

The water's edges

A great deal can be learned about the sea from its edges. A day spent beachcombing or rock-pooling on an interesting section of coastline will yield sightings of animals from the majority of the groups described in this book.

On sandy beaches, for example, look along the strand line – that zone on the beach where the high tide deposits its debris before retreating – for the shells of molluscs, live crabs, beach fleas, stranded jellyfish and sea stars, as well as animals such as bryozoans and whelks attached to fronds of seaweed, the distinctive eggs

Below: If you would prefer not to go into the water, rock pools on the shore teem with life – from crustaceans to tunicates and small fish.

Above: Scuba diving requires proper equipment and training, but it is a fantastic way to experience marine wildlife close up.

of sharks and rays, and occasionally the bodies of dead fish. In the sand itself you will likely see the characteristic squiggly casts of lugworms, and if you dig fast enough you may find the animal itself.

Although you might not be lucky enough to come across a real trophy – the large bones of dead cetaceans, for example, or a fabulous queen conch shell – the important thing to remember is that size is not important. Many of the most rewarding discoveries are tiny, so be prepared to get down on your hands and knees for a close look at what is on offer.

On rocks right up to the high-tide mark you will find hardy creatures, such as limpets, whelks and barnacles, clamped tight shut to avoid drying out. Closer to the low tide mark, and

especially in the pools of water left behind by the tide, you can begin to experience a whole new world – look for more anemones with their tentacles extended in the water (or retracted when exposed to air), sea squirts, sea urchins and brittlestars, ragworms, sea slugs and mussels, as well as small fish, such as blennies, gobies and rockling.

Below: Rock barnacles (Balanus species) may be spotted close to – or even encrusting – other shell animals such as limpets.

Shallow water

The next step for the avid rockpooler is to venture into large tidal pools, or below the low-tide mark. The physical properties of air and water mean that light is transmitted differently through each. Eyes such as ours, which are adapted for seeing in air, tend not to focus very well in water – hence, when opening your eyes in the sea or in a swimming pool, everything seems blurry. But by keeping the water away from your eyes – by using goggles, a mask or a glass-bottomed viewing tray, your reward will be a perfectly clear picture of the watery world around you.

Using a snorkel to help you breathe will allow you to move more carefully and observe this new habitat for longer periods – coming up for air every few seconds is disorientating and it disturbs the wildlife. Snorkelling gives you a fine view of the world below the surface and it is the perfect way to explore calm, shallow waters just 1m/3.25ft or so deep.

Going deeper

However, in order to get a close look at animals living a little deeper – say 2–20m/6–70ft down – you need a bit more equipment and a course of training in scuba diving techniques.

Diving is not difficult, nor should it be especially strenuous. Admittedly, it is not for everyone – those with asthma or a heart condition, as well as those who suffer from claustrophobia may be better off staying at the surface.

Below: Reef squid are often curious about divers and snorkellers. They may change colour quickly as a means of communication.

Above: Boat trips offer a great way to get a look at the type of open-water marine life you could never see close to the shore. You might see a spotted dolphin (Stenella dubia).

However, dive schools will be able to arrange guided dives for almost any reasonably fit individual, or train those with a keener interest to a level where they can plan and undertake their own shallow dives with other qualified divers within a period of a week.

Modern, well-maintained scuba equipment is extremely safe, as long as it is used correctly, and it will allow you to explore reef and subtidal zones in intimate detail. Face-to-face meetings with marine invertebrates, turtles, seals and cetaceans, and of course all kinds of fish (including large sharks), are all part of the thrill of this popular sport.

Alternatives

But if all that sounds rather too adventurous or expensive, don't worry. The beaches and rockpools are still yours to enjoy, and some of the most exciting sea-watching experiences can be had from boats.

Whale watching features near the top of almost every list of great wildlife experiences. Because whales are mammals and breathe air, they must come to the surface regularly. And while they are there, many species seem to delight in taking a good look at the world above the water.

Most cetaceans are intelligent and inquisitive animals and will often investigate boats. And although we do not fully understand their behaviour, they seem playful when performing their acrobatic antics. Activities such as breaching (leaping clear of the water),

Above: The enormous head of a sperm whale (Physeter macrocephalus). These sea mammals are often attracted by ships, and may swim close or perform in recognition.

lobtailing (slapping the surface with the tail) and spyhopping (bobbing upright with the head out of the water) are just some of the performances that endear these amazing mammals to us.

But to witness them close up is another matter entirely – there is the chance to hear the sound of a massive exhalation, and even catch the fishy scent of whale breath! These are the unforgettable memories that lucky whale watchers treasure forever.

Watching from the shore

Whales and other large marine animals such as seal and basking sharks can also be watched from the shore. Pick a calm, slightly overcast day, settle yourself comfortably on a prominent headland, and don't forget your binoculars, a picnic and good book to read while you wait.

Below: It may be possible to spot whales swimming close to the shore by the jet of vapour they send out when exhaling.

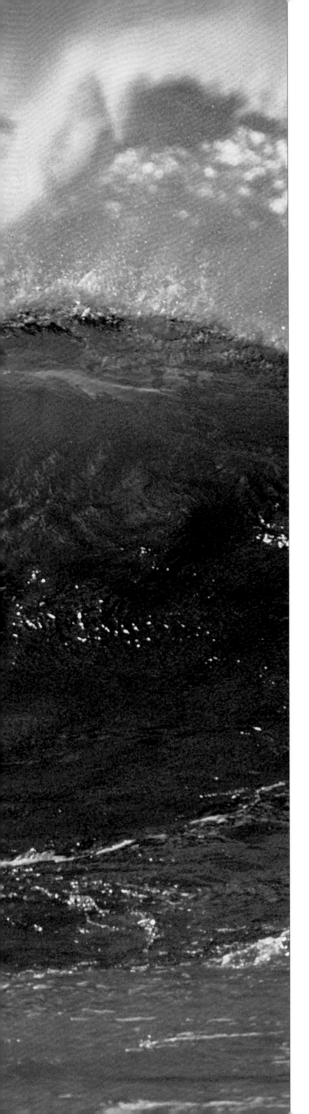

MARINE HABITATS

Marine habitats tend not to exist in isolation. Apart from a few inland seas such as the Caspian and Aral, our seas, oceans, estuaries and straits are, by their very nature, continuous. They often blend with each other in such a way that it can be difficult to say where one ends and the next begins. Likewise, it is not possible to draw a line on a map and say 'Here a species or ecosystem exists, but there, on the other side of the line, it does not'. So the distinctions described in this book are, like those made by most marine scientists, rather broad.

One useful way to divide up marine habitat zones is by depth. But within these broad divisions there will be differences from ocean to ocean, and between latitudes – the tropics and polar seas are quite different in character and yet many species take advantage of both by undertaking seasonal migrations. Local habitats and their ecosystems are also influenced by local geology. In the mid-ocean ridges, for example, molten rock forced from splits in the Earth's crust creates virgin sea bed, available to any creature that can tolerate the depth, heat and the mix of chemicals released into the water. At the other extreme, ancient crust raised above sea level to form land is continuously being eroded, creating sand, silt and mud.

The marine environment has many extremes, but between these are countless composite habitats. Life, in some form or another, has found a way to exploit each and every one.

Above, left to right: Lone tree on tropical beach shore; orca (Orcinus orca) pair swimming; leopard seal (Hydrurga leptonyx) reclining on ice.
Left: The movement of the water is responsible for shaping environments, depositing water, silt, salt and nutrients, and for increasing the availability of dissolved oxygen.

OCEAN OR SEA?

About 98 per cent of all the water on Earth is contained in the oceans and seas. The other 2 per cent, be it held within polar ice caps or inland lakes and rivers, has all been part of an ocean at some point in the past, and will be again in the future.

In everyday parlance, the terms 'ocean' and 'sea' are often used interchangeably to describe the marine realm. However, they are not the same thing. Strictly speaking, an ocean is an expanse of water lying over a thin area of the Earth's crust.

Oceanic crust is relatively new in geological terms. It forms along an area known as a mid-ocean ridge, from molten rock forced to the surface. Thus, rocks closer to the mid-ocean ridges are newer than those at the ocean edges. Because new crust is continually being formed along these ridges, areas of continental crust, or plate, are gradually being pushed apart. Obviously the Earth is not getting any bigger, so an amount of crust equivalent to that being produced is either being eliminated, by sinking back under the continental plate, or folded up to create extra-thick pieces of crust – creating continents and mountain ranges.

Continental drift

In geological terms, the shape and structure of oceans is not constant. Most people are familiar with the idea of seven continents (Europe, Asia, Africa, North and South America, Australia and Antarctica), and five major oceans – the Pacific, Atlantic, Indian, Southern and Arctic. But this now-familiar arrangement has evolved over time. An alien observing the Earth 200 million years ago would have noted two continents, now known to geologists as Laurasia and Gondwanaland, surrounded by ocean and separated by a wedge-shaped sea, now called Tethys. An observer from an even more ancient civilization, some 500 million years ago, would have seen just one great ocean, Panthalassa, swirling around a single landmass, now known as Pangaea or Rodinia.

The idea that the Earth's crust is mobile, that continents float around on fragments of thick crust separated by a layer of thinner crust, and that this thinner crust holds the world's oceans, is really very new. Most early 20th-century geologists considered the notion preposterous when first proposed by the German Alfred Wegener in 1915.

The seas

By definition, a 'sea' is a body of salt water overlying a depression within a chunk of continental crust. In many cases, this depression is close to the edge of the plate, so the sea may be adjoined to an ocean – as with the North Sea, the Caribbean Sea and the South China Sea. In others, the depression is wholly landlocked – as with the Caspian and Aral Seas of Central Asia. These inland seas are not to be confused with lakes – which by definition are bodies of freshwater.

Seas are almost always shallower than oceans. The depth of the world's oceans and seas varies greatly, to a

The moving continents

Over the last 500 million years, Earth's continents have merged together then split and drifted apart. About 225 mya (million years ago) at the end of the Permian, all land was joined in one supercontinent geologists call Pangaea. Pangaea began to drift apart about the time dinosaurs appeared on Earth, so different kinds of dinosaur evolved in newly separated parts of the world. The maps here show the current continental shapes to help identify them, but in fact their shapes have varied as low areas were flooded and mountain ranges rose up.

Permian 225 mya *During the Permian period, all the world's landmasses moved together to form the giant continent Pangaea.*

Late Triassic 205 mya *During the Triassic, a wedge of ocean called the Tethys Seaway grew wider, elbowing into the east of Pangaea.*

Jurassic 150 mya *In the Jurassic period, the great landmass Pangaea began to split into a northern supercontinent, Laurasia, and a southern one, Gondwana.*

Cretaceous 80 mya *By the Cretaceous, Laurasia and Gondwana had split up to form today's northern and southern continents. India began drifting northwards towards Asia.*

Present day *Over the last 50 million years, the North Atlantic has opened up to divide Europe and America, and India has forged into Asia. The major oceans of the world have formed.*

Hawaii – marine microcosm

In the space of a few hours, a marine biologist visiting this archipelago, in the middle of the Pacific Ocean, could theoretically visit examples of all the major habitat zones described in this book – open water, deep ocean trenches, coral reefs, turbulent shorelines, tidal pools, sandy beaches and estuaries, each with their own distinctive communities of superbly adapted animals.

Below: The islands of Hawaii are less than 5 million years old – the result of continuing volcanic activity.

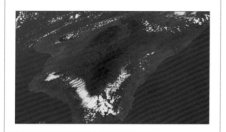

maximum of almost 11km/36,000ft in the deepest trenches. The average depth is about 3.7km/2.3 miles.

Marine chemistry

Water is a superb solvent, in which an enormous range of other chemicals can be dissolved. The water that fills the oceans and seas, usually referred to as seawater, is salty. It contains chemicals that originate from the Earth's atmosphere, from the rocks of its crust and from biological organisms. Present in large quantities are ionic (electrically charged) forms of the minerals chlorine, sodium, sulphate, magnesium, calcium and potassium. Between them, these chemicals account for more than 99 per cent of the mineral content of the oceans. It is no coincidence that these same compounds appear in large quantities in the bodies of most living organisms – indeed, the body fluids of some of the simplest forms of marine life are little more than seawater.

Right: World ocean currents have a major impact on the temperament of different oceans and on world climates. Some currents, (red arrows) carry water heated by the sun away from the tropics, and into cooler temperate and polar zones, while others (blue arrows) transport cooler water from high latitudes back towards the tropics.

Frozen oceans

Water is unusual in that it expands slightly when it freezes, therefore becoming less dense. This means ice floats – and this is very significant. If oceans froze from the bottom up, instead of the top down, it would be very difficult for life to become established on the sea floor in cooler parts of the world. Another important property of water is its capacity to absorb heat energy. It takes an enormous input of heat to raise the temperature of an ocean by even a tiny amount, but, having been warmed up, the water then takes a long while to

Above: The relative densities of frozen and liquid water are strikingly illustrated by towering ice bergs floating on the seawater.

cool down. Thus the oceans act as vast storage heaters for the planet – ultimately it is the interaction of these areas of hot and cold air that generate 'weather'. The influence of the oceans on land is most apparent at the edges of the continents, where winters are much milder than they are inland. Compare the climates of the UK and Moscow for example – they lie on similar latitudes, but with no ocean nearby, Moscow winters average 10°C/32°F cooler than those in Britain.

SEASHORES

Life on the seashore is about dealing with extremes – in particular, the area that exists between the highest and lowest points of the tide. Known as the littoral, or tidal, zone, this ever-changing environment presents its inhabitants with a tricky set of contrasting challenges.

The littoral zone is in a state of constant flux. For part of each day, it is submerged beneath the tide. At these times, conditions are rather similar to those elsewhere in the oceans – animals benefit from the physical support of water, while endeavouring to extract the oxygen from it to meet their respiratory needs.

But the challenges of life under water only apply for part of the time. When the tide goes out, many aquatic animals go with it, but others remain on the shore. They have to cope with a completely different set of physical conditions. Suddenly, they are in danger of drying out. They have to find a way of obtaining oxygen from

air rather than water. They may be exposed to baking sun or freezing temperatures way below 0°C/3°F.

Rock pools may become super-saline, as water evaporates, or enormously diluted by rain or streams of fresh water running off the land. In very salty water, organisms must stop water being drawn from their body

Above: Sandhopper (Talitrus saltator). Lives among fronds of rotting seaweed on upper shore.

Above: Common seal (Phoca vitulina). Hauls out on sandy beaches of temperate coasts.

Above: Common hermit crab (Eupagurus bernhardus). Found on lower shores and shallow beds.

Above: Beadlet anemone (Actinia equina) attaches to rocks and crevices on middle shore.

by osmosis, while in fresh water, they risk absorbing so much moisture that their cells may swell and rupture.

Added to these challenges are the perils of sea spray, occasional flooding by spring tides, storms and tsunamis. But far from rendering the world's coastlines barren, these challenges mean that the littoral and sublittoral zones are home to some of the most vibrant and exciting natural communities on Earth. In a habitat where change occurs hourly with the movement of the tide, there is rarely an opportunity for any single species or group of species to dominate fully.

Types of shoreline

Seashores can be broadly divided into two types. Rocky coastlines tend to be young, geologically, and steeply sloping. They generally face regular pounding by the sea – indeed, loose sediments are quickly washed away, exposing the bare rock of the earth. Animals that tolerate these conditions must be tough, able to resist the physical impact of waves, periodic exposure to dry air and drastic fluctuations in temperature and salinity. Shelled animals such as molluscs, crabs, echinoderms and anemones do well. Clean, rocky coasts

also act as pupping sites for seals, whose juvenile fur would fail to insulate effectively if matted with mud.

By contrast, sedimentary shores are generally created by the dispersal, and subsequent accumulation, of sand, shingle and mud from rocky coasts eroded by the tide. They experience more moderate assaults by the sea, but their very substance, sand and silt, is easily washed away, so they are inherently unstable as habitats. The marine life that thrives in these ever-shifting conditions include borrowing molluscs and annelid worms, crabs and sand dollars.

*Above: Common lobster (*Homarus gammarus*). Found on rocks and in crevices in the sublittoral zone.*

*Above: Common limpet (*Patella vulgata*). Found in rocks pools and attached to rocks on the shore.*

*Above: Edible sea urchin (*Echinus esculentus*). Found on seaweeds and rocks on the lower shore.*

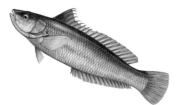

*Above: Rainbow wrasse (*Thalassoma pavo*). Ventures into very shallow water of 1m/3.25ft.*

ESTUARINE HABITATS

Areas where rivers meet the sea – swamp, marsh and mangrove – are often characterized by dark, oozing mud and an offensive smell of decay. But these apparently hostile environments are among the richest of coastal habitats and home to an abundance of hardy animal species.

An estuary is the very last section of a river, where outward-bound fresh water arriving from inland is subject to salination, and increased volume, by incoming sea water. Estuaries are also areas of deposition – rivers carry not only water but sediment, which is often dumped close to the mouth, forming wide expanses of mud flats that become exposed when water level falls, at low tide. Not all rivers have estuaries – some simply spill down deep rocky coasts into the sea. At the other extreme, along sheltered, low-energy coastlines, the build up of sediment can be immense, causing the river to split and branch, forming distinctive landscapes called deltas.

Estuarine water is generally brackish, but salt concentrations rise twice daily with the influx of the tide. For animals that can tolerate the variability, the rewards are great. Estuaries are not only calm, they are also extremely rich in nutrients, thanks to a ready supply of organic material washed downstream. Tidal mudflats

Above: Large scale archer fish (Toxotes chatareus). Favours brackish shallow estuarine water.

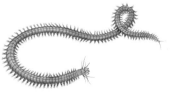

Above: Ragworm (Nereis diversicolor). Often found on muddy seabeds of shallow water.

Above: Mud fiddler crab (Uca pugnax). Prefers muddy shores of estuarine habitats.

Above: Opossum shrimp (Neomysis integer). Can tolerate freshwater and salty tidal pools.

support vast numbers of burrowing species – beds of mussels and oysters can extend for miles. Annelid worms, especially species of lugworm and ragworm, also thrive, as do crabs and other crustaceans. Estuaries also serve as nursery grounds for some bony fish.

Typical estuarine habitats

Swamps tend to occupy low-lying land close to estuaries, and are periodically flooded by river water. However, they are also nutrient-rich and offer shelter for a wide variety of aquatic life. In time, deposition of sediment and colonization by hardy salt-tolerant plants may raise the level of the swamp so that it becomes flooded less often. Eventually, it may develop into more stable salt marsh, drained by creeks and supporting mostly terrestrial life.

Mangroves are trees, an unusual group of some 50 species able to extract the fresh water they need from the salt water inundating their roots. Most can tolerate high levels of salt in their tissues, but they must still prevent saturation occuring. Some species filter water as it enters the roots, others secrete salt from pores in the leaves. Others simply shed the salinated leaves and start afresh.

Despite these tactics, mangroves rely upon the regular flushing of their vascular system by fresh water at low tide. They must also deal with mud which is anaerobic, or lacking in oxygen. Thus the trees have aerial roots which rise above the mud and absorb gases directly from the air.

These extraordinary adaptations allow mangroves to create a unique sheltered three-dimensional habitat where there would otherwise just be mud. They support an enormous array of animal life, both above and below the water line, and are crucial nursery grounds for fish.

*Above: Sand goby (*Pomatoschistus minutus*). Found close to the shore and in estuarine waters.*

*Above: Common mussel (*Mytilus edulis*). Attaches to solid objects in fresh and salt water.*

*Above: Finless porpoise (*Neophocaena phocaenoides*). Coastal and estuarine waters.*

*Above: Barred mudskipper (*Periophthalmus argentilineatus*). Tidal mudflats and mangroves.*

SHALLOW SEAS

Between the cluttered and turbulent coasts and the vast open waters of the oceans lie broad, shallower zones rich in marine life. Aquatic life at the edge of the continents supports some highly productive ecosystems, among them the vibrant rocky and coral reefs.

At the point where the thick crust of continental land thins to become the oceans, there are areas of shallow water that comprise many of the world's seas. These waters are highly productive, especially in zones where sunlight penetrates. In the tropics, productivity is moderately high all year around, but in higher latitudes it can

fluctuate a great deal, with dark, cold, unproductive winters giving way to a spectacular burst of life during the summer. Long daylight hours fuel this massive productivity, starting with a bloom of photosynthetic algae, and immense swarms of algae-eating zooplankton which in turn attract a variety of migratory species.

Shallow seas are generally more productive and nutrient-rich than deep oceans, and while life is often concentrated close to the bottom, the middle depths and surface waters may also throng with life – schooling fish, drifting jellyfish, squid, and the animals that prey on them: bony fish, sharks, turtles, cetaceans, penguins and

Above: Common octopus (Octopus vulgaris). From rocky shallows to depths of 200m/650ft.

Above: Atlantic hake (Merluccius merluccius). Continental shelf; sometimes deeper water.

Above: Dead man's fingers (Alcyonium digitatum). Rocky reefs; also encrusts shell animals.

Above: Common skate (Dipterus (Raja batis). Remains close to sea bed in shallow seas.

of course humans – these offshore waters include all the world's major fishing grounds.

Living space

Hard substrata such as rocky ledges, boulders and even ship-wrecks support encrusting animals and algae. Stable soft bottoms are also well inhabited by more elusive creatures that bury themselves in the sediment: bivalve molluscs, crabs and tube worms; or those which adopt cryptic colouration to avoid the attention of predators: flatfish such as flounders, bottom-dwelling rays and small sharks.

Another important feature of shallow seas is the dropoff, where a coastal shelf falls away into much deeper water. These great walls are common at the edges of reefs. They support sunlight-dependent algae and corals and their associated fauna in the upper reaches, and filter-feeders, predators, scavengers and detritivores in the depths below. Currents deflected along the wall or even welling up from below direct a heavy load of organic material easily snared by the outstretched tentacles, arms and tubes of anemones, soft corals, echinoderms, tunicates and other invertebrates.

The need for light means that most large-scale plantlife is restricted to shallow water. The largest of all algae, the immense giant kelps, grow up to 100m/330ft long. Attached to the sea floor but supported by the water so their fronds reach up to the light, these enormous plants form forests as impressive as any on land. Starfish, eels and sea lions and others prey on the small animals seeking shelter there.

Sea grasses are flowering plants that have adapted to life in saltwater. They offer sanctuary to many fish and invertebrates, and food for grazers such as dugongs, turtles and urchins.

Above: Common whelk (Buccinum undatum). Mud and sandy seabeds to 100m/330ft.

Above: Turbot (Psetta maxima). Sandy and rocky bottoms; can also tolerate brackish water.

Above: Spotted torpedo ray (Torpedo marmorata). Soft sea beds and seagrass meadows.

Above: Purple starfish (Henricia oculata). Rocky and sandy shallows of exposed coastlines.

CORAL REEFS

Often described as the tropical rainforests of the sea, coral reefs rank among the world's most complex, species-rich ecosystems. They are the teeming, sprawling cities of the marine world, and act as feeding and spawning grounds for many marine creatures, but are also subject to predation by others.

Coral reefs occur in the brightly lit, warm, shallow seas of the tropics. They are the largest living structures on the planet, and the only ones visible from space. Biological in origin, reef-building coral animals are small, colonial jelly-like creatures of the phylum Cnidaria – relatives of jellyfish, hydras and anemones.

Adult coral animals are similar to anemones in their basic form. They are polyps – sessile, tube-like animals with a mouth at the top surrounded by a crown of feeding tentacles. Polyps reproduce either by producing eggs and sperm or by budding off new individuals, which are genetically identical clones of themselves. These

clones remain attached to the original polyp and share a single gastrovascular cavity. In reef-building corals, each polyp secretes a supportive casement of calcium carbonate (limestone). As the colony grows, new polyps build on the stony lattice-shaped structure left by their predecessors, and thus only the outermost layer of the reef is alive.

Above: Sweetlip emperor (Lethrinus miniatus). Reef-dweller by day; lagoons for night feeding.

Above: Banded sea snake (Laticauda colubrina). Favours coral reefs and coastal waters.

Above: Copperband butterflyfish (Chelmon rostratus). Usually found among shallower reefs.

Above: Vase sponge (Ircinia campana). A reef giant; found only in shallow, warmer waters.

How reefs are formed

Reef-building coral have a mutual arrangement with the symbiotic algae living within them. The algae depend on the coral for shelter, and in turn it is the algae's photosynthesizing actions that provide the coral animals with food. For this reason, reef-building coral are found in shallow, sunlit seas.

Space is at a premium on the reef and competition for every square inch is intense, even between the coral themselves. Members of adjacent colonies do battle by secreting digestive enzymes that break down the soft tissues of neighbouring colonies growing too close. Different species of coral may adopt characteristic shapes, growing upwards or branching out to maximize the amount of sunlight they can provide for the symbiotic algae. Common coral names often reflect this tendency, such as staghorn and brain coral, or sea fans.

In addition to the coral themselves, the reef supports a vast array of other life. This includes many permanently attached residents, such as tube-dwelling polychaete worms, sessile molluscs, bryozoans, anemones and feather stars. Other residents, which may not be physically attached but nevertheless remain closely associated include other echinoderms, free-living worms, molluscs, crustaceans and fish. Occasional visitors include turtles, sharks, small cetaceans and ocean-going fish such as tuna. They are attracted by the abundant food and by opportunities for a wash-and-brush-up by cleaner fish and shrimps.

Despite their protective stony fortifications, corals have their share of predators. One is the voracious crown of thorns starfish; also parrotfish, whose beak-like teeth are strong enough to bite off chunks of reef to get to the tissues and algae within.

Above: Banded brittlestar (Ophiolepis superba). Limbs often snag and break on reefs.

Above: Red tree sponge (Haliclona compressa). Attaches to reefs where current is swift.

Above: White-tip reef shark (Triaenodon obesus). A curious, active reef predator.

Above: Crown-of-thorns starfish (Acanthaster planci). Feeding populations can damage reefs.

OPEN OCEANS

For the most part, the open ocean – the world's largest habitat – is a rather barren, lifeless place. But here and there, when the current flushes nutrients to the surface, or where a stray piece of seaweed or flotsam provides a small oasis of shelter, animal life suddenly and dramatically appears in profusion.

Seawater sometimes appears green because it contains large quantities of algae. But further out the open oceans are deep, dark blue – they look this way because of the way water refracts (or bends) different wavelengths of light. With no algae, and no sediment, and no other organic material to tint them, these enormous stretches of blue are almost devoid of life. Yet when nutrients arrive, usually associated with currents or floating objects, they fuel an intense bloom of algae. The colour of the algae, usually green but sometimes red, is determined by the pigments within that help harvest the sun's rays for photosynthesis, or shield the plant from the damaging effects of solar radiation. Algae are primary producers – they form the basis of the marine food chain, just as green plants on land support whole terrestrial ecosystems. They are eaten by animals – mostly very small ones such as copepods, tiny shrimps and the larvae of fish, molluscs, echinoderms and other crustaceans – which are

*Above: Pelagic worm (*Tomopteris pacifica*). Strong swimming member of zooplankton.*

*Above: Pelagic polychaete (*Poeobius meseres*). Traps drifting plankton via sticky mucous web.*

*Above: Atlantic herring (*Clupea harengus*). Schooling plankton-feeder of shallow and mid-water.*

*Above: Pantropical dolphin (*Stenella attenuata*). One of the most abundant of the delphinidae.*

collectively known as zooplankton. Many of these creatures, especially in their larval forms, perform a vertical migration at night, rising under cover of darkness to feed on plankton at the water's surface, and descending again by day to avoid the eyes of predators.

The open water food chain

Larger members of the zooplankton eat smaller ones, and are in turn eaten by larger animals still – small fish such as anchovies, or large creatures such as whale sharks. The plankton-eating fish are preyed on by an enormous variety of animals, from tunas, billfish and sharks to dolphins and toothed whales. All are the victims of more insidious forms of animal life – parasites that cling to their skin, or set up home in their gut, attach to their gills or burrow deep into their flesh.

Floating objects – such as seaweed or the 'flotsam' (floating cargo) jettisoned from ships or wrecks – can become hubs for small, ephemeral but surprisingly diverse communities of open ocean life. The objects themselves may be settled by encrusting organisms such as barnacles, and may even offer shelter to small schools of fish larvae and other plankton. These schools will eventually attract the attention of larger species, which may stake a claim to the floating territory and guard it fiercely. Some drifting communities become cleaning stations; others offer concealment to patient 'ambush predators' such as jacks and triggerfish.

Sometimes a single animal supports a group of drifters. A few species have adapted to tolerate the stings of the Portuguese man o war, either feeding directly on the hydrozan, or on the animals that venture too close. Sharks and turtles, meanwhile, may carry hitchhiking remoras, or less benign parasites such as lice and barnacles.

*Above: Olive Ridley turtle (*Lepidochelys olivacea*). Spend much of their life in open water.*

*Above: Man o war fish (*Nomeus gronovii*). Drifts among the trailing tentacles of its namesake.*

Above: Whale barnacles. Encrust the skin of whales; different species attach to different hosts.

*Above: Cosmopolitan flying fish (*Exocoetus volitans*). Capable of gliding above surface waters.*

OCEAN DEPTHS

The deep oceans represent the last great frontier of human exploration on Earth. This is an alien world – less familiar to scientists than the surface of the moon, and yet only a few hundred metres away from sunlit surface waters and busy shipping lanes.

The average depth of the world's oceans is about 3.7km/2.3 miles. Much deeper waters than this tend to occur some distance from where the edges of the continents drop down to a wide, abyssal underwater plain. In parts, the plain is interrupted by mid-ocean ridges, where new crust is being made, and by deep ocean trenches, where one tectonic plate is sliding beneath another. The deepest of these trenches occurs near the Marianas islands in the Pacific. At its deepest point, known as Challenger Deep, the Marianas Trench is some 10,923m/35,838ft below the surface. Incredibly, there is life at the bottom. Animals observed include echinoderms and fish, eking out a sedate, low-energy lifestyle in pitch black, very cold water under pressure of about 1,065 atmospheres/16,000 pounds per square inch.

Extreme temperatures
Below about 150m/450ft, very little sunlight can penetrate. This also means little heat: at 1,000m/3,300ft, the

Above: *Pompeii worm (Alvinella pomejana). First observed in the Galapagos vent.*

Above: *Giant vent clam (Calyptogena magnifica). Thermal vents of deep ocean volcanoes.*

Above: *Tube-eye (Stylephorus chordatus). Deep dweller with goggle-like eyes.*

Above: *Abyssal grenadier (Coryphaenoides armatus). Abundant; emits light from belly.*

average water temperature is about 5°C/41°F in any ocean, be it tropical or icebound. At 4,000m/13,000ft, it is between 1 and 2°C/34 and 36°F. But even these chilly waters are neither devoid of life nor completely dark. The first scientists to descend to these depths in high-tech submersibles, like the one shown below, observed blue, green and red patches of light. The light, known as bioluminescence, was produced by animals – such as fish, crustaceans, molluscs and worms – as a means of communicating, luring prey close enough to attack, or simply throwing predators off course. Even

where sparse, the presence of light means that total blindness at great depths is rare. Many deep sea fish have eyes large enough to help them make the most of what little there is.

In 1977, scientists made another great discovery. In an area of newly-made crust, where tectonic plates were slipping apart, they found vents and chimneys from which super-heated water spewed forth in spectacular plumes. The 'black smokers', shown below, were the hottest of these – the water they expel is up to 400°C/750°F. Only the enormous pressure keeps the water in liquid form. It is coloured

black by a heavy load of dissolved minerals, particularly iron and sulphides. White smokers are slightly cooler and contain chemicals such as calcium, barium and silicon.

What also amazed researchers was that this superheated, toxic water is teeming with life, including giant worms, clams and crabs. Bacteria, often living inside the bodies of these vent animals, use energy bound up in certain chemicals to fuel their own process of 'chemosynthesis'. This enables them to supply the host with food in return for a safe home and ready supply of raw materials.

Above: Silver hatchetfish (Argyropelecus aculeatus). Emits blue light to conceal silhouette.

Above: Deep sea amphipod (Eurythnes gryllus). May descend to 6,500m/21,300ft.

Above: Copepod (Pleuromamma xiphias). Uses bioluminescence to deter predators.

Above: Deep-sea louse (Bathynomus giganteus). Physical similarity to extinct trilobites.

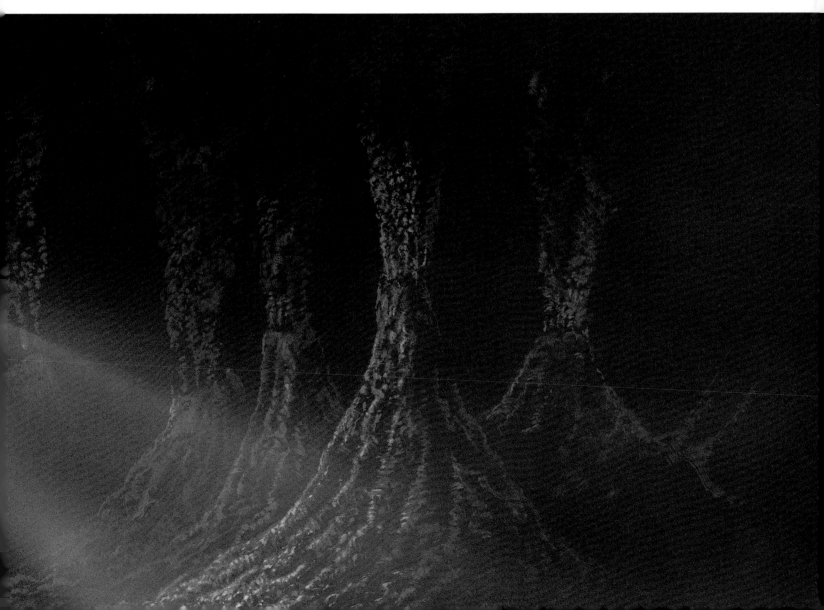

DIRECTORY OF MARINE SPECIES

The following pages provide a wealth of fascinating information on hundreds of marine animals, from sessile coral polyps to circumglobal navigators such as whale sharks and leatherback turtles, and of course some of the 25,000 known species of bony fish that dominate the fauna of our seas.

While the popular perception of the marine realm concerns life in the oceans and seas, a number of the shallow-water creatures included here have adapted to an existence in brackish estuaries, or occupy intertidal zones devoid of water for part of the day. These habitats are quite accessible and their communities are well studied. Their deep-water counterparts, a large proportion of which have long evaded human observation, offer much more scant data. The concise profiles presented here are accurate in light of the information currently available, but in some cases are based necessarily upon a degree of carefully considered conjecture.

The directory is organized into three major categories, based loosely on habitat type. Beginning with the inhabitants of seashores and estuaries, we move on to the shallow waters approximating to continental shelf and reef systems. We conclude with the most remote parts of the larger bodies of water on Earth – the open ocean and deep sea.

*Above, left to right: hermit crab (*Eupagurus bernhardus*); walruses (*Odobenus rosmarus*); the head of an orca (*Orcinus orca*).*
*Left: School of powder blue tangs (*Acanthurus leucosternon*), one of the so-called 'surgeonfish' that inhabit tropical waters.*

HOW TO USE THE DIRECTORY

The following pages contain entries on hundreds of marine species from all over the world. To make these concise, expertly-drawn profiles as digestible as possible, the directory is designed to a format that makes all information easy to identify and locate.

As explained above, the directory of species is divided into three key habitat types, and, within these sections, all featured animals are further grouped according to fundamental taxonomic principles. In order to ensure as wide a coverage as possible in the book, these subgroupings are not constrained by formal scientific categories; rather, they should be treated as indicative of the perceived evolutionary relationships and shared physical similarities that exist between certain species. The introductory text to each new grouping points out some of these common behavioural and anatomical traits, and may define the actual taxonomic groups, such as the order or family, to which the animals belong.

The marine world contains a greater diversity of life than any other part of the planet, and an exhaustive treatment of its members would be more or less impossible in a book of this size and scope. However, the species selected represent many of the major groups of invertebrates, vertebrate fish, reptilians and aquatic mammals found within marine waters. Some species may be familiar to certain readers; others – including less adaptable, rarely-sighted or even endangered species – may offer an entirely new perspective on the animal life of the saltwater world.

The text describes each specimen in a straightforward way. Where technical terms are included, these are usually defined with their first mention in the text, and the reader can also refer to the extensive glossary of terms towards the close of the book for a fuller explanation. An index listing all featured animal species by their common and scientific names appears on the final pages of the book.

Main headings

The main headings identify the group, or groups, of organisms covered on those pages. Depending on the level of representation, groupings may be broad, as with Cephalopod Molluscs or Crustaceans, or more specialized, as with Perchlike Fish (below) or Ground Sharks.

Introductory text

A few lines of general text introduce the group and describe some of its shared characteristics. Where the treatment of a group is more extensive than usual, such as with Perchlike Fish (below), the information accumulates over several pages.

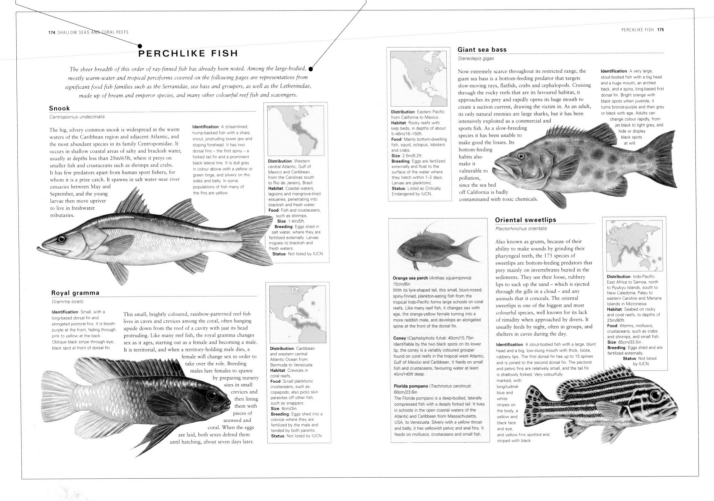

Species name
The common English language name is given first, with the internationally accepted scientific name (pairing generic and species names) underneath. Alternative common names may be noted in the description.

ID Caption
This text builds a physical profile of the species, including details, such as variations in colour or the ability to emit light, that may not be visible in the drawing.

Description
The main text supplies useful information on the behavioural traits of the animal, such as its predatory or reproductive habits. This behaviour may be noted as typical of its group, or as quite specific to that species.

Distribution map
Based on reported sightings, the maps indicate where, in the broadest sense, the species is likely to occur. Ranges given may be quite specific to a certain body of water, or may reflect a global distribution.

• Royal gramma
Gramma loreto

Identification: Small, with a long-based dorsal fin and elongated pectoral fins. It is bluish-purple at the front, fading through pink to yellow at the back. Oblique black stripe through eye; black spot at front of dorsal fin.

This small, brightly coloured, rainbow-patterned reef fish lives in caves and crevices among the coral, often hanging upside down from the roof of a cavity with just its head protruding. Like many reef fish, the royal gramma changes sex as it ages, starting out as a female and becoming a male. It is territorial, and when a territory-holding male dies, a female will change sex in order to take over the role. Breeding males lure females to spawn by preparing nursery sites in small crevices and then lining them with pieces of seaweed and coral. When the eggs are laid, both sexes defend them until hatching, about seven days later.

Distribution: Caribbean and western central Atlantic Ocean from Bermuda to Venezuela.
Habitat: Crevices in coral reefs.
Food: Small planktonic crustaceans, such as copepods; also picks skin parasites off other fish, such as snappers.
Size: 8cm/3in.
Breeding: Eggs shed into a crevice where they are fertilized by the male and tended by both parents.
Status: Not listed by IUCN.

Illustration
All species have been drawn to a uniform size to maximize visual detail. They do not reflect actual size; this information can be gleaned from the Factfile data.

Factfile data
This formulaic panel lists the major categories of data often used to identify a species, and gives relevant information where available. An expansion of the treatment of data in this panel appears below.

Typical panel entry
Features species name (common and scientific), maximum size within adult range, and a brief general description of anatomy and behaviour. Directionals may be given to clarify the species illustrated, where necessary.

Other features of the directory

All descriptions of species are accompanied by a Factfile data panel, which acts as a quick-reference source of diagnostic information. In addition, a tinted panel provides concise profiles of several species related to the main animals described. In a handful of cases, these tinted panels offer fuller information about the ecology of the animal group as a whole.

Distribution: Caribbean and western central Atlantic Ocean from Bermuda to Venezuela.
Habitat: Crevices in coral reefs.
Food: Small planktonic crustaceans, such as copepods; also picks skin parasites off other fish, such as snappers.
Size: 8cm/3in.
Breeding: Eggs shed into a crevice where they are fertilized by the male and tended by both parents.
Status: Not listed by IUCN.

Food
Identifies the primary food source of the animal.

Size
A species may exhibit quite a range of sizes; this data aims to reflect the maximum end of the adult size range. Where there is a marked discrepancy in the sizes of the male and female of the species, this is stated.

Distribution
Summarizes the range given in the accompanying map.

Habitat
Gives a broad description of the physical environment favoured by the animal.

Breeding
Summarizes the key aspects of the animal's breeding behaviour, where known.

Status
Data is based on IUCN listings (see Glossary).

Orange sea perch (*Anthias squamipinnis*): 15cm/6in
With its lyre-shaped tail, this small, blunt-nosed, spiny-finned, plankton-eating fish from the tropical Indo-Pacific forms large schools on coral reefs. Like many reef fish, it changes sex with age, the orange-yellow female turning into a more reddish male, and develops an elongated spine at the front of the dorsal fin.

Coney (*Cephalopholis fulva*): 40cm/15.75in
Identifiable by the two black spots on its lower lip, the coney is a variably coloured grouper found on coral reefs in the tropical west Atlantic, Gulf of Mexico and Caribbean. It feeds on small fish and crustaceans, favouring water at least 45m/145ft deep.

Florida pompano (*Trachinotus carolinus*): 60cm/23.6in
The Florida pompano is a deep-bodied, laterally compressed fish with a deeply forked tail. It lives in schools in the open coastal waters of the Atlantic and Caribbean from Massachusetts, USA, to Venezuela. Silvery with a yellow throat and belly, it has yellowish pelvic and anal fins. It feeds on molluscs, crustaceans and small fish.

SEASHORES, COASTS AND ESTUARIES

Many of the animals in these pages will be familiar to anyone that has spent time beside the sea. But despite their relative accessibility, these habitats are among the toughest in the marine environment, indeed in the world. Nowhere else on the planet do animals and plants have to deal with such dramatically fluctuating environmental conditions on a routine basis. Such conditions exert powerful selective forces. These have led to the evolution of a remarkable guild of diverse but outstandingly robust forms of animal life, which occupy habitats that are neither fully land nor sea.

The marginal habitats between land and sea also draw a range of visitors. Birds including waders, gulls and even certain eagles make a living from the sea and its shores and terrestrial mammals such as rats, foxes, and even elephants visit beaches to scavenge from the heaps of debris that wash up on every tide. These animals are beyond the scope of this book, but depending on where you are in the world, a visit to a seashore can always bring surprises.

*Above, left to right: Sponge crab (*Dromia personata*); potato cod (*Epinephelus tukula*); northern elephant seal (*Mirounga angustirostris*).*

*Right: Australian sea lion (*Neophoca cinerea*) on the shore at Kangaroo Island, Australia.*

SPONGES

Sponges are simple, multicelled bottom-dwelling animals that spend their entire adult lives attached to rocks, piers or other firm surfaces. Although some species of sponges live in fresh water (those of the family Spongillidae), the majority are found in the sea. As well as reproducing sexually, many can form new individuals by budding and fragmentation.

Sea orange

Suberites ficus

Identification: Body shape globular, massively lobed, cushion-like or encrusting. Colour also variable, from orange to shades of yellow or brown, but may be grey, green or white. Contracts when taken from water.

This sponge's common name comes from its resemblance to an orange, although sometimes it may be elongated or flatter. Like other members of its class, the Demospongiae, the body of the sponge is supported by spicules of silica and horny spongin fibres. The pores through which water leaves the body are large and usually at the top of the lobes. The sea orange is frequently associated with whelk shells occupied by hermit crabs, forming a rounded structure over them that may erode away the shell so that the hermit crab is protected solely by the sponge. The crab enjoys a degree of camouflage from this association, while the sponge has transport to new feeding areas.

Distribution: Atlantic Ocean, Mediterranean Sea.
Habitat: Among rocks, piers and empty gastropod shells from shallow water down to about 200m/656ft.
Food: Tiny organic particles filtered from the water.
Size: Up to 40cm/16in across.
Breeding: Eggs are fertilized externally by sperm released into the water; free-swimming larvae settle to form new sponges.
Status: Not listed by IUCN.

Breadcrumb sponge

Halichondria panicea

Identification: The form can be very variable – from thin sheets about 2.5cm/1in high with volcano-like exhalent openings, to large, interconnected lobed structures up to 25cm/10in high and 60cm/24in across. Sometimes stout, chimney-like processes with oscular openings present. The colour ranges from green to creamy yellow. The sponge has a distinct 'seaweed' smell.

Often found growing in large encrustations under rocky overhangs, the openings of the exhalent pores, or oscules, of this sponge give the appearance of craters in tiny volcanic cones. The breadcrumb sponge grows from the middle shore downwards on rocks, stones and in rockpools. Under water, the sponge is often found in places where currents and wave action are strong, attaching itself to the fronds of seaweeds such as the sea oak (*Phycodrys rubens*). The shape of the sponge can be variable and may consist of connecting lobes. In shallow waters it may be green as a result of symbiotic algae in the tissues, although it tends to be paler in deeper or shaded water and in winter.

Distribution: Atlantic Ocean, Baltic and Mediterranean Seas.
Habitat: Among rocks, seaweeds and shells from the middle shore downwards.
Food: Tiny organic particles filtered from the water.
Size: 2.5–25cm/1–10in high; up to a maximum of about 60cm/24in across.
Breeding: Eggs are fertilized externally by sperm released into the water; free-swimming larvae settle to form new sponges.
Status: Not listed by IUCN.

Bath sponge
Spongia officinalis

The rough, spongin fibre 'skeleton' of this species has long been used as the popular bath sponge, although cheaper, synthetic sponges are often used today instead. An irregular-shaped species, the bathing sponge grows on rocks from shallow water downwards. When first collected from the sea, the sponge is a rather unattractive dark, amorphous structure. Processing into a bath sponge begins with the body liquids and cells being pressed out of the sponge before it is washed and immersed in the sea for several hours. The pressing, beating and washing is repeated until only the skeletal fibres are left. The sponge is then trimmed and dried before being treated with chemicals to clean it and lighten its colour.

Identification: The body of the sponge usually takes the form of a globose, branching mass with distinct, crater-like exhalent, or oscular, openings raised from the surface. The colour ranges from reddish-brown to green and black.

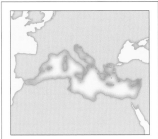

Distribution: Mediterranean.
Habitat: On rocks from shallow water down to about 50m/164ft or more.
Food: Tiny organic particles filtered from the water.
Size: Usually up to 20cm/ 8in across, but eastern Mediterranean subspecies *S. o. mollisima* may grow to twice this size.
Breeding: Eggs are fertilized externally by sperm released into the water; free-swimming larvae settle to form new sponges.
Status: Not listed by IUCN.

Purse sponge (*Grantia compressa*): 5cm/2in high
Usually shaped like a flattish or rounded sac with an opening at one end, this sponge resembles a hot-water bottle. This variably shaped sponge may also be tubular or consist of flat, stalked lobes. It often collapses when out of water, at which time it may look like a flattened purse. White or cream but sometimes pale brown in colour. Its surface appears smooth and clean, and it grows on the lower shore and in shallow water in groups on rocky overhangs or attached to seaweeds. Found in Atlantic Ocean and Mediterranean Sea.

Purple sponge (*Haliclona permollis*): 4cm/1.6in high
Ranging in colour from pink through to lavender to purple, this encrusting sponge resembles miniature volcanic cones fused at their bases. It has clearly visible pale-bordered oscular openings, and its texture is soft. The purple sponge is found growing on pilings and rocks from the mid-tidal zone down to about 6m/20ft deep in many of the world's oceans. It is often grazed on by molluscs attracted by its soft texture.

Branching vase sponge (*Callyspongia vaginalis*): 25cm/10in high
This is an attractive and distinctive species consisting of clusters of long, erect, thin-walled tubes, each resembling the kind of tall, cylindrical and narrow vase often used to display the single stem of a flower. The branching vase sponge is a common reef species and can be found in a number of different colours, ranging from purple, blue, grey, brown or greyish-green.

Gold sponge
Verongia aerophoba

This distinctive and attractive species takes the form of erect, cylindrical, pillar-like structures joined at the base. The exhalent openings are situated in small depressions at the peak of the 'pillars', which have the appearance of having had their tops trimmed off. The skeleton of the gold sponge consists only of spongin fibres, although the tissue is more dense, with hard nodules embedded in it.

Identification: Erect, cylindrical pillars joined at the base. The tops of the pillars are usually flattened and contain the exhalent openings. The colour of this sponge varies from yellow to yellow-green.

Distribution: Mediterranean.
Habitat: On rocks in shallow water.
Food: Tiny organic particles filtered from the water.
Size: Usually up to 15cm/6in high.
Breeding: Eggs are fertilized externally by sperm released into the water; larvae settle to form new sponges.
Status: Not listed by IUCN.

SEA ANEMONES

Although they often resemble flowers, sea anemones are, in fact, true animals. Most attach themselves to rocks and other hard substrates – sometimes even to the shells of living animals – and catch their prey using stinging tentacles. Some species burrow in sand or mud. As with sponges, many species can reproduce by budding and fragmentation, as well as sexually.

Black coral

Antipathes subpinnata

Despite its common name and appearance, the black coral is, in fact, a type of sea anemone belonging to the class Anthozoa. It consists of a thin, blackish-brown branching skeleton forming a tree- or bush-like shape overlaid with greyish-white tissue in which are embedded numerous tiny polyps. The polyps have tentacles armed with stinging cells that capture small marine creatures. These are then transferred to the polyps' mouths to be digested, although anthozoan polyps cannot retract their tentacles. The black coral is found on stony substrates. Black coral is sometimes harvested for making into jewellery, and in the past it has also been used medicinally and in religious ceremonies. In addition, there is a small trade in live specimens for aquaria. Most black coral is exported from Taiwan, but significant quantities also come from Hawaii.

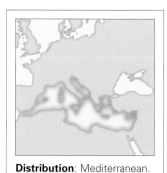

Identification: Hard, horny, tree-like skeleton, blackish-brown with tiny polyps embedded in overlying tissue and attached to the stony substrate. The pinhead-sized polyps feed by immobilizing their prey with stinging cells.

Distribution: Mediterranean.
Habitat: Growing on muddy seabeds interspersed with stones, from 10–250m/ 33–813ft.
Food: Tiny planktonic creatures.
Size: Skeleton up to 1m/ 3.25ft high; polyps about 1mm/0.04in high.
Breeding: Can reproduce asexually by division or sexually by producing eggs and sperm.
Status: Listed in CITES appendix II in 1981.

Beadlet anemone

Actinia equina

Identification: Smooth column with adhesive basal disc. About 200 tentacles arranged in five or six circlets around the mouth. Distinct ring of blue spots visible when tentacles retracted. Colour ranges from brown, red, orange or green; sometimes red with yellow-green spots.

The beadlet anemone is a common species, often seen as a dark, jelly-like blob a few centimetres high nestling in rocky crevices or at the base of breakwaters at low tide. However, it is very variable in colour, and is found in other hues, such as green or even red with yellow-green spots – the strawberry variety. Like many other anemones, the beadlet has a strong, sucker-like base, which it uses to attach itself firmly on to the substrate. The top of the column is densely packed with about 200 stinging tentacles, arranged in five or six circlets, or whorls, around the mouth. If disturbed, or when exposed at low tide, the tentacles retract, showing the ring of 24 blue spots that surrounds the oral disc.

Distribution: Atlantic Ocean, Mediterranean Sea.
Habitat: On rocks and in crevices from middle shore down to 8m/26ft.
Food: Tiny marine creatures.
Size: Column up to 7cm/ 2.8in high and 6cm/2.4in across; tentacles about 2cm/0.8in long.
Breeding: Can reproduce asexually by division or sexually by producing eggs and sperm.
Status: Not listed by IUCN.

Cerianthus lloydii: 15cm/6in long; tentacle span up to 7cm/2.8in
Like others in the order Ceriantharia, this species lives permanently within a long, soft tube buried in the sand or mud with only its tentacles exposed. The animal quickly withdraws its body and tentacles into the tube if threatened. Around the mouth are 60 or so long, brownish, green or white tentacles, surrounding a ring of shorter tentacles. It occurs from low water down to about 40m/131ft in the Atlantic Ocean.

Dahlia anemone (*Tealia felina*): 15cm/6in high
A variable anemone with a warty column often covered with fragments of gravel and shells; when closed it may be quite inconspicuous. Base strongly adhesive and sucker like. Between 80 and 160 robust, retractable stinging tentacles surround mouth. Colour is blue, grey or green with blotches. Mouth is pink, green or blue. Translucent tentacles often banded with various colours. From Atlantic middle shore downward.

Plumose anemone (*Metridium senile*): 10cm/4in high
The column is smooth with a well-defined collar below the tentacles. The tentacles are short and fine, giving a feather duster appearance. It attaches to rocks and underwater structures, such as pier supports, down to about 3m/ 10ft in the Atlantic Ocean and Mediterranean Sea. Its various colour forms include pink, orange and cream.

Opelet

Anemonia viridis

Also known as the snakelocks anemone because of its long, flexuous tentacles, the opelet is a large, attractive species, variably coloured and with violet tinges on the tips of its stinging tentacles. On the seashore, it is usually encountered in rockpools and in water-filled rocky crevices. The opelet rarely withdraws its tentacles, and so these anemones are quite easy to spot. The base of the column is only weakly adhesive and sucker-like and is wider than the column. Although the opelet is found mainly in places such as intertidal rockpools, it is sometimes encountered growing on the sea grass. This species often lives in the more intense light found in shallow waters.

Distribution: Atlantic Ocean, Mediterranean Sea.
Habitat: In rockpools and in crevices from middle shore down to the sublittoral.
Food: Tiny marine creatures.
Size: Column up to 10cm/4in high; base about 7cm/2.8 in across; tentacles about 15cm/6in long.
Breeding: Can reproduce asexually by division or sexually by producing eggs and sperm.
Status: Not listed by IUCN.

Identification: Column with weakly adhesive basal disc. Approximately 170 tentacles arranged in about six circlets around the mouth. Colour ranges from brown, grey or bright green; fleshy tentacles have violet-tips – most apparent in green variety.

Red-speckled pimplet anemone

Anthopleura balli

This anemone, like several others, occurs in more than one colour variety. In this species, the most common colours are hues of yellow-green and orange-pink. The column is characterized by its distinctly warty appearance, with the warts becoming larger near the top. The tentacles are translucent, but attractively marked with varying tinges of colour. It tends to shun strong light conditions, and so prefers to live in shady places, such as under rocky overhangs or in dark holes. Like other anemones, it feeds by extending its column and waving its tentacles about in the water, waiting to ensnare any small animals that blunder into them.

Identification: Warty column with weakly adhesive basal disc. There are about 50 tapering tentacles around the mouth. Colour of column usually yellow-green or orange-pink. Translucent tentacles tinged with hues of grey, brown, pink or green.

Distribution: Atlantic Ocean, Mediterranean Sea.
Habitat: In crevices of rocks or under rocky overhangs where light levels are low from middle shore downwards.
Food: Tiny marine creatures.
Size: Column up to 5cm/ 2in high.
Breeding: Can reproduce asexually by division or sexually by producing eggs and sperm.
Status: Not listed by IUCN.

'Parasitic' anemone

Calliactis parasitica

This anemone frequently forms part of an unusual relationship known as commensalism, in which two unrelated species live in close association together for their mutual benefit – although both species can, and often do, live without their commensal partner. The anemone is often found attached to a whelk shell that has been taken over by a hermit crab, usually of the genus *Eupagurus*. The anemone's stinging tentacles give the soft-bodied crab a degree of protection from predators, such as octopuses, while the anemone gets to feed on scraps when the crab has a meal. Sometimes the hermit crab may have two or more anemones attached to its shell. When the hermit crab grows too big for its shell and chooses a larger one, the anemone also 'moves house' with its host at the same time.

Identification: Strongly adhesive base and stout column, usually coloured grey or brown with spots and pale vertical lines. Mouth fringed with several hundred translucent, yellow-grey tentacles.

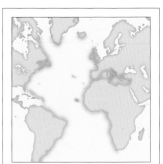

Distribution: Atlantic Ocean, Mediterranean Sea.
Habitat: On muddy and sandy substrates in the sublittoral region.
Food: Small marine creatures and other organic matter.
Size: Column up to 8cm/3in; tentacles approximately 3cm/1.2in long.
Breeding: Can reproduce asexually by division or sexually by producing eggs and sperm.
Status: Not listed by IUCN.

Cloak anemone

Adamsia palliata

Identification: Highly modified base and column form a flattish, enveloping structure around the shell occupied by the hermit crab. Mouth surrounded by approximately 500 tentacles, often on underside near shell aperture. Colour fawn to yellow with distinct purple blotches.

The cloak anemone is another commensal species (see above), and it is almost always associated with the hermit crab *Eupagurus prideauxi*. The highly modified base and column completely envelop the shell in which the crab is living. When the crab grows, instead of changing to a bigger shell, the anemone secretes a horny substance to effectively increase the size of the existing shell. The part of the column leading to the mouth is extremely short and often appears on the underside, with the numerous tentacles hanging down towards the substrate. In addition to its stinging tentacles, the anemone may eject a series of thin, purple threads when it is disturbed. As in similar commensal relationships, the crab is protected by the outer 'cloak' afforded by the anemones and the anemone captures scraps of food when the crab feeds.

Distribution: Atlantic Ocean, Mediterranean Sea.
Habitat: On sandy substrates from 4–100m/13–328ft.
Food: Small marine creatures and other organic matter.
Size: Column up to 7cm/2.8in across.
Breeding: Can reproduce asexually by division or sexually by producing eggs and sperm.
Status: Not listed by IUCN.

Daisy anemone

Cereus pedunculatus

Distribution: Atlantic Ocean, Mediterranean Sea.
Habitat: Sand or muddy bottoms, rockpools and crevices.
Food: Small marine creatures and other organic matter.
Size: Column up to 12cm/4.7in high; up to 15cm/6in diameter at top.
Breeding: Can reproduce asexually by division or sexually by producing eggs and sperm.
Status: Not listed by IUCN.

This is a species that habitually buries most of its column deep in soft sand, mud or in a rocky crevice, so that only the oral disc and the surrounding tentacles are visible at the surface. The daisy anemone is found in a variety of habitats – from rockpools and watery crevices to estuarine mud – and it occurs from the midshore down to about 50m/164ft or more. This species has a tall, flared or trumpet-shaped column terminating in a wide, oral disc with numerous short tentacles, numbering on average around 750. The column has warty, sucker-like structures present towards the top, often with small fragments of shell or stones attached to them. The daisy anemone is fairly common and sometimes occurs in large numbers.

Identification: Tall, smooth column with adhesive base; column often flared towards the top when extended. Warty suckers near top of column. Numerous (500–1,000) short tentacles. Colour of column orange, buff or greyish, becoming darker near top; tentacles buff to purple or black with lighter banding or flecking.

Sagartia elegans: 6cm/2.4in high; tentacles 1.5cm/0.6in long
Small species with column bearing warty suckers and a ring of about 200 tentacles. Found among rocks and in crevices from the lower shore down to about 50m/164ft in the Atlantic Ocean. If disturbed, this species can eject stinging threads (see right) through its mouth. Various colour forms of this anemone exist, ranging from ones with an orange disc and white tentacles, to all-white individuals.

White-spotted rose anemone (*Urticina lofotensis*): 15cm/6in high
In this attractive species the short, scarlet column is marked with vertical rows of small white spots, and the long, fleshy tentacles are yellow suffused with pink-red edging and tips. It is found in the Pacific Ocean and the Atlantic Ocean attached to rocks, wooden piers and similar structures in the intertidal and subtidal zones.

Strawberry sea 'anemone' (*Corynactis californica*): up to 2cm/0.8in long
A corallimorph rather than a true anemone (see overleaf), *C. californica* is often found living in groups along the North American Pacific seaboard. Occurs in shades of red, pink and purple; also orange, brown, buff and even pale blue. Tentacles are not fully retractile. Feeds on small creatures including copepods and larvae.

Diadumene cincta

Distribution: Atlantic Ocean, Mediterranean Sea.
Habitat: On shells and rocks on lower shore and in shallow water down to about 40m/131ft.
Food: Small marine creatures and other organic matter.
Size: Column up to 3.5cm/1.4in high.
Breeding: Reproduces asexually by forming clones.
Status: Not listed by IUCN.

This is a small, slim anemone species found attached by its adhesive base to hard surfaces, such as rocks and shells, on the lower shore and in shallow water. It is sometimes found in groups. The surface of the column is smooth and is punctuated with randomly spaced pores, known as cinclides, which allow water to be expelled from the body cavity when the animal contracts. In the contracted state, the parapet – a collar-like fold of tissue that surrounds the tentacles – is visible. This anemone can expel thin filaments armed with stinging cells through its mouth in order to deter predators. The tentacles of this anemone are fully retractable.

Identification: Small anemone with smooth column bearing a collar (parapet) near the top – although this may not be visible if the animal is fully expanded. Small pores present on column. About 200 slender, retractable tentacles on oral disc. Orange in colour.

CORALS AND RELATIVES

Corals are distinguished from sea anemones because the polyps secrete around themselves a hard calcareous or limestone cup into which they can almost, or completely, retreat if threatened by a predator. Some species of corals may form enormous aggregations, known as coral reefs. The closely related Corallimorpharia, such as the Jewel 'anemone' below, lack a calcareous cup.

Scarlet-and-gold star coral

Balanophyllia regia

The scarlet-and-gold star coral is a brightly coloured, solitary species that sometimes occurs at the extreme low water mark on the seashore attached to rocks or in caves, although it is more commonly found in shallow sublittoral zones. The polyp is surrounded by a cylindrical calcareous exoskeleton into which it can only partially withdraw. Each polyp has about 48 tentacles armed with cells called nematocysts that fire venomous threads to subdue unwary creatures that blunder into them, before being transferred to the mouth. These nematocysts are fluid-filled capsules containing a barbed, hollow thread that is shot out delivering a paralyzing sting. They are used for both defence and to capture food.

Identification:
Calcareous, spongy skeleton broad and low. About 48 short, tapering tentacles arranged in rows around the mouth; tentacles lack terminal knobs. Polyp are yellow, orange or scarlet; tentacles translucent yellow.

Distribution: Atlantic Ocean.
Habitat: On rocks and in caves at lower shore and down to 10m/33ft.
Food: Tiny marine creatures.
Size: Skeleton 1cm/0.4in high.
Breeding: Can reproduce asexually by division or sexually by producing eggs and sperm.
Status: Not listed by IUCN.

Jewel 'anemone'

Corynactis viridis

Identification: Column smooth and low with broad, adhesive base. About 100 tentacles arranged in three circlets; tentacles terminate in small knob. Brightly coloured – green, pink, orange, white – with column and tentacles often in contrasting colours. Tentacles contain stinging cells to immobilize prey.

The common name of this coral is derived from its anemone-like appearance. The species does not have a hard skeleton. It occurs on rock faces, inside caves or under overhangs where the light is not strong, and may be found in large numbers. Low and squat and with a smooth column, the jewel 'anemone' is a solitary species (in other words, each individual consists of a single polyp) that is encountered in a wide variety of contrasting, often vivid colours. Each of the 100 or so tentacles terminates in a small knob, and, like other cnidarians, are armed with stinging cells.

Distribution: Atlantic Ocean, Mediterranean Sea.
Habitat: On rocks and in caves at lower shore and down to 100m/330ft.
Food: Tiny marine creatures.
Size: Body about 5mm/0.2in across.
Breeding: Can reproduce asexually by division or sexually by producing eggs and sperm.
Status: Not listed by IUCN.

Devonshire cup coral (*Caryophyllia smithi*): 1.5cm/0.6in high
A solitary coral with a stout, ridged skeleton into which the polyp might retreat (as here). The polyps may be various colours – white, pink, green or brown. The tentacles, also variable in colour, terminate in a small knob. This Atlantic species on the extreme lower shore and in water down to about 100m/328ft.

Balanophyllia italica: 2.5cm/1in high
The cylindrical skeleton forms an inverted cone that is oval at the top. The polyps are iridescent and may be colourless or brownish-yellow. It is found on rocks and stones from about 1m/3.25ft to 100m/330ft in the Atlantic and Mediterranean.

Cladocora cespitosa: 10cm/4in high
This species forms low, stony colonies and has tubular skeletons. The polyps are brown and are found on shells and rocks from 1–70m/ 3.25–230ft in the Mediterranean.

Red sea fingers (*Alcyonium glomeratum*): 30cm/12in high
Found in gullies and caves in the Atlantic from about 10m/33ft down, this species is similar to dead man's fingers (*Alcyonium digitatum*), but the lobes are more slender and often branched. The colour is red, orange or yellow. The polyps, each with eight tentacles, are white.

Dead man's fingers

Alcyonium digitatum

Each retractable polyp bears a number of branching tentacles and is embedded in a fleshy mass whose skeleton is composed of unattached calcareous ossicles, resulting in a soft and pliable coral. The thick, fleshy mass forms erect, branching, finger-like lobes that give rise to the coral's common name. When disturbed, the polyps retreat inside the skeleton. The coral colonizes rocks, stones and shells, especially where weak light prevents seaweeds from growing. It sometimes also colonizes the shells of living crabs and gastropod molluscs.

Identification: Mature colonies form stout, fleshy, finger-like branching masses about 20cm/8in high and 20cm/8in across. Colours are white, pink, yellow or orange.

Distribution: Atlantic Ocean.
Habitat: On rocks, stones and shells from lower shore down to 150m/165ft or more.
Food: Tiny marine creatures.
Size: Polyps about 1cm/ 0.4in tall.
Breeding: Can reproduce asexually by division or sexually by producing eggs and sperm.
Status: Not listed by IUCN.

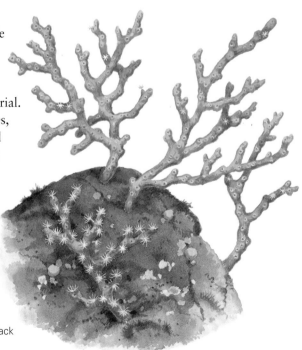

Red coral

Corallium rubrum

Distribution: Mediterranean.
Habitat: On rocks or other firm substrates from about 50m/164ft.
Food: Tiny marine creatures.
Size: Colony up to 50cm/ 19.7in high.
Breeding: Can reproduce asexually by division or sexually by producing eggs and sperm.
Status: Not listed in CITES, however the species may be subject to local legislation controlling the collection of, or trade in, both red and pink corals.

Red coral, or precious coral as it is also known, is a colonial species. The retractable polyps are embedded in tissue that is supported by a skeleton made up of needle-like calcium-carbonate rods fused together and covered with a horn-like material. The colony is firmly fixed to hard substrates, such as rocks. Depending on environmental conditions, the colony may form branching shapes or may be fan-like or bushy. It can look spectacular when the small polyps extend their white tentacles into the water to hunt for food. Red coral is one of several species of coral that is prized for making into jewellery and ornaments. When cut, polished and waxed, it takes on a brilliant lustre.

Identification: Colonial, with variable branching shape. Colour of main skeleton red, pink, brown, black or white. Polyps with white tentacles.

FLATWORMS AND RIBBON WORMS

Flatworms are, as their name implies, generally flattish, leaf-shaped creatures with a mouth on the underside of the body. They glide along with the aid of thousands of cilia (hair-like projections). Ribbon worms are thin, frequently long, worms that live in the sand or mud and under stones. Most species capture prey using an extendible proboscis.

Thysanozoon brocchii

Marine flatworms, such as *Thysanozoon brocchii*, are grouped within the class Turbellaria. They generally have leaf-shaped bodies – sometimes elongated, sometimes more rounded – and simple sense organs at the front end in the form of eyespots and tentacles. The mouth is situated on the underside, and the gut is often visible through the body. Marine flatworms glide about the sea floor by beating thousands of hair-like cilia on the under surface of the body, although some can also swim.

Identification: Unsegmented, leaf-like body, slightly thicker in the centre, with folded margins. Head blunt and bearing two tentacles. Body colour brown or pinkish.

Distribution: Mediterranean.
Habitat: Found among mussel beds and under seaweeds along the lower shore.
Food: Small particles of organic matter.
Size: 5cm/2in.
Breeding: Reproduces sexually by producing eggs and sperm.
Status: Not listed by IUCN.

Candy-stripe flatworm

Prostheceraeus vittatus

Identification: Unsegmented, broad, flattened body with wavy margins. Head blunt, with two tentacles; eyes arranged in two groups. Body colour cream or yellowish-white with numerous dark grey or black longitudinal stripes.

With its strikingly marked body and a pair of short, forward-projecting tentacles, the candy-stripe flatworm looks more like one of the colourful species of sea slugs than an example of flatworm. However, the creature lacks the prominent and often elaborate gills and other structures found on the dorsal surfaces of sea slugs, and the tentacles are formed from folds of body tissue. It moves by crawling along rocky substrates, often covered with a layer of sand and muddy sediments, using its cilia, and may swim by undulating movements of its body. The candy-stripe flatworm lives under rocks and among seaweeds from the lower shore to the sublittoral. It is most often found in water 10–30m/33–98ft deep.

Distribution: North-east Atlantic around British Isles and Ireland; also North Sea coasts and English Channel.
Habitat: Under stones and among seaweeds on sandy shores and shallow water.
Food: Small organic particles.
Size: 7cm/2.8in.
Breeding: Reproduces sexually by producing eggs and sperm.
Status: Not listed by IUCN.

Bootlace worm

Lineus longissimus

Distribution: From Icelandic coasts east to North Sea shores and British Isles.
Habitat: Under stones and among seaweeds on sandy shores, in pools and in shallow water.
Food: Small marine creatures.
Size: 5m/16.4ft or more.
Breeding: Reproduces sexually by producing eggs and sperm.
Status: Not listed by IUCN.

Lift a large rock at the lower shore and it is possible to find a bootlace worm partly buried in the soft, watery sand. This writhing mass of coils is also found in rockpools and rock crevices. The bootlace worm belongs to the phylum Nemertina, or ribbon worms – elongated, unsegmented creatures with an eversible proboscis at the front of the rectangular head which is used for capturing food. The bootlace worm is the longest nemertine worm known: it often grows up to 5m/16.4ft, although much bigger specimens – up to 30m/100ft – are sometimes found. However, like the other species of ribbon worms, this animal is slender (only about 5mm/0.2in wide) and lives a secretive life, so despite its length it is often overlooked.

Right: View from above showing the deep clefts in the surface of the worm's head.

Identification: Very long, slender, unsegmented body, often looped into coils when disturbed; tapers towards the end. Head rectangular, with groups of dark eyes on each side of snout, and deep clefts behind; tip of head may be pale. Body colour brown or black, sometimes with purplish sheen; young specimens may be olive or brown. Front dorsal surface of body may be streaked with light-coloured longitudinal lines.

Convoluta convoluta: 6mm/0.25in
A narrow, leaf-like flatworm. The head is broader than the tail, but there are no tentacles or eyes. This species has no gut. The body is coloured green due to the presence of symbiotic algae within the worm. Found among seaweeds on the lower shore and down to about 15m/49ft in the Atlantic Ocean and Mediterranean and Baltic Seas.

Red ribbon worm (*Lineus ruber*): 16cm/6.2in
A reddish-brown ribbon worm that lives under rocks and stones on the middle shore downwards in the Atlantic Ocean and Mediterranean and Baltic Seas. The head is slightly wider than the body, which itself tapers towards the tail.

Orange ribbon worm (*Tubulanus polymorphus*): 3m/10ft
This ribbon worm has a broadly rounded head. The body is a uniform bright orange colour, and can contract to about the thickness of a pencil. Found under stones and gravel or in mussel beds from the lower shore downwards in Pacific Ocean waters.

Pseudoceros sapphirinus: 6cm/2.4in
A flatworm with a striking, velvety black body fringed with electric blue colouring, this species mimics the body colouration of the sea slug *Philinopsis gardineri* – a poisonous mollusc – which is also found in the Indo-Pacific region.

Football jersey worm

Tubulanus annulatus

Called the football jersey worm because of its bright, colourful body markings, this species is another of the ubiquitous but rarely seen nemertine worms that inhabit the lower shore and sublittoral zone. On the shore, it is found under stones or inside laminarian seaweed holdfasts. For protection, it sometimes occupies the uninhabited tubes of other worm species. This ribbon worm has an unsegmented body that is flattened on the ventral surface but rounded above, and the head is broad and rounded. Like several marine worm species, the size to which individuals can grow varies greatly – often 15cm/6in or so, but some specimens of the ribbon worm may reach 75cm/29.5in or more in length. However, the worm is only about 3–4mm/0.12–0.16in wide.

Distribution: Northern Pacific coast of North America; North-eastern Atlantic; North Sea and Mediterranean.
Habitat: Under stones, among seaweeds or in disused worm tubes on sandy shores and in shallow water to about 40m/130ft.
Food: Small marine creatures.
Size: 15cm/6in or more.
Breeding: Reproduces sexually via eggs and sperm.
Status: Not listed by IUCN.

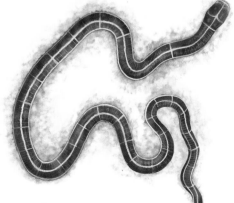

Identification: Long, slender and flattened, unsegmented body. Head broad and rounded; eyes not visible; clefts behind snout. Body colour attractive shades of brownish-red to brick-red, marked with contrasting longitudinal white stripes (usually three; one in the centre of the dorsal surface and the other two lateral) and white transverse rings (usually about 50).

BRISTLE WORMS AND SIPUNCULOID WORMS

Bristle worms have bodies composed of segments, most of which bear appendages known as parapodia. Some are hunters, searching for prey under stones, among weeds and in the substrate. Others are sedentary, living in burrows in the sand or surrounding their bodies with protective coverings of shell fragments and sand. Sipunculoids are sac-like or cylindrical worms with a mouth surrounded by tentacles.

Sea mouse

Aphrodite aculeata

Identification: Body elongated oval in shape covered in a mat of long, grey-brown hairs obscuring the scales on the upper (dorsal) surface. Top of body convex, lower surface flat and sole-like. About 40 segments with fringing iridescent hairs on ventral (lower) surface. Two horn-like palps at front of animal.

It is easy to see how this species gets its common name; its broad, grey, bristly body resembles that of a mouse at first sight. Yet despite its outward appearance, the sea mouse is a segmented worm. Beneath the hairy or felt-like covering is a scaly body made up of about 40 segments. Some of the bristles, or chaetae, especially on its sides, are iridescent, imparting a brilliant gold, green and brown sheen to the body. The animal's head is not visible from above, although two horn-like palps (feelers) protrude from the front of the body. The sea mouse is an errant species found in muddy sand at depths down to about 1,000m/3,280ft.

Distribution: Atlantic Ocean, Mediterranean and Baltic seas.
Habitat: On muddy substrates in water.
Food: Small organic matter.
Size: 15–20cm/6–8in long.
Breeding: Reproduces sexually by producing eggs and sperm.
Status: Not listed by IUCN.

Ragworm

Nereis diversicolor

The ragworm is an active bristle worm found on sandy and muddy substrates on the seashore and in estuaries. It often makes burrows in the sand or mud, lining them with a mucous coating, parts of which may be visible at the surface of the burrow. Throughout its range the ragworm is a common and often abundant species, much sought by sea anglers who prize it as a fishing bait. The head bears several distinct appendages, including eyes, antennae, tentacular cirri (slender, flexible appendages), palps, jaws and a proboscis with teeth. The long, sinuous body may be variously coloured, and is composed of a number of segments (about 100) bearing on each side parapodia with chaetae (hairs). The ragworm is both a predator and a scavenger, and will eat live or dead plant or animal matter. Several other *Nereis* species may be found on beaches and in estuaries.

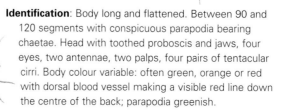

Identification: Body long and flattened. Between 90 and 120 segments with conspicuous parapodia bearing chaetae. Head with toothed proboscis and jaws, four eyes, two antennae, two palps, four pairs of tentacular cirri. Body colour variable: often green, orange or red with dorsal blood vessel making a visible red line down the centre of the back; parapodia greenish.

Distribution: Atlantic Ocean, Mediterranean and Baltic seas.
Habitat: On muddy and sandy substrates on lower shore and in shallow water.
Food: Small marine animals; also scavenges on organic debris.
Size: 20–40cm/8–16in long.
Breeding: Reproduces sexually by producing eggs and sperm.
Status: Not listed by IUCN.

Sand mason

Lanice conchilega

Distribution: Atlantic Ocean, Mediterranean Sea.
Habitat: On sandy substrates on middle shore downwards.
Food: Small food particles.
Size: 30cm/12in long.
Breeding: Reproduces sexually by producing eggs and sperm.
Status: Not listed by IUCN.

This bristle worm lives partly buried in sand from the middle shore downwards. To protect its soft body from predators, it builds around itself a thin tube of shell fragments and sand grains. The top of the tube, which typically has a 'frayed' appearance, protrudes above the sand (right). The head bears a crown of long tentacles that the creature waves about in the water to trap food particles. There are three pairs of red, tufted gills (below). The body consists of up to 300 segments, with chaetae borne on the segments in the thoracic region. The sand mason is only one of several species of bristle worm that protect themselves in tubes. Others live in mucus-lined burrows.

Identification: Body consists of 150–300 segments. Head bears three pairs of red-coloured gills and crown of pale pink or white feeding tentacles. Swollen thoracic region of 17 segments bears chaetae. Abdomen thinner and fragile. Body encased in tube made of sand grains, shell fragments and other similar material with characteristically 'frayed' upper end.

Left: The tentacles are retracted when the sand mason is not feeding.

Green leaf worm (*Eulalia sanguinea*): 10cm/4in
This relatively long species is a paddle worm, so called because of the prominent, paddle-like parapodia arranged along each side of the segments. The creature's small head bears conspicuous eyes, antennae and cirri, as well as an eversible proboscis. Its grass-green colour, sometimes tinged with blue, helps it to remain camouflaged among seaweeds. Found in shallow water in the Atlantic Ocean, and in the Mediterranean and Baltic seas.

Lugworm (*Arenicola marina*): 20cm/8in
This common, soft-bodied, green-brown coloured worm (below) makes a U-shaped burrow beneath the surface of the sand. It draws watery sand in at the head end, extracts any edible food particles it contains, and then deposits the 'waste' sand out from the tail end. Small, neat coils of mud or sand on the beach at low tide indicate the presence of lugworms. Found on middle shore to low water on Atlantic, Mediterranean and Baltic shores.

Southern fanworm (*Sabellastarte indica*): 15cm/6in
Also known as the Indian fanworm, this widely distributed species has an attractive, often banded branchial crown that the creature uses to trap detritus suspended in the water, and on which it feeds. It lives inside a protective tube on rocky reefs and exists down to about 30m/98ft in tropical seas.

Red tubeworm

Serpula vermicularis

This slender, sedentary bristle worm belongs to the family Sabellidae, whose members have bodies with a thoracic region consisting of a few segments (seven) and a long abdomen composed of many segments. The head is reduced, and bears clearly visible gills on which are situated the eyes. The gills are used to obtain oxygen and to trap tiny food particles. As its common name suggests, the worm lives inside a calcareous tube cemented firmly to hard surfaces such as rocks, stones, discarded shells and even ships' hulls. Sometimes it occurs in large numbers, forming small reef-like colonies. The top end of the calcareous tube can be securely closed by a lid called an operculum, which is attached to the animal's head and operated by special muscles.

Distribution: Atlantic Ocean, Mediterranean Sea.
Habitat: Fixed to stones, rocks, etc. on lower shore and down to about 250m/820ft.
Food: Small food particles.
Size: 6cm/2.4in long.
Breeding: Reproduces sexually by producing eggs and sperm.
Status: Not listed by IUCN.

Identification: Head of worm bears two fan-like gills with many filaments; eyes on gills; trumpet-shaped, calcareous operculum with small teeth. Body slender and composed of about 200 segments bearing chaetae. Tube cylindrical, calcareous, funnel shaped and marked with rings; often twisted and rambling. Colour of worm variable: yellow, orange, pink or red; red gills. Colour of tube pinkish-white.

CHITONS AND GASTROPOD MOLLUSCS

The chitons are molluscs whose bodies are protected by a shell formed from overlapping plates. They creep about on the rocks grazing algae. The gastropods are a large and important group of molluscs represented by some of the best-known of all marine creatures. Many species live inside elaborate, coiled shells, although a few have no shell and are active swimmers.

Lepidochitona cinereus

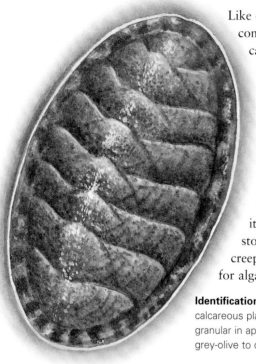

Like other chitons, this small species has a shell composed of eight transverse, overlapping calcareous plates. The slightly articulated nature of the shell gives rise to the chitons' other common name: coat-of-mail shells. In living specimens, the edge of the shell is fringed with a fleshy girdle. The shell of this chiton is slightly less flattened than it is in many species and has a granular appearance. One of the most common chitons, it is found on rocks and under stones on the shore, where it creeps slowly about searching for algal films to graze on.

Identification: Shell consists of eight, slightly convex calcareous plates forming an elongated oval shape. Shell is granular in appearance and may be encrusted. Colour ranges from grey-olive to dull red; underside of shell plates is blue-green.

Distribution: Atlantic Ocean, Mediterranean and Baltic seas.
Habitat: Mainly on and under rocks and stones on the seashore; also on stones in rock pools.
Food: Algal films.
Size: 2cm/0.8in.
Breeding: Reproduces sexually by producing eggs and sperm.
Status: Not listed.

Pinto abalone

Haliotis kamtschatkana

Identification: Thin, flattened shell with lumpy or wavy pattern on exterior surface; three to six raised holes along one edge of shell. Exterior of shell mottled green or brown; interior white.

The pinto abalone is one of a group of primitive gastropod molluscs with flattened, whorled shells; the low profile of the shell is an adaptation to help it minimize resistance to the action of the waves and to protect it against predators. Water, waste products and gametes (reproductive cells) pass through a series of holes along one edge of the shell. This species lives on rocks and seaweeds, where it grazes on algae. It often occurs in groups. In the northern parts of its range it is found in the intertidal zone, but further south it is subtidal only. Its predators include the sea otter (*Enhydra lutris*) – for which it is a favourite food – as well as starfish. When confronted by a starfish the pinto abalone may respond by jerking away from the danger. Once heavily harvested for food, numbers are still declining, probably due to illegal poaching.

Distribution: Pacific Ocean: Alaska to California, US; northern Japan and Siberia.
Habitat: On seaweeds on rocky exposed coasts and in water down to about 15m/50ft.
Food: Algae.
Size: About 15cm/6in, sometimes larger.
Breeding: Reproduces sexually by producing eggs and sperm.
Status: Listed as Threatened by IUCN.

Common limpet

Patella vulgata

Distribution: North-eastern Atlantic around northerly Scandinavian coasts and British Isles to southern Icelandic shore; also western Atlantic off Nova Scotia.
Habitat: On rocks and in rockpools on middle and upper shore.
Food: Algae.
Size: 7cm/2.8in long.
Breeding: Reproduces sexually by producing eggs and sperm.
Status: Not listed by IUCN.

Throughout its range, the distinctive conical shell of the common limpet is a familiar sight on rocky shores, clamped firmly down to help retain moisture and to prevent predators plucking the creature from its resting place. However, during feeding, the limpet leaves the safety of its niche to graze on algae with its rasping tongue. Once it has fed, it returns unerringly to the same spot, the lower edge of its shell snugly fitting the folds of the rock on which it rests. The height of limpet shells varies according to location: those in sheltered places are relatively tall, whereas those found in exposed areas are lower to help reduce resistance to the pounding waves. Spawning is usually induced by inshore winds and accompanying rough seas.

Identification: Rough, irregularly ribbed conical shell with apex lying towards the front. Top of shell slightly rounded and flattened. Exterior of shell generally blue-green to grey, often with encrusting barnacles. Interior of shell white or yellow with visible muscle scar left by animal.

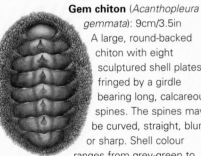

Gem chiton (*Acanthopleura gemmata*): 9cm/3.5in
A large, round-backed chiton with eight sculptured shell plates fringed by a girdle bearing long, calcareous spines. The spines may be curved, straight, blunt or sharp. Shell colour ranges from grey-green to grey-brown. Found in the Indo-Pacific from Africa to Australia, it occurs among rocks in the intertidal zone down to about 2m/6.6ft, where it feeds on algae.

Marbled chiton (*Chiton marmoratus*): 6cm/2.4in
This somewhat flattened species has smooth shell plates with almost parallel sides. Colours vary from grey to brown to olive-green. The girdle is narrow and covered in scales. This species of chiton is quite common throughout its entire Caribbean range, which stretches from the coastal waters of Florida down to the West Indies.

Common ormer (*Haliotis lamellosa*): 7cm/2.8in
Only a few of the hundred or so species in the family Haliotidae are represented in the Mediterranean region, this being one of them. The flattened, ear-shaped shell has a creased appearance to its outer surface and bears a row of holes on one edge, and is often encrusted with worm tubes and other debris. The inner surface is nacreous. It is found among rocks on the lower shore and in shallow water.

Blue-rayed limpet

Patina pellucida

The blue-rayed limpet is an attractive species, and it is characterized by the beautiful, electric-blue streaks, or rays, that radiate outwards from the apex of the shell to the margins. These markings are especially vivid in young specimens; they tend to fade in older animals, when the shell often darkens as well. This species generally lives on the fronds and holdfasts of seaweeds, such as laminarians, on the lower shore and in shallow water, where it feeds by rasping algae.

Identification: Smooth, semi-transparent shell with slightly off-centre apex. In young specimens, shell typically light brown or beige in colour with well-defined electric-blue streaks radiating from the apex to the margins; in older specimens, rays may become less distinct and shell may turn a generally darker, horn-like colour.

Distribution: North-eastern Atlantic around northerly Scandinavian coasts and British Isles to southern Icelandic shore; also western Atlantic off Nova Scotia.
Habitat: On the fronds and holdfasts of seaweeds on lower shore and in shallow water.
Food: Algae.
Size: 1.5cm/0.6in long.
Breeding: Reproduces sexually by producing eggs and sperm.
Status: Not listed by IUCN.

GASTROPOD MOLLUSCS AND NUDIBRANCHS

The Nudibranchia is an order of gastropod molluscs within the subclass Opisthobranchia.
In all opisthobranchs, the shell is reduced or even absent. Many species have brightly coloured bodies
and conspicuous external gills. Their number include the intriguing cone shells, armed with an
appendage, often hidden inside the shell, which effectively 'harpoons' their prey.

Pelican's foot shell

Aporrhais pespelecani

A species of gastropod mollusc with a many whorled shell marked with numerous tubercles and grooves; the last (outer) whorl has a flared aperture that is extended into four foot-like projections. One of these projections grows close to, and more or less parallel with, the spire, two grow outwards and one forms the siphonal canal, through which the animal samples the water. In young individuals, these projections are less well formed. This species lives on muddy, sandy and gravelly substrates down to about 80m/262ft.

Identification: The shell of mature individual has a flattened aperture lip giving a webbed-foot appearance (hence the common name of pelican foot). Aperture lip has four extensions. Subdued colouration of whorled and grooved external shell ranges from brown to greyish, although the inside may be lighter and have a slightly glazed appearance. Tests surrounding water for scent of potential predators through siphonal canal. Feeds on algae.

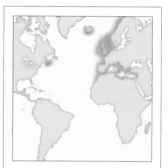

Distribution: Atlantic, from northerly Scandinavian coasts, British Isles and southern Iceland to the Mediterranean. Also found in the west off Nova Scotia.
Habitat: Muddy, sandy and gravelly substrates.
Food: Algae.
Size: 4cm/1.6in.
Breeding: Reproduces sexually by producing eggs and sperm.
Status: Not listed by IUCN.

Queen conch

Strombus gigas

Identification: Robust, heavy shell with low spire and wide, flared aperture lip in mature specimens; outer edge of lip tends to be brittle. Spire whorls with tubercles, sometimes spiny. Colour of external shell is creamy but overlaid by darker outer membrane, or periostracum. Inner shell pink.

Also known as the pink conch, this is one of the biggest species in its genus, prized both for its spectacular – and useful – shell and as a source of food. The shell has a broad, flared aperture lip when the animal is mature, although this feature is not developed in juvenile individuals. The whorls of the spire feature large tubercles, which sometimes form spines. The shell of the queen conch is sometimes used as a type of trumpet, and the animal occasionally produces pink-coloured pearls.

Distribution: Atlantic Ocean from Florida (US) to Caribbean Sea.
Habitat: Shallow, sandy substrates.
Food: Algae.
Size: 23cm/9in.
Breeding: Reproduces sexually by producing eggs and sperm.
Status: Not listed by IUCN.

Textile cone

Conus textile

Distribution: Indo-Pacific region.
Habitat: Under rocks or sand in shallow water.
Food: Small fish and invertebrates.
Size: 8cm/3.2in.
Breeding: Reproduces sexually by producing eggs and sperm.
Status: Not listed by IUCN.

The 300 or so cones are characterized by their beautifully, subtly and variably marked conical shells, and the textile cone is as attractive as any of the species. Like other cone shells, the textile cone is carnivorous, preying on small fish, molluscs and other invertebrates by injecting venom through a harpoon – actually a modified tooth from the radula, which is the rasping tongue used by most grazing molluscs. Once a victim has been harpooned and immobilized, it is drawn back into the stomach of the cone to be digested. The textile cone usually hides under rocks while waiting for food. What sets the textile cone apart from most other cone shells is the toxicity of its venom; it has been known to cause fatalities in humans.

Identification: The shell of this species has a short spire with slightly concave or straight sides. Body whorl convex. Exterior of shell white with elaborate pattern of overlapping brown lines and three intricate yellowish or brown spiral bands. Like other cone shells, this pattern is largely obscured by the outer covering (the periostracum) in living specimens. The hollow radular teeth, of which there are a number, are 'loaded' into position by the radular muscle.

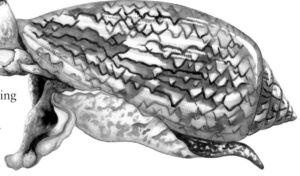

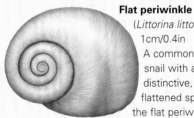

Flat periwinkle
(*Littorina littoralis*):
1cm/0.4in
A common sea snail with a distinctive, flattened spire, the flat periwinkle is found on seaweeds and in rock crevices on the middle and upper parts of Atlantic and Baltic shores. Many specimens are yellow, but this highly variable species may also be brown, green, red and orange, as well as banded.

Snipe's bill murex (*Haustellum haustellum*):
13cm/5in
Like most murex shells, this species has a highly distinctive shell. The spire is low and robust, the body whorl is big and the siphonal canal very long. The outer shell is creamy pink with brown blotches and stripes. Found among the sandy shallows of the Indo-Pacific region.

Tiger cowrie (*Cypraea tigris*): 9cm/3.5in
Smooth and tactile, the tiger cowrie is a large species with a bulbous shell marked typically with diffused brown spots on a white ground. Found among coral in the Indo-Pacific region.

Dogwhelk (*Nucella lapillus*): 3cm/1.2in
This little sea snail lives on sheltered rocky shores in the Atlantic Ocean feeding on barnacles and other invertebrates. The shell has a short, pointed spire and a broad body whorl. Colour and banding both variable, ranging from brown to ash-grey, often with brown spiral bands.

Green-spotted nudibranch

Nembrotha nigerrima

Nudibranchs are a group of marine molluscs that lack shells. They are often vividly coloured and bear elaborate external gills (the word nudibranch means 'naked gill') and other appendages. At the front of the body are sensory tentacles called rhinophores. Nudibranchs lack the protection afforded by a shell, and many deter predators by being highly poisonous, advertising this fact with warning colours. The green-spotted nudibranch is a widespread species that feeds on ascidians (primitive chordate animals) in shallow waters. Like other nudibranchs, it can swim using undulating body movements, but also crawls about on rocks and seaweeds.

Identification: Soft, slug-like body with raised central area in the middle of the back bearing green gills. Two prominent rhinophores on top of head near front of body. Colour of body velvet black with distinct green blotches and other markings.

Distribution: Indo-West Pacific region.
Habitat: On rocks and seaweeds in water from about 3–8m/10–26ft.
Food: Ascidians.
Size: 10cm/4in.
Breeding: Hermaphrodite; exchange of sperm followed by egg laying.
Status: Not listed by IUCN.

BIVALVE MOLLUSCS

Bivalve molluscs have a shell composed of two halves, or valves. In some species, both valves are similar, and in others they differ. Occasionally the valves are extremely reduced. Many bivalves live a sedentary life on or in the sand, but some can swim by clapping their valves together. Others attach themselves firmly to rocks and other substrates. A few bore into wood and rock.

Common mussel

Mytilus edulis

Throughout its range, clumps of the common mussel are a familiar sight festooning rocks, piers and crevices, although the species is also grown commercially in special beds as a source of food. The shell, roughly triangular in shape, consists of two similar valves. Common mussels are filter feeders, drawing in oxygen-rich water and tiny particles of food via their tube-like siphons when submerged by sea water. Once the tide recedes, the valves clamp shut again. A gland in the animal's foot secretes thin, silky filaments called byssal threads which anchor the mussel to the substrate; a single mussel may have hundreds of these threads.

Identification: Roughly triangular shell consisting of two valves, but shape varies according to environmental conditions. Shell smooth with pattern of radiating lines. Inconspicuous ligament with almost straight ligamental region. Terminal beak. Colour varies from purple to blue or brown. Inside of shell pearly with dark border.

Distribution: Coasts and estuaries worldwide.
Habitat: On rocks, stones, piers and breakwaters from middle shore downwards. Also found in estuarine waters.
Food: Tiny food particles filtered from the water.
Size: Variable: usually from 1–10cm/0.4–4in, sometimes larger than this.
Breeding: Reproduces sexually; eggs are shed and fertilized externally; larval phase follows.
Status: Not listed by IUCN.

Queen scallop

Aequipecten opercularis

This species is found from the intertidal zone down to 200m/660ft, sometimes in great numbers. The two shell valves are convex, although the lower one is less so, and sculpted with radiating ribs. The colour of this shell is quite variable and is often encrusted with sponges. When young, the queen scallop often attaches itself to the substrate with fine byssal threads for safety, often in the company of horse mussels. However, the adult scallop swims freely by rapidly clapping the two shell valves together. In this way, it can travel over quite considerable distances.

Identification: Roughly round shell consisting of two convex valves. Lower valve less convex and paler in colour. About 20 conspicuous, radiating ribs. Shell margin crenulate (with small teeth). Each valve bears an ear; anterior ear longer than posterior. Colour varies from light brown to yellow or orange, sometimes with spots or bands.

Distribution: Atlantic Ocean, Mediterranean Sea.
Habitat: Attaches to sand and gravel on seabed; found at depths of up to 200m/660ft.
Food: Tiny food particles filtered from the water.
Size: 9cm/3.5in.
Breeding: Reproduces sexually; eggs are shed and fertilized externally; larval phase follows.
Status: Not listed by IUCN.

European thorny oyster

Spondylus gaederopus

Distribution: Mediterranean.
Habitat: Attaches to rocks and other firm surfaces on the seabed.
Food: Tiny food particles filtered from the water.
Size: 10cm/4in long.
Breeding: Reproduces sexually; eggs are shed and fertilized externally; larval phase follows.
Status: Not listed by IUCN.

The thorny oysters are characterized by having shells covered with irregularly positioned spines of various lengths – although these are sometimes absent. The European thorny oyster, like other thorny oysters, cements itself to the rocky seabed or to some other firm object by one of its valves and remains there for life, relying on its thorny outgrowths for both physical protection and camouflage. The permanence of the oyster's existence is often underlined by the growth of worm tubes and barnacles that encrust the shell's outer surface.

Identification: Oval-shaped shell slightly longer than it is wide. Lower valve convex, upper valve flatter. Shell surface usually bears long, sharp spines – especially on upper valve. Colour of external shell surface purple, crimson or brown; lower valve usually paler. Interior of shell white.

Date mussel (*Lithophaga lithophaga*):
7cm/2.8in long
Elongated, smooth-edged shell consisting of two equal-sized valves. Fine sculptured lines on exterior shell surface. The exterior of the shell is brownish in colour and the interior is blue-white. This mussel lives in shallow waters in the Mediterranean Sea where it bores into limestone rock and coral skeletons.

Common European oyster
(*Ostrea edulis*): 10cm/4in long
The shape of this greyish mollusc can be variable, but it is often oval in outline or pear-shaped and the surface is rough or scaly. The two valves are dissimilar: the lower one is concave and fixed to the substrate, while the upper one is flatter and fits inside. Found down to about 80m/262ft in the Atlantic Ocean and Mediterranean Sea and in commercial oyster beds.

American oyster (*Crassostrea virginica*):
15cm/6in long
Shells of this oyster are typically flat, ribbed and elongate in shape but, as with several other oyster species, they can be variable in their appearance. The lower valve is securely fixed to hard objects. The exterior is dirty white in colour or grey and the inside is white. The American oyster is found in estuaries and bays from the Gulf of St Lawrence, in Canada, south to Brazil.

Mediterranean jewel box

Chama gryphoides

The bivalve molluscs in the family Chamidae are known as jewel boxes and are confined mostly to tropical waters, although the Mediterranean jewel box is, as its common name suggests, found in temperate waters. They resemble the thorny oysters in so far as the shells are often adorned with protective spines or other outgrowths, and they live by attaching themselves firmly to the substrate. The Mediterranean jewel box has two dissimilar valves. One valve is cup-shaped and attached to the substrate, while the other valve is smaller and opens like a lid, complete with hinge.

Distribution: Mediterranean.
Habitat: Attaches to rocks and other firm surfaces on the seabed.
Food: Tiny food particles filtered from the water.
Size: 4cm/1.6in long.
Breeding: Reproduces sexually; eggs are shed and fertilized externally; larval phase follows.
Status: Not listed by IUCN.

Identification: Shell comprises two dissimilar valves: lower valve cup-shaped and cemented to rocks or other firm surfaces on seabed; upper valve smaller and opens with a hinge mechanism. Shell displays series of ridged, radiating growth lines. Colour of external surface grey-white; inner surface brownish.

Common cockle

Cerastoderma edule

The common, or European, cockle is common and often abundant in shallow, sandy coastal waters and has formed the basis of a thriving fishing industry for centuries. Many of these cockles are simply raked from beneath the surface at low tide, while others are reared in commercial cockle beds. Cockles dig themselves a few centimetres down into the sediment with their foot and then extend their feeding siphons up to the surface to draw in water and tiny suspended food particles. The cockle can tolerate a wide range of salinity: it is usually found in salinities of between 15 and 35 parts per 1,000, but it can survive in conditions of just 10 parts per 1,000. At low tide, the cockle is one of the molluscs sought by seabirds as food items.

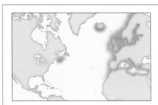

Distribution: Eastern Atlantic from Iceland to Morocco, and in the west off Nova Scotia; Mediterranean and Baltic.
Habitat: Burrows about 5cm/2in down into sand, mud or gravel; found from middle shore down to shallow water.
Food: Tiny food particles filtered from the water.
Size: 5cm/2in long.
Breeding: Eggs are shed and fertilized externally; larval phase follows.
Status: Not listed by IUCN.

Identification: Has a thick, solid shell that is globular and more or less oval in shape. Bears 22–28 radiating ribs that are transversed by ridges, giving shell a banded effect. Edge of shell is crenellated (toothed) where ridges meet. Has a prominent external ligament. Colour of shell is generally creamy white or fawn, sometimes with patches of yellow or pale blue, and the foot is bright red or orange. Unlike some bivalve species, the two valves of the shell are similar in size. In contrast with the highly sculpted exterior, the interior of the shell is smooth in texture and whitish in colour, with partial grooves.

Right: One of the best times to spot common cockles is when the tide recedes, leaving these filter feeders exposed to seabirds and scavenging humans engaged in 'cockle-picking'. Mass collection along a seashore or estuary bed is often done with the aid of a garden rake.

Pod razor shell

Ensis siliqua

The long, distinctive shapes of the razor shells (*Ensis* species) have led to them being called jack-knife clams in the US and finger oysters in Australia, although their range is broad around Atlantic and Pacific coasts; they are also common around British shores. Their unusual streamlined shape gives them a distinct advantage when burrowing: using their muscular foot to first push themselves deep into the sand, they then pull their shell downwards, and in this way they reach safety with astonishing speed. Once 'dug in', a razor shell is extremely hard to dislodge from its safe haven – even if its siphons are gripped by predators, they will break off and regenerate. The pod razor shell is a large species and is found on the lower shore downwards, where it uses its siphons to draw in water and suspended food particles (known as 'suspension feeding').

Identification: Long, narrow shell consisting of two equal valves. Edges of shell straight and ends blunt. Colour of shell white inside and out, but exterior overlaid with green-yellow periostracum layer, often partially eroded. Foot – usually hidden – is pale brown. Most razor shells live in more or less permanent burrows along the lower shore and in shallow water. May occasionally be seen sticking out of the sand, but presence is more likely to be indicated by the keyhole-shaped markings made in the sand by the siphons during feeding.

Distribution: Eastern Atlantic from Iceland to Morocco, and in the west off Nova Scotia; also found Mediterranean and Baltic seas.
Habitat: Burrows into sand or gravel; found from lower shore down to about 35m/115ft in shallow water.
Food: Tiny food particles filtered from the water.
Size: Up to 20cm/8in long.
Breeding: Reproduces sexually; eggs are fertilized externally and become larvae.
Status: Not listed by IUCN.

Common piddock

Pholas dactylus

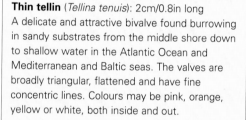

Distribution: Eastern Atlantic from Iceland to Morocco, and in the west off Nova Scotia; also Mediterranean and Baltic.
Habitat: Bores into soft rock, wood or peat on the lower shore; also found in shallow water.
Food: Tiny food particles filtered from the water.
Size: Up to 15cm/6in long.
Breeding: Reproduces sexually; eggs are fertilized externally and become larvae.
Status: Not listed by IUCN.

The shells of piddocks are adapted to enable the animals to bore into clay and soft rock, such as chalk and sandstone, as well as wood or peat. The ability to shelter in hard substrates means that these molluscs can remain relatively secure against predators. When boring, the piddock gapes (opens) its shell valves and uses the fine, sharp, ribbed edges to wear away the surface of the substrate into which it is boring. Because the shell is partly open when it is drilling, the piddock can then close the valves slightly and use its foot to push itself into the hole it has just excavated. The piddock also has four accessory shell plates to give it extra protection. When the animal is alive, the long siphons are covered by a protective horny sheath.

Identification: Shell consists of two narrow, long equal valves. Front of shell edges may be crenulate. Four protective accessory plates present. Shell has external sculpturing and concentric radiating ribs, roughest where they are used for boring. Colour of shell greyish-white but covered with yellow-brown periostracum (hard membrane). Interior white.

Thin tellin (*Tellina tenuis*): 2cm/0.8in long
A delicate and attractive bivalve found burrowing in sandy substrates from the middle shore down to shallow water in the Atlantic Ocean and Mediterranean and Baltic seas. The valves are broadly triangular, flattened and have fine concentric lines. Colours may be pink, orange, yellow or white, both inside and out.

Wedge clam (*Donax cuneatus*): 4cm/1.6in long
This Indo-Pacific species is broadly triangular with a rounded front end like most donax clams. Its colour is greyish white with brown rays. It lives buried in intertidal sand, where it migrates up and down the beach according to the tides.

Banded venus (*Venus fasciata*): 2.5cm/1in long
Like most venus clams, the banded venus burrows out of sight and feeds by drawing water and food in through its siphons.  The round shell is white, yellow or pink with dark rays and has prominent umbones and concentric ridges. Mediterranean Sea and Atlantic Ocean.

American soft-shell clam (*Mya arenaria*): 10cm/4in
Also known as the sand gaper, this mollusc is found in intertidal mud and sand, including estuaries, down to about 70m/230ft in the Atlantic Ocean. The dirty white shell is oval with concentric rings on the external surface. The right valve is usually more convex than the left.

Ship worm

Teredo navalis

This specialized wood-boring animal gets its common name because of its rather worm-like appearance and its adaptation to burrowing into the hulls of wooden-built boats – sometimes in large numbers. This burrowing activity can seriously weaken not only ships' timbers, but also piers and other wooden structures infested by the ship worm. An inner tooth on each of the extremely reduced shell valves is used for drilling. At the same time, the mantle secretes a protective, chalky tube that follows the path of the boring mollusc. A pair of tough pallets attached to the end of the worm is used to seal the tube when the siphons are withdrawn, enclosing the mollusc safely inside.

Identification: Shell valves much reduced and covering only small anterior part of animal. Shell valves white but covered by light brown periostracum. Mollusc body elongated and worm-like; brown in colour. Posterior of worm bears two off-white calcareous pallets. Two small siphons at end of body.

Distribution: North-eastern Atlantic; Mediterranean and Baltic seas.
Habitat: Bores into wooden structures below water.
Food: Tiny food particles filtered from the water; also wood shavings.
Size: Shell 2cm/0.8in long; soft, worm-like body 15cm/6in long; pallets 5mm/0.2in long; chalky tube up to 60cm/24in long and 8mm/0.3in in diameter.
Breeding: Reproduces sexually; eggs are shed and fertilized externally; larval phase follows.
Status: Not listed by IUCN.

BARNACLES AND SHRIMP-LIKE CRUSTACEANS

The class Crustacea includes many different seashore and shallow-sea animals. The familiar barnacles are sessile, highly modified crustaceans enclosed in a protective chalky shell. Shrimp-like crustaceans include the ubiquitous sand hoppers, as well as the aquatic sea-slaters, mantis shrimps and opossum shrimps.

Goose barnacle

Lepas anatifera

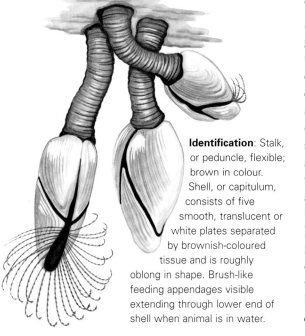

Identification: Stalk, or peduncle, flexible; brown in colour. Shell, or capitulum, consists of five smooth, translucent or white plates separated by brownish-coloured tissue and is roughly oblong in shape. Brush-like feeding appendages visible extending through lower end of shell when animal is in water.

The goose barnacle common name comes about because to some eyes it resembles a goose. In ancient times, geese were believed to have arisen from these small marine crustaceans. The goose barnacle is a pelagic creature; it drifts in the ocean attached to any suitable floating object, such as pieces of wood, plastic or cork, on which it first settles while in the larval stage. These animals are encountered when the object to which they are attached is washed ashore as flotsam. Like other barnacles, the goose barnacle is a highly modified crustacean. It attaches itself by means of a partially retractable stalk, and the 'shell' consists of a series of chalky plates through which it extends appendages that sweep backwards and forwards in the water to collect small food items.

Distribution: Temperate North Atlantic and North Sea.
Habitat: Pelagic, attached to drifting objects, but found when washed ashore.
Food: Tiny food particles in the water.
Size: Stalk 10–20cm/4–8in long; shell 5cm/2in long.
Breeding: Hermaphrodite. Free-swimming larvae settle to form new barnacles.
Status: Not listed by IUCN.

Acorn barnacle

Balanus balanoides

The acorn barnacle is one of several barnacle species that can be seen dotted over rocks at low tide – often in huge numbers. Its shape, like many other types of barnacle, usually resembles a tiny flattish pyramid or cone; this shape offers minimum resistance to the pounding of the waves, while allowing for the maximum adhesion to the rocks or other substrates to which it cements itself. When the tide is out, the shell remains tightly closed, but when the tide is in, the top of the shell opens and tiny, feathery appendages extend into the water and flick backwards and forwards, ensnaring plankton and other small creatures.

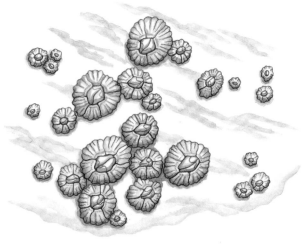

Identification: Shell consists of six plates forming a fairly flat or conical shape, marked with ridges and fissures. Two further protective plates form diamond-shaped opening in centre. Colour usually dirty white.

Right: All acorn barnacles have a pair of non-fixed 'interior' plates at the opening of the shell. These part to enable the animal to trap tiny food particles.

Distribution: Atlantic Ocean, Baltic Sea.
Habitat: Attaches to rocks and other suitable objects along the shore. .
Food: Tiny food particles in the water.
Size: Shell up to 1.5cm/0.6in across.
Breeding: Hermaphrodite. Free-swimming larvae settle to form new barnacles.
Status: Not listed by IUCN.

Parasitic barnacle
(*Sacculina carcini*):
This highly modified
and unusual barnacle
lives on the bodies of
crabs, such as
common shore crabs.
Adult size varies considerably and may be
influenced by the size of the host animal. The
barnacle forms a thread-like structure within the
host's body, and appears as a yellow-brown lump
tucked under the latter's abdomen (above left).

Neomysis integer: 1.8cm/0.7in
This is one of several species known as
opossum shrimps. The thin carapace (shell) is
nearly half as long as the body, which itself
is often reflexed downwards. Large eyes are
carried on short, movable stalks. Often found
in lagoons and estuaries in the Atlantic Ocean
where the salinity is lower.

Sea-slater (*Ligia oceanica*): 2.5cm/1in
This small crustacean belonging to the order
Isopoda resembles the terrestrial woodlouse.
The head bears a pair of long antennae. The
body is broad and flattened and has two
branched processes at the rear end. The sea-
slater lives under rocks and seaweeds and in
crevices on the upper shore, coming out at
night to forage for food. It is found around
Atlantic, North Sea and Mediterranean coasts.

Ghost shrimp (*Caprella linearis*): 2cm/0.8in
At first glance, this unusual-looking crustacean
resembles a small piece of red or brown knotted
thread. The head is almost triangular in shape
with long upper antennae; the body is long and
thin and the abdomen is reduced. It lives among
weeds on the lower shore and sublittoral of the
Atlantic Ocean.

Mantis shrimp
Squilla empusa

The mantis shrimp is not a true shrimp at
all, despite its common name, although it is
closely related to them and has several
shrimp-like features. The 'mantis' part of
its common name comes from the two
clubbing, claw-like appendages coming from
its thorax – the middle part of the body
between the head and the abdomen – that
can be suddenly extended and then snapped
closed around its prey, crushing it, in a
similar way to the hunting method
employed by the insect known as the
praying mantis. The claw-like appendages
of the mantis shrimp are so powerful that
sometimes the crustacean is known as the
'thumb splitter' by local fishermen who have
experienced this painful action at first hand.
The mantis shrimp has a shrimp-like
carapace (a protective covering formed from
a fusion of the head and thorax) and a
segmented abdomen with various
appendages modified for tasks such as
feeding, swimming and reproduction. This
sizable crustacean is a rapacious,
forceful nocturnal hunter of small
fish and invertebrates.

Distribution: Atlantic coasts
of Europe; Mediterranean.
Habitat: On sandy and
muddy intertidal seabeds,
and at shallow depths of up
to 150m/500ft.
Food: Small fish,
crabs, shrimps.
Size: Up to 25cm/10in.
Breeding: Reproduces
sexually; females carry eggs
between anterior legs; larval
phase follows.
Status: Not listed by IUCN.

Identification: Flattened,
shrimp-like body. Two pairs of
antennae at front. One pair of
stalked eyes. Thorax bears eight
pairs of appendages; second
pair of thoracic legs are long,
claw-like, food-capturing
appendages. Abdomen bears five
pairs of appendages. Terminal
part of abdomen forms a broad
telson. Colour usually translucent,
tinged with green.

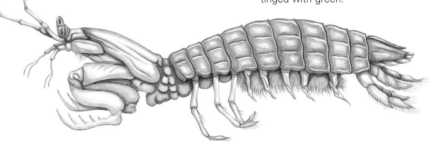

Sand hopper
Talitrus saltator

Distribution: Atlantic coasts
of Europe; Mediterranean.
Habitat: On the upper
shore, favours the fronds of
rotting seaweed.
Food: Rotting vegetation and
other organic debris.
Size: 1.5cm/0.6in.
Breeding: Reproduces
sexually by eggs and sperm.
Status: Not listed by IUCN.

Lift up a pile of rotting seaweed on the
upper shore strandline and the chances are
that scores of small crustaceans will leap up
into the air, in flea-like fashion, from it.
These animals are sand hoppers – tiny
crustaceans belonging to the order
Amphipoda, many of which are found on
the seashore. Unlike real fleas, which feed
on blood, the sand hopper, or beach flea,
scavenges on partly decayed
seaweeds and the tiny organisms it
finds among the rotting fronds.
The sand hopper may also bury
itself in the sand down to depths
of about 30cm/12in.

Identification: Body appears quite broad and flat
when viewed from above. Colour varies from
greyish-green to brown. Head with short upper
antennae and much longer lower antennae. Eyes
round and black. Juveniles lack the ability to burrow
into the soft sand and may conceal themselves
among seaweed lying on the shore.

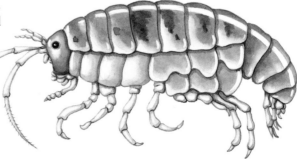

PRAWNS AND SHRIMPS

The true prawns and shrimps have light exoskeletons and their bodies are usually slightly flattened sideways. One of their two pairs of antennae is much longer than the other. Various species of prawns and shrimps are found in every part of the world's oceans and seas, from tidal pools and estuaries to coral reefs and the deepest trenches.

Snapping prawn (Pistol shrimp)

Alpheus ruber

Identification: Bulky prawn with a very short rostrum – the part of the carapace that is drawn out and projects between the animal's eyes. Long, jointed antennae. First pair of walking legs bear one 'normal' claw and one enlarged and modified claw. Second walking legs bear tiny pincers. Rich, almost luminous red colour.

This is one of many species of snapping prawns or pistol shrimps in the family Alpheidae, many of which occur on coral reefs. It owes its name to the snapping sound that it produces with a modified claw or pincer – usually the right claw. The movable part of the claw has a bulb at the base that fits into a socket when the claw is shut. When the prawn opens the claw wide, a sticky pad on the bulb locks against another pad on the socket, holding it open like the hammer of a cocked pistol. If the prawn then pulls on the big adductor muscle that closes the claw, the locking pads give way and the claw snaps shut with a report that can stun nearby animals. The animal uses this technique to immobilize and then capture its prey.

Distribution: North-eastern Atlantic; Mediterranean Sea.
Habitat: Crevices in rocky reefs and sand, and cavities in sponges.
Food: Small marine animals such as shrimps, small crabs and small fish.
Size: 2.5–3.5cm/1–1.4in.
Breeding: Reproduces sexually; females carry eggs beneath their bodies; these hatch into swimming larvae.
Status: Not listed by IUCN.

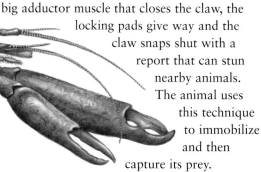

Common prawn

Leander serratus (Palaemon serratus)

The virtually transparent body of the common prawn makes it hard to see as it picks its way delicately over the bottom of a rockpool. It feeds by gathering small edible items with the pincers on its first two pairs of legs, while monitoring the water movement with its very long, sensitive antennae. At any hint of danger it propels itself backwards through the water into a nearby refuge with a quick flick of its tail. It can also swim slowly by beating the small limbs, or swimmerets, beneath its abdomen.

Identification: Elongated body; downturned tail with leaf-like structures at the end. Long, upcurved, toothed rostrum and two pairs of long antennae, the inner pair each divided in two. Small pincers at the tips of the first two pairs of walking legs. Body almost transparent, with a pinkish brown tint and reddish spots and lines.

Distribution: North-eastern Atlantic; Mediterranean and Black seas.
Habitat: Sandy and rocky shores, including rockpools, to depths of about 40m/130ft.
Food: Edible debris and small animals.
Size: Up to 10cm/4in.
Breeding: Reproduces sexually; females carry up to 4,000 eggs attached to hairs on their swimmerets, for around four months. They hatch into planktonic larvae.
Status: Not listed by IUCN.

Opossum shrimp

Neomysis integer

Distribution: North-eastern Atlantic Ocean, as far south as Spain.
Habitat: Upper reaches of estuaries, and some tidal pools.
Food: Detritus, diatoms, algae and small crustaceans.
Size: Up to 1.7cm/0.7in.
Breeding: Reproduces sexually; females carry up to 100 larvae in a brood pouch for about two months before releasing them into the water.
Status: Not listed.

One of several different species of opossum shrimp that live in a variety of aquatic habitats, this small, free-swimming crustacean is adapted for life in the brackish waters of estuaries. It lives in groups, gathering microscopic food particles from the water. Like many marine organisms, it feeds near the surface at night, seeking the protection of deeper water in daylight. It has a well-developed instinct for dealing with the ebb and flow of the tide, retreating to the deep main channels as the tide level falls to avoid being stranded, but swimming against the current to prevent itself being swept out to sea. The name 'opossum shrimp' refers to the female's brood pouch, in which the young larvae spend their first weeks after hatching from their eggs.

Identification: Slender, almost transparent shrimp, with a carapace bulkier than its abdomen, and a short, pointed rostrum protruding between the eyes. Large stalked eyes and long antennae, feathery limbs adapted for swimming. Brood pouch for carrying up to about 100 larvae after hatching.

Common shrimp (*Crangon vulgaris*): 5cm/2in long
Varying from grey to dark brown in colour, this bottom-dwelling shrimp lives in shallow coastal waters to depths of 20m/66ft, in clean or muddy sand. It spends the day buried, emerging at night to creep over the sand in search of food. It uses its short, stout pincers to tackle worms, young fish and other crustaceans, as well as any edible debris it can find.

Aesop prawn
(*Pandalus montagui*): 15cm/6in long
This Arctic and North Atlantic species of prawn lives mainly on hard seabeds at depths of down to about 20m/66ft. Looking very like the common prawn, but with bright orange stripes on its mainly transparent body, it has a long, slightly upturned rostrum. It is one of the species that is commonly fished for food.

Chameleon prawn (*Hippolyte varians*): 3cm/1.2in long
This small prawn owes its common name to the way its colour varies and adapts to its habitat – an effective means of camouflage. During the day it may appear in hues of red, yellow, brown, green or blue, depending on the colour of the environment it finds itself in. At night, when the water turns darker, it always reverts to a bluish-green colour as it grazes on marine algae. It usually lives in shallow Mediterranean and Atlantic coastal waters, and may also be found in brackish estuarine habitats.

Banded coral shrimp

Stenopus hispidus

Sometimes known as the banded boxer shrimp because of its pugnacious, territorial behaviour – it will attack and even kill other trespassing shrimps – this colourful shrimp obtains most of its food by 'cleaning' other marine animals such as fish. It stays in one place on the reef and solicits for customers, which recognize the shrimp by its banded pattern and allow it to pick parasites and dead tissue from their skin. It will even valet particularly voracious fish such as moray eels, but it is occasionally eaten by opportunist triggerfish, large angelfish, wrasses and groupers.

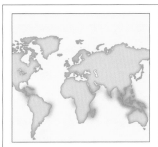

Distribution: Tropical coral seas worldwide.
Habitat: Coral reefs, to depths of 30m/100ft.
Food: Parasites and dead skin removed from fish, plus other small animals and debris.
Size: Up to 7.5cm/3in.
Breeding: Reproduces sexually; females carry green eggs beneath the body. When hatched, the young live attached to the female for about six weeks, then swim to the surface to live among plankton.
Status: Not listed by IUCN.

Identification: A spiny shrimp, vividly patterned with dark red and white bands, and deep blue bases to its very long, enlarged front limbs, which are equipped with powerful pincers. Long, slender white legs, with small pincers on the first two pairs. Six long white antennae. Black eyes.

LOBSTERS, SQUAT LOBSTERS AND HERMIT CRABS

The lobsters and crayfish are powerfully built crustaceans with pincers on the first pair of walking legs. The last part of the abdomen forms a telson. The squat lobsters and hermit crabs often have their abdomen folded under the body. Hermit crabs protect their abdomens with the shells of dead molluscs.

Common lobster

Homarus gammarus

One of the largest of all crustaceans, the common lobster is also prized as a delicacy. When lobsters are cooked they turn red, but in life they are blue-black. The common lobster lives in the sublittoral zone, hiding under rocks or in caves and large crevices. It scavenges for much of its food, but also preys on creatures such as mussels. It first crushes the shell with its larger claw, or pincer, and then uses its smaller claw to remove the mollusc.

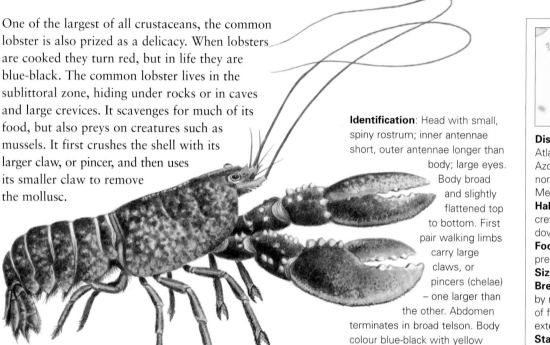

Identification: Head with small, spiny rostrum; inner antennae short, outer antennae longer than body; large eyes. Body broad and slightly flattened top to bottom. First pair walking limbs carry large claws, or pincers (chelae) – one larger than the other. Abdomen terminates in broad telson. Body colour blue-black with yellow spots; paler below.

Distribution: North-eastern Atlantic from Norway to the Azores and Morocco; also north-western Black Sea and Mediterranean.
Habitat: Among rocks and crevices in sublittoral zone down to about 60m/197ft.
Food: Both a scavenger and predatory feeder.
Size: Up to 50cm/20in.
Breeding: Sperm transferred by male to seminal receptacle of female; eggs fertilized externally; larval phase follows.
Status: Not listed by IUCN.

Squat lobster

Galathea strigosa

The often colourful and attractively marked squat lobsters are immediately recognizable because of their blue stripes, short, almost oval body shape (caused by the abdomen being folded underneath the thorax and so accounting for their common name of 'squat') and their long appendages bearing pincers. This species hides away under rocks or in crevices during the day, but emerges at night to hunt other marine creatures and to scavenge for food. Despite its relatively small size, it can be an aggressive species if handled and so needs to be treated with a degree of caution. Although they are called lobsters, squat lobsters are in fact more closely related to hermit crabs.

Identification: Head with rostrum bearing three pairs of spines; conspicuous antennae longer than body; black eyes. Body oval. Walking limbs scaly; first walking limbs bear pincers. Body colour orange-red with transverse blue bands; limbs covered with green-brown spines.

Distribution: North Atlantic from North Cape, Scandinavia to Spain and Canaries; also Mediterranean and Red Seas.
Habitat: Among rocks and crevices in lower shore and down to about 35m/115ft.
Food: Both a scavenger and predatory feeder.
Size: Up to 12cm/4.7in.
Breeding: Sperm transferred to seminal receptacle; eggs shed and fertilized externally.
Status: Not listed by IUCN.

Long-clawed porcelain crab

Porcellana longicornis

Distribution: North-eastern Atlantic; Mediterranean.
Habitat: Under stones and among laminarian seaweed holdfasts on lower shore.
Food: Small edible particles filtered from the water.
Size: 1cm/0.4in.
Breeding: Sperm transferred by male to seminal receptacle of female. Female sheds eggs which are then fertilized externally and held until they hatch into larvae.
Status: Not listed by IUCN.

Some members of the family Porcellanidae bear a superficial resemblance to true crabs (see later in this section), but porcelain crabs are actually more closely related to squat lobsters (Galatheidae) and hermit crabs (Paguridae). A few porcelain crab species do, however, resemble lobsters or prawns in shape, having long abdomens. They possess very long antennae (whereas those of true crabs are usually very short), which originate at the front of the head. They also have a very reduced fourth pair of walking legs. This species has particularly long claws that are made more conspicuous by being so disproportionate in size to the rest of the body; these are used for fighting rather than feeding. The long-clawed porcelain crab can be found under rocks and stones on the lower shore downwards, but it is also often associated with the root-like holdfasts of laminarian seaweeds (those of the genus Laminaria), among which the crab can hide from predators.

Identification: A small creature with long antennae. Carapace roundish and smooth. First walking legs are also smooth and bear long, slender pincers. Colour is reddish-brown. Claws are much longer than the rest of the body.

Slipper lobster (*Parribacus antarcticus*): 18cm/7in long
Sometimes called a bulldozer lobster, this crustacean has a flattened body and short antennae and claws. It relies on its blue-grey mottled colouring and bristly outline to help it remain concealed in holes by day. At night, it scavenges and also preys on small invertebrates and fish. Indo-Pacific and tropical Atlantic Ocean.

Crawfish (*Palinurus vulgaris*): 40cm/16in long
Also called the spiny lobster, the red-brown crawfish is recognized by the apparent lack of pincers on its walking legs – although females have a small pair on their fifth walking legs. The abdomen bears sharp spines. Found among rocks and in crevices in the Atlantic Ocean and Mediterranean Sea.

Galathea intermedia: 1cm/0.4in long
This little squat lobster bears a superficial resemblance to *Galathea strigosa*, although it is smaller and its legs are the same bright red colour as the rest of the body. Among stones and rocks on the lower shore downwards in the Atlantic Ocean and Mediterranean Sea.

Diogenes pugilator: 2.5cm/1in long
This small hermit crab has hairy antennae and white tips to its pincers. Like other hermit crabs, it lives in shells of dead gastropod molluscs to protect its abdomen. Found in shallow water in the Atlantic Ocean and Mediterranean Sea.

Common hermit crab

Eupagurus bernhardus

Instead of having their soft, vulnerable abdomens enclosed within a hard carapace, as the true crabs do, the hermit crabs have evolved a way of protecting this part of their body by living inside the shell of a dead gastropod, such as those of whelks. With its abdomen safely inside the shell, the hermit crab can move about the substrate with just the head, thorax and legs – which are encased in a hard exoskeleton like other crabs – protruding. Like many other hermit crabs, this species discards its shell for a bigger one as it grows. The hermit crab often shares its shell with certain species of anemones, sponges and marine worms.

Identification: First pair of walking legs end with big, granulated unequal pincers (the crab's right-hand pincer is the larger one). Second and third pairs of walking legs end in spiny claws; fourth and fifth pairs of walking legs are reduced. Colour of carapace red, orange or grey; pincers brown.

Distribution: Temperate Atlantic coasts of Europe; Mediterranean and Baltic.
Habitat: On the seabed from the lower shore downwards.
Food: Both a scavenger and predatory feeder.
Size: 10cm/4in.
Breeding: Sperm transferred by male to seminal receptacle of female. Female sheds eggs which are then fertilized externally and held until they hatch into larvae.
Status: Not listed by IUCN.

TRUE CRABS

True crabs are familiar animals of seashores and estuaries, and they make up a widespread and fascinating group of crustaceans. Typically robust with broad, flattened shells, or carapaces, true crabs also have reduced tails and powerful anterior pincers for dealing with prey and for defending themselves. The spider crabs get their common name from their long limbs and relatively smaller bodies.

Sponge crab

Dromia personata

This somewhat squat, broad crab has short, dark-brown, hairlike growths covering almost all of its carapace and legs, enhancing this impression still further. A small, fifth pair of legs is raised, and appears itself to be carried on the crab's back. The crab is sometimes encountered grasping a sponge on its back, using its rear-most pairs of legs – a method of concealment against predators such as octopuses. The sponge may eventually dwarf the crab's carapace in size, although it never becomes attached to it. In fact, if in some danger, the crab may abandon the sponge and flee without it. At night, the sponge crab feeds mainly by scavenging on the remains of other marine animals.

Distribution: Atlantic range is from southern North Sea and British Isles to Western Sahara, Azores and Canaries; all of Mediterranean Sea.
Habitat: On sandy and rocky shores and among pilings, down to about 30m/100ft.
Food: Scavenges.
Size: 8cm/3.25in.
Breeding: Eggs are fertilized externally.
Status: Not listed by IUCN.

Identification: Carapace broad and domed. Fourth and fifth pairs of walking legs are displaced and may be used to grasp items such as sponges for shelter. Carapace and legs brown; pincers pink.

Spider crab

Macropodia tenuirostris

Identification: Carapace triangular; longer than it is wide, and tapering severely at front. Carapace usually smooth or slightly granular but may be encrusted with seaweeds or other growths. Long, prominent rostrum with hooked hairs. Eyes on prominent stalks at side of rostrum. First pair of walking legs with pincers. Second and third pairs of walking legs long and straight; fourth and fifth pairs end in curved claws. Body colour red-brown or yellow-red.

The spider crabs are characterized by having small bodies in relation to their long, slender limbs, giving them a rather spider-like appearance – hence the common name. Some species can grow very large indeed – measuring 3.7m (12ft) across their outstretched legs. The species here is one of the smaller varieties, but it clearly shows the typical body form of these crabs. It is found among seaweeds in water varying in depth from about 9–97m/30–320ft, but also occasionally down to 300m/1,000ft. The spider crab scavenges edible food matter as well as hunting other marine animals.

Distribution: North Sea and British Isles south to Western Sahara and Cape Verde Is.
Habitat: Among seaweeds, usually from about 9m/30ft.
Food: Scavenger and also predatory on small marine creatures.
Size: 2cm/0.8in or less.
Breeding: Reproduces sexually. Some evidence that sperm may be stored in the receptacles of female crabs to fertilize further broods.
Status: Not listed by IUCN.

Velvet swimming crab

Macropipus puber

Distribution: Atlantic coasts of north-western Europe.
Habitat: Among rocks and stones from lower shore down to 10m/33ft or more.
Food: Varied diet, including seaweed, molluscs and crustaceans.
Size: 8cm/3.2in or less.
Breeding: Reproduces sexually; fertilization is external.
Status: Not listed by IUCN.

In addition to the typical scuttling action that most crabs employ when moving around on the substrate, some species have specially adapted limbs to enable them to swim. The various species of swimming crabs, found in many of the world's oceans, have their fifth pair of limbs modified to form flattened, paddle-like structures to allow them to swim rapidly backwards. The velvet swimming crab puts on an impressive display when threatened; it rises up on its legs and holds its claws apart in an attempt to make itself appear bigger. It feeds on a variety of food items from seaweeds to other crustaceans. When mating, the male velvet crab may cling on to the female for several days.

Identification: Front of carapace serrated with five teeth either side of the eyes and ten smaller teeth between the eyes. First pair of walking legs bears pincers. Flat, paddle-like back legs. Carapace and limbs covered with hairy bristles. Colour of carapace red-brown. Eyes are red.

Common shore crab (*Carcinus maenas*): 5cm/2in long
Characteristic sideways walking action when seen on the estuaries and salt marshes it favours. Can tolerate a wide range of salinities, and is abundant in brackish conditions. This opportunist scavenger eats seaweeds and preys on other invertebrates, especially bivalve molluscs such as mussels and cockles, using its powerful pincers to break open their shells. A native of Europe and North Africa, it has also been introduced to other parts of the world.

Ghost crab (*Ocypode albicans*): 7cm/2.8in long
This stalk-eyed shore crab occurs on warm sandy beaches, from the Carolinas in the eastern USA to Brazil, where it scavenges for dead animals on the strandline. It lives in a burrow in the sand, emerging to feed in large numbers at low tide. It owes its common name to its cryptic sandy coloration, which makes it seem to disappear when it stops moving.

Spiny spider crab (*Maia squinado*): 18cm/7in long
A long-legged and spider-like species of the Atlantic and Mediterranean, the red-brown carapace of this crab is approximately triangular with a tapering front, and is covered with bristles and spines. Powerful pincers on its first walking legs. Found from lower shore down to about 50m/165ft.

Chinese mitten crab

Eriocheir sinensis

This species' common name comes from the bristly covering on the pincers, which gives the impression that the animal is wearing mittens. This crab is a native of the coastal and estuarine regions of the Yellow Sea in Asia. However, it has long been naturalized in parts of the European Atlantic, where it quickly established itself, and is now found in parts of California in the US. The Chinese mitten crab is an omnivorous species that eats a range of food from marine plants to worms and small molluscs. Sometimes members of this species will clamber over dry land if dams or other obstructions impede their migration – even turning up in swimming pools and on roads. This crab may have a harmful effect on native marine life.

Distribution: Indigenous to China; also found Yellow Sea; estuarine habitats in northern Europe and North America.
Habitat: In mud and sand, often burrowing.
Food: Seaweeds, molluscs and crustaceans.
Size: 7cm/2.8in.
Breeding: Reproduces sexually; females carry between 250,000 and 1 million eggs until hatching, and both sexes die soon after reproduction.
Status: Not listed by IUCN.

Identification: Carapace squarish in shape, with four teeth between the eyes. First pair of walking legs bears equal-sized pincers covered in 'hairy' bristles. Other legs long and also hairy. Colour of carapace olive-green; lower parts of legs and claw tips paler.

TRUE CRABS, HORSESHOE CRABS AND SEA SPIDERS

Horseshoe crabs are not true crabs, despite their common name. These ancient, shallow-water arthropods are the sole survivors of a group of invertebrates that flourished millions of years ago. Their relatives, the sea spiders, are small, curious marine animals found in shallow water and the ocean deeps.

Mud fiddler crab

Uca pugnax

Identification: Carapace squarish with an H-shaped depression in the middle. Eyes born on long, thin, prominent stalks. Males have one claw hugely enlarged and covered in granules. Other walking legs banded. Females and young crabs have claws of equal size. Colour of carapace brown to yellowish; claws yellowish to white.

Fiddler crabs are so called because males have an enlarged claw they use to protect their burrows, and which they wave to attract females when mating. This claw may account for 65 per cent of the crab's body weight. Males also engage in ritualized arm waving when confronting rivals, although serious injury is rare. The smaller of the two claws is used to collect and sift mud and other material when looking for decaying plant and animal matter to eat. Fiddler crab burrows may be 30cm/12in deep, and provide a safe haven from predators and a site for mating. At low tide, fiddlers leave their burrows to look for food, quickly returning to them – or to any other convenient burrow – if any danger should threaten.

Right: Aerial view of the mud fiddler crab, illustrating the disproportionally large claw.

Distribution: Mid-Atlantic US coast.
Habitat: Muddy and sandy estuaries and shores.
Food: Detritus and algae.
Size: 2.5cm/1in.
Breeding: Reproduces sexually; fertilization of eggs is external.
Status: Not listed by IUCN.

Horn-eyed ghost crab

Ocypode ceratophthalma

Identification: Carapace squarish and robust. First pair of walking legs bear large, but unequal-sized, pincers. Other legs relatively long. Large, erect oblong eyes on stalks with prominent horn above; larger in males. Colour cream-brown with greyish markings and traces of yellow.

This species of ghost crab hides in conspicuous burrows, which it digs in the sand of the upper shore of sheltered beaches, with only its large eyes protruding above the surface on stalks. Special hairs growing on its legs help it to absorb moisture from wet sand through capillary action, which reduces the amount of time it needs to spend near water. The ghost crab is both a scavenger and an active hunter, emerging at dusk to prey on small marine animals it encounters near the water's edge. Good vision and the ability to run quickly make the horn-eyed ghost crab an efficient hunter. A prominent horn situated above each of the stalked eyes of this species gives rise to its common name.

Right: Aerial view of the horn-eye ghost crab, illustrating the protrusion of the eyes.

Distribution: East Africa and Red Sea to Japan, Hawaii and Tahiti. Also Australian tropics.
Habitat: Sandy shores.
Food: Scavenger; also preys on small marine animals.
Size: 7cm/2.8in.
Breeding: Reproduces sexually; fertilization of eggs is external.
Status: Not listed by IUCN.

Horseshoe crab

Limulus polyphemus

Distribution: Eastern US coastline from Maine to Gulf of Mexico.
Habitat: Sandy and muddy substrates down to 30m/98ft or more.
Food: Worms, molluscs, crustaceans.
Size: 60cm/24in.
Breeding: Reproduces sexually; females lay between 2,000 and 20,000 eggs.
Status: Listed as Low Risk by IUCN.

The horseshoe crabs in the class Merostoma are primitive marine arthropods, whose ancestors arose in the Silurian Period, more than 400 million years ago. In fact, the horseshoe crabs, or king crabs as they are also known, are more closely related to the extinct trilobites and to modern spiders and ticks than they are to true crabs and crustaceans. The body is covered by a protective, hinged carapace, and a long caudal spine extends from the back. The caudal spine can be used to right the animal if it is accidentally turned over. Under the carapace are the chelicerae and five pairs of walking legs. The horseshoe crab burrows in sand and mud, although it can swim. Worms and other invertebrate food are crushed by the pincer-like chelicerae on either side of the mouth. During mating, these crabs congregate in the intertidal zone, where the female lays her eggs in holes in the sand. The horseshoe crab can live for about 20 years.

Identification: Horseshoe-shaped carapace broad, domed and hinged, back of carapace bears spines. Long, tapering caudal spine. One pair each of pedipalps (mouth appendages) and chelicerae (modified fangs). Five pairs of walking legs. Colour of carapace dark-brown.

Hairy crab (*Pilumnus hirtellus*): 2cm/0.8in long
With almost all of its red-brown, spiny upper carapace and legs covered in dense bristles, this crab is sometimes very hard to spot, especially when silt collects between the hairs. The pincers have dark-brown tips and are stout and powerful, with one being larger than the other. Found on seaweeds, stones, rocks and in crevices on the lower shore and in shallow Atlantic and Mediterranean waters down to 80m/262ft.

Masked crab (*Corystes cassivelaunus*):
carapace 4cm/1.6in long
Recognized by its slender, oval carapace with four teeth on each lateral margin and a further two teeth between the eyes.
First pair of walking legs (chelipeds) twice as long as the carapace in males, but much shorter in females. Long, hairy antennae held together in front – when the animal is buried in sand they form a tube enabling water to reach the gills. Carapace brown to yellow in colour. Found in sand on lower shore and shallow water in the Atlantic Ocean.

Sea spider (*Nymphon gracile*): 1cm/0.4in long
Looking very much like a small terrestrial spider, this species is found on rocky shores and in shallow waters in the Atlantic Ocean and Mediterranean Sea. The eight long, thin legs are about three or four times the length of the body. Although the body is translucent, the gut is visible, giving the animal a pinkish tinge. Like terrestrial spiders, it has chelicerae (fang-like appendages close to the mouth) and palps (members used as sensory and feeding aids) for cutting off small pieces of prey and transferring them to the mouth at the end of the proboscis. Both sexes have ovigerous (egg-bearing) legs, although the eggs are brooded by the male. This species may live for a year.

Sea spider

Pycnogonum littorale

Like other sea spiders, this species is characterized by the head and thorax being fused to form a narrow, elongated structure called a cephalothorax. It also bears the legs, into which the digestive system extends and, in females, also the ovaries. The abdomen is tiny, consisting of a single segment. As well as the walking legs, males have an extra pair of 'ovigerous' legs, held under the body. As the female lays her eggs, they are collected by the male and held on the ovigerous legs where they are brooded until they hatch. The sea spider feeds by sucking up body tissues through its proboscis.

Distribution: Common around coasts of Great Britain and Ireland; not present in north-east Scotland.
Habitat: Under stones and on seaweed on the lower shore and in shallow water.
Food: Sucks body tissues from marine organisms, such as sea anemones.
Size: 2cm/0.8in.
Breeding: Reproduces sexually; after mating, males brood the eggs.
Status: Not listed by IUCN.

Identification: Heavily built body with short, thick legs. No palps or chelicerae present. Cephalothorax terminates in a narrow, conical proboscis. Four pairs of walking legs and one pair of ovigerous legs in males. Males pale brown in colour; females white or cream.

FEATHER STARS AND BRITTLESTARS

The feather stars are slender-looking echinoderms with five pairs of branched arms that are used for filtering food, swimming and moving slowly about on the seabed. Brittlestars get their common name because their long, fragile arms regularly break – and this is sometimes used as a defensive method, to aid escape from predators. They can regenerate these appendages easily.

Feather star

Antedon bifida

Identification: Five pairs of branched, feathery arms arising from a small central disc. Below disc are about 25 short, claw-like appendages used for gripping substratum. Colour reddish-brown, pink or orange, sometimes banded.

Looking almost plant-like when submerged, the feather star has the body shape of a typical crinoid, with five paired branching arms growing from a cup-like central disc. These arms wave about trapping food from the surrounding water in a sticky mucus substance; the arms also help the animal to change locations. The feather star secures itself to the substratum with a group of short appendages called cirri, on the underside of the disc. The feather star usually lives in shallow water, but during extreme low-tide periods it may be uncovered on the lowest part of the shore. When out of the water, the animal looks like a tangle of string.

Distribution: British Isles and Ireland, except for eastern and south-eastern England.
Habitat: Clinging to rocks or sometimes other growths in shallow water down to about 450m/1,476ft.
Food: Small particles of organic matter trapped from the surrounding water.
Size: Arms up to 10cm/4in long.
Breeding: Reproduces sexually; fertilization of eggs is external.
Status: Not listed.

Ophiura texturata

This species is a burrowing brittlestar that is usually found in sand on the lower shore and downwards searching for small particles of food. The animal's central disc is approximately pentagonal in shape when viewed from above, and it bears two flattish plates at the point of origin of each of its arms. The mouth is located on the underside of the disc, which appears scaly. Compared with most other species of brittlestars, the arms of this species are relatively thick. The colour of this species is variable, but is usually in shades of brown. Rather confusingly for marine biologists, a related species, *Ophiura albida*, which is similar in appearance to *O. texturata*, can often be found living in the same type of habitat as the latter.

Identification: Pentagonal central disc scaly and bearing two plates at the point of origin of each of the five arms. Thick, tapering arms bear tapering spines. Colour brownish-orange above, but paler below; occasionally there are also tinges of purple or red.

Distribution: North Atlantic Ocean, Mediterranean and Baltic seas.
Habitat: Burrowing in sand from the lower shore down to 200m/656ft.
Food: Small particles in the substrate.
Size: 25cm/10in across.
Breeding: Reproduces sexually; fertilization of eggs is external.
Status: Not listed by IUCN.

Common brittlestar

Ophiothrix fragilis

Distribution: North Atlantic including North Sea; also Mediterranean.
Habitat: On rocks or sediments and in crevices down to about 350m/1,148ft.
Food: Small particles suspended in the water.
Size: Disc about 2cm/0.8in across; arms about five times disc diameter.
Breeding: Reproduces sexually; fertilization of eggs is external.
Status: Not listed by IUCN.

The common brittlestar has a body consisting of a flattened central disc with a five-rayed pattern of spines on the upper surface. The animal's mouth is located on the underside of the disc. Radiating from the disc are five long, thin, thorny arms bearing tube feet on the underside. As with all brittlestars, *O. fragilis* uses its arms to aid movement from location to location. The arms often break, and specimens may be seen displaying appendages in various stages of regeneration. This species is found from the lower shore down to several hundred metres, sometimes congregating in large numbers. In intertidal regions, the common brittlestar often lives in crevices or under rocks.

Identification: Central disc flattened and pentagonal in shape, with pattern of spines on upper surface radiating from the centre and running between points of attachment of arms. Arms thin, fragile and thorny. Colour variable: ranging from white, yellow, orange, red or purple, sometimes banded – especially the arms.

Antedon mediterranea: 20cm/8in across
A feather star found in the Mediterranean Sea, this species has a small central disc from which arise its many-branched arms. It may be red, brown or yellow; sometimes a combination of colours in alternating bands. It is found on rocks and seaweeds down to about 40m/130ft, sometimes also attached to corals.

Acrocnida brachiata: disc 1cm/0.4in across
This spiny, grey-brown brittlestar is characterized by its extremely long, thin arms – they often extend about 15 times the disc diameter. It is usually found buried in sand from the lower shore down to about 40m/130ft with its arms coiled or twisted. Distributed in the Atlantic Ocean.

Small brittlestar (*Amphipholis squamata*): disc about 5mm/0.2in across
Small and inconspicuously coloured bluish-grey or white, this species of brittlestar lives under stones and among seaweeds and other growths in rockpools and on the lower shore downwards. The central disc is circular, with scaly plates present at the point where the arms attach to the disc. The arms are thin and spiny and about four times the disc diameter in length. It is a scavenger that feeds on detritus and other small organic particles.

Ophiocomina nigra

Like the common brittlestar (*Ophiothrix fragilis*), this species exhibits the basic body shape seen in most brittlestars, but it differs from the common brittlestar in several anatomical details. First, the central disc is much less pentagonal. Second, instead of having a series of prominent spines on the upper surface, the disc is covered with fine granules above. Third, the arms, while still appearing fragile, are thicker at the point of attachment to the disc, and taper more distinctly towards the tip. Fourth, the spines on the arms are finer and almost glassy, and are arranged in a regular pattern, like the teeth on a comb. This fairly large species is often found in groups of up to 100 individuals per square metre, sometimes in association with the common brittlestar (above).

Distribution: North Atlantic including North Sea; also Mediterranean.
Habitat: On rocks or sediments down to about 350m/1,148ft.
Food: Small particles suspended in the water.
Size: Disc about 3cm/1.2in across; arms about five times disc diameter in length.
Breeding: Reproduces sexually; fertilization of eggs is external.
Status: Not listed by IUCN.

Identification: Large central disc weakly pentagonal in shape, with upper surface covered in fine granules. Arms relatively robust, but spines give impression they are wider; arms thicker at point of attachment. Spines on arms arranged in regularly spaced pattern. Colour of disk usually brown or black; arms brown.

STARFISH

With no front or back and able to change direction without turning, starfish are most unusual creatures. These echinoderms are immediately recognizable from their shape, which basically consists of a body drawn out to form distinct arms, or rays. There are usually five or six arms present, although some species have considerably more – perhaps as many as 20. The mouth is found on the underside.

Common starfish

Asterias rubens

Identification: Robust body drawn out into five arms; body highest in the middle, tapering to ends of arms. Body covered with spines and bears tiny, pincer-like structures (pedicellariae) that help remove parasites. Underside of body bears rows of tube feet; arms grooved on underside. Colour is yellow-brown above, paler on the underside.

One of the most familiar images of the seaside, the common starfish has a body covered in small spines and drawn out into five broad arms, or rays. Like other starfish, it moves by means of tube feet – small, fluid-filled structures on the underside of the arms that expand and contract, pulling the animal along. The tube feet may also be used to grip prey when feeding. The common starfish is predatory, tracking down its food mainly by smell. Once it finds a suitable prey item, such as a bivalve mollusc, it engulfs it with its arms, everts its stomach over the prey, or into the shell in the case of many molluscs, and digests it before absorbing the contents. The common starfish is found among rocks and in mussel beds, often in large congregations.

Distribution: North Atlantic.
Habitat: Among rocks and in mussel and oyster beds from lower shore to sublittoral.
Food: Crustaceans, molluscs, worms; predator as well as scavenger.
Size: 50cm/19.7in across, though usually smaller.
Breeding: Eggs are fertilized externally and develop into planktonic larvae.
Status: Not listed by IUCN.

Blue star

Linckia laevigata

Identification: Body consists of five finger-like, radiating arms; arms are almost same thickness along their whole length and have rounded tips. Underside of body bears rows of tube feet, and mouth. Colour usually bright blue; some starfish of this species also bear prominent white spots, as shown here.

Also known by a variety of similar names, such as blue sea star and blue starfish, the blue star is an attractively coloured species that is very popular with marine aquarists because of its colouration and because it is less predatory than many other types of starfish. This tropical species is found in Indo-Pacific waters from the lower shore downwards. For example, it is a common part of the marine fauna of the Great Barrier Reef, off the coast of Australia, although it is often encountered in small coral rockpools as well. The blue star tends to hide away out of sight during the day, becoming active at night when it crawls over rocks grazing small food items growing on them as well as eating detritus.

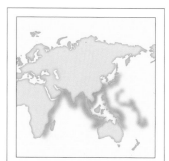

Distribution: Tropical coasts of Indian Ocean and Indo-Pacific region.
Habitat: Among rocks on reefs from lower shore down to 60m/197ft.
Food: Detritus and small organisms encrusting rocks.
Size: 30cm/12in across.
Breeding: Eggs are fertilized externally and develop into planktonic larvae.
Status: Not listed by IUCN.

Common sunstar

Crossaster papposus

Distribution: North-eastern Atlantic; Pacific seaboard of USA down to Gulf of Maine; population also found at Budget Sound, Alaska.
Habitat: Among rocks, on sand and in mussel and oyster beds in shallow water from about 10–40m/33–130ft.
Food: Echinoderms, molluscs, sea pens.
Size: 25cm/10in across.
Breeding: Eggs are fertilized externally and develop into planktonic larvae.
Status: Not listed by IUCN.

This highly distinctive and attractive starfish, sometimes called the rose sea star, is immediately recognizable by its large, round disc and its array of between 8 and 16 arms, or rays, each of which is shorter than the width of the disc itself. The body of this species is further characterized by the very prominent spines that cover the disc and the arms. The common sunstar is found in sheltered locations, often in the company of other echinoderms, such as brittlestars. It feeds by everting its stomach on to its prey and digesting it. Among its food items are other, smaller starfish, such as cushion stars. The common sunstar is itself preyed on by other starfish, such as *Solaster dawsoni*.

Identification: Usually 13 arms, but varies from 8 to 16; each arm about half the width of the disc. Body covered in conspicuous spines. Colour varies from purple, brownish-red, yellow or red above; yellowish-white below. Patterning also variable – combinations of colours or a single colour with a concentric white ring.

Giant sea star (*Pisaster giganteus*): 30cm/12in across
This large, five-armed species has a brown body covered with short, white spines, each encircled by a blue-coloured ring. Because of its appearance, it is sometimes called the jewelled star. Found in Pacific Ocean waters among sand and rocks at the low-water mark and in shallow water, it is carnivorous, feeding on invertebrates such as mussels.

Spiny starfish (*Marthasterias glacialis*): 30cm/12in across
This species has a body with five stiff arms, each of which bears three rows of prominent spines, each encircled by small, pincer-like pedicellariae. It is mainly brown or green-grey with purple arm tips above, and yellow-white below. The spiny starfish can sometimes grow as large as 70cm/27.5in across. It is found from low water down to about 200m/660ft in the Atlantic Ocean and Mediterranean Sea.

Porania pulvillus: 10cm/4in across
A cushion-like starfish with short arms and a fleshy body, which feels somewhat greasy to the touch. White papillae (small bumps) cover the upper surface. The colour ranges from scarlet to orange, with a pattern of white streaks and lines above; paler coloured below. This species is found on rocks and sponges from about 10–250m/33–800ft in Atlantic Ocean waters.

Goosefoot star

Anseropoda placenta

This species gets its common name because its body bears a resemblance to a goose's webbed foot. The goosefoot star's body is thin, almost pentagonal in shape, with slightly ragged, concave edges between the five arms. It has no pedicellariae – tiny, pincer-like organs on some echinoderms that keep the body clean and free from parasites. The upper surface has short spines, and the underside of the arms bear tube feet that can expand and contract to enable the echinoderm to move about. This species frequents sandy and muddy substrates.

Distribution: North-eastern Atlantic Ocean; US Pacific population at Gulf of Maine.
Habitat: On or in sand and muddy gravel in shallow water down to 100m/330ft.
Food: Small crustaceans.
Size: 20cm/8in across.
Breeding: Eggs are fertilized externally and develop into planktonic larvae.
Status: Not listed by IUCN.

Identification: The body is thin and flat and its shape is almost pentagonal. Bears five arms. Body colour is mainly white, with a vivid red centre and five radiating red lines – one running along the centre of each arm. The perimeter of the body is also red. Distribution of this colour is variable between individuals. Underside of body tends to be yellowish.

SEA URCHINS, HEART URCHINS AND SEA CUCUMBERS

These echinoderms are among the oldest surviving marine creatures on Earth. Sea urchins are round-bodied with conspicuous, moveable spines, while the heart urchins, which include the sea potatoes, are covered in shorter bristles. The sea cucumbers are sac-like species lacking obvious arms.

Black sea urchin

Arbacia lixula

Identification: Test roughly rounded, slightly flattened below, with a dense covering of short spines with sharp, pointed tips that totally obscure it. Colour of spines brownish-black. Colour of test pink with red lines indicating position of pores that allow water to enter the tube feet.

The sea urchins are members of the class Echinoidea, in which the body consists of chalky plates forming a shell called the test. From the test sprout bristling, mobile spines as well as long tube feet, which the animal uses when moving about. The black sea urchin has fairly short, sharp spines arising from an almost spherical test. Like other sea urchins, the mouth is on the underside of the body and from it protrude five white teeth – they are part of a chewing structure known as Aristotle's lantern, because of its resemblance to an old-fashioned oil lamp. The anus is on the top of the body. The black sea urchin crawls about among seaweeds and on rocks from the lower shore down to about 40m/130ft.

Distribution: Common in Mediterranean Sea.
Habitat: On seaweeds and rocks.
Food: Organic debris.
Size: Test 5cm/2in across; spines 3cm/1.2in long.
Breeding: Reproduces sexually; fertilization of eggs is external.
Status: Not listed by IUCN.

Edible sea urchin

Echinus esculentus

Identification: Test globular (may be flatter in those from shallow water) with close covering of robust spines. Pedicellariae (pincer-like organs that keep the urchin clean) are present on the test. Colour of spines reddish usually with purple tips and white bases. Colour of test usually shades of red, pink or purple.

This is a large, globular sea urchin often eaten as a seafood delicacy in many countries. It is found on rocks and crawling among seaweeds on the lower shore and in water down to about 40m/130ft, although it may also be encountered at greater depths than this. The animal's test is covered in short, solid spines; in some species of urchins the spines are clearly divided into primary and secondary types according to their sizes, but in the edible sea urchin this distinction is much less clear. The spines also provide a refuge for several other marine invertebrates: these include *Astacilla intermedia*, an amphipod related to sand hoppers, and the worm *Flabelligera affinis*.

Distribution: Associated with North Atlantic drift, from Norway to northern Portugal.
Habitat: On seaweeds and rocks from lower shore down to 40m/130ft or more.
Food: Organic debris.
Size: Test 10cm/4in across; spines 1.5cm/0.6in long; specimens sometimes bigger.
Breeding: Reproduces sexually; external fertilization.
Status: Not listed by IUCN.

Sea potato

Echinocardium cordatum

Distribution: North-eastern Atlantic including British Isles and North Sea; Mediterranean.
Habitat: In sand from lower shore down to about 200m/660ft.
Food: Organic debris.
Size: Test 9cm/3.5in across.
Breeding: Reproduces sexually; fertilization of eggs is external.
Status: Not listed by IUCN.

The sea potato is an echinoderm also known as a heart urchin. The test is heart-shaped with many short, and longer, backward-directed spines, giving the animal initially an almost furry appearance. Most of the heart urchin's tube feet – small, fluid-filled organs that enable the animal to move about – are on the upper surface, although some are below. It spends its life burrowing in clean sand to a depth of about 15cm/6in. Unlike the closely related sea urchins, the heart urchins do not have teeth and they feed on detritus passed to the mouth by the tube feet. The mouth is situated on the underside near the front, and the anus is also on the underside, at the back of the animal. The presence of a heart urchin can sometimes be detected by the small conical depression it makes near its head end; the depression is used to collect detritus prior to it being eaten.

Identification: Test heart-shaped, with an indentation at the front end; upper surface has a deep furrow; five rows of tube feet. Short and longer spines on test, mostly pointing backward. Colour yellowish-brown.

Savigny's sea urchin (*Diadema savignyi*): test 6m/2.4in long; spines 20cm/8in long
This Indo-Pacific species of sea urchin has a rounded test covered in long spines. Colour variable: often the test is black, but in some individuals the tests are a lighter colour. The spines, which are venomous and can cause severe pain if they puncture the skin, are often banded in a warning pattern of alternating light and dark colours. Savigny's sea urchin hides among rocks on sandy reefs by day.

Purple heart urchin
(*Spatangus purpureus*): test 12cm/4.7in long
This somewhat flattened species is an attractive violet-red colour. It lives buried in sand and gravel in water that varies from about 5m/16ft to about 800m/2,600ft in the Atlantic Ocean and Mediterranean Sea; sometimes a few of the longer spines on its upper surface are visible at the surface.

Lyre urchin (*Brissopsis lyrifera*): test 7cm/2.8in long
This species gets its name from the lyre-shaped pattern on the upper surface of the test, which is visible when the spines are removed. The lyre urchin is red-brown in colour with dense, fur-like spines covering the test. It lives in sand in water down to about 300m/985ft in the Atlantic Ocean and Mediterranean Sea.

Sea cucumber

Holothuria forskali

The sea cucumber is a member of the class Holothuroidea. The holothuroids have sac- or cucumber-like bodies. They do not have arms or rays, and many have no obvious spines – although calcareous spicules are embedded in the skin. However, most have tube feet – sometimes arranged in rows down the sides of the animal or in a ring around the mouth, at the front of the body. The sea cucumber has a long, narrow body with three rows of suckered tube feet on the lower surface, which are used for movement, and some suckerless tube feet scattered on the animal's warty upper surface. There is a ring of about 20 modified tube feet around the mouth, which are used for feeding. As a means of defence, this species can eject a mass of sticky white threads from the hind end that entangle a would-be predator.

Distribution: North-eastern Atlantic including British Isles and North Sea; Mediterranean.
Habitat: Sand and rocks from extreme lower shore down to about 70m/230ft.
Food: Deposit feeder.
Size: 20cm/8in across.
Breeding: Reproduces sexually; fertilization of eggs is external.
Status: Not listed by IUCN.

Identification: Body cucumber-shaped. Upper surface warty with suckerless tube feet randomly arranged; lower surface bearing three rows of suckered tube feet. Ring of modified, feathery tube feet around mouth. Colour yellow-brown, darker on top.

GROUND SHARKS

The seven families of sharks of the order Carcharhiniformes are collectively known as ground sharks, and vary widely in size, shape and behaviour. All the sharks of this family have a nictitating membrane, or third eyelid, capable of being drawn across the eyeball. These animals are found in temperate, sub-tropical and tropical oceans, and the range of some species even includes fresh water.

Bull shark

Carcharhinus leucas

Big, powerful and aggressive, the bull shark's tolerance of both sea and fresh water means it is found in rivers as far apart as the Zambezi in Africa and the Mississippi in the US. It has even been found 4,200km/2,600 miles up the River Amazon. Although implicated in a number of marine attacks on humans, assaults in fresh water are comparatively rare. In marine environments, bull sharks are found swimming close to the shore, where they feed on almost anything they can catch. Inland, the shark's list of food items may include sizeable mammals such as dogs and antelopes that stray into the water, and even hippos. In the Ganges, corpses consigned to the river in funerals have also ended up on the menu. In the Nile, bull sharks are themselves preyed upon by crocodiles. Bull sharks frequently give birth to their young in brackish water.

Distribution: All tropical and subtropical regions; also tropical rivers inland.
Habitat: Along coastlines and estuaries; also found in rivers and lakes.
Food: Almost anything edible, such as fish, turtles, birds, squid, crustaceans, dolphins and other mammals, including land mammals when populations range upriver.
Size: 3.5m/11.5ft.
Breeding: Ovoviviparous; bears 1–13 young.
Status: Listed as Lower Risk by IUCN.

Identification: Stocky body. Head with short, broad snout and relatively small eyes. First dorsal fin much bigger than second. Upper lobe of caudal fin larger than lower one. Body is slate-grey on top, white below.

Pyjama shark

Poroderma africanum

Identification: Body long and slender. Head slightly flattened with rounded snout. Large eyes. Mouth bears small sensory barbels. First dorsal fin bigger than second dorsal fin. Pectoral fins well developed. Body brown-grey with seven black stripes running length of animal from from nose to tail; pattern resembles pyjamas, hence common name. Takes several years for pyjama shark to reach maturity.

Also known as the striped cat shark, the pyjama shark is a small, attractively marked species that is often seen in public aquariums. This slender-bodied shark feeds on a variety of bottom-dwelling invertebrates, such as crabs and shrimps, often using the sensory barbels around its mouth to locate prey hidden from view. It also takes other fish, such as gurnard and hake. The pyjama shark is found from the intertidal zone downwards, where it prefers to hide by day among seaweeds, rocks and crevices and in sea grass meadows, using its cryptic body patterning to avoid the attentions of other larger predatory fish. Female pyjama sharks lay two leathery egg cases every three days or so during the breeding season.

Distribution: South-eastern Atlantic off coast of southern Africa. Possibly also coasts of Mauritius and Madagascar, Indian Ocean, although reports are not confirmed.
Habitat: Bottom-dwelling, usually from the intertidal zone down to about 250m/820ft.
Food: Fish, squid, octopuses, crabs, shrimps.
Size: 1m/3.25ft.
Breeding: Oviparous; two egg cases laid every three days in the breeding season.
Status: Listed as Lower Risk by IUCN.

Leopard shark (*Triakis semifasciata*): 2.1m/7ft
Slender shark that feeds on bottom-dwelling prey, such as crabs and fish. Found from eastern Pacific to Gulf of California, it frequents inshore sandy and muddy bays and estuaries near the bottom. Sometimes forms loose, nomadic schools with other shark species. Females give birth to between four and 33 live young.

Dogfish (*Scyliorhinus canicula*): 1m/3.25ft
Atlantic and Mediterranean shark with slender body, long tail, flattened head and rounded snout. Sandy-brown above with brown spots, creamy-white below. Rests among rocks by day, and at night hunts crabs, molluscs and small fish. Reproduction involves males entwining their bodies around females.

Grey smooth hound (*Mustelus californicus*): about 1.5m/5ft
Slender body and head with large, oval eyes. Body grey or brown above, lighter below. An eastern Pacific species often found in bays and rocky shallows, sometimes in company of other small sharks. Eats mainly worms, fish and crustaceans. Produces live young.

Blotchy swell shark
Cephaloscyllium umbratile

This is one of several species of sharks whose collective common name comes from their ability to swell, or inflate, their bodies as a defence mechanism against predators. When threatened, they can wedge themselves tightly into a crevice or hole by pumping up their bodies and so becoming almost impossible to dislodge. The rest of the blotchy swell shark's common name comes from its characteristic upper body markings – a series of blotches and bands that helps it to remain camouflaged on the bottom. The shark's fine, pointed teeth are perfectly adapted for dealing with prey items, such as octopuses, flatfish and skate, that it finds on the substrate. It is, however, a relatively sluggish species that soon gives up the chase if prey tries to escape.

Identification: Fairly slender body with longish tail. Head flattish. First dorsal fin set well back. Well-developed pectoral fins. Upper part of body and fins covered in dark blotches and saddles, underside pale.

Distribution: Western Pacific from Japan to South China Sea, possibly also New Guinea.
Habitat: Rocky bottoms and reefs from 20–200m/ 65–660ft.
Food: Bony fish, cartilaginous fish such as rays, squid, octopuses.
Size: 1.2m/4ft.
Breeding: Oviparous; pairs of egg cases laid throughout the long breeding season.
Status: Not listed by IUCN.

Tope
Galeorhinus galeus

Distribution: Temperate and subtropical oceans between latitudes 68°N and 55°S.
Habitat: Shallow bays and offshore waters.
Food: Mainly fish, such as herring, smelt, barracuda and hake; also squid, crabs, snails and sea urchins.
Size: 1.8m/6ft.
Breeding: Ovoviviparous; between 6 and 50 young born after year-long gestation.
Status: Listed by IUCN as Vulnerable globally and Near Threatened in New Zealand.

The tope is known by many common names, including soupfin shark – a sadly appropriate name for a shark whose fins are highly prized for making shark fin soup. It is caught throughout its range, both commercially and as a sport fish. The tope adapts well to life in large aquariums. A wide-ranging and abundant species, often occurring in small schools, the tope inhabits the surf zone and deep water, and is found both on the bottom and swimming in open water. In the higher latitudes of its range, it is highly migratory, occurring near the poles in summer and moving near the equator in winter. Tope can cover 50km/30 miles or more in a day. They have a lifespan of about 55 years, but like many sharks they mature slowly and have low breeding productivity; this, coupled with pressures of fishing, have caused numbers to decline.

Identification: Body slender. Head with long snout and large, almond-shaped eyes. Mouth with blade-like teeth bearing cusps. First dorsal fin much bigger than second dorsal fin. Second dorsal fin more or less aligned with anal fin and approximately same size. Terminal caudal lobe as long as rest of fin. Body colour grey to bluish above, becoming white on underside. Juveniles have black-tipped dorsal and caudal fins and white trailing edges on pectoral fins.

BULLHEAD SHARKS AND ANGEL SHARKS

Bullhead sharks are relatively small, bottom-dwelling sharks with a distinctive ridge over each eye, resembling a bull's horns, and a groove connecting the nostrils to the corners of the mouth. The 18 or so species of angel sharks have flattened bodies with wing-like fins. They swim gracefully but spend much time buried in the sand waiting for prey to come into range.

Port Jackson shark

Heterodontus portusjacksoni

The best-known of the nine species of horn, or bullhead, sharks, the Port Jackson shark has a large, blunt head and a prominent ridge over each eye. It is a bottom-dwelling species that often pumps jets of water over the substrate when feeding to expose hidden prey. Port Jackson sharks are highly migratory at breeding times, often travelling up to 800km/500 miles to the same winter spawning areas; sometimes individuals will even select the same caves and crevices used on previous occasions. Fertilization takes place internally, and although it is often stated that females use their mouths to place the eggs in a safe spot for hatching, this has never been observed.

Identification: Body tapers towards tail. Head big and blunt, with prominent ridge originating in front of each eye; eyes set high on head. Mouth has fine pointed teeth at front and flatter teeth at back. Stout spine in front of each dorsal fin. Large pectoral fins. Body colour greyish brown with dark banding.

Distribution: Pacific Ocean; mainly southern Queensland to Western Australia.
Habitat: Rocky, sandy and muddy bottoms from shallow water down to around 167m/550ft.
Food: Crabs and other crustaceans, molluscs, starfish, sea urchins, fish.
Size: 1.5m/5ft.
Breeding: Oviparous; bears 10–16 leathery eggs.
Status: Listed as Lower Risk by IUCN.

California horn shark

Heterodontus francisci

Identification: Tapering body. Large, blunt, pig-like head with prominent ridge originating in front of each eye; eyes set high on head. Mouth has fine pointed teeth at front and flatter teeth at back. Stout spine in front of each dorsal fin. Large pectoral fins. Body colour greyish brown with dark spots (although spots may be absent).

This small, solitary shark bears a resemblance to the Port Jackson shark, although it has a different form of body patterning. The California horn shark usually lies hidden in caves or under rocky ledges and other safe spots by day, emerging at night to hunt for food on the seabed and among kelp. Food consists of fish and invertebrates, such as crabs and squid. California horn sharks are found in water down to about 11m/36ft deep, and although they can swim freely, they are usually seen moving sluggishly along the bottom using their powerful pectoral fins. These sharks are egg layers, and the auger-shaped egg case – which is typical of *Heterodontus* species – has two filaments at one end. These are used to help anchor the egg case in place among rocks, where it hatches out about seven to nine months later.

Distribution: Eastern Pacific Ocean, mainly southern California; also Peru.
Habitat: Rocky, sandy and muddy bottoms and kelp beds down to around 11m/35ft.
Food: Crabs, squid, worms, sea urchins, anemones, fish.
Size: 1.2m/4ft.
Breeding: Oviparous; spiral egg cases laid.
Status: Listed as Lower Risk by IUCN.

Common angel shark

Squatina squatina

Distribution: Eastern North Atlantic coast (Norway to Spain); also Morocco, Mauretania and Senegal.
Habitat: Sandy and muddy seabeds.
Food: Other bottom-dwelling fish, crabs, molluscs.
Size: 2.4m/7.8ft.
Breeding: Ovoviviparous; bears 7–25 pups.
Status: Listed as Vulnerable by IUCN.

Lying motionless on the sandy bottom using its colouration and flattened shape to help it remain concealed from any potential prey, the common angel shark appears a placid creature. If prey comes within range, however, this ambush predator can strike with lightning speed to snatch the unsuspecting victim. It can also be highly aggressive if disturbed by divers, and when caught and landed in a boat it will snap dangerously at anything coming within range. Mostly active at night, the common angel shark frequents shallow water from about 2m/6.5ft down to 100m/330ft in summer, but it descends down to about 150m/500ft or so in the winter.
Also known as 'monkfish' (although not to be confused with *Lophius*), the common angel shark is popular for commercial fishing in many parts of the world.

Identification: Flattened body with large, wing-like pectoral and pelvic fins. Mouth bearing pointed teeth located near tip of snout. Eyes on top of head. Prominent spiracles behind eyes. Small spines on snout and above eyes. Body colour mottled greyish-brown to green above, underside lighter.

Japanese angel shark (*Squatina japonica*): 2m/6.5ft
Characteristic flattened body shape with broad, wing-like pectoral and pelvic fins. As in other angel sharks, it has fleshy appendages around its mouth. The body is blackish-brown with large, irregular dark blotches on upper side. Moderately large denticles on snout and above eyes, and on midline of back and tail from head to dorsal fins. One of the less well-known angels, this species is found in the subtropical western Pacific around Japan, Korea, northern China and the Philippines, on or near sandy bottoms. It produces live young.

Atlantic angel shark (*Squatina dumeril*): 1.8m/6ft
Its habit of rearing up out of the sand and biting anyone who disturbs it has earned the Atlantic angel shark the nickname of 'sand devil'. The term is sometimes also applied to other species in the genus, most of which are equally aggressive. Found along the Atlantic coast of North America from Massachusetts to the Florida Keys and the Gulf of Mexico; also parts of the Caribbean and northern South America. Possesses the flattened body and large pectoral fins characteristic of angel sharks. Body colouring is speckled grey-blue above, and whitish below. There are rows of denticles on the upper surface. A typical litter consists of about 16 pups.

Pacific angel shark

Squatina californica

Similar in shape and general habits to the common angel shark, the Pacific angel shark lives in the warm waters of the eastern Pacific Ocean, where it partly buries itself in sand or mud at the bottom. Like other bottom-dwelling angel sharks, instead of taking in water through the mouth when breathing as most other fish do, it pumps water in via the openings known as spiracles, which are located on top of the head behind the eyes. This evolutionary adaptation prevents sand and other debris from entering the respiratory system and clogging up the animal's delicate gill tissues. Sluggish when resting or waiting to ambush its prey, the Pacific angel shark attacks aggressively if provoked or even touched. Some specimens are reported to have lived for 35 years.

Distribution: Eastern Pacific from southern Alaska to Gulf of California; and from Costa Rica to southern Chile.
Habitat: Sandy and muddy seabeds, among rocks and in kelp forests down to about 200m/660ft.
Food: Other bottom-dwelling fish, crustaceans, molluscs.
Size: 1.5m/5ft.
Breeding: Ovoviviparous; bears 6–10 pups.
Status: Listed as Near Threatened by IUCN.

Identification: Flattened body with large, wing-like pectoral and pelvic fins. Mouth bearing numerous pointed teeth located near tip of snout. Eyes on top of head. Prominent spiracles behind eyes. Body greyish-brown with red, brown or grey speckles above, underside lighter.

EELS AND ELOPIFORMS

Eels are slender-bodied fish with long dorsal and anal fins but no pelvic fins. They occur worldwide, except in polar seas. The tarpon, ladyfish and bonefish are members of the order Elopiformes. They are related to eels and have slender bodies and forked tails. All produce eggs which hatch into thin, transparent planktonic larvae called leptocephali.

European conger eel

Conger conger

Lurking in caves and crevices, the powerful European conger eel is one of several species found worldwide. This species is usually a nocturnal predator, lying out of sight until likely prey comes near, at which time it launches itself from its hiding place to snatch its meal with large teeth. Congers, landed in boats and lashing about and snapping viciously, have been known to overturn small craft as well as well as biting their occupants. Once sexually mature, the conger migrates from its north Atlantic coastal waters to spawn in deep ocean of the continental slope. The young eels hatch into a stage known as leptocephali and are carried back across the Atlantic on ocean currents.

Identification: Muscular, snake-like body lacking scales. Head with large eyes and protruding upper jaw. Both jaws have powerful teeth. Prominent, pointed pectoral fins. Long dorsal fin originates well forward, near pectoral fins. Elongated anal fin. Colour black, grey or dull brown above, often depending on habitat; creamy below.

Distribution: Atlantic Ocean from Iceland and Scandinavia to Mediterranean and Senegal.
Habitat: Among shipwrecks and rocks in both shallow and deep water.
Food: Octopuses, crabs, fish.
Size: 3m/10ft.
Breeding: Oviparous; spawns in deep, subtropical Atlantic Ocean; eggs hatch into planktonic leptocephali.
Status: Not listed by IUCN.

California moray eel

Gymnothorax mordax

There are about 200 species of moray eels found in the world's tropical and warm-temperate oceans. Some have highly colourful body markings and prominent nasal appendages. All morays are predatory fish, with an often well-deserved reputation for aggressive behaviour if disturbed. Indeed, there are instances of moray eels chasing divers out of the water and then lunging at them from the surf. This species hunts at night, sometimes lurking in rocky crevices waiting to ambush prey, but also seeking it out using a well-developed sense of smell. The eel constantly opens and closes its mouth to ensure a constant supply of oxygenated water is forced over its gills. The red rock shrimp (*Lysmata californica*) is often found sharing the lair of the California moray eel. The shrimp keeps the eel free of parasites and dead skin, and in return the eel provides its 'cleaner' with protection and possibly scraps of food.

Identification: Muscular, snake-like body lacking scales. Head small with numerous sharp, pointed teeth. Body lacks pectoral fins. Dorsal and anal fins long, fused at tail with caudal fin. Colour light or dark brown or green, often mottled.

Distribution: Eastern Pacific Ocean from Baja California northward; also Galapagos Is.
Habitat: In crevices on rocky reefs from 1–20m/3–65ft.
Food: Octopuses, crabs, urchins, fish.
Size: 1.5m/5ft.
Breeding: Oviparous; external fertilization; eggs hatch into planktonic leptocephali.
Status: Not listed by IUCN.

Tarpon

Megalops atlanticus

Distribution: Eastern Atlantic from Senegal to Angola; western Atlantic from North Carolina, US, to northern Brazil.
Habitat: Over reefs, in estuaries and in rivers.
Food: Fish, molluscs.
Size: 2.4m/7.8ft.
Breeding: Oviparous; spawns in shallow water; eggs hatch into planktonic leptocephali.
Status: Not listed by IUCN.

Although looking much more like a 'typical' fish, the huge Atlantic tarpon is, in fact, closely related to the eels. The tarpon has existed since the Cretaceous (about 130 million years ago), making it one of the longest-surviving living fish species. This species of tarpon is a common fish, often gathering in groups in its native Atlantic waters, frequently encountered around reefs, but also found in estuaries and rivers. This abundance, coupled with its large size, makes it a prime target for fishermen – both for food and sport. Luckily, the tarpon is also a prolific breeder – a female can produce 12 million eggs – and so it is not currently at risk. The fish has large, silvery scales, prized in some regions for making into jewellery. The tarpon often leaps high out of the water, especially when hooked by fishermen. True to its eel-related lineage, the eggs of the tarpon hatch into ribbon-like leptocephali.

Identification: Slightly elongated and compressed body. Large head with large eyes and large mouth with protruding lower jaw. The last ray of the dorsal fin is an elongated projection. Caudal fin deeply forked. Scales large and silvery, becoming darker and 'metallic' on back.

European eel (*Anguilla anguilla*): 1m/3.25ft
The European eel has a snake-like body with deeply embedded tiny scales. Adults have silvery bodies with blackish backs. The dorsal fin runs along much of the fish's back. There are no pelvic fins. Found in freshwater rivers

and lakes, from which it travels, sometimes over land, to breed in the Sargasso Sea.

Ribbon eel (*Rhinomuraena quaesita*): 1.3m/4.3ft
With its bright blue body, orange-yellow jaws and fleshy nasal and jaw appendages, this Indo-Pacific eel is a striking-looking species. It usually lives in sand or rubble on reefs in water down to about 60m/200ft with just its head protruding, while it waits for small fish to grab as they pass.

Edward's spaghetti eel (*Moringua edwardsii*): female 50cm/20in
Spaghetti eels derive their common name from the fact that they resemble strands of spaghetti. Females of Edward's spaghetti eel are much larger than males, which grow to about 15cm/6in. Young and females are found in sand and among reefs in the Atlantic. Males live in deeper water.

Bonefish (*Albula vulpes*): 1m/3.25ft
A slender subtropical fish with silvery scales and dark streaks, a blunt, conical snout and a deeply forked tail. The fish appears blue-green above. The bonefish prefers shallow waters down to about 80m/260ft and feeds by rooting out crabs, worms and molluscs from the sea bed.

Ladyfish

Elops saurus

The slender-bodied, silvery blue ladyfish is a popular gamefish species, and has the habit of leaping clear of the water when hooked in an attempt to escape. It is often sold fresh, frozen or salted in markets, although its flesh is not considered to be a particular delicacy. The ladyfish often forms shoals near the shore, and sometimes swims several kilometres offshore, but it can tolerate a wide range of salinities and also frequently inhabits brackish waters, such as estuaries and mangroves, as well as rivers. The ladyfish is generally considered to be a warm-water species, but it can tolerate colder conditions for short periods. Spawning takes place offshore. The metamorphosing larvae – which at first have a transparent, ribbon-like appearance – and juveniles are usually encountered in inshore estuarine waters. When adult, the ladyfish's diet consists mainly of crustaceans and other fish; young larvae absorb nutrients in the water through their skin.

Distribution: Western Atlantic from Cape Cod, Massachusetts, to Gulf of Mexico and Caribbean and south to Brazil.
Habitat: Shallow inshore waters to about 50m/165ft.
Food: Fish, crustaceans.
Size: 1.2m/4ft.
Breeding: Oviparous: spawns offshore; leptocephalic larvae metamorphose inshore.
Status: Not listed by IUCN.

Identification: Slim-bodied but robust, streamlined fish; body covered with small scales. Head small and pointed with large mouth bearing small, sharp teeth. Caudal fin deeply forked. The dorsal surface is silvery blue or greenish. The sides and lower surface are silvery.

COD AND RELATIVES

The cod and their relatives comprise more than 1,200 species of fish, encompassing important commercial food species such as cod, haddock and whiting, as well as the rarely seen and highly modified anglers, goosefish and toadfish. Members of the group are found in a variety of environments, ranging from surface waters to the ocean depths.

Pearlfish

Echiodon drummondii

Identification: Thin, flattish, shallow, eel-like body – almost knife-like in shape; dorsal and ventral surfaces are fringed with a continuous fin. Its body is translucent, with silvery bands and patches of pale reddish pigment on the flanks, iris and operculum (gill cover). It has a silvery abdomen. Dark markings on head.

The 30 or so species of pearlfish, which are also known as cucumber fish, are inhabitants of tropical, subtropical and temperate seas. Many of them spend much of their lives inside other marine creatures, such as bivalve molluscs or sea cucumbers. Some species do this for protection only, while others also feed on the organs of the host. The pearlfish *Echiodon drummondii* has the typical thin, elongated shape of many pearlfish. This knife-like shape makes it easy to squeeze into the host's body through its anus. Most pearlfish have a fairly sedentary lifestyle, but their eggs hatch at the surface into glassy larvae that are dispersed widely on the ocean currents to exploit new habitats.

Distribution: North Sea and British Isles.
Habitat: Waters from about 50–400m/164–1,312ft.
Food: Probably small marine creatures.
Size: 30cm/12in.
Breeding: Oviparous; eggs hatch at surface and larvae are carried and distributed by ocean currents.
Status: Not listed by IUCN.

Shore rockling

Gaidropsarus mediterraneus

The shore rockling is one of several species of rockling that inhabit shallow Atlantic waters. The shore rockling has a preference for algae or sea grasses in which it can hide. Like the other rocklings, the shore rockling has a long, slender body with two dorsal fins. Rocklings have sensory barbels on the snout and chin; in the case of the shore rockling, there are two on the snout and one on the chin. The similar-looking five-bearded rockling (*Ciliata mustela*), with which it can be confused, has five barbels, however. The three-bearded rockling (*Gaidropsarus vulgaris*) also has three barbels around the mouth, but it is distinguished from the shore rockling by its colour, which is reddish brown with well-marked blotches.

Identification: Body is long and slender with smooth, scaleless skin. First dorsal fin is short, with a prominent first ray; second dorsal fin is long. Long anal fin. Caudal fin is rounded. Head bears two sensory barbels on the snout and one barbel on the chin. Colour is dark brown; the pigment on the dorsal area may be slightly mottled in appearance.

Distribution: North-eastern Atlantic, including North Sea, from British Isles to southern Morocco; also Mediterranean.
Habitat: Among rocks and in shallow water down to about 30m/98ft.
Food: Crustaceans, worms and fish.
Size: 50cm/19.7in.
Breeding: Oviparous; eggs hatch at the surface.
Status: Not listed by IUCN.

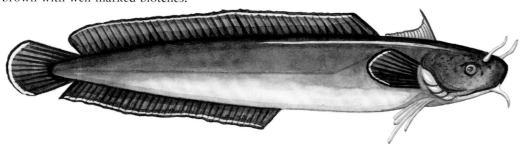

Spotted cusk eel (*Chilara taylori*): 36cm/14in
Despite their common name, cusk eels are not true eels at all, although they do have slender, eel-like bodies. The nocturnal spotted cusk eel usually rests on the bottom with its tail touching the substrate, and at the first sign of danger it corkscrews itself into the sand or mud or into a convenient crevice for safety. It is found in the eastern Pacific Ocean.

Atlantic cod (*Gadus morhua*): 1.2m/4ft
This is one of the world's most important food fish for humans, but it is now classed as Vulnerable due to long periods of overfishing. The omnivorous cod is found in north Atlantic coastal waters, usually in schools. The fish has a stout body with three dorsal fins, two anal fins and a large, triangular tail. The head bears a single chin barbel.

Whiting (*Merlangius merlangus*): 35cm/14in
Like many other species in the family Gadidae, the slender whiting has three dorsal fins and two anal fins; the first anal fin is much longer than the second anal fin. The whiting is an important commercial food fish and it is found in shallow Atlantic waters from Iceland in the north to Spain in the south, including the Mediterranean and Black Seas.

American oyster toadfish

Opsanus tau

Also known as the oyster-cracker, this sluggish species of toadfish lives in shallow water, usually hiding on the bottom until unwary prey comes close enough to be snapped up by its huge, wide mouth. Hard shells are crushed by the fish's powerful jaws. The American oyster toadfish makes grunting noises when threatened, and males also make a foghorn-like or whistling sound to attract females to spawn. After the female has laid her eggs, the male fertilizes them and guards them until they hatch. The toadfish has venomous dorsal spines, often erected when the animal is threatened.

Identification: Head is large with large, protruding eyes and a big, wide mouth; fleshy appendages around mouth and short snout. Skin is scaleless. First dorsal fin short; second dorsal fin long. Anal fin long. Large pectoral fins. Caudal fin rounded. Colour yellow-brown with brown markings extending on to the fins.

Distribution: Atlantic Ocean from Cape Cod to Miami.
Habitat: Among rocks and sand in shallow inshore waters.
Food: Crustaceans and other invertebrates, fish.
Size: 38cm/15in.
Breeding: Oviparous; eggs laid in a secluded nest, which the male guards.
Status: Not listed by IUCN.

Angler

Lophius piscatorius

Distribution: North-eastern Atlantic from Scandinavia to Morocco; also North, Baltic and Mediterranean seas.
Habitat: Among rocks and sand in shallow, inshore waters.
Food: Crustaceans and other invertebrates, fish.
Size: 2m/6.6ft.
Breeding: Oviparous; eggs float at the surface in gelatinous masses.
Status: Not listed by IUCN.

Also known as the popular dish 'monkfish', the angler is a huge-headed creature with a range of unusual adaptations for capturing prey. Lurking on the bottom with its ragged-edged, flattened and mottled body helping it to blend with its surroundings, it waves and twitches an enticing lure (formed from its first dorsal fin spine) to attract victims. If a fish or crab comes close to the lure (presumably believing it to be a small food item), it is engulfed by the angler's mouth. Amazingly, even diving seabirds have ended up in the stomachs of anglers. Spawning takes place in deep water and the eggs float at the surface. Once hatched, the young spend their early lives feeding on plankton.

Identification: Head is massive and flattened, with large, upward-facing, gaping mouth and sharp, incurved teeth. Body flattened and tapering towards tail; body much narrower than head. Head and body bordered by a fringe of lobes. Dorsal surface has several elongated rays; first bears a fleshy lobe (the 'lure'). Pectoral fins broad and large. Pelvic fins small. Colour is variable.

GASTEROSTEIFORM FISH

Most of the fish in this group are characterized by having bodies covered in bony plates instead of scales. They range in shape from the familiar stickleback to the bizarre sea horses, pipefish and sea dragons. The snout of these fish is often elongated. Gasterosteiforms are found from temperate freshwater habitats and brackish waters to tropical seas.

Slender seamoth

Pegasus volitans

The common name of the slender seamoth comes from its habit of gliding over the sea bed using its broad, wing-like pectoral fins in a manner reminiscent of a flitting moth. With its hard, bony-plated body suffused with mottling and reticulated patterning, it is well camouflaged on the sea bed as it searches out the small invertebrates that form its diet, sucking them into a small mouth at the end of its elongated snout. Like other seamoths, the slender seamoth can use its stiff fins to walk about on the substrate. During mating, males and females swim up from the bottom, and the eggs are fertilized in the water. The eggs float at the surface and soon hatch. The larvae spend time among the plankton before sinking to the bottom to develop into adults.

Identification: Head narrow and tapering, with long snout. Mouth found at end of snout on the underside; eyes prominent. Body flattened and covered by bony plates. Pectoral fins large and wing-like. Dorsal and anal fins short. Tail squarish. Colour variable – brown or grey, with mottled or reticulated patterning.

Distribution: Indo-Pacific Ocean including Mozambique, Persian Gulf and Bay of Bengal; coast of Burma to Japan; tropical Australasia.
Habitat: Shallow muddy, sandy or silty substrates.
Food: Small invertebrates.
Size: 12cm/4.7in.
Breeding: Oviparous; external fertilization.
Status: Listed as Data Deficient by IUCN.

Three-spined stickleback

Gasterosteus aculeatus

Identification: Pointed head with small mouth and large eyes. Body slender and flattish, tapering to narrow caudal peduncle. Three dorsal spines in front of dorsal fin. Anal fin shorter than dorsal fin. Pectoral fins with rounded edges. Pelvic fins reduced to a single spine and ray. Colour outside breeding season: silvery on flanks and white below; male in breeding colours described on the right.

Found in many parts of the Northern Hemisphere from ponds and rivers to shallow seas, the three-spined stickleback is a lively little fish immediately recognizable by the three characteristic spines on its back. The body lacks scales, but is protected by bony plates, and carries pelvic spines as well as the dorsal spines. During breeding, the underside of the male becomes an intense red or orange colour, his back and sides turn blue-green, and his eyes become blue. When breeding, the male builds a nest and is highly territorial. The tunnel-shaped nest rests on the bottom and is made from plant material glued together with mucous secretions. Then he displays to attract several females who lay their eggs in the nest. Once the eggs are laid, he immediately fertilizes them. The male then fans and guards them until they hatch. He even protects the hatchlings for several days, until they disperse.

Distribution: Northern Pacific and Atlantic coasts; also Mediterranean and Black Seas; also inland in North American and European rivers.
Habitat: Shallow freshwater and marine habitats; preferably with gentle or no currents.
Food: Mainly invertebrates, fish eggs and larvae, small fish.
Size: Up to 10cm/4in.
Breeding: Oviparous; external fertilization.
Status: Not listed by IUCN.

Tubesnout (*Aulorhynchus flavidus*): 18cm/7in
Looking somewhat like an elongated stickleback, the tubesnout has bony plates on its body and about 26 spines on its back. It is found in shallow eel grass and kelp beds in the eastern Pacific. The male tubesnout builds a nest from plant material in which the female lays her eggs.

Fifteen-spined stickleback
(*Spinachia spinachia*): 23cm/9in
This slender species has a pointed head, a long caudal peduncle and 14–17 spines on its back. It is the largest member of the stickleback family. It is found usually among seaweed in coastal areas near the shore in the eastern Atlantic.

Shortsnouted seahorse
(*Hippocampus ramulosus*): 15cm/6in
Like other seahorses, this species has a horse-like head and swims with its body held vertical or nearly so. The pectoral fins are situated just behind the eyes. The body is covered with bony plates. Favours habitats among the seaweeds and grasses in Atlantic and Mediterranean waters.

Chinese trumpetfish (*Aulostomus chinensis*): 80cm/31in
The Chinese trumpetfish has an elongated body and a long head with the mouth at the tip. It lives on Indo-Pacific coral reefs, where it often floats towards unsuspecting prey before darting forward and sucking it into its tube-like mouth.

Longsnouted seahorse

Hippocampus guttulatus

Among the most instantly recognizable of all marine creatures, seahorses get their common name from the shape of the head, which is essentially like that of a horse. With their strange appearance, unusual fins and habit of floating upright in the water or resting with their tails entwined around vegetation, it is not surprising that many people do not realize that seahorses are, in fact, fish. However, the mating behaviour of seahorses is even more atypical of fish. During mating, as with other seahorse species, male and female longsnouted seahorses perform an elaborate display by linking their tails and undertaking a courtship 'dance'. Then they bring their bellies together and the female transfers some of her eggs into the male's abdominal pouch. He then fertilizes the eggs. The young develop in the male's pouch for several weeks before he 'gives birth' to live young that resemble miniature versions of their parents.

Distribution: Eastern Atlantic from Great Britain to Morocco; also Mediterranean.
Habitat: Shallow waters, especially among algae and sea grasses, down to 20m/66ft; in water down to about 80m/260ft during winter.
Food: Mainly invertebrates.
Size: Up to 15cm/6in.
Breeding: Male broods fertilized eggs in abdominal pouch until they hatch.
Status: Listed as Data Deficient by IUCN.

Identification: Long snout; fleshy appendages on back of neck resemble a 'mane'. Head and body bony, angular and ridged. Body elongated, especially from region of dorsal fin to end of tail. Pectoral fins and anal fin small. Pelvic fins and caudal fin lacking. Colour yellowish-green to reddish-brown, marked with blue patches and spots.

Leafy sea dragon

Phycodurus eques

Distribution: Indo-Pacific.
Habitat: On reefs among kelp beds down to about 50m/165ft.
Food: Mainly fish and crustacean larvae.
Size: 45cm/18in.
Breeding: Male broods fertilized eggs in abdominal pouch until they hatch.
Status: Listed as Data Deficient by IUCN.

Drifting among the reefs of Indo-Pacific waters, the leafy sea dragon resembles a clump of seaweed. This bizarre-looking fish is a master of disguise – avoiding the attentions of predators while at the same time floating horizontally unnoticed towards its own prey, using imperceptible movements of its body and tiny fins. Beneath the 'leafy' outgrowths that sprout from its body, the fish has a body not unlike that of a seahorse, to which it and the other sea dragon species are closely related. Also like seahorses, the male receives eggs from the female which he fertilizes and then broods in a special part of his body between the belly and the lower part of the tail.

Identification: Head with long, trumpet-like snout. Body elongated and angled. Pelvic and caudal fins lacking. Head and body angular, bony and ridged, with elaborate plant-like appendages resembling seaweed. Yellowish-orange with white ridges and olive-green appendages.

MAIL-CHEEKED FISH

The mail-cheeked fish in the order Scorpaeniformes include some of the most dangerous fish known and all have venom glands and spines. Species such as the stonefish are masters of disguise and spend much of their lives lying partly concealed waiting for prey, while others, like more flamboyant lionfish, actively hunt their food.

Estuarine stonefish

Synanceia horrida

Lurking motionless on the seabed, the estuarine stonefish aptly lives up to its common name, for it resembles nothing more than the stones among which it nestles. This extremely effective disguise enables the fish to remain concealed until likely prey approaches. Then, the estuarine stonefish darts and grabs the victim with its upward-pointing mouth, specially adapted to take prey from below, lunging upwards. Together with all other species in its family, the stonefish has venomous spines in its dorsal fin that it can raise to protect itself from attack. Indeed, the estuarine stonefish is one of the two most venomous fish known, and has been known to kill humans who have inadvertently trodden on it.

Identification: Body elongated and tapering. Head large with big, upward-facing mouth and upward-looking, protuberant eyes. Body surface covered in rough warts and lumps, resembling rocks and stones; may also be covered with algae. Venomous spines on back and on anal and pelvic fins. Colour variable to match surroundings; often shades of brown-yellow or reddish-grey.

Distribution: Indo-West Pacific Ocean: India to China, Philippines, Papua New Guinea and Australia.
Habitat: In shallow water, partly buried among rocks and sand.
Food: Fish and crustaceans.
Size: 60cm/24in.
Breeding: Oviparous; external fertilization.
Status: Not listed by IUCN.

Longspine waspfish

Paracentropogon longispinis

Identification: Body laterally compressed. Large head with relatively small mouth. Dorsal fin tall and running from top of head, above the eyes;12–15 prominent spiny rays in dorsal fin. Body colour mottled reddish-brown with white patches.

The longspine waspfish is a highly venomous member of the family Scorpaenidae – a family containing some of the most poisonous fish in the world. This species is found in inshore waters among reefs and other hard-bottomed substrates, where it conceals itself partly by its mottled body markings and partly by its body texture, which resembles the coral on which it hides. The poison from the venomous spines can prove fatal if not treated. Seek emergency medical attention immediately if affected. If this is not possible, steeping the wounded area in very hot water as quickly as you can may render the poison harmless. Despite its reputation, this species is one of several venomous fish that are popular with aquarists.

Distribution: Indo-Pacific Ocean.
Habitat: Among silt, rocks and coral down to about 70m/230ft.
Food: Fish and crustaceans.
Size: 15cm/6in.
Breeding: Oviparous; external fertilization.
Status: Not listed by IUCN.

Northern sea robin

Prionotus carolinus

Distribution: Western Atlantic Ocean from Nova Scotia to Gulf of Mexico.
Habitat: On sandy bottoms in water down to about 180m/590ft.
Food: Fish, crustaceans, molluscs, worms.
Size: 30cm/12in.
Breeding: Oviparous; external fertilization.
Status: Not listed by IUCN.

This species spends much of its life on the bottom, where it feels for food on the seabed using three elongated rays on its large, wing-like pectoral fins. The sea robin can also support itself above the substrate with its fins, giving the impression of walking. At the first sign of danger, the fish will quickly bury itself in the sand, leaving just the top of its head and eyes exposed. Unlike most bottom fish, it is a very strong swimmer. By using special muscles attached to the swim bladder, the sea robin can also make loud noises, especially during the breeding season. A popular commercial fish, its flesh is used for pet food and fish bait, the tissues as fertilizer and the eggs are sold as gurnard 'caviar'.

Identification: Body tapering. Head large, encased in bony plates, with big eyes situated at the top of the head. Front of dorsal fin bears prominent spines. Broad caudal fin. Long anal fin. Large pelvic fins. Large pectoral fins, with lowest three rays free and elongated. Body colour mottled reddish-brown above with saddle-shaped blotches, whitish below.

Red gurnard (*Aspitrigla cuculus*): 30 cm/12in
This reddish-coloured fish has a large, distinctly sloping head and prominent eyes. First dorsal fin tall and spiny; second dorsal fin lower and longer. Anal fin about same length and size as second dorsal fin. First three rays of pectoral fins separate and used for sensing the substrate for food and for resting on bottom. Found in eastern Atlantic, Mediterranean and Baltic waters.

Kelp greenling (*Hexagrammos decagrammus*): 50cm/19.7in
One of several species of greenlings found in the North Pacific, the kelp greenling has large fins, including a dorsal fin with a deep undulation about halfway along its length. The males have blue spots on their heads and bodies; the females reddish-brown spots. The kelp greenling has five lateral lines along each side of its body.

Cabezon (*Scorpaenichthys marmoratus*): 76cm/30in
This species lives in the North Pacific at depths ranging from surface waters down to about 200m/656ft. A bulky fish with smooth, grey-brown mottled skin, it has a broad head, wide mouth and large fins. It eats mainly crabs, crustaceans and small fish.

Lumpsucker (*Cyclopterus lumpus*): 55cm/22in
The lumpsucker has a deep, rounded, scaleless body with four rows of bony plates embedded in it. Although the fish has two dorsal fins, in older specimens the first dorsal fin becomes incorporated into the body. The pelvic fins are modified into a ventral sucker, with which the fish attaches itself to rocks. Males in breeding condition develop a reddish belly.

Pogge

Agonus cataphractus

With its large, heavily armoured head and upturned snout, barbel-fringed mouth and narrow, tapering body, the pogge is a highly distinctive fish. It usually lives on the bottom, preferring sandy or muddy seabeds, although it is also encountered in estuaries. An underslung mouth restricts its food to bottom-living animals, and it uses the sensory barbels around its mouth to probe the substrate for small hidden crustaceans, worms, brittlestars and molluscs on which to feed. The pogge often burrows in the mud or sand, where its body colouration makes it difficult to see.

Identification: Head and body covered in hard, bony plates. Head large and longish, with eyes set on top of head; snout upturned and bearing a pair of hooked spines; mouth fringed with numerous barbels. Spine on each gill cover. Two dorsal fins. Body colour mottled grey-brown with four or five dark saddles across back; underside whitish.

Distribution: North-eastern Atlantic, including Shetland and Faroe Is., southwestern Iceland and southern Baltic.
Habitat: On sandy and muddy bottoms from 5–500m/16–1,650ft.
Food: Echinoderms, crustaceans, molluscs, worms.
Size: 15cm/6in.
Breeding: Oviparous; external fertilization.
Status: Not listed by IUCN.

PERCHLIKE FISH

Perciforms, commonly known as perchlike fish, account for just over 40 per cent of all fish, with over 7,000 species. It is the largest order of vertebrates on Earth. Fin spines are prominent in the physical make-up of this group: in many species, the dorsal section is divided into spiny and soft-rayed portions. Although a small percentage of perciforms have adapted to freshwater habitats, the majority are marine.

Potato cod

Epinephelus tukula

One of the largest of the groupers is the potato cod. It is also one of the biggest bony fish to be found on Indo-Pacific coral reefs, growing to weights of 100kg/220lb or more. It tends to lurk in deep channels and around seamounts, in places where the current is quite strong. It is highly territorial, and can be aggressive towards intruders, both of its own species and others, including human divers. However, it usually confines itself to an intimidating close approach and, paradoxically, this makes it a favourite with reef divers who enjoy close encounters with big fish. It is hand fed at some sites on the northern Great Barrier Reef, Australia. However, this behaviour also makes it vulnerable to spear fishers where it is not protected, and since it is a slow breeder this can have a serious impact.

Identification: A bulky fish with large, pointed head, thick-lipped mouth and relatively small eyes. Spiny first dorsal fin, continuous with taller, soft-rayed second dorsal fin. Generally creamy white or pale grey-brown with black or dark brown blotches. These are usually widely spaced, but large adults may be nearly black. The head has linear blotches radiating outwards from the eyes, and there are dark spots on the fins.

Distribution: Indo-West Pacific: Red Sea and East Africa to southern Japan and Queensland, Australia. Also Paracel Is., South China Sea.
Habitat: Coral reefs at depths of 10–150m/35–500ft.
Food: Smaller fish and crustaceans, such as crabs and spiny lobsters.
Size: 1.8m/6ft.
Breeding: Adults are initially female, maturing at a length of about 1m (3ft), but become males as they grow larger. Oviparous; eggs fertilized externally.
Status: Not listed by IUCN.

Rainbow wrasse

Thalassoma pavo

Identification: A sleek, streamlined fish with a rounded head, large eyes, and a long, low dorsal fin extending to the tail. Young adults are female, with golden-yellow bodies barred with pale blue-green, darker above, and with a rust-red head marbled with a pattern of turquoise lines. Older adults become male, with bright turquoise dorsal and anal fins, a brighter head pattern and fewer bars on the body.

This colourful, streamlined subtropical fish is one of many wrasses that is a protogynous hermaphrodite – that is, a species that is first female, and then changes to become male. This remarkable transformation is emphasized by a change in colour pattern, although unlike some wrasses the basic range of colours remains the same. It is commonly found in warm, shallow waters, where it preys on animals such as prawns, small crabs and marine snails. Recent research indicates that it is extending its range northwards in the Mediterranean in response to rising water temperatures.

Distribution: Eastern Atlantic, from Portugal to south of Cape Lopez, Gabon including Azores, Madeira and Canaries. Also Mediterranean.
Habitat: Rocky reefs and seagrass beds, at depths of 1–150m/3–500ft.
Food: Small molluscs and crustaceans.
Size: 25cm/10in.
Breeding: Adults are initially female, becoming male and changing colour with age. Oviparous; eggs fertilized externally.
Status: Not listed by IUCN.

Red mullet (*Mullus surmuletus*): 40cm/16in
Most common in warm, shallow Mediterranean
and eastern Atlantic waters, the red mullet
occasionally occurs in Scandinavia.
Reddish-brown above with yellow stripes on its
flanks, it is a slender fish with a steeply arched
head profile and large eyes. It has two long
sensory barbels beneath the jaw, enabling it to
feel for prey such as shrimps and molluscs on
sandy or muddy seabeds.

Ballan wrasse (*Labrus bergylta*): 60cm/24in
The bulky ballan wrasse occurs in the North
Atlantic. It has large conical teeth for crushing
the shells of molluscs and crabs. It usually
forages among rocks about 20m/65ft down,
although the young often occur in large intertidal
rockpools. Young fish are often emerald green.
Adults are mottled
greenish-brown
females, but
change sex
to become
reddish males.

Stargazer (*Uranoscopus scaber*): 30cm/12in
Lying half-buried in soft sediments on the
seabed, the stargazer has a robust, flattened
head with eyes set on top, pointing upwards.
Usually dark brown or blackish with grey-brown
flanks, it is well camouflaged and attracts prey
with a mobile lure on the lower lip of its large
mouth. It has a venomous spine behind each gill
cover, and an electric organ behind each eye.
Occurs in Mediterranean and eastern Atlantic.

Greater weever

Trachinus draco

The weevers have venom glands associated
with grooved spines on their gill covers and
in the first dorsal fin. The venom provides
defence against bottom-feeding rays and
large flatfish, since during the day the fish
typically lie buried in the sand with just
their eyes and the tip of the first dorsal fin
exposed. If not disturbed, the fish stay
buried all day, emerging at night to swim
about in search of prey. The greater weever
favours deeper water than the very similar
lesser weever, which frequently occurs in the
shallows off sandy beaches and is regularly
trodden on by bathers. The resulting
wounds are extremely painful, often causing
swelling and bruising.

Distribution: Eastern Atlantic
from southern Norway to
Morocco, Madeira and
Canaries; also Mediterranean
and Black Seas.
Habitat: On sandy, muddy or
gravelly seabeds, at depths of
1–150m/3–500ft.
Food: Small invertebrates
and fish.
Size: 40cm/16in.
Breeding: Oviparous; eggs
fertilized externally.
Status: Not listed by IUCN.

Identification: An elongated fish with a small, compressed head, an upward-slanting
mouth and large eyes. The first dorsal fin is short, black, spiny and fan-like, while the
second dorsal fin and anal fin are long and low, extending to the tail. It has a small tail fin,
but large pectorals. There are two or three small spines above each eye, and a large spine
on each gill cover. Greenish above with yellowish-white oblique stripes; paler below.

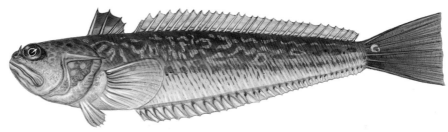

Large-scale (seven-spot) archerfish

Toxotes chatareus

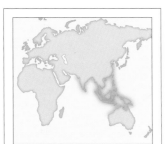

Distribution: India
and South-east Asia to
New Guinea and
northern Australia.
Habitat: Brackish, tidal
mangrove swamps and
river estuaries.
Food: Mainly insects
dislodged from vegetation by
well-aimed jets of water.
Size: 30cm/12in.
Breeding: Oviparous; eggs
fertilized externally.
Status: Not listed by IUCN.

This is one of several species of archerfish
that live and hunt primarily among the tidal
mangrove swamps of tropical Asia and
Australasia. It specializes in targeting insects
that perch on the arching roots and foliage
of the mangroves, bombarding them with
jets of water shot from its mouth. Its object
is to knock the insects into the water, where
it can seize and eat them. A ridge along the
top of its tongue fits into a deep groove in
the roof of its mouth, forming a tube like
a rifle barrel. By rapidly contracting its
gill covers, the fish forces water along the
tube, which gives good accuracy up to a
range of about 1.5m/5ft. The profile of its
upper body allows it to approach
a potential victim just below the
surface, so it can see its target well
without creating ripples that might
distort its view or alert its prey.

Identification: A deep-bodied, small-headed fish
with a virtually straight profile from the tip of its
sharp snout to the top of its dorsal fin. It has large
eyes and an upward slant to its mouth. It is silvery,
darker above, with six or seven black spots
of varying size on each upper flank.

Tompot blenny

Blennius gattorugine

A common fish of rocky shores, the tompot blenny is usually found from just below the low-tide mark to depths down to about 12m/40ft, where it conceals itself in crevices or under rocky ledges. It is most active at dusk and dawn, but its cryptic colouration and pattern make it hard to be seen by the small crustaceans that largely make up its diet. Young fish sometimes occur in large tidal pools on the lower shore among thick seaweed. The blennies use the same areas for spawning, with each male selecting a suitable crevice and encouraging one or more females to attach their adhesive eggs to the rock. The male then fertilizes the eggs and guards them until they hatch. The presence of tentacles above each eye makes identification of this species definitive.

Distribution: North-eastern Atlantic from Ireland to Morocco; also Mediterranean Sea. Found inland throughout mainland Portugal.
Habitat: Shallow coastal waters off rocky shores, from 3–30m/10–100ft.
Food: Mainly small crustaceans.
Size: 20cm/8in.
Breeding: Oviparous; sticky eggs are laid in a submerged rock crevice.
Status: Not listed by IUCN.

Identification: A stoutly built blenny with a long, high dorsal fin that is stiff and spiny at the front. It has a long anal fin and large pectoral fins, and a flattened, branched tentacle above each eye. It is typically yellowish brown with seven or more dark brown bars on each flank; spawning males are chocolate-brown. Guards fertilized eggs for a month until hatching.

Barred mudskipper

Periophthalmus argentilineatus

This is the most widespread and familiar of all the mudskippers – specialized gobies that live part of their life out of the water on the mudflats of brackish mangrove swamps. It uses its strong pectoral fins to jump, or skip, over the mud, often very rapidly, and may even climb on to the exposed roots and trunks of the mangroves, clinging to them with its pectoral sucker. Like all fish, it absorbs oxygen through its gills, but it also carries a supply of oxygenated water in its gill cavity for use when it is not submerged. It can also absorb oxygen through its skin, like a frog, provided it stays moist. Mudskippers are territorial fish, warning off rivals by displaying their colourful dorsal fins. The males also display to females in this fashion, before spawning in flooded, crater-like burrows in the mud.

Identification: An elongated fish with a large head and protruding, high-set eyes. It has powerful, limb-like pectoral fins. The pectoral fins are fused to form a sucker. Colour is generally brownish-grey with darker blotches or bands along the flanks. The dorsal fin has a conspicuous black band and may be edged in bright red.

Distribution: Southern Red Sea to South Africa: east to the Marianas and Samoa; north to Ryukyu Islands; south to western Australia and Oceania.
Habitat: Intertidal, brackish mudflats among estuarine mangroves, mainly when exposed at low tide.
Food: Marine worms, crustaceans and insects such as mosquito larvae.
Size: 15cm/6in.
Breeding: Oviparous; eggs laid and fertilized in specially excavated pools. Eggs and larvae guarded for about 50 days until the young are able leave the water.
Status: Not listed by IUCN.

Sand goby

Pomatoschistus minutus

Distribution: Eastern North Atlantic from Norway to Spain; parts of Mediterranean and Black Seas.
Habitat: Sandy and muddy shallows close to the shore, and estuaries, mainly from mid-tide level to about 20m/66ft.
Food: Small crustaceans and marine worms.
Size: 6cm/2.4in.
Breeding: Oviparous; female attaches eggs to the inside of an empty clam shell where they are fertilized by the male, who guards the eggs.
Status: Not listed by IUCN.

A very common fish of inshore sandy and muddy areas, the sand goby has a sleeker profile than most of its relatives and sometimes swims in small schools. Active by day, it feeds mainly on tiny crustaceans, such as copepods, amphipods and young shrimps, as well as marine worms. In turn, it is eaten by a wide variety of marine predators, including various species of cod and bass, as well as seabirds such as terns. It spawns in shallow waters in summer, the male luring the female into the empty shell of a bivalve mollusc to lay her eggs, but retreats to deeper waters in winter. Juvenile fish may enter the lower reaches of estuaries, but adults avoid brackish water.

Identification: A slender goby with high-set, prominent eyes. The two dorsal fins are well separated, the first with six rays. Rounded pectoral fins. Pelvic fins are fused into an oval sucker. Colour generally light sandy brown with dark dots and faint bars on the back. The male has a white-rimmed dark-blue or black spot on the first dorsal fin.

Butterfish (*Pholis gunnellus*): 25cm/10in
The skin of the almost eel-like butterfish is coated in slippery mucus, making it difficult to grip and accounting for its common name. Usually brown or greenish with blurred vertical bars on its flanks and about 12 white-ringed black spots on each side at the base of the dorsal fin. On rocky coasts on both sides of the North Atlantic, and Baltic, from intertidal pools to depths of about 100m/330ft. It is often found beneath stones or among seaweeds, where it feeds on small crustaceans and marine worms.

Black-rayed shrimp goby (*Stonogobiops nematodes*): 5cm/2in
One of several tropical coral reef gobies that live in association with a pistol shrimp or snapping prawn. The fish has an elongated, pale body with dark oblique bars, a bright yellow head and eye, and a long, black first dorsal fin ray. It lives in mated pairs, in a burrow excavated by the shrimp. The pair hover around the burrow entrance, and dive into the burrow at the first sign of danger.

Shanny (*Lipophrys pholis*): 18cm/7in
Common on rocky shores in the eastern North Atlantic and Mediterranean, the shanny is found in rockpools where it eats barnacles, small crabs, molluscs and seaweed. It can survive out of the water for some time, and uses its paired fins to move between rockpools. Its elongated body is usually a dull brown or greenish, with darker blotches, but its colour is variable.

Northern (shore) clingfish

Lepadogaster lepadogaster

This is the most common of the five genera of clingfish, with a total of eight species occurring in the north-east Atlantic. The powerful sucker beneath its body enables it to attach itself to rocks to resist the waves and tidal streams of rocky shores, although it is more frequently found in partly sheltered sites. It is always discovered clinging upside down beneath boulders and ledges, often among kelp growing low down on the shore. It uses the same habitats as breeding sites, attaching its eggs to the rocks. The adult fish guard the eggs, but despite this they are often eaten by sea slugs and other animals.

Identification: Rather flattened, tapered, scaleless body. Head long and triangular with a 'duck-billed' snout. It has a fringed flap in front of its large eyes. Long dorsal and anal fins set well back on the body. A sucker on the underside is formed partly from the pelvic fins. Body colour varies from pink to red, with two yellow-rimmed, deep blue spots on top of the head.

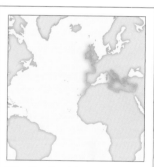

Distribution: Eastern North Atlantic from Britain to Morocco; also eastern and central Mediterranean Sea.
Habitat: Intertidal pools on rocky shores.
Food: Small crustaceans and other planktonic animals.
Size: 6cm/2.4in.
Breeding: Oviparous; eggs attached to the underside of boulders, where they are fertilized. They are guarded by a parent until they hatch.
Status: Not listed by IUCN.

DOLPHINS AND PORPOISES

These widely distributed, powerful marine mammals are social animals, highly adapted for an aquatic life. The body is streamlined and is totally lacking hair, the limbs are modified to form flippers and a broad tail is used for swimming. They are found all over the world in rivers, inshore waters and the open ocean. The young are born at sea.

Common dolphin

Delphinus delphis

With its markings, long beak and pointed flippers, the common dolphin has been the inspiration of artists and sculptors. It is an intelligent animal with a well-developed, hierarchical social structure, often occurring in schools several hundred strong. It is frequently encountered cavorting around boats. The common dolphin's behaviour includes many instances of individuals coming to the aid of injured companions. Dolphins are air-breathing mammals, but can dive for five minutes or more at depths down to several hundred metres as they search for fish and squid, which they often find using a sophisticated system of echo location.

Identification: Body slender and torpedo shaped. Slender, sickle-shaped dorsal fin. Long, slender beak and distinct forehead. Body colour variable: brownish-black or black upper parts; chest and belly cream-white; tan or yellowish hourglass pattern on flanks; black stripe from lower jaw to front of flipper and from beak to eye; flippers black, grey or white.

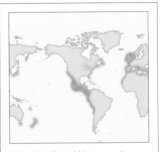

Distribution: Warm and temperate waters of Atlantic, Pacific and probably Indian oceans.
Habitat: Coastal and offshore waters.
Food: Fish, squid.
Size: 2.2m/7.2ft.
Breeding: One calf; calving period once every 2 years.
Status: Not listed by IUCN.

Killer whale

Orcinus orca

This is the largest member of the dolphin family Delphinidae, a robust animal with a rounded head and no beak. The huge, triangular dorsal fin of an adult male is 2m/6.5ft high, but is smaller and more curved in female and juveniles. The killer whale can travel at speeds of up to 65km/h/40mph – the fastest of all sea mammals – and can track prey by echo location. Its body markings help it to remain concealed in the shallow, turbid waters in which it often stalks. Killer whales sometimes cooperate when hunting. This species is known to live for up to 100 years.

Identification: Body robust but streamlined. Rounded head with no beak. Mouth with about 50 teeth. Large, paddle-shaped flippers. Dorsal fin tall and erect in males; smaller and sickle-shaped in females and juveniles. Body colour black on sides and back; white under head and chest extending up to flanks; white patch above and behind the eye.

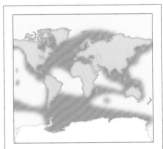

Distribution: All oceans.
Habitat: Coastal and offshore waters.
Food: Fish, squid, marine mammals, such as seals, porpoises, walruses.
Size: Male 7m/23ft or more; female slightly smaller.
Breeding: One calf; calving period every 3–5 years.
Status: Listed as Lower Risk; Conservation Dependent by IUCN.

Common porpoise

Phocoena phocoena

Distribution: Panglobal in temperate regions of North Atlantic and North Pacific Oceans; occasionally also ventures into adjoining seas, especially Baltic and Black seas.
Habitat: Coastal waters.
Food: Fish, crustaceans.
Size: 1.8m/6ft.
Breeding: One calf; calving period once every 2 years.
Status: Listed as Vulnerable; Conservation Dependent.

The common or harbour porpoise is also known as the sea pig, due to the snorting noises it makes when it breathes. The smallest of all the cetaceans, the common porpoise also has a relatively short lifespan – rarely living for more than about 12 years. It is a gregarious species, usually found in groups, and although it lives close to land, it spends much of its time submerged, diving for up to six minutes at a time, and so is not frequently seen. Numbers of the common porpoise have been reduced by habitat loss and prey reduction as well as by pollution and fatal encounters with fishing nets, in which they become entangled.

Identification: Body small and robust with rounded head sloping to mouth. Small, slightly rounded flippers. Triangular, blunt-tipped dorsal fin. Body colour dark greyish on back; white or light grey on belly. Black lips; black invariably extends to cover part of the chin. Has a slightly upcurved mouth that gives impression of smiling.

Bottlenose dolphin (*Tursiops truncatus*): 3.9m/12.8ft
This familiar dolphin of zoos and films has a broad, high dorsal fin and a short, wide beak. Intelligent and sociable, bottlenose dolphins live in groups. It has an echo-location system that emits a range of sounds at different frequencies for analysing objects precisely. Found worldwide in temperate and tropical waters.

Irrawaddy dolphin (*Orcaella brevirostris*): 2.5m/8.2ft
This species has a rounded head, no beak, and a small, triangular dorsal fin with a rounded tip. It varies in colour from light and dark blue-grey to pale blue. Found in coastal waters, estuaries and some rivers from the Bay of Bengal to northern Australia, where it feeds on crustaceans, fish and squid. Although generally listed Data Deficient, it is Critically Endangered in some places.

Spectacled porpoise (*Phocoena dioptrica*): 2.3m/7.5ft
An inhabitant of the temperate and subarctic waters of the Southern Ocean, the species gets its common name from the black rims around its eyes. Sharply marked with black dorsal and lateral regions contrasting with a white abdomen. Little is known about its habits, although anchovies and crustaceans were found in the stomach contents of a dead individual.

Finless porpoise

Neophocaena phocaenoides

Easily distinguished from other porpoises by its prominent, humped forehead, beak-like mouth and lack of a dorsal fin, the finless porpoise is a quick and agile mammal, diving for short periods to catch fish and other marine creatures using its system of echo location. Although found all year throughout its range, in some areas the finless porpoise undertakes seasonal movements that are reflected by changes in abundance. Usually sighted near coasts, the species feeds on a variety of prey, including fish, shrimps and squid. Unfortunately, the finless porpoise is often found drowned, ensnared in fishing nets. In the Yangtze River in China, finless porpoises sometimes become caught on baited hooks that are intended for fish.

Identification: Body lacks dorsal fin. Humped forehead and mouth with beak-like appearance. Body colour light grey with paler abdomen; newborn calf mainly black.

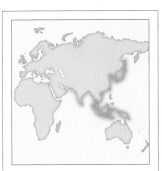

Distribution: Indo-Pacific from Persian Gulf to Indonesia and Japan.
Habitat: Coastal and estuarine waters; also rivers.
Food: Fish, crustaceans, molluscs.
Size: 1.8m/6ft.
Breeding: One calf; calving period once every 1–2 years.
Status: Listed by IUCN as Data Deficient throughout range, except China where listed as Endangered.

TRUE SEALS

Seals are marine mammals that are adapted to live in the sea, although they all spend some part of their life ashore, moving about clumsily on their flippers when on land. True seals are distinguished from the similar-looking sea lions because they lack external ear pinnae, or structure, and their hind flippers cannot be brought forward in front of the body.

Leopard seal

Hydrurga leptonyx

Sleek, powerful and streamlined, the leopard seal is built for hunting a range of marine animals from penguins to krill – although it will also take carrion. It usually waits to take penguins under water as they move off the ice. It is one of the largest species of seal, with an almost reptilian-like head armed with massive jaws and large teeth. The leopard seal is known to be aggressive towards small boats and their occupants when approached too closely. Females give birth to young on the pack ice, but the males are not present at the time. The coats of young leopard seals are similar to those of adults. This species is known to live for 26 years or more.

Identification: Sleek and elongate seal. Neck well defined. Wide-gaping mouth with large canines and large post-canine teeth. Long foreflippers. Coat colour silver to grey above, lighter below, with a mixture of light and dark spots.

Distribution: Polar and subpolar waters of Southern Hemisphere.
Habitat: At the edge of the pack ice, on Antarctica and around some islands.
Food: Penguins, krill, seals, carrion.
Size: Females 3.3m/10.8ft; males slightly smaller.
Breeding: Little known of behaviour; pups born September–January.
Status: Not listed by IUCN.

Common/harbour seal

Phoca vitulina

The common seal is a non-migratory, usually solitary species with a wide distribution. There are five subspecies known, ranging from one found in the north-east Atlantic Ocean to one that lives in the north-west Pacific Ocean. The common seal frequently hauls out to sleep and bask on sheltered tidal rocky and sandy sites, and sometimes travels up rivers and is seen in lakes. It feeds mostly during the day, and can dive for up to 30 minutes in search of squid and other food, although dives are usually only of durations of five minutes or so. Pre-mating behaviour includes males and females blowing bubbles and biting each other's necks.

Identification: Body rounded and relatively short, with large head proportionately. The face somewhat dog-like in appearance. The flippers are short. The coat colour is highly variable, ranging from grey-white, brown or black overlaid with rings, blotches or spots in adults.

Distribution: Northern Atlantic and Pacific Oceans.
Habitat: Temperate and subarctic coastal waters.
Food: Crustaceans, squid, fish.
Size: Males 1.8m/6ft; females slightly smaller.
Breeding: Mating takes place in the water; typically one pup born per year.
Status: Not listed by IUCN.

Crabeater seal (*Lobodon carcinophagus*): 2.4m/8ft

These sleek seals with long muzzles are among the most abundant of all pinnipeds, with numbers estimated at about 12 million. Fast-moving and agile, the crabeater seal feeds on krill mainly at night, using its cusped, interlocking teeth to sieve the prey from the water. It occurs around pack ice in Antarctic seas. The coat is silver grey or brown.

Grey seal (*Halichoerus grypus*): 2.4m/8ft
This is a large seal found on both sides of the North Atlantic Ocean, usually around coasts or near ice floes. It has a long head and snout, resulting in its nickname of 'horsehead'. Males usually have a grey, dark brown or black coat with lighter blotches. Females are usually light tan or grey with dark patches and spots. Squid, fish and crustaceans form the bulk of the diet.

Weddell seal (*Leptonychotes weddellii*): 2.9m/9.5ft
This most southerly breeding seal has a circumpolar distribution in the Antarctic. Usually solitary, large numbers may gather around breathing holes in the ice outside the breeding season. A diver capable of spending over an hour under water searching for fish and other food. The Weddell seal has a small head and short muzzle; coat blue-grey above, whitish grey below.

Harp seal

Phoca groenlandica

The harp-shaped markings on the back, together with the dark head, make this species one of the more easy to recognize. The harp seal lives much of its life in the open sea on the edge of the pack ice, maintaining holes through which it dives for fish and crustaceans, sometimes descending to 274m/900ft. At mating time, in autumn, thousands of harp seals may congregate together. Males fight each other with their flippers and teeth to gain access to females.

Identification: Body plump. Head small and flattened. Large eyes set close together. Foreflippers small and pointed. Coat colour: background silvery white; two black bands joined over shoulders and extending over rear flanks forming harp-shaped pattern; head black. Pups camouflaged with white fur.

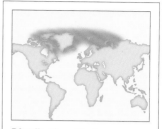

Distribution: Northern Atlantic and southern Arctic Oceans.
Habitat: Arctic and subarctic waters.
Food: Crabs and other invertebrates, fish.
Size: Males 1.9m (6.2ft); females slightly smaller.
Breeding: Usually one pup born per year; pups weaned at about 12 days.
Status: Not listed by IUCN.

Northern elephant seal

Mirounga angustirostris

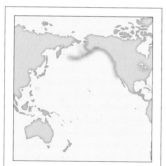

Distribution: Mainly Pacific coast of North America.
Habitat: Coastal waters and shores.
Food: Molluscs such as squid, fish.
Size: Males 5m/16.4ft; females 3m/10ft.
Breeding: Gestation period about 1 year. Usually one pup born per year.
Status: Not listed by IUCN.

The largest pinniped in the Northern Hemisphere. Females usually weigh up to about 900kg/1,984lb, but the males can reach 2,300kg/5,070lb. Much of this weight is accounted for by a thick layer of blubber under the skin. Such a large source of blubber and meat became a ready target for commercial seal hunters, and numbers dwindled almost to extinction by the end of the 19th century, although they recovered after the animal was protected. The northern elephant seal makes regular long dives (an hour or more has been recorded) when hunting for food. Mating takes place on land, with each dominant male controlling access to a group of females, and threatening rival males by rearing up and displaying his proboscis. After the pup is weaned, it is left to fend for itself as the mother returns to sea.

Identification: Males, especially, are massive and often scarred from battles with rivals. Male has a large, trunk-like snout, or proboscis, at the front of the face. Foreflippers relatively small. Hind flippers lobed. Coat colour tan, brown, or greyish on top, lighter underneath.

SEA LIONS, WALRUS AND SEA COWS

Sea lions are distinguished from true seals by having external ear pinnae, and because they can bring their hind flippers underneath the body. The walrus, the only member of its family, is a huge, tusked mammal found in the Arctic. The sea cows are slow-moving, plant-eating aquatic mammals such as dugongs and manatees that exist entirely in the water.

California sea lion

Zalophus californianus

Identification: Streamlined body with well-developed flippers. Head dog-like; external ears. Males have horny crest on head creating domed effect. Colour of coat: males generally chestnut-brown, although some have lighter patches. Females and juveniles, tan.

This sea mammal, once common in circuses, is still a popular attraction at many marine theme parks and zoos. It is a sociable animal, living in groups along the western coast of North America, where it often comes ashore, basking on jetties and piers as well as beaches. It is a capable swimmer and diver, reaching depths of 270m/890ft as it hunts day and night for its main prey: fish and squid. The California sea lion can swim at 32km/h/20mph. During the breeding season, males establish territories on remote beaches and islands for several weeks and vigorously defend them against any rivals who attempt to encroach on them. Gestation lasts about 11 months, with pups being born between May and June.

Distribution: Pacific Ocean, from Baja California to Alaska; also Galapagos Islands.
Habitat: Breeds on coasts and islands.
Food: Fish, squid.
Size: Males 2.4m/8ft; females 1.8m/6ft.
Breeding: One pup, nursed for 5 or 6 months or up to 1 year. Pups and their mothers communicate in rookeries through vocalizations.
Status: Not listed by IUCN.

Northern fur seal

Callorhinus ursinus

The northern fur seal spends most of its life at sea, usually feeding at night, and rarely comes ashore except to breed. A northern fur seal pup may spend up to 22 months at sea before returning to land. At breeding time, nearly three-quarters of the species' total population (about 1 million individuals) congregate on the Pribilof Islands of St George and St Paul in the Bering Sea. After the pup is born, it is left for days at a time while the mother goes back to sea to hunt. On her return, she is able to locate her offspring by its unique call. Although no longer hunted in huge numbers, the northern fur seal is still caught in some places. It also becomes ensnared in trawl nets that have been set for fish.

Identification: Moderately built seal; males have stockier neck, shoulders and chest than females. Muzzle short and downcurved. Flippers long, wide and tapering. Fur on foreflippers extends only to 'wrist'. Coat colour: males grey, black, reddish or brown with yellow or grey frosting on mane; females silver-grey with cream or tan chest; pups born blackish with lighter chin and muzzle.

Distribution: North Pacific Ocean: Bering Sea to waters of northern Japan and southern California.
Habitat: Breeds on islands in range.
Food: Mainly squid, fish.
Size: Males 2.1m/7ft; females 1.5m/5ft.
Breeding: One small, black pup produced in June.
Status: Listed as Vulnerable by IUCN.

Walrus

Odobenus rosmarus

Distribution: Bering and Chukchi Seas in Arctic Ocean.
Habitat: Pack ice, rocky islands, open water.
Food: Molluscs, worms, fish, crustaceans; occasionally seals.
Size: Males 3.2m/10.5ft; females 2.7m/8.9ft. Tusks up to 55cm/21.6in in males.
Breeding: Females give birth to young every other year; one well-developed pup produced.
Status: Listed as lower risk by IUCN.

The gregarious walrus is an impressive creature, immediately recognizable by the pair of prominent tusks – larger in males – that extend downward from the mouth. The tusks have many uses. They are employed in defence, as tools to smash holes in the ice, as icepicks to help haul the animal out of the water, but primarily they are used to signal social position in the hierarchy. Those with the biggest tusks are the most dominant animals and can secure the most advantageous sites for mating. If challenged by another individual, however, a walrus' tusks can become fearsome stabbing weapons. Cumbersome on land, the walrus is an agile and strong swimmer. It feeds on a variety of mainly bottom-dwelling bivalve molluscs, which it senses with the 'moustache' of bristles around its mouth, and then digs out with its horny lips.

Identification: Massively built with short neck and squarish head. Flat, wide snout bears stiff, sensory bristles. Upper canines modified to form two tusks. Colour of skin brown to tawny, darker on chest and abdomen. Skin becomes pinker when exposed to sun.

Steller sea lion (*Eumetopias jubatus*): 2.8m/9ft
This species, the largest of the family Otariidae, or eared seals, overlaps its range with the California sea lion, but its larger size and lighter body colour help distinguish it. The Steller sea lion inhabits the North Pacific Ocean. After breeding, individuals disperse far and wide, sometimes travelling thousands of kilometres. The species is an opportunist feeder, hunting near the shore and over the continental shelf for fish and molluscs and, occasionally, seals.

Australian sea lion (*Neophoca cinerea*): 2.4m/8ft
This sea lion has a large head, tapering muzzle and small external ears. It breeds on sandy beaches on islands off the coast of western and southern Australia. A non-migratory species, it lives close to its breeding site in fairly large colonies, feeding on fish, squid and penguins. It is much less awkward out of water than many sea lion species, and may occur inland when rough weather forces it from the sea.

Dugong (*Dugong dugon*): 4m/13ft
Also known as the sea cow, the dugong bears a close resemblance to the manatees, although it can be told apart by its crescent-shaped tail fluke. The dugong can be found in the southwest Pacific Ocean, Indian Ocean and Red Sea – also in coastal shallows, where it grazes on sea grasses. It is classed as Vulnerable.

West Indian manatee

Trichechus manatus

This large, docile aquatic mammal is found in coastal areas and rivers. Together with three other species, including the dugong, it comprises the order Sirenia. Early mariners thought these creatures were mermaids – hence the name sirenians (sirens of the sea). Among mammals that never leave the water, sirenians are the only ones that exploit plants as their chief food source. The West Indian manatee only has foreflippers, the rear part of the body terminating in a broad, rounded tail fluke. It feeds by foraging for plants. The animal's eyesight is poor, but both its hearing the sense of touch are good. The manatee is a sociable animal, living in small groups. When not feeding it usually lies on the seabed, coming to the surface to take in air through its large nostrils. Newborn calves stay with their mothers for up to 18 months. In captivity, the species has been known to live for about 30 years.

Distribution: US coasts: mainly Florida, also west to Texas and north to Virginia. From coastal Central America to Brazil, South America.
Habitat: Shallow coastal waters, estuaries, rivers.
Food: Water hyacinths, sea grasses.
Size: Up to 4.3m/14ft.
Breeding: One calf produced every 2–5 years.
Status: Listed as Vulnerable by IUCN.

Identification: Heavy bodied with short neck and blunt, oblong head. Broad snout bears sensory bristles (vibrissae) on upper lip and nostrils are set far back. Foreflippers long with rudimentary nails. Tail fluke broad and rounded. Body colour grey-brown; hairless.

SHALLOW SEAS AND CORAL REEFS

The sunlit waters of the world's shallow seas can be phenomenally productive, and their proximity to shore means they are also among the best studied marine waters. Sadly, they are also the most polluted and exploited and all are susceptible to the effects of global climate change.

Temperate shallow seas teem with life, much of it microscopic – such as the algae and other plankton that give such waters their characteristic greenish tint. In contrast, the clear blue water of the tropics contain relatively little nutriment and can be relatively devoid of life. But if such waters are the marine equivalent of deserts, at their margins are great forests and swathes of pasture in the form of kelp and sea grass beds. These provide shelter and grazing for a diverse host of fish, mammals and invertebrates. In the tropics coral reefs may develop, and these rival tropical rainforests as the world's most biodiverse ecosystems. Each of these habitats supports its own characteristic assemblages of animals, and there are many species that cruise from one environment to another, turning each to different advantage – feeding, spawning, rearing young or seeking shelter from predators.

*Above, left to right: Giant clam (*Tridacna maxima*); spotted eagle ray (*Aetobatus narinari*); clown triggerfish (*Balistoides conspicillum*).*

Right: This shallow reef in Indonesia is clearly visible above the surface of the water.

SPONGES

There are approximately 5,000 species of sponge living in marine habitats today. Although a small percentage inhabit deep waters, the majority live at relatively shallow depths. They exhibit an astonishing range of physical forms, from the small calcareous species encrusting rocks and shells to the dome-shaped vase and giant barrel sponge, which belong to a different group within the class Demospongiae.

Red tree sponge

Haliclona compressa

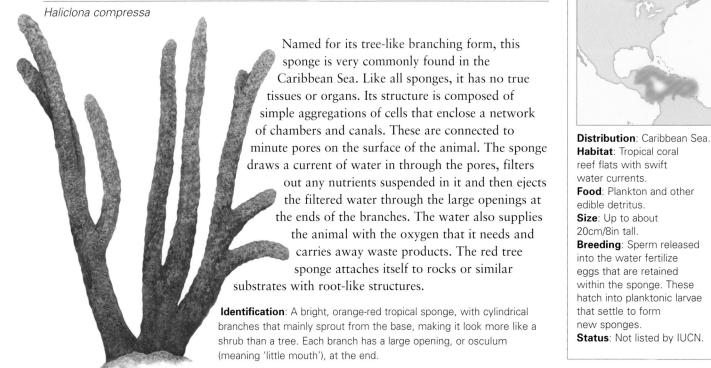

Named for its tree-like branching form, this sponge is very commonly found in the Caribbean Sea. Like all sponges, it has no true tissues or organs. Its structure is composed of simple aggregations of cells that enclose a network of chambers and canals. These are connected to minute pores on the surface of the animal. The sponge draws a current of water in through the pores, filters out any nutrients suspended in it and then ejects the filtered water through the large openings at the ends of the branches. The water also supplies the animal with the oxygen that it needs and carries away waste products. The red tree sponge attaches itself to rocks or similar substrates with root-like structures.

Identification: A bright, orange-red tropical sponge, with cylindrical branches that mainly sprout from the base, making it look more like a shrub than a tree. Each branch has a large opening, or osculum (meaning 'little mouth'), at the end.

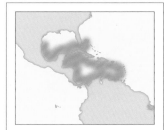

Distribution: Caribbean Sea.
Habitat: Tropical coral reef flats with swift water currents.
Food: Plankton and other edible detritus.
Size: Up to about 20cm/8in tall.
Breeding: Sperm released into the water fertilize eggs that are retained within the sponge. These hatch into planktonic larvae that settle to form new sponges.
Status: Not listed by IUCN.

Vase sponge

Ircinia campana

Like other sponges, this large species is little more than a loose association of cells that feed cooperatively by filtering organic particles from the water. However, the structure is reinforced by spongin – the fibrous, flexible protein that is the basis of natural bath sponges – strengthened with glassy silica spicules. This strong skeleton enables the vase sponge to grow into a large organism that can withstand the flow of ocean currents, although it is occasionally uprooted by storms and is found washed ashore, where it becomes tough and shrunken as it dries out. The chemicals that make it smell of garlic – and account for its alternative name of stinker sponge – probably help to protect it from fish that might otherwise eat it.

Identification: Large, bell-shaped sponge with a deep central cavity and a rough outside surface with small pores and coarse longitudinal ribs. It ranges in colour from purple to brown or red, and it has a characteristic smell of garlic.

Distribution: Caribbean Sea, from Florida and the Bahamas to Mexico.
Habitat: Sandy shallows with rocks for attachment, down to 15m/50ft.
Food: Plankton and other edible debris.
Size: Up to 90cm/36in tall; 60cm/24in across.
Breeding: Sperm released into the water fertilize eggs that are retained within the sponge. These hatch into planktonic larvae that settle to form new sponges. Can also grow from 'buds', or fragments, of tissue.
Status: Not listed by IUCN.

Distribution: Southern California, US.
Habitat: Rocky shores from intertidal zone downwards,
Food: Small organic particles filtered from the water.
Size: Individuals up to 2cm/ 0.75in thick; 10cm/4in across.
Breeding: Sperm released into the water fertilize eggs that are retained within the sponge. These hatch into larvae that settle to form new sponges. Like other sponges, it can also grow from fragments of tissue, or by sprouting 'buds' from the main body mass.
Status: Not listed by IUCN.

Encrusting sponge

Leucetta losangelensis

One of many species known as breadcrumb sponges, this low-profile, encrusting sponge is more precisely described by its specific name, which indicates its southern Californian distribution. It is one of the calcareous sponges – species that have skeletons reinforced with tiny rods of chalky material rather than glassy silica. These calcareous rods make the sponge rough and sandpapery to the touch. It is usually small and white, with large outlet pores, or oscules. It inhabits narrow crevices between boulders and under rocks, and favours places where wave action is strong. These are often inhabited by the crustacean *Paracerceis sculpta*, which also lives on rocky shores.

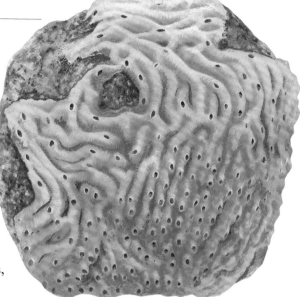

Identification: An encrusting sponge of variable shape, but typically with a finger-like growth pattern. White to pale brown, its surface has scattered, oval-shaped oscules. It can spread to cover completely large submerged rocks.

Leucosolenia complicata: 2cm/0.75in high
This pale, fragile, calcareous sponge is tree-like or bushy, depending on its habitat, and it is usually found beneath overhangs on rocky shores below the tideline, but also in estuaries. Each soft, off-white branch has an opening, or oscule, at the end, for ejecting water that has been filtered for food. Widespread in Arctic and Atlantic Oceans.

Orange puffball sponge (*Tethya aurantia*): 8cm/3in
This Atlantic and Pacific Ocean sponge occurs on tidal shores and in coastal waters down to 130m/430ft. It grows as an orange or a yellow sphere, with mushroom-shaped projections and very small oscules that are barely visible. It is preyed on by the colourful blue-ring topsnail (*Calliostoma annulatum*).

Giant barrel sponge (*Xestospongia muta*): 1.8m/6ft
One of the largest of sponges, this aptly named Caribbean species is one of many that lives in association with photosynthesizing algae, in the same way as reef-building corals. The algae in its tissues supply the sponge with sugars, while the sponge supplies the algae with other nutrients. Like corals, it also suffers from 'bleaching' when water temperatures are too high. Affected sponges turn white, crumble and die.

Myxilla incrustans

Several sponges may live on the shells of mobile molluscs and crustaceans. This species often lives on scallops, mainly on the upper, flat valve of the shell. The sponge probably benefits from the attachment by being carried into areas with clean, flowing, food-rich water, while the scallop may enjoy some protection from predatory starfish, which cannot get a good grip on the sponge-encrusted shell and so cannot pull the scallop open to eat it. The sponge does not only live on scallops, however; it is also found on the shells of crabs and on hydroids (relatives of anemones). It also lives on rocks, where it forms a thick, spreading cushion with raised ridges.

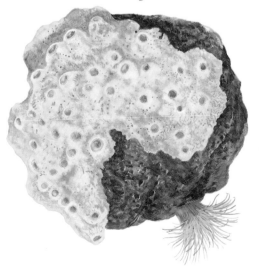

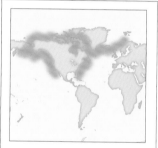

Distribution: North American range: Bering Sea to southern California; Gulf of St Lawrence to Maine and Florida; from Kotzebue Sound, Alaska, to Davis Strait, Canada. Also occurs North Atlantic.
Habitat: On shells or on rocks below the tideline down to 130m/427ft.
Food: Tiny edible particles filtered from the water.
Size: Up to 15cm/6in across; 5cm/2in thick.
Breeding: Sperm released into the water fertilize eggs retained within the sponge. Larval phase follows.
Status: Not listed by IUCN.

Identification: A soft, felt-like, encrusting sponge. It is pale to sulphur yellow or golden brown, The surface has numerous deep furrows, with large, unevenly distributed pores, or oscules, scattered over it.

STONY AND GORGONIAN CORALS, SEA-PENS

Most of the reef-forming corals belong to the large stony group (or true corals). The polyps of these corals produce a protective skeleton in the shape of a cup. They are often found with Gorgonian corals (of the order Gorgonacea) which have flexible skeletons of tough material.

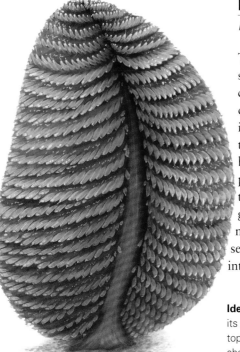

Phosphorescent sea-pen

Pennatula phosphorea

The sea-pens are colonies of polyps forming a feather- like structure with a strong central shaft, or rachis. The common name is derived from the use of feathers as quill pens in the past. The back of the shaft is covered in inhalent polyps (siphonozooids) that draw water into the colony, inflating it and keeping it erect. The branches carry tentacled stinging polyps that capture small planktonic animals. If touched, the polyps of the bioluminent sea-pen produce flashes or waves of glowing bioluminescence controlled by the colonial nervous system, which are clearly visible at night. The sea-pen is also able to contract its branches and withdraw into a tube below the mud surface.

Identification: Resembles a translucent, pink or yellowish feather, with its shaft embedded in the sea floor. The shaft is often bent over at the top. Stout, fleshy, triangular branches sprout alternately from the main shaft, and carry white polyps. Glows with blue-green light if disturbed.

Distribution: Common in North Sea and Western Scotland; north-eastern Atlantic and Mediterranean.
Habitat: Sandy and muddy seabeds at depths of 10–100m/33–330ft.
Food: Plankton and drifting organic particles.
Size: Up to 40cm/16in tall, with up to 25cm/10in projecting above the seabed.
Breeding: Sperm released into water and drawn into the polyps to fertilize eggs. Larvae form new colonies.
Status: Not listed in IUCN.

Brain coral

Oulophyllia bennettae

Identification: Massive, roughly spherical, brain-shaped, stony colonial coral that can be many metres across, with large, angular margins between the polyps, giving a convoluted appearance. The colour is greenish-grey.

The brain corals are among the largest of the stony corals, which form colonies of polyps supported by skeletons of calcium carbonate, or limestone. The common name comes from the corals' resemblance to the folded surface of a human brain. Each polyp resembles a sea anemone, with a central mouth cavity and a crown of stinging tentacles. In brain corals, the polyps are crammed together on the surface and linked by a continuous sheet of living tissue. This contains microscopic algae, or zooxanthellae, that make sugars by photosynthesis. This provides the coral with much of its food, but the coral also digests planktonic animals, and passes vital nutrients to the zooxanthellae. This symbiotic relationship is typical of reef-building corals.

Distribution: Indo-Pacific Ocean.
Habitat: Upper slopes of coral reefs, in sunlit waters.
Food: Small planktonic animals and floating organic particles, plus sugars made by symbiotic algae, using photosynthesis.
Size: Several metres across, depending on conditions.
Breeding: Eggs and sperm shed into the water, and fertilized eggs develop into free-swimming larvae that eventually settle to grow into new colonies.
Status: Appendix II CITES.

Staghorn coral

Acropora nobilis

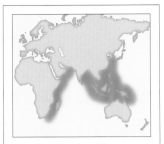

Distribution: Indo-Pacific; also Arabian Gulf and from eastern Africa to Madagascar.
Habitat: Coral reefs and sandy lagoons.
Food: Sugars made by symbiotic algae, using photosynthesis, plus small planktonic animals and drifting organic particles.
Size: Up to 5m/16.5ft across.
Breeding: Eggs and sperm shed into the water; fertilized eggs develop into planktonic larvae that settle to form new colonies.
Status: Appendix II CITES.

One of the most common and widespread of the branching stony corals, the staghorn coral occurs on a variety of reef sites from the upper reef slopes to deep lagoons, favouring places where there is plenty of water movement. Its common name comes from the way its branches grow like the antlers of deer, but it sometimes also grows in dense, shrub-like stands. The coral polyps that sprout from the branches take two forms, large and small, with the larger ones protruding like tubes. The variable colours are derived from the symbiotic algae that live within the coral's tissues, and which supply it with food.

Identification: Branching colonial coral with upright, widely spread cylindrical branches, often forming large colonies. In very shallow water the branches sometimes grow horizontally, and are fused together. Different colonies may be pinkish, cream, blue, yellow, green or brown, with pale branch ends.

Stony coral

Montipora venosa

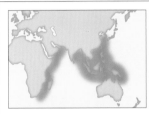

Distribution: Indo-Pacific; also Arabian Gulf and from eastern Africa to Madagascar.
Habitat: Coral reefs.
Food: Tiny drifting animals and organic particles, plus sugars made by symbiotic photosynthesizing algae.
Size: Colony may be massive.
Breeding: Eggs and sperm are shed into the water; fertilized eggs develop into planktonic larvae that eventually settle and grow into polyps that multiply into new colonies.
Status: Appendix II CITES

This quite small coral forms nodular structures covered with a honeycomb of pits containing the individual coral polyps. These are of two types: protruding and funnel-shaped. They have stinging tentacles that immobilize and gather live food. The nitrogenous proteins in the food supplement the sugars produced by the symbiotic algae living in the coral's tissues, providing essential nutrients for both the coral and the algae. Like all corals that live in a symbiotic relationship with photosynthesizing algae (zooxanthellae), it can thrive only in shallow, sunlit water.

Identification: Usually pale brown or blue, this coral forms irregular masses, rather than plates or branches, dotted with flower-like polyps.

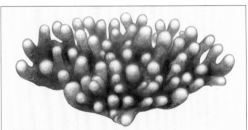

Porites cylindrica: 1m/3.25ft or more
A common Indo-Pacific reef coral, this is often the dominant species in lagoons and quiet back-reef zones. It forms branching yellow, cream, green or blue colonies with white tips. In calm water these tend to be compact and roughly hemispherical, but they are more irregular in places affected by wave action.

Orange sea-pen (*Ptilosarcus gurneyi*): 50cm/20in
This sea-pen has the same feather-like form as the bioluminescent sea-pen, but has pale branches fringed with orange feeding polyps, and an orange stem. It lives on sand or mud below the tideline of north-west Pacific coasts, from the Gulf of Alaska to California, to depths of 70m/230ft, and feeds on microscopic animals and organic debris.

Whip coral (*Juncella fragilis*): 1m/3.25ft
Growing among coral reefs are many gorgonians, such as the whip coral, which have skeletons of a tough, flexible, horny material called gorgonin. This forms a rod that supports the coral stem and the feeding polyps that sprout from it. This species occurs on Indo-Pacific reefs at depths of 5–30m/16–100ft. It often lives in association with a fish called a whip goby (*Bryaninops amplus*).

JELLYFISH

These cnidarians consist of a bell-shaped, jelly-like structure enclosing internal organs. Suspended from the bell are the animal's tentacles, covered in stinging cells. Most jellyfish undergo a life cycle involving a free-swimming medusa stage and a sessile polyp stage. In scyphozoan jellies, often referred to as 'true jellyfish', the former is the dominant stage – and the state in which they are most likely to be seen.

Moon jelly
Aurelia aurita

Among the world's most common true jellyfish species, the moon jelly (or common jellyfish) often occurs in large numbers, drifting together on currents and tides. Each animal is a disc of jelly with a central mouth on the underside surrounded by four short arms. Inside the body is a branching system of channels – the jellyfish version of a digestive and vascular system – which distributes nutrients and oxygen around the body. There is no brain or central nervous system, just a loose network of nerves that coordinates responses to stimuli, such as light and the 'scent' of chemicals in the water. The moon jelly feeds mainly on particles that accumulate around the edges of the bell among the short tentacles. Moon jellies have only a very mild sting.

Identification: Saucer-shaped bell fringed with short, fine tentacles. Four frilly edged arms hanging down from bell. Four pinkish or purple, horseshoe-shaped reproductive organs visible inside the body among radiating channels of branched gut.

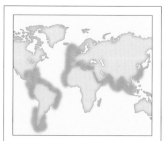

Distribution: Tropical and temperate oceans and seas.
Habitat: Surface waters, most commonly in coastal areas; may enter estuaries.
Food: Small particles of organic debris and plankton.
Size: Up to 50cm/20in across.
Breeding: Alternating sexual and asexual generations: medusae produce eggs and sperm. Fertilized egg develops into a larva, then a sessile polyp, which buds off more sexually reproducing medusae.
Status: Not listed by IUCN.

Sea wasp
Chironex fleckeri

Also known as the box jellyfish, this member of the class Cubozoa is probably the world's most venomous marine animal. Drifting in shallow coastal waters, and relatively inconspicuous due to its pale coloration, bathers unfortunate enough to bump into the sticky, stinging tentacles of this species may be injected with cardiotoxic and neurotoxic venom of enormous potency, often resulting in death. It is thought that the stinging cells are stimulated to 'fire' by sensing chemicals present on the skin. Such lethal and fast-acting venom is designed to immobilize quickly the jellyfish's natural prey of shrimps and other small creatures, thus avoiding damage to the sea wasp's delicate tissues caused by struggling food animals. Food is transferred to the mouth to be digested. Adult sea wasps spawn in shallow water near river mouths, and the fertilized eggs develop into polyps, which attach themselves to rocks. Later, small jellyfish develop from the polyps and migrate to the sea to grow.

Identification: The bell is cube- or box-shaped. In each corner there are between 10 and 60 stinging tentacles hanging down. Apart from a blue tinge, bell and tentacles are almost transparent.

Distribution: Indo-Pacific Ocean, including northern Australian waters.
Habitat: Shallow waters at the edges of beaches.
Food: Small fish and crustaceans.
Size: Bell 20cm/8in across; tentacles up to 3m/10ft long.
Breeding: Alternating sexual and asexual generations: medusae produce eggs and sperm. Fertilized egg develops into a larva, then a sessile polyp, which buds off more sexually reproducing medusae.
Status: Not listed by IUCN.

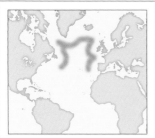

Distribution: North Atlantic.
Habitat: Floating in surface waters.
Food: Small marine animals.
Size: Umbrella about 15cm/6in across.
Breeding: Alternating sexual and asexual generations: medusae produce eggs and sperm. Fertilized egg develops into a larva, then a sessile polyp, which buds off more sexually reproducing medusae.
Status: Not listed by IUCN.

Blue jellyfish

Cyanea lamarckii

Floating majestically in the waters of the North Atlantic Ocean, the medusa stage of the blue jellyfish (*cyaneus* means 'dark blue' in Latin) is an attractive species, but do not be deceived as it can deliver powerful stings from its numerous dangling tentacles. The animal's umbrella is saucer-shaped, and a characteristic of the species at this stage of its life cycle is that all around the edge it is drawn out into about 32 lobes. The tentacles, armed with nematocysts (stinging organs found in jellyfish), hang down from the umbrella in clusters. Inside the tentacles are four shorter, frilly arms, which are used to transfer prey immobilized by the nematocysts to the central mouth, where they are consumed before being digested.

Identification: A blue-white jellyfish with a saucer-shaped umbrella with 32 peripheral lobes. Tentacles hang down in eight clusters. It has four frilly arms, shorter than tentacles.

Upside-down jellyfish (*Cassiopea andromeda*): 30cm/12in across
This jellyfish is often mistaken for a large sea anemone, which it resembles as it lies on the bottom, mouth upward, with its frilly tentacles on outstretched arms waving in the current created by its pulsating bell. It is brown-yellow with white streaks and spots. Found in lagoons and intertidal shallows in the Indo-Pacific Ocean, the upside-down jellyfish feeds on plankton as well as food produced by the symbiotic algae in its tissues. Can deliver a painful sting.

Compass jellyfish (*Chrysaora hysoscella*): 30cm/12in across
The compass jellyfish has a large, saucer-shaped umbrella with a pattern of radiating lines. The edge of the lobed umbrella bears 24 trailing tentacles armed with stinging cells and a series of sense organs. The four mouth arms of this species are shorter than the tentacles. Drifting with the tides and currents, the compass jellyfish is found in the Atlantic Ocean.

Sea wasp (*Carybdea alata*): Up to 23cm/9in high
This Indo-Pacific species carries a powerful venom in its stinging cells. It may come close to shore in regular monthly swarms, when it can pose a real hazard to bathers. The bell is rounded in cross-section but flattened at the top, and is typically taller than it is wide. Hanging from the transparent bell are four pink or yellow-pink tentacles, often marked with brown rings.

Stalked jellyfish

Haliclystus auricula

Unlike most jellyfish, in which the medusa stage is a graceful, free-swimming organism floating in the ocean currents, a few species spend this part of their life cycle firmly anchored in one place. One such jellyfish is the stalked, or sessile, jellyfish. It attaches itself to seagrasses, seaweeds such as *Fucus* species or firmer supports, such as rocks, by means of an adhesive stalk. The trumpet-shaped bell is drawn out into eight lobes, each one bearing a cluster of small, club-like tentacles that the creature uses to catch plankton and other small marine animals. There are also kidney-shaped anchors found between the tentacles. Although the stalked jellyfish is fairly common throughout its range, it is not a large creature and so is often overlooked, particularly when it is not fully extended.

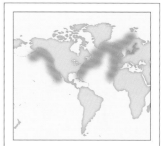

Distribution: North Pacific to California; North Atlantic; Baltic Sea.
Habitat: Attached to seaweeds or rocks in rockpools and shallow water.
Food: Small marine animals.
Size: Bell about 2.5cm/1in across; stalk about 1.5cm/0.6in high.
Breeding: Alternating sexual and asexual generations: medusae produce eggs and sperm.
Status: Not listed by IUCN.

Identification: Bell is a trumpet- or flower-like cup extended into eight lobes, each one bearing club-like tentacles. Attaches to substrate by an adhesive stalk. Colour variable: mainly translucent shades of green, brown, orange or red.

GASTROPOD MOLLUSCS

Although well represented in terrestrial habitats by snails and slugs, more than two-thirds of all gastropod species are marine, and indeed the group's geological origins were exclusively marine. As demonstrated by many nudibranchs, not all gastropods have shells, but the species included here have some of the most distinctive and beautiful shells seen in this class of molluscs.

Purple topshell

Gibbula umbilicalis

Many of the marine gastropod molluscs known as topshells have attractively marked shells, and the purple topshell is no exception. As its common name suggests, the shell is characterized by purple stripes radiating down from the apex. On the underside is a large, round umbilicus (the point around which the whorls of the shell are coiled) – although a form without the umbilicus has also been recorded. The inner part of the shell is lined with a layer of mother-of-pearl. The purple topshell is a relatively small species that frequently occurs on sheltered rocky shores, where it grazes on seaweeds. This species is tolerant of brackish water conditions and it is also found in estuarine areas.

Identification: The shell has flattish whorls; overall, the shell is wider than it is high. Large umbilicus present on the underside of the shell. Colour dull grey-green with reddish-purple stripes radiating from the apex. It is not unusual for areas at the top of the shell to become abraded, revealing attractive mother-of-pearl surfaces.

Distribution: North-eastern Atlantic; also from Nova Scotia to Maine.
Habitat: On seaweeds and rocks on the middle and lower shore; also estuaries.
Food: Seaweeds, mainly of the *Fucus* species.
Size: 1.5cm/0.6in high; 2.2cm/0.9in across.
Breeding: Reproduces sexually; eggs are shed and fertilized externally; larval phase follows.
Status: Not listed by IUCN.

Giant triton

Charonia tritonis

Identification: Elegant shell with rounded whorls, a tall spire and a large, flared lip. Colour of outer shell creamy with dark brown swirls and crescent-shaped blotches; shell aperture is orange-brown, alternating with cream around the lip.

The tritons are a group of gastropod molluscs that are widely distributed in warm, tropical oceans – mainly because their larvae have a long free-swimming period and may, therefore, travel great distances before settling. The giant triton is the largest member of the family, and is characterized by its tall, elegant spire, wide, flared lip and the beautiful markings on both the outside and the aperture of the shell. Because of its size and its appearance, this shell is very popular with collectors. The giant triton is also famous for being one of several species of gastropod shell that is used as a trumpet (once the apex has been cut off). In fact, it is also known as the trumpet triton. It is a carnivorous species found on coral reefs, where it will hunt other invertebrates.

Distribution: Western part of Indo-Pacific Ocean.
Habitat: On reefs in water down to about 25m/82ft.
Food: Other molluscs and sea urchins.
Size: 40cm/15.75in high.
Breeding: Reproduces sexually; eggs are shed and fertilized externally; larval phase follows.
Status: Not listed by IUCN.

Eyed cowrie

Cypraea argus

Distribution: Red Sea and East Africa, including Madagascar; widespread in shallow waters of Indo-Pacific.
Habitat: On reefs in water down to about 25m/82ft.
Food: Algae.
Size: 7.5cm/3in high.
Breeding: Reproduces sexually; eggs are shed and fertilized externally; larval phase follows.
Status: Not listed by IUCN.

Smooth, lustrous and beautifully and variously marked, the 200 or so species of cowrie – a member of the gastropod family Cypraeidae – have long been popular with shell collectors. In some cultures, cowrie shells have been used as money. Many have evocative common names that describe the type of markings seen on the shell. The eyed cowrie is a widespread species, with a heavy, somewhat elongated, cylindrical shell. Like other cowries, the underside of the shell has a long, narrow aperture, the edges of which are marked by prominent tooth-like projections. It is from this aperture that the animal extends its muscular foot, which it uses to move around the substrate. By day, the eyed cowrie hides among rocks and crevices on reefs, but at night it leaves its refuge to feed on algae.

Identification: Shell roughly cylindrical, the apex a flattened coil of about three whorls. The aperture is wider at the front than at the rear. Light brown or beige above with several darker, broad encircling bands; brown circles over upper surface and sides. Underside light brown with dark-brown bands either side of aperture.

Common topshell (*Calliostoma zizyphinum*): 2.5cm/1in high
Topshells come by their common name because of their resemblance to spinning tops – an old-fashioned children's toy. Also known as the painted topshell, this species has a straight-sided, conical shell that is approximately as wide at the base as it is high. It is either cream or brown in colour with pink or brown markings. It is found in Atlantic waters on rocks from the lower shore down to about 100m/330ft.

Geographer cone shell (*Conus geographicus*): 10cm/4in
All species of cone shell are predatory, injecting venom into their prey from an extensible proboscis or 'harpoon'. The geographer cone shell is one of the most venomous of all. The shell of this Indo-Pacific species has a low spire and a very large aperture. The colour of the shell is cream to light brown or blue-white with thin reticulation, and there are two or three encircling brown bands.

Rough star shell (*Astraea rugosa*): 5cm/2in
The thick, conical shell of this species is about as wide at the base as it is high. It is reddish-brown in colour and has about seven whorls with thorny ridges. In life, the aperture can be sealed by a spiral calcareous operculum, or cover. It is found on rocks from the lower shore downwards in the Mediterranean Sea and Atlantic Ocean.

Common whelk

Buccinum undatum

A common and widespread mollusc, the common whelk has long been a popular seafood snack, often sold cooked and ready to eat at seaside 'whelk stalls'. In life, the common whelk is a scavenger, feeding on virtually anything edible, including the remains of fish. The shell is thick, with a tall spire and a bulging body whorl. The shell does not have any distinctive colour patterning, but is clearly marked with growth ridges. Because of their size and durability, empty common whelk shells are a common sight on beaches. The shape and size of the common whelk's shell is ideally suited to soft-bodied hermit crabs, which frequently choose empty whelk shells as a 'home'. Another feature of the common whelk is sometimes seen on the seashore – the spongy, spherical mass of egg cases from which the embryos hatch.

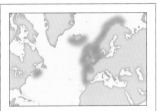

Distribution: North-eastern Atlantic; also from Nova Scotia to Maine.
Habitat: On muddy and sandy bottoms in water down to about 100m/330ft.
Food: Virtually anything that is edible.
Size: 8cm/3in high.
Breeding: Reproduces sexually; eggs are shed and fertilized externally; larval phase follows.
Status: Not listed by IUCN.

Identification: Shell heavy and durable with a tall spire and an inflated body whorl. Shell is marked with growth lines and ribs. Short siphonal canal. Large, smooth aperture. Colour is pale brown, cream or grey with some darker-coloured bands.

BIVALVE MOLLUSCS

The members of the class Bivalvia described here include the heaviest of all molluscs, which can grow to a prodigious weight, as well as some smaller-growing species that swim by clapping the two valves of their shell together to expel water. In some species, particularly the giant clams, the shell's interior, known as the mantle, is very brightly coloured, and can dwarf the outer edges entirely when on display.

Giant clam

Tridacna maxima

Identification: Valves are massive and thick; elongated oval in shape with about five undulating ribs. Edges of valves are scalloped and interlocking. Interior of shell is white; exterior is usually encrusted with marine growths, such as barnacles, sponges and bryozoans.

Giant clams are the heaviest-known mollusc and specimens can reach a weight of 230kg/507lb, although this particular species is smaller than some of its relatives. Giant clams lie, hinge downwards, among coralline and rocky bottoms in shallow water. The gaping valves normally remain open to allow light to reach the symbiotic algae embedded in the clam's mantle tissues. The algae manufacture sugars and other nutrients on which the clam feeds, in addition to the food particles it obtains by filter feeding. The size and permanence of the clams mean that it is also an attractive site for other organisms to colonize, and the shells are often encrusted with marine growths. Giant clams are an important food source to humans in some regions, which has led to overfishing.

Distribution: Red Sea and East Africa, including Madagascar; widespread in shallow waters of Indo-Pacific.
Habitat: On coral reefs in shallow water, down to about 20m/65ft.
Food: Filter feeds on minute particles; also absorbs nutrients manufactured by symbiotic algae.
Size: Up to 1m/3.25ft across.
Breeding: Reproduces sexually; eggs are shed and fertilized externally; larval phase follows.
Status: Listed as Lower Risk by IUCN.

Fan mussel

Pinna fragilis

This species of mussel is a member of the group of bivalves known as pen shells. These are large, thin, paddle- or fan-shaped molluscs that live in the calm waters of warm and temperate oceans. They remain in an upright position with the narrow end of their shells attached to rocks by strands of tough byssus threads or by embedding themselves partly in supportive muddy sand or gravelly substrates. The fan mussel is a gregarious species, and once anchored by its byssus threads *en masse*, individual specimens are very difficult to dislodge. The gold-coloured byssus threads are very durable and fine in texture, and they were once used for weaving into fine garments for royalty – the 'Field of the Cloth of Gold' mentioned in the time of English king Henry VIII is believed to be a reference to him wearing a garment made of fan mussel byssus threads and byssus fabric is also mentioned in the Book of Genesis.

Identification: Valves are fan-shaped, equal in size and shape and smooth-edged. The outer surface bears concentric ribs and lines and the colour is brown.

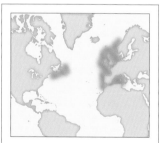

Distribution: North-east Atlantic and northern Pacific from Nova Scotia to Maine; western Mediterranean.
Habitat: In sand or gravelly sea floors or on rocks, lower intertidal or subtidal regions.
Food: Minute food particles filtered from the water.
Size: 30cm/12in long.
Breeding: Sexes are separate; little else known.
Status: Not listed by IUCN.

Great scallop

Pecten maximus

Distribution: Patchy; north-eastern Atlantic and parts of the Mediterranean.
Habitat: Sand or gravelly ocean and sea floors at depths of 5–150m/16–490ft.
Food: Minute food particles filtered from the water, including algae, bacteria and other microscopic organic matter.
Size: 15cm/6in long.
Breeding: Hermaphrodite.
Status: Not listed by IUCN.

The shell of the great scallop is one of the best-known mollusc shells. As well as the food value of the animal living inside, the fluted shell is used for purposes ranging from ashtrays to dishes. The shell also features in the painting *The Birth of Venus* by Sandro Botticelli. Like other scallops, it has a fan-shaped shell characterized by two large 'ears', one on each side of the umbones, the often tapering, first part of the shell to be formed. When the great scallop gapes its shell, a fringe of sensory tentacles dotted with numerous small eyes can be seen. The scallop rests with the flatter of its two valves uppermost. When threatened, it claps the valves together, expelling water in a jet propulsion action, and swimming to safety.

Identification: Broad, fan-shaped valves; upper (left) valve flatter than lower (right) valve; 'ears' prominent; valves each bear about 16 conspicuous ribs; the edges of the valves are broadly serrated. Upper valve brownish-red; lower valve brownish-white.

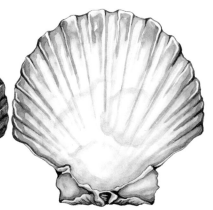

Common saddle oyster (*Anomia ephippium*): 6cm/2.4in long
The brown-white upper (left) valve of this bivalve mollusc is thick, domed and scaly; often encrusted with marine organisms. The lower (right) valve is thin, flat and saddle-shaped.

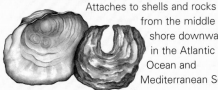

Attaches to shells and rocks from the middle shore downwards in the Atlantic Ocean and Mediterranean Sea.

File shell (*Lima lima*): 2.5cm/1in long
This species has the characteristically asymmetrical shape of other file shells, although each valve is similar. It swims by clapping its valves together to expel water. Found in crevices in shallow Mediterranean waters.

Warty venus (*Venus verrucosa*): 5cm/2in
The thick-walled, robust shell is rounded and its exterior has concentric ridges bearing tubercles towards the anterior and posterior margins. Exterior is grey, white or yellow; interior is white. Found in sand or gravel from the lower shore to about 100m/328ft in the Atlantic Ocean and Mediterranean Sea.

Sand gaper (*Mya arenicola*): 15cm/6in
The sand gaper is one of a group of molluscs that typically burrow in soft, muddy substrates in cool waters. The off-white shell is elongate, with rough growth lines covering the exterior surface. Found from the lower shore and in estuaries down to 70m/230ft in Atlantic Ocean waters.

White hammer oyster

Malleus albus

The small family of hammer oysters gets its common name from the shape of the shells, which is reminiscent of a hammer or mallet. Indeed, when first encountered, the shell has sometimes been mistaken for a small, abandoned, growth-encrusted hammer. The narrow shell of the white hammer oyster is very elongated, with slightly wavy or undulating edges. The long 'hammerhead' part of the shell is formed by the very extended hinge lines. Like most other hammer oysters, this species lies partly buried in mud or sand in tropical intertidal reef areas. Its unusual shape means that the shell is popular with collectors.

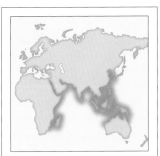

Distribution: Red Sea and East Africa, including Madagascar; widespread in shallow waters of Indo-Pacific.
Habitat: In sand or mud in intertidal reef areas.
Food: Minute food particles filtered from the water.
Size: 15cm/6in long.
Breeding: Reproduces sexually by eggs and sperm.
Status: Not listed by IUCN.

Identification: Valves elongated and narrow with long, narrower wings at right angles, formed by extended hinge lines. Edges of shell undulating. Exterior of shell consists of overlapping lamellae. Colour of shell creamy-beige or dirty white with a blue-black muscle scar on the inner, nacreous surface.

CEPHALOPOD MOLLUSCS

Cephalopods are mainly active creatures with well-developed senses. They have cylindrical or sac-like bodies, and most species have no external shell – although some have a small internal shell. The foot is modified to form a ring of suckered tentacles surrounding the mouth, which itself has a parrot-like beak. Octopuses can swim by jet propulsion, forcing water rapidly from a siphon.

Greater blue-ringed octopus

Hapalochlaena lunulata

Identification: Slightly pointed, sac-like body covered with papillae. Mouth a horny beak surrounded by eight relatively short arms, each bearing two rows of suckers. Colour usually beige, dark brown or yellow; turns vivid yellow with electric blue rings if threatened.

Hiding in rockpools and shallow coral, or marooned on wet sand as the tide recedes, this small octopus looks innocuous. However, it is one of the world's most venomous animals, with a toxin in its saliva estimated to be 10,000 times more deadly than cyanide. Delivered via a horny beak, the toxins have been evolved to kill crabs – the octopus's main prey – and also to ward off predators. Normally a beige or dark yellow colour with brown patches, its body erupts with electric-blue rings as a warning. Although this display may be sufficient to deter natural predators, it may in fact encourage the unwary beachcomber to pick the animal up. The greater blue-ringed octopus is an ambush predator.

Distribution: Western part of Indo-Pacific, particularly Japan to Australia.
Habitat: Hiding in crevices in tidal pools and among coral in shallow water down to about 20m/65ft.
Food: Mainly crabs; also shrimps and molluscs.
Size: 20cm/8in across arms.
Breeding: 50–100 eggs guarded by female until they hatch.
Status: Not listed by IUCN.

Common octopus

Octopus vulgaris

Identification: Sac-like body lacking a shell; warty upper surface. Eight arms, each bearing two rows of muscular suckers; arms relatively long. Colour variable: greenish or grey-brown, according to mood.

This eight-legged cephalopod is one of the most widespread of all marine animals. Highly territorial, it lurks in holes and under ledges waiting for its prey, which is captured at night with long, suckered arms. New research suggests that it 'stockpiles' supplies of bivalves and other sedentary food items near its lair, and sometimes it camouflages its lair with stones and shells. The octopus can change shape to squeeze into tiny gaps, and change colour according to its mood and surroundings. The common octopus has highly developed sense organs. In laboratories, it has been shown to have the ability to learn simple tasks and undertake problem solving.

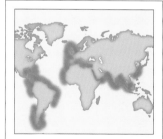

Distribution: Found worldwide in most temperate and tropical oceans and adjoining seas.
Habitat: In crevices of rocks close to the shore and in shallow water down to 200m/650ft.
Food: Crustaceans, molluscs and other marine animals.
Size: Up to 1m/3.25ft long.
Breeding: Internal fertilization; up to 500,000 eggs laid on substrate in shallow water and protected by female.
Status: Not listed by IUCN.

Paper nautilus

Argonauta argo

Distribution: Worldwide in tropical and subtropical oceans.
Habitat: Swimming in surface water as well as creeping on the bottom. Rarely found near shores.
Food: Plankton and other small organisms.
Size: Female up to 20cm/8in; male 1cm/0.4in. Shell up to 30cm/12in.
Breeding: Internal fertilization; eggs carried by the female, protected within her shell until they hatch.
Status: Not listed by IUCN.

Despite its common name, *Argonauta* is not a nautiloid, but is a member of the order Octopoda. The female is about 20 times larger than the male. Her body is partly encased in a thin, coiled shell, which she holds tightly using two modified arms with flattened ends. During reproduction, the male inserts his sperm into the female's pouch with a modified arm called a hectocotylus. The fertilized eggs are protected inside the shell as they develop. Due to its fairly small size and pelagic habits, the paper nautilus is rarely seen by seashore visitors, although it is not especially rare. The shell, sometimes washed ashore – usually without its attendant female – is prized by collectors.

Identification: Female has sac-like body bearing eight arms, two of which are modified and have spatulate ends for gripping shell. Shell is coiled, laterally compressed, and has a narrow keel and numerous sharp nodules. Male is much smaller and lacks shell. Colour and pattern of animal variable: from silver-white to grey, red or blue. Shell white.

Long-finned squid (*Loligo vulgaris*): 50cm/20in
The pink or whitish body of this squid has brown mottling on the upper surface. Wide, conspicuous fins running halfway along the body and joined at the end form a spearhead shape. The head bears eight short arms, and two long, retractable, suckered tentacles for capturing prey. Found in shallow and deeper water in the Atlantic Ocean.

Lesser octopus (*Eledone cirrhosa*): 50cm/20in
This octopus is normally red-brown above and paler below, but it can rapidly change colour to match its surroundings. The lesser octopus has only one row of suckers on each of its eight, slender arms. The body is warty in appearance. Found among rocks and in crevices in the Atlantic Ocean from the lower shore downwards, where it lies in wait for prey.

Caribbean reef octopus (*Octopus briareus*): 60cm/24in
This species is blue-green, with mottled brown markings. It is solitary and, like other octopuses, it can rapidly change colour to match its surroundings. It feeds at night on crustaceans, other molluscs and small fish, which it hunts on reefs and seagrass beds. Found in warm, shallow waters of the western Atlantic Ocean.

Common cuttlefish

Sepia officinalis

The cuttlefish are active, swimming molluscs with a reduced, internal shell (the 'cuttlebone' often offered to cagebirds). The common cuttlefish has a head bearing eight short, suckered arms and two long tentacles; these surround a mouth armed with a horny beak. Food is grabbed in the tentacles and transferred by the arms to the mouth. Large eyes help it detect prey and navigate with speed and precision. Swimming is achieved by the rippling action of lateral fins that run along each side of the body. On the underside of the body is a large funnel through which water is expelled to help the cuttlefish shoot rapidly backwards to escape predators. It can also quickly change colour to help it blend in with its surroundings.

Identification: Flattened, oval, cylindrical body bearing lateral fins. Large head bears eight short arms and two long, suckered tentacles with spatulate pads that can be extended and retracted; eyes large and well developed. Colour variable: often brown or black lateral stripes or mottled pattern over cream or off-white ground colour, but colour and pattern may be rapidly changed at will.

Distribution: North-eastern Atlantic including North Sea down to equatorial Africa; Mediterranean Sea.
Habitat: Swimming or lying on bottom, often near shore.
Food: Molluscs, fish, crabs and other crustaceans.
Size: 30cm/12in.
Breeding: Internal fertilization; egg masses protected by female.
Status: Not listed by IUCN.

SHRIMPS, PRAWNS AND LOBSTERS

The protective exoskeleton, which is common to all animals in the phylum Crustacea, must be shed and replaced to allow for growth. Their abundance and good-tasting flesh means that several of the species described here – particularly those of temperate, muddy waters – are important commercial species.

Spiny lobster

Palinurus elephas

Identification: Typical elongated lobster shape with carapace covered in tiny, hair-like spines, and segmented, flexible abdomen terminating in broad telson (tail). The species is notable for its long, stout antennae. Lacks large, crushing pincers. Predominantly red-brown in colour.

This heavily armoured, bottom-dwelling crustacean is distinguished by its extremely long, flexible antennae, which it uses to locate food by touch and scent. Its pincers are very small and not obvious, although the limbs that carry them are slightly stouter than its walking legs. The pincers are not strong enough to crush hard-shelled prey, so the spiny lobster feeds on soft-bodied animals, such as starfish and marine worms. It frequently hunts on the open seabed, but retreats to crevices if threatened. These lobsters are heavily fished in some areas, and this has made them increasingly scarce.

Distribution: North-eastern Atlantic Ocean and Mediterranean Sea.
Habitat: Rocky seabeds below the intertidal zone, mostly below 20m/66ft.
Food: Worms, small crabs, starfish, soft-bodied molluscs and dead animals.
Size: 50cm/20in.
Breeding: Females carry eggs for 5–9 months until they hatch. The larvae drift in the plankton for many weeks before settling on the seabed.
Status: Not listed by IUCN.

Scampi

Nephrops norvegicus

The well-armed scampi, Dublin Bay prawn or Norway lobster is an opportunist predator that spends much of the day in a burrow on a soft, muddy seabed, particularly in shallow, sunlit water. At night it emerges to hunt for prey, especially other crustaceans, such as prawns and small crabs. Having a relatively heavy, calcified skeleton, it lives mainly on the bottom, but it can swim if necessary. It can also use its broad tail-fan to propel itself rapidly through the water to escape from enemies. It is heavily fished to be peeled and prepared as scampi, or served whole as langoustine.

Identification: A slender, elegant, bright orange and white lobster with large black eyes, two pairs of antennae – one pair being longer than its body – and slim, though quite powerful, spiny pincers. It also has small claws or pincers on the second and third pairs of legs. It is reasonably heavily armoured and has a broad tail-fan (or telson).

Distribution: North-eastern Atlantic Ocean, from Iceland to Morocco, and in the Mediterranean Sea
Habitat: Soft seabeds down to 20–800m/66–2,625ft.
Food: Other crustaceans, molluscs, marine worms, starfish, sea urchins.
Size: Up to 25cm/10in.
Breeding: Fertilized eggs are carried under the female's abdomen for 8–9 months, during which time females tend to stay in their burrows. They emerge to allow their planktonic larvae to hatch and disperse in the currents.
Status: Not listed by IUCN.

Broad-clawed porcelain crab

Porcellana platycheles

Distribution: North-eastern Atlantic from Shetland to the Canaries; Mediterranean Sea.
Habitat: Sheltered muddy, stony shores down to a few metres.
Food: Edible detritus filtered from the water.
Size: Carapace up to 1.5cm/0.6in long.
Breeding: Females carry eggs beneath their bodies until they hatch into planktonic larvae, which then disperse in the currents before settling to metamorphose into adult form.
Status: Not listed by IUCN.

Although this species looks like a very hairy crab in its basic shape, it is, like all porcelain crabs, more closely related to the squat lobsters. Like the latter, it has a pair of long antennae and only three functioning pairs of walking legs. It does have a fourth pair of legs, but they are small and usually tucked out of sight. It walks sideways, however, like the true crabs – an adaptation that allows it to move quite fast when necessary. Its flattened body is perfect for hiding beneath rocks, which it grips with the claws on its legs. It uses the hairs on its claws to filter edible debris from the the water, wiping them through its mouthparts to feed.

Identification: A small, conspicuously hairy looking crab with an almost round carapace. Large, flattened, hairy claws, one pair of long antennae and only three visible pairs of walking legs. Usually greyish-brown on top, and a dirty yellowish-white below.

Slipper lobster (*Parribacus antarcticus*): up to 25cm/10in
This species lives on Indo-Pacific coral reefs. Its legs are hidden beneath a broad, flattened carapace with shovel-like extensions that are actually modified antennae. Its eyes are mounted on top of its carapace. During the day, it hides in crevices, but at night it emerges to forage over the reef for prey, such as shellfish, worms and fish. It also scavenges dead animals.

Painted dancing shrimp (*Hymenocera picta*): 6cm/2.4in
This beautiful coral reef shrimp from the Pacific Ocean is white with pale red-brown blotches that resemble patches of wet watercolour paint. Its body cuticle and claws are extended into flared plates that the shrimp uses in a dancing display. It lives in pairs, hiding in crevices by day and slipping out at night to hunt. It preys on starfish, flipping them on to their backs and eating them alive.

Camel (candy) shrimp (*Rhynchocinetes durbanensis*): 4cm/1.6in
Often found living inside large sponges, this Indo-Pacific shrimp is transparent with a dazzling pattern of red and white lines and dots, and a long, toothed, moveable rostrum that is usually held up at an angle. It prefers to congregate in coral crevices or under overhangs, and feeds on invertebrates such as sea anemones.

Scarlet skunk cleaner shrimp

Lysmata amboinensis

This fragile-looking tropical shrimp feeds mainly on parasites and dead skin tissue and scales picked from the bodies of reef fish. The fish recognize that this is a useful service, and make deliberate visits to the 'cleaning stations' where the shrimps live and ply their trade. Several shrimps often work together, for unlike some species – such as the banded coral shrimp – they are not aggressively territorial. They will remove parasites from fish that would normally pose a threat to small crustaceans, but sometimes fall victim to fish that are more concerned with finding a meal than maintaining skin hygiene.

Distribution: Indo-Pacific.
Habitat: Coral reefs.
Food: Parasites and dead skin picked from other fish, plus detritus and planktonic organisms from the water.
Size: Up to 8cm/3.2in.
Breeding: Females carry green eggs beneath their bodies; these hatch into tiny transparent larvae that disperse over the reef.
Status: Not listed by IUCN.

Identification: A delicate shrimp with slender white pincers, six long, white antennae and black eyes. Very colourful: yellow flanks and legs and a scarlet back, with a white 'skunk stripe' running from between the eyes to the base of the tail. The tail fan is scarlet with white patches.

CRABS

Most of us tend to be more familiar with the types of crabs we seeing scuttling around our seashores and swimming in rockpools at low tide. Many of these same crustaceans, however, are also found in sub-littoral habitats, including several of the species shown here. Some of these shallow-water crabs tend to hunt for food, or seek shelter from predators, by digging deep into the sand and gravel of the sea bed.

Shame-faced crab

Calappa granulata

Identification: Rounded crab with ridged carapace, short legs and broad, flattened pincers, each with a crest like a cock's comb. Very light brown in colour with reddish spots.

One of the most common crabs in the Mediterranean, this burrowing species is named for the way it holds its very broad, crested pincers over its 'facial' region, with just its eyes peeping over. One of the pincers is specialized for breaking into the shells of the clams and cockles that form much of its food, with a blunt projection on the mobile part of the pincer that acts against the basal part of the pincer like a nutcracker. It finds its prey by digging through the sand or mud, and spends much of its time wholly or partly buried in the seabed. If alarmed, it retracts both its pincers and legs to form a tight, armoured ball.

Distribution: Eastern Atlantic from Bay of Biscay to Western Sahara including Azores, Madeira, Canaries, Cape Verde Is.; also Mediterranean Sea.
Habitat: Soft seabeds from 10–400m/33–1,300ft.
Food: Small burrowing animals, such as clams, and other molluscs; also scavenges.
Size: Carapace about 11cm/4.3in wide.
Breeding: Females carry eggs beneath their bodies; these hatch into planktonic larvae, which are dispersed by tides and currents to new habitats.
Status: Not listed by IUCN.

Decorator crab

Camposcia retusa

Identification: Long-legged, short-clawed crab with a narrow, pointed carapace and twin horns projecting between its black, teardrop-shaped eyes. Often found in coral rubble area. Very variable camouflage of sponges, algae, seaweed and other organisms and debris attached to its carapace and legs by a dense covering of hooked hairs.

Almost impossible to detect until it moves, this small spider crab conceals its identity by 'decorating' itself with encrusting animals, algae and debris. It uses its pincers to nip off bits of living sponges and seaweed, or selects suitable shell fragments, and then sticks them firmly on to the fine, hooked hairs that cover its body and legs. The attached sponges and algae often continue to grow, and tiny animals frequently settle among them to create a whole mobile community. Only the black eyes and tips of the pincers remain undecorated, enabling the crab to find and then deal with its food.

Distribution: Coral seas of the western Pacific and Indian Oceans.
Habitat: Sandy places on coral reefs, such as lagoons and among coral rubble.
Food: Small animals as well as carrion.
Size: About 5cm/2in wide.
Breeding: Females carry eggs that hatch into planktonic larvae; these are dispersed over the reefs by water currents before settling.
Status: Not listed by IUCN.

Marbled rock crab

Pachygrapsus marmoratus

Distribution: North-eastern Atlantic Ocean from Brittany to the Canaries; Mediterranean and Black Seas.
Habitat: Rocky shores and adjacent shallow, rocky seabeds. Also under stones on sandy mud in estuaries and lagoons.
Food: Omnivorous.
Size: About 8cm/3in wide; carapace about 3.8cm/1.5in wide.
Breeding: Female carries eggs beneath her body; these hatch into swimming larvae that drift with the plankton.
Status: Listed by IUCN as Vulnerable in certain regions.

This species is the most common shore crab found in southern Europe. It is also known as the running crab because of its ability to run rapidly over rocks and then slip quickly into tight cracks to escape from predators. It is able to survive for long periods out of the water by carrying a supply of oxygenated water in its gill cavity, and takes the opportunity to scavenge over the shoreline at low tide looking for dead and damaged molluscs and other edible material stranded on the shore. These crabs are often caught and eaten by land predators, such as introduced American mink.

Identification: A usually dark, violet-brown or green crab, often with a marbled pattern. Fairly small pincers – larger on the male – flattened legs and an almost square, convex carapace. The front edge between the eyes is virtually straight, but there are three pointed teeth on each side.

Edible crab (*Cancer pagurus*): 14cm/5.5in Carapace reddish-brown in colour and broadly oval and with approximately nine indentations on the edge at each side giving a 'pie-crust' appearance. Primarily a scavenger, but it will also prey on molluscs that are crushed by the crab's massive, black-tipped claws. Found from the shore down to 90m/300ft in the Atlantic Ocean.

Red-and-white painted crab (*Lophozozymus pictor*): up to 20cm/8in
Deep red or orange with white spots, this thick-bodied crab is common on coral reefs, where it shelters in crevices between the coral heads or beneath broken slabs of coral rock. It feeds on marine algae and small planktonic organisms, as well as scavenging for debris. Its flesh can be extremely poisonous, causing paralytic shellfish poisoning (PSP), because the crab feeds on molluscs that accumulate toxins produced by certain planktonic organisms.

Pea crab (*Pinnotheres pisum*): up to 2cm/0.8in
Female pea crabs live in the mantle cavities of bivalve molluscs, such as clams, as well as starfishes and sea squirts. The variable Atlantic and Mediterranean species favours mussels and oysters, where it feeds on material trapped by the shellfish. Several may live in one mussel. The smaller males are free-swimming, but enter the molluscs to mate.

Lissa chiragra

Found in shallow waters of the Mediterranean Sea, this small spider crab is frequently disguised from predators by the encrusting organisms that cover its carapace. The carapace itself is pear shaped and sculpted with nodular growths and has two central humps on the dorsal surface. The nodular pattern is continued on to the legs. This species frequently hides from view among other organisms on the seabed.

Distribution: Mediterranean Sea and eastern Atlantic Ocean off Portugal.
Habitat: Mainly coral beds at depths of 14–90m/46–295ft; also muddy sea floors.
Food: Various small marine creatures.
Size: Carapace about 4.5cm/1.75in long.
Breeding: Females carry eggs beneath their bodies, which hatch into planktonic larvae that are dispersed by tides and currents.
Status: Not listed by IUCN.

Identification: A small spider crab with a roughly triangular carapace (less wide than it is long), ornamented with a complex pattern of nodules and spines. The legs are similarly ornate. Two rostral spines appear fused together at the top to form a 'T' shape. The colour is rich orange-red.

FEATHER STARS AND BRITTLESTARS

The feather stars and brittlestars comprise two of the five classes within the phylum Echinodermata (the echinoderms, or spiny-skinned animals). Feather stars typically have 'feathery' arms and a small, centrally located body; brittlestars are characterized by having five slender, brittle arms and a central disc. The distribution of these groups is widespread; the species described here live in warmer waters.

Basket star

Astroboa nuda

Identification: Large, radially symmetrical, flower-like echinoderm with very complex, feathery arms. Generally creamy or pale brown, but colour variable.

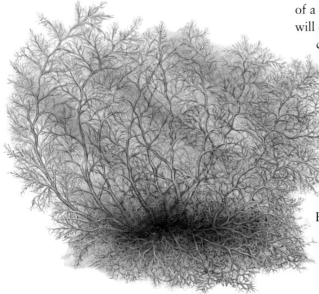

The basket stars are highly specialized types of brittlestars with finely multi-branched arms that resemble the skeletonized leaves of a bush or shrub. By day, a basket star will often lie on the coral with its arms curled inwards in a sphere. At night, however, it extends its arms outwards into a shallow parabolic dish in order to sieve the water for any tiny planktonic animals that may be drifting with the current. The prey is passed to the animal's mouth, which lies beneath the central disc, and wastes are expelled through the same orifice. Basket stars act as hosts for vast numbers of tiny crustaceans called copepods, which feed on the animals trapped by the feathery arms.

Distribution: Indo-Pacific Oceans, Red Sea and Persian Gulf.
Habitat: Coral reefs.
Food: Small planktonic animals such as crustacean larvae.
Size: Up to 1m/3.25ft across.
Breeding: Separate sexes release eggs and sperm into the water through openings at the base of each arm.
Status: Not listed by IUCN.

Orange feather star

Cenolia trichoptera

Identification: Many feathery limbs, extended like the petals of a flower by night or curled up by day. Typically orange, but often yellow, purple, white or brown, or a combination of these colours.

Feather stars are essentially inverted starfish that attach themselves to rocks and corals using jointed appendages called cirri. They then extend their feathery limbs into the current to strain suspended food material from the surrounding water. They feed mainly at night, and curl up by day to avoid predation. The arms carry hydraulic 'tube feet' that are coated with a sticky mucus substance; when a food fragment sticks to the mucus it is transferred to a food-groove running the length of the arm, and then passes along the groove to the central mouth. The mouth is located on the upper side of the central disc, instead of underneath, as it is in starfish. This species occurs in Australian waters, where it is associated with a marine worm that feeds on the food accumulated in the food grooves.

Distribution: Southern, temperate coasts of Australia and Tasmania.
Habitat: Coral and rocky reefs to depths of 35m/115ft.
Food: Drifting edible particles in water.
Size: Up to 30cm/12in across.
Breeding: Eggs and sperm are released into the water; fertilized eggs develop into planktonic larvae.
Status: Not listed by IUCN.

Banded brittlestar

Ophiolepis superba

Distribution: Western Pacific Ocean.
Habitat: Coral reefs.
Food: Organic debris.
Size: Up to 35cm/ 14in across.
Breeding: Separate sexes release eggs and sperm into the water, where fertilization takes place. Free-swimming larvae drift in the plankton to colonize new sites.
Status: Not listed by IUCN.

The brittlestars are named for the fragility of their slender, very flexible limbs, which often break off if the animal is seized by a predator. The lost limb can regenerate, and the limb itself may grow into a new individual if it is not too damaged and is attached to a sizeable portion of the central disc. The most mobile of the echinoderms, brittlestars wander in search of edible detritus, using their sense of smell to track down food. Like many other species of brittlestars, the banded brittlestar is a good scavenger. This species is particularly boldly marked, but otherwise it is typical of this very widespread group of marine invertebrates.

Identification: Five-armed echinoderm with slender, flexible limbs and a small, distinct central disc. Colour is a striking pattern of dark brown to red bands against a tan background. Common name comes from fact that limbs are likely to break off if attacked.

Ophioderma longicauda: 25cm/10in
Very common among rocks and seaweeds in the Mediterranean Sea and in the eastern Atlantic Ocean, this dark, slender brittlestar is normally brown to olive green with darker blotches, but like many brittlestars it is very variable in colour. Serpent stars such as this are often found entwined in the branches of gorgonian corals, where they feed on the rich mucus of their hosts, cleaning them in the process.

Noble feather star
(*Comanthina nobilis*): 40cm/16in
This typically yellow feather star occurs throughout the Indo-Pacific coral reef zone. Like all feather stars it is closely related to the stalked crinoids, or sea lilies, an ancient group of animals that spend their lives rooted to one spot. By contrast, feather stars move to prominent places on the reefs or rocks to feed in the current flow by day, and retreat to a safer spot at night.

Spiculate brittlestar (*Ophiothrix spiculata*): 20cm/8in
Often occurring in dense swarms where there is plenty to eat, this eastern Pacific brittlestar lives on rocky sea floors from the coastal shallows to great depths. It is usually red-brown or orange, and has unusually spiny limbs. Like all brittlestars, it is most active at night, foraging by reaching out with its very flexible limbs and passing any food particles that it finds to its central mouth.

Schayer's brittlestar

Ophionereis schayeri

The spiny arms of brittlestars are made up of articulated ossicles (tiny bone-like structures) that move like the links of a chain. This makes the arms very flexible, but also liable to fracture at the joints. This Australian species of brittlestar filters sand and mud from the ocean floor, extracting any edible detritus it finds. The food is digested in a central stomach, and any waste is excreted through the animal's mouth. It is often found lurking under rocks, but moves quickly away to hide from the light when the rock is overturned. It is the most common brittlestar found in the shallow seas around southern Australia.

Distribution: Southern, temperate coasts of Australia and Tasmania.
Habitat: Intertidal rocky shores, and coastal waters to a depth of 180m/600ft.
Food: Small particles of organic debris.
Size: Up to 18cm/ 7in across.
Breeding: Eggs and sperm are released into the water; fertilized eggs develop into planktonic larvae.
Status: Not listed by IUCN.

Identification: A slender, long-armed echinoderm. Colour usually pale grey with dark grey rings around the arms, but may be variable.

STARFISH

The members of this major group of echinoderms do not have a central processing centre, or brain. Instead, a series of nerves running down the rays, or arms, coordinates the animal's movements and actions. Despite their attractive, often delicate appearance, many are extremely capable hunters, and may engulf prey almost as large as themselves. Some species even cannibalize other starfish.

Purple starfish

Henricia oculata

Also known as the bloody Henry starfish, this colourful species has a very stiff body with blunt, skin-covered spines on its upper surface. It often lives in kelp forests below the low-tide mark, but it also thrives in very exposed rocky sites, such as tide races, where the currents are powerful enough to sweep many animals away. The fast water flow carries a large amount of food material with it, and the starfish exploits this by using its sticky tube feet to gather edible items from the water. It also attacks and eats encrusting animals such as sponges.

Identification: A rigid, five-armed starfish with a rough skin, like sandpaper. The colour is very variable: from purple to red, brown or yellow. The outer portions of the arms are sometimes paler than the inner parts and the central disc.

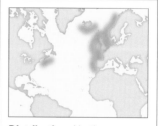

Distribution: North-eastern and north-west Atlantic Ocean.
Habitat: Rocky or sandy seabeds on open coasts with plenty of water movement, at depths down to 100m/330ft.
Food: Encrusting animals, including sponges and hydroids, as well as edible particles suspended in the water.
Size: Up to 20cm/8in.
Breeding: Females produce up to 1,000 eggs that develop into miniature starfish without going through a larval stage.
Status: Not listed by IUCN.

Sand-burrowing starfish

Astropecten irregularis

As its common name indicates, this starfish spends much of its time partly hidden in the sediment, burrowing into the sand with its pointed, suckerless tube feet. It rarely buries itself completely, but uses the tips of its arms to maintain contact with the surface. It often emerges to feed at dawn or dusk, digging into the sand to find small molluscs and crustaceans. It does not feed by turning its stomach inside out over its victims as many starfish do; instead it swallows them whole. It is easily dislodged by heavy wave action and is sometimes stranded on beaches after storms.

Identification: A flattened species with five short, tapering arms and a grainy upper surface. There is a double series of large marginal plates at the edge of each arm, with long spines extending from the upper plates. The colour is variable, from sandy to yellowish-orange, pink or brown. It often has a purple spot at the centre of the disc, and purple tips to each arm.

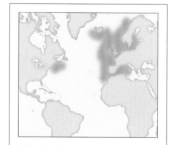

Distribution: North-eastern Atlantic: Norway to Cape Verde Islands, Mediterranean Sea. Also north-west Atlantic.
Habitat: Soft seabeds of sand or muddy sand, from low water to depths of about 1,000m/3,280ft.
Food: Small burrowing molluscs and crustaceans.
Size: Up to 20cm/8in.
Breeding: Eggs and sperm are released into the water where fertilization takes place. Fertilized eggs develop into planktonic larvae that are dispersed by ocean currents.
Status: Not listed by IUCN.

Distribution: Indo-Pacific Ocean, including Red Sea.
Habitat: Coral reefs.
Food: Coral polyps.
Size: Up to 50cm/ 20in across.
Breeding: Female produces up to 20 million eggs each summer, which are fertilized in the water. They hatch into planktonic larvae that drift in the ocean for several weeks before settling and changing into their adult form.
Status: Not listed by IUCN.

Crown-of-thorns starfish

Acanthaster planci

Notorious for its destructive impact on coral reefs – particularly the Great Barrier Reef along the east coast of Australia – the crown-of-thorns starfish is a voracious predator that feeds exclusively on live corals, usually by night. Settling on the reef, it everts its stomach over a coral head so its digestive juices can break down the soft tissues, allowing the starfish to ingest them. Meanwhile, the scent of semi-digested coral disperses through the water, attracting other starfish. Each individual eats about its own diameter of coral each night, leaving bare, white coral rock, but they can multiply to plague numbers and denude huge areas of coral. After a few years these plagues subside, and the reef usually recovers.

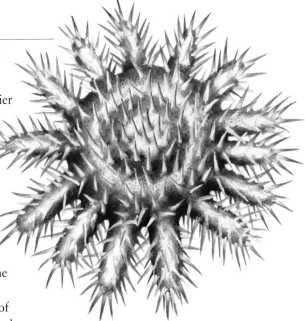

Identification: Very large, orange to purple-brown, with 12–23 arms and a broad, central disc covered in stout, dark spines. The spines are coated in toxic mucus that causes intense pain and inflammation, followed by itching that can last for a week.

Seven-armed starfish (*Luidia ciliaris*): 40cm/16in
Distinguished by its seven long arms that taper only at the ends, and its conspicuous fringe of stiff white spines, this large orange-brown or reddish starfish preys mainly on other starfish and brittlestars. It often lies partly buried in gravel, but can move quickly on its long, tapering tube feet in pursuit of its prey. It lives on sandy sediments or rocks from the lower shore to depths of about 400m/1,300ft in the Atlantic Ocean and Mediterranean Sea.

Six-armed Luzon sea star
(*Echinaster luzonicus*): 15cm/6in
A tropical reef species of the western Pacific Ocean, this long-armed starfish may be orange, red, brown, pink or even yellow, often with darker tips. Like many starfish, it can regenerate lost limbs, but it may multiply by voluntarily shedding a limb, which then grows into a new individual. It also reproduces sexually, shedding eggs and sperm into the water.

Purple sun star (*Solaster endeca*): 40cm/16in
Although often purple, the colour of this rough-skinned starfish is more variable than the name suggests and ranges from pale yellow to bright red. It usually has nine triangular arms, but may have from 7 to 13. It occurs in the north Atlantic, on gravelly or rocky bottoms. It is a voracious predator, eating other starfish as well as bivalve molluscs, which it pulls apart with its tube feet before everting its stomach over the animal.

Cushion star

Asterina gibbosa

This stumpy coastal starfish usually lives beneath stones and boulders by day. It emerges at dusk to feed on organic debris in the sand or gravel. It also scavenges from the carcasses of dead animals – including those of its own kind. Like many other starfish, it digests large food items externally, by everting its stomach lining to smother the food with digestive juices. Unusually, it places its well-developed eggs in a sheltered site rather than shedding them into open water, and the eggs hatch as miniature starfish instead of planktonic larvae.

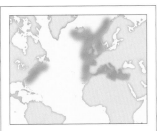

Distribution: North-eastern and north-west Atlantic Ocean and Mediterranean Sea.
Habitat: In rockpools and under rocks and stones on the lower shore, on sheltered and semi-exposed rocky coasts, to depths of 100m/330ft.
Food: Microorganisms, decaying seaweeds and dead invertebrates.
Size: Up to 5cm/2in.
Breeding: Individuals are male when young, but turn into females with age. These lay up to 1,000 orange eggs beneath stones. The eggs hatch into tiny starfish, without passing through a larval stage.
Status: Not listed by IUCN.

Identification: Short, broad arms with rounded tips. Upper surface with short, stiff, often orange, spines. Colour variable: most are blue-grey, green or orange, but some mottled. Specimens from deeper water paler.

SEA URCHINS AND SEA CUCUMBERS

Some of the spiny echinoids described here are capable of extraordinarily long life. The distantly related sea cucumbers, of the class Holothuroidea, exhibit quite an astonishing range of physical features, from elongated, sac-like bodies to squat potato- or egg-shaped forms with sprouting tentacles. One of the functions of the latter is to trap food particles drifting in the current.

Giant red sea urchin

Strongylocentrotus franciscanus

The largest of the spiny sea urchins found in the north Pacific, and possibly the world, this animal is an important part of the coastal kelp forest ecosystem. It feeds almost exclusively on kelp, often in large numbers, keeping these fast-growing marine algae in check. In turn, it is preyed on by the sea otters that live among the kelp, forming a major part of their diet. It is also caught and eaten as a delicacy, especially in Japan. It often harbours the amphipod *Dulichia rhabdoplastis*, which feeds on the microscopic diatoms that live among its spines. These sea urchins have long lifespans, regularly living for 100 years or more; some are believed to be 200 years old.

Identification: Very large, spiny urchin with long pink, red, maroon or purple spines and dark-red tube feet.

Distribution: North Pacific Ocean, from Gulf of Alaska to Mexico and northern Japan.
Habitat: Rocky reefs, especially around kelp, from low tide level down to about 125m/410ft.
Food: Mainly kelp, plus encrusting animals.
Size: Body diameter up to 17cm/6.7in; spines up to 7cm/2.75in long.
Breeding: Eggs and sperm are released into the water. Fertilized eggs develop into planktonic larvae that settle and develop their adult form after 6–10 weeks.
Status: Not listed by IUCN.

Grooved burrowing urchin

Brissus unicolor

Identification: Potato-shaped, burrowing sea urchin with short, close-set, sand-coloured spines giving the appearance of coarse fur. Five-rayed pattern of grooves visible through the spines.

The burrowing urchins have a radial body plan, like that of spiny sea urchins, but they are modified into an irregular, bilaterally symmetrical form with definite head and tail ends. They have short, mobile spines that they use for digging, and they live by burrowing through the sand and gravel in shallow water, where they gather edible organic particles with their long tube feet. This species is widespread through the Atlantic Ocean and Mediterranean Sea, where the empty shells, or tests, of dead specimens are frequently found on beaches. These reveal the petal-like pattern of grooves in the body, dotted with pores through which the tube feet extended in life.

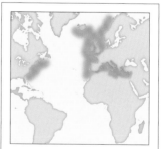

Distribution: North-eastern and north-western Atlantic Ocean; also Mediterranean.
Habitat: Burrows in sand and gravel in shallow water.
Food: Organic remains gathered from sand.
Size: 12cm/4.7in across.
Breeding: Eggs and sperm shed into the water for external fertilization. Eggs develop into planktonic larvae that disperse in the ocean currents.
Status: Not listed by IUCN.

Leopard sea cucumber

Bohadschia argus

Although they look quite unlike sea urchins and sea stars, the sea cucumbers are in fact soft-bodied echinoderms, with calcareous spicules embedded in the skin. This colourful species lives on Indo-Pacific coral reefs, where it crawls over the bottom ingesting coral sand and stripping it of edible particles. It often lives in association with various other animals, such as shrimps, small crabs, marine worms and fish. These include the emperor shrimp (*Periclimenes imperator*), which rides on the sea cucumber and gathers up food disturbed by the animal as it feeds. If it becomes alarmed, the sea cucumber releases from its anus white threads, which are covered with sticky, toxic mucus.

Distribution: Indo-Pacific Ocean, from Madagascar to the South Pacific Islands.
Habitat: Coral reefs.
Food: Small, edible, organic particles in sand.
Size: 25cm/10in.
Breeding: Separate sexes release eggs and sperm into the water, where external fertilization results in planktonic larvae. These drift with the currents before settling to become bottom-living adults.
Status: Not listed by IUCN.

Identification: Sausage-shaped, soft-bodied animal with distinctive leopard spots or eye spots on a brownish background.

Sea apple (*Pseudocolochirus axiologus*): 10cm/4in
This is a sea cucumber of the tropical coral seas, which feeds by straining suspended food particles from the water with its crown of feathery tentacles. These range from yellow to crimson, and the creature's relatively short, ovate body is greyish pink with rows of pink, orange or yellow tube feet. As it feeds, it pushes each tentacle in turn into its central mouth to remove food particles.

Green sea urchin (*Psammechinus miliaris*): 5cm/2in
This eastern Atlantic spiny urchin has a slightly flattened form and strong, short, purple-tipped green spines. It is common on rocky and stony shores from just below the tideline to depths of 100m/330ft. It feeds on seaweeds and encrusting animals, grinding them up with the cage of five teeth that protrudes from its ventral mouth, and often forms dense local populations in sheltered sites. It may live for up to 10 years.

Pea urchin (*Echinocyamus pusillus*): 1.5cm/0.6in
A tiny, oval, burrowing urchin covered with velvety, close-set greyish spines, this north Atlantic and Mediterranean species owes its common name to the way it turns bright green if injured. It lives among coarse gravel from the lower tide limit to depths of 1,250m/4,100ft, burrowing through the sediment and feeding on organic debris and microscopic animals.

Sea cucumber

Thyone fusus

Many sea cucumbers feed by crawling over the seabed ingesting sediments containing organic remains. This species, however, gathers particles suspended in the water. It does this with a net of branched tentacles – formed from modified tube feet – that sprout from the mouth end of its body. The rest of its body is usually buried, so the tentacles are the only part visible, extending some 10–20cm/4–8in above the sediment.

Distribution: North Atlantic Ocean, Mediterranean Sea.
Habitat: Sheltered, soft seabeds of mud, sand, gravel or shell fragments, down to 150m/492ft.
Food: Planktonic organisms and small organic particles suspended in the water.
Size: Up to 20cm/8in.
Breeding: Separate sexes release eggs and sperm into the water, where the eggs develop into planktonic larvae. These are dispersed by the currents before they settle on the bottom.
Status: Not listed by IUCN.

Identification: Egg-shaped, off-white, pale pink or brown coloured body, tapering at both ends, with tube-feet scattered all over the skin. Usually concealed in substrate, apart from a crown of 10 pale-brown, delicately branched tentacles.

PRIMITIVE CHORDATES AND JAWLESS FISH

The phylum Chordata includes humans and all other vertebrates, though not all chordates are vertebrates. Sea squirts are often jelly- or sac-like creatures that may be free swimming or live attached to soft seabeds, according to species. Some are solitary and others form colonies. Lancelets are burrowing fish-like animals. The hagfish and lampreys are primitive fish that lack jaws.

Common sea squirt

Ciona intestinalis

Identification: Translucent, cylindrical, soft-bodied animal resembling a small plastic bag, with a large, yellow-edged siphon tube at the top and a smaller siphon at the side. Usually greenish yellow, but sometimes with an orange tinge.

The adult common sea squirt is a simple, sessile animal – one that is permanently fixed to a substrate – that resembles a tube of translucent jelly. It functions by pumping water into its body through an aperture, or siphon, in the top, straining it through a net-like structure to remove suspended food particles, and then pumping it out through another siphon on the side. The common sea squirt is remarkable for its larvae, each one of which resembles a tadpole with a definite head and a long tail reinforced by a pliable rod called a notochord. This feature, which is common to all sea squirts, is the equivalent of the backbone possessed by other vertebrates, and confirms that the sea squirt is a primitive chordate.

Distribution: Temperate oceans worldwide.
Habitat: Attached to rocks, jetties and other solid substrates, from low water to depths of 500m/1,650ft.
Food: Edible particles filtered from the water.
Size: Up to 15cm/6in long.
Breeding: Hermaphrodite; Individuals release sperm and eggs, and fertilization takes place in the water. Fertilized eggs develop into tadpole-like larvae that disperse in the plankton before settling and turning into adult sea squirts.
Status: Not listed by IUCN.

Lancelet

Branchiostoma lanceolatum

A lancelet (also known as an amphioxus) is a small fish-like creature with a flexible notochord rather than a true backbone, and *B. lanceolatum* is one of about 20 species of lancelet. The muscles are arranged in blocks along each flank. A nerve cord runs from head to tail, but there is no well-developed brain, no obvious sense organs and no jaws. It feeds by drawing water into its mouth and filtering it through a series of gill slits. These strain off food particles and absorb oxygen. Although lancelets can swim, the adults spend most of their time buried in the sediment with their heads protruding to feed. Larval lancelets do the same by day, but swim up into the plankton at night.

Identification: Small, elongated, blade-like animal with dorsal, ventral and caudal fins, and visible muscle blocks in flanks. Capable of swimming, though lives buried in sand or sediment in shallow water where there is a current to supply oxygen and food particles. Typically almost colourless, or a translucent grey-blue colour.

Distribution: Temperate and tropical oceans worldwide.
Habitat: Sandy and gravelly seabeds at depths of about 40m/130ft.
Food: Edible particles filtered from the water.
Size: 10cm/4in.
Breeding: Separate sexes release eggs and sperm into the water. Fertilized eggs develop into swimming larvae that feed for several months before metamorphosing into adults.
Status: Not listed by IUCN.

Atlantic hagfish

Myxine glutinosa

This is one of about 30 species of hagfish that all have the
same basic body form and habits. Although blind, it is an
active predator, particularly of worms. This bottom-living
animal is also a scavenger. It finds carcasses or moribund
fish by scent, drills into them with its jaw-like toothed
plates, and then forces itself inside to eat the flesh. Its body
is extremely slimy for lubrication and to protect itself from
predators, and it is able to form part of it into a knot to
gain extra purchase as it forces its way in for its
meal. A hagfish has no stomach,
and its skeleton consists
of a pliable reinforcing
rod, or notochord,
running the
length of the
body. A dorsal
nerve cord lies
above this, terminating
in a simple brain at the head end.

Identification: Eel-like animal
with a glutinous, scaleless body
and a fin-like fold of skin
extending along the body and
around the tail. The head end
has a single nostril and mouth
surrounded by short barbels, but
no eyes. Greyish or reddish
brown in colour, but variable
depending on colour of seabed.

Star ascidian (*Botryllus schlosseri*): Colonies up
to 15cm/6in across
A colonial sea squirt, the individual animals, or
zooids, live in clusters of up to 12 around a
common opening, embedded in a jelly-like 'test'.
The zooids are usually brightly coloured with
yellow and red, contrasting with the duller test,
and this radial arrangement creates the star-like
pattern referred to in the common name. They
encrust rocks on the lower shore and to depths
of 300m/985ft or more, in the north Atlantic.

Light-bulb sea squirt (*Clavelina lepadiformis*):
Colonies up to 5cm/2in across
Although this species looks like a cluster of
solitary sea squirts, resembling transparent
versions of *Ciona intestinalis*, it is actually
colonial, with the individual animals linked at the
base by short stolons. It is found attached to
rocks and seaweeds from below the tideline to
depths of about 50m/164ft, in the north Atlantic
and Mediterranean.

Pacific hagfish (*Eptatretus stoutii*): 50cm/20in
Brown, grey, or brownish red, often tinted with
blue or purple, this northeast Pacific species
(below) is like the Atlantic hagfish, and has the
same preference for soft sediments at depths of
15–650m/50–2,100ft. It, too, is a scavenger,
relying on scent to find dead fish which it
burrows into and hollows out, leaving just a bag
of skin and bones.

Sea lamprey

Petromyzon marinus

Although it has no jaws, the sea lamprey is
much closer to a true fish than the similar-
looking hagfish. Its gills are supported by a
cage of cartilage, and as an adult it has
functioning eyes. Its dorsal and tail fins have
fin rays, and it has a complex spawning
behaviour resembling that of salmon. Yet it
has a pliable notochord rather than a series
of vertebrae, and instead of jaws it has a
rasping tongue. It uses this to bore into the
flanks of living fish such as cod and sharks,
and feed on their blood and flesh. An
anticoagulant in its saliva keeps the blood
flowing. In total contrast, larval sea
lampreys are filter feeders that live in rivers
partly buried in the river bed.

Identification: Eel-like fish with a rasping tongue
instead of jaws, prominent eyes and seven circular
gill apertures on each side behind the head. Two
shallow dorsal fins, and small tail fin. Brownish
yellow with black marbling on the back, pale below.

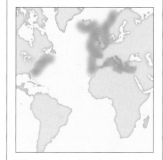

MACKEREL SHARKS

Mackerel sharks comprise about 16 species of varied appearance and lifestyle. Among the seven families in the order are some of the best-known of all sharks, including the great white and the mako. However, there are also some rarely seen species, such as the goblin shark and the megamouth. As a group, mackerel sharks are found in most of the world's oceans at depths ranging from shallow water to deep water.

Great white shark

Carcharodon carcharias

The great white, the largest predatory shark, has a reputation as a ruthless killer. Attacks on humans may occur because the shark mistakes swimmers for its natural food of seals or turtles. When a great white attacks, it usually lunges up from below, delivering a lightning-fast bite before pulling back. Once the prey has been rendered helpless, it returns to shear off chunks with its triangular, serrated teeth. Smaller prey may be taken whole. After a large meal, the shark may not feed again for several weeks. Wide-ranging and usually solitary, the great white breeds at about 10 to 12 years, producing live young after a gestation of about 12 months.

Identification: Torpedo-like body with pointed, conical snout. Mouth bears large (7.5cm/3in), serrated teeth in both jaws. Well-developed lateral keels on caudal peduncle. Upper part of body blue-grey or brownish, lower part white. Large caudal (tail), dorsal and pectoral fins; pectoral fins with blackish tips on underside.

Distribution: Temperate and tropical oceans worldwide.
Habitat: One of the more coastal mackerel sharks, but also found in open water to depths of 1,300m/4,260ft.
Food: Fish, turtles, seabirds, seals, sealions, dolphins.
Size: Up to 6m/20ft, but occasionally larger.
Breeding: Two to ten young; livebearer.
Status: Listed as Vulnerable by IUCN.

Basking shark

Cetorhinus maximus

This giant, the second-largest species of shark, gets its common name from its habit of cruising leisurely at the surface of the water in summer as if sunbathing, although it may also swim at depths of about 200m/650ft. Basking sharks may be found alone, in pairs or in groups. Despite its size, the basking shark feeds solely on tiny plankton, which it filters from the water using comb-like structures on its gill arches. To help it obtain sufficient food, the basking shark swims along at about 5km/h/3mph with its huge mouth wide open, taking in thousands of litres of water per hour.

Identification: Huge, with pointed snout and cavernous mouth. Gill slits very large and prominent. Large caudal fin with longer upper lobe. Has small teeth, but these used for mating, not feeding. Body variably coloured blackish, brown or blue on back, becoming pale towards belly. Fins prized for making shark-fin soup.

Distribution: Temperate oceans worldwide. Common along Pacific coasts of US during winter months.
Habitat: Highly migratory species. Found inshore in surface waters, but possibly also deeper water.
Food: Plankton.
Size: 10m/33ft, but occasionally up to 15m/50ft.
Breeding: Little known about breeding behaviour; it may produce up to six young in a litter; livebearer.
Status: Listed by IUCN as Vulnerable to Endangered.

Common thresher shark

Alopias vulpinus

Distribution: Widely distributed continental shelf species. Especially prominent along eastern and south-western coasts of Australia.
Habitat: Deep coastal waters to open surface waters.
Food: Fish, squid, crustaceans.
Size: 6m/20ft.
Breeding: Two to seven young; livebearer.
Status: Probably declining in numbers.

The common thresher is the largest of the three species of thresher sharks. All three are recognizable by the upper lobe of the tail fin, which is almost as long as the body itself. It is thought that the shark may use its tail to lash out and stun prey before devouring it. Threshers may even join together to herd prey together with their tails before feeding on them. The common thresher is wide-ranging, swimming in deep water close to the shore as well as in open water near the surface. The thresher's breeding habits are only partly known, but like other mackerel sharks the young feed on the yolk of unfertilized eggs as they develop, which helps ensure they are well formed at birth. Threshers are hunted for their meat and fins, and their numbers have dropped as a result.

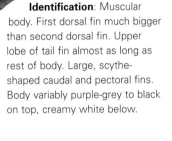

Identification: Muscular body. First dorsal fin much bigger than second dorsal fin. Upper lobe of tail fin almost as long as rest of body. Large, scythe-shaped caudal and pectoral fins. Body variably purple-grey to black on top, creamy white below.

Grey nurse shark
(*Carcharias taurus*): 4.3m/14ft
Stout-bodied with jaws lined with forward-projecting, needle-sharp teeth. It has two large dorsal fins and a tail fin with an elongated upper lobe. It feeds on fish – including small sharks – and invertebrates that it usually hunts near the seabed in sandy coastal waters of the Atlantic, Pacific and Indian Oceans.

Porbeagle (*Lamna nasus*): 3.7m/12ft
A fast-swimming, stout-bodied shark of mainly cool coastal and inshore waters of the North Atlantic, Pacific and Indian Oceans, the porbeagle's distinguishing features include a white patch on the trailing edge of the first dorsal fin and relatively large eyes. A popular gamefish, the porbeagle is also caught for its oil and for making into fishmeal.

Small-tooth sand tiger shark (*Odontaspis ferox*): about 1.8m/6ft, but 3.7m/12ft also recorded
The small-tooth sand tiger can be distinguished from the similar grey nurse shark (*Carcharias taurus*) by the fact that its first dorsal fin is significantly larger than the second; in the grey nurse they are the same size. The small-tooth sand tiger is sometimes encountered by divers on coral reefs near the drop-off zone of continental shelves, but is also known to live in waters 530m/1,750ft deep. This shark is most active at night, feeding on fish, shrimps and squid.

Shortfin mako shark

Isurus oxyrinchus

A sleek, spindle-shaped, metallic blue shark, the mako bears a resemblance to the porbeagle (see panel left), but is distinguished from it by its longer body and lack of a secondary keel on the caudal fin. The mako also lacks lateral cusps on its dagger-like teeth. One of the fastest of all the sharks, the highly predatory mako can accelerate to speeds of up to 35km/h/22mph – sometimes even faster – for short distances, and it can also maintain a higher body temperature than that of the surrounding water. An opportunist hunter, its food includes schooling fish, such as tuna and herring, but it is also known to take porpoises. The mako is a popular sport fish and is often caught on rod and line from boats; at such times, it often leaps spectacularly from the water, and jumps up to a height of 6m/20ft are sometimes recorded. The mako may even try to attack the boat. These sharks may live up to 20 years or more.

Distribution: Worldwide distribution in temperate waters; also found tropical oceans.
Habitat: From surface waters down to 150m/490ft or more.
Food: Fish such as mackerel and tuna; also porpoises and turtles.
Size: 4m/13ft, perhaps exceptionally to 6m/20ft
Breeding: Usually about 10–12 young; livebearer.
Status: Listed as Lower risk by IUCN.

Identification: Streamlined body. Head has long, conical snout. Curved teeth lack lateral cusps. First dorsal fin much bigger than second dorsal fin. Crescent-shaped caudal fin with no secondary keel. Body colour metallic blue above, white below.

REQUIEM SHARKS

All of these sharks belong to the family Carcharinidae, often known as Requiem sharks, which is one of the seven families of ground sharks that, altogether, amass more than 200 members. Taxonomists sometimes group hammerheads in a separate family, Sphyrinidae. The species shown here include some of the best-known and most voracious sharks to be found anywhere in the world's oceans.

Great hammerhead shark

Sphyrna mokarran

The largest of the eight or nine species of hammerheads (family Sphyrinidae), this shark, like all hammerheads, has extended lateral lobes on either side of the head forming the so-called 'hammer'. However, in other species the lobes may be more scalloped, wing-like or shovel shaped. Ranging from inshore reefs to depths of about 300m/980ft, the great hammerhead hunts a variety of animals including rays and sea snakes, feeding mainly at dusk. It migrates to cooler waters at the poles during the summer months. Unlike most other sharks, mating often takes place near the surface. After about an 11-month gestation, young are born in the Northern Hemisphere.

Identification: Muscular body with prominent first dorsal fin; pectoral and pelvic fins relatively small; caudal fin with long upper lobe bearing notch. Head with conspicuous lateral lobes; eyes and nostrils on lobes. In all species, eyes and nostrils located at the ends of hammer; this may give them a wider sensory field for locating prey. Hammer also acts as a bow-plane, improving manoeuvrability. Body brown, grey or olive above, fading to white below.

Distribution: Circumtropical, coastal warm temperate and tropical waters between latitudes 40°N and 37°S.
Habitat: From shallow coastal areas to far offshore at depths of 300m/985ft, but usually less than 80m/260ft.
Food: Wide variety of marine creatures from invertebrates to bony fish, sharks and rays.
Size: 6m/20ft.
Breeding: From 6 to 42 young; livebearer.
Status: Listed as Data Deficient by IUCN.

Bonnethead shark

Sphyrna tiburo

The bonnethead is the smallest of the hammerhead species. Like other hammerheads, the head has conspicuous lateral lobes bearing the eyes and nostrils, but in this species the profile resembles a flattened shovel or bonnet. The shape may have evolved to improve prey-finding capabilities and to make swimming more efficient by increasing lift. The bonnethead usually feeds by day. Darting swiftly forward, it grabs prey with its pointed front teeth, and then uses the flattened molars at the back of the mouth to crush hard shells. Often occurring in schools of up to 15 individuals, during migration this number may be hundreds. It is thought that bonnetheads may communicate with each other using chemical scents. It travels great distances daily, staying in warm waters. In winter it is found near the equator. Gestation is between four and five months – a short time for sharks.

Identification: Compact body shape with tall first dorsal fin. Short pectoral fins. Caudal fin has long upper lobe. Head flattened; shovel- or bonnet-shaped, with eyes and nostrils located at ends of rounded lobes. Front teeth pointed. Body colour greyish-brown, occasionally with dark spots, fading to white below.

Distribution: Temperate Atlantic Ocean from New England to Gulf of Mexico and Brazil. Common in Caribbean Sea. Also found warm-temperate and subtropical Pacific Ocean from southern California to Ecuador.
Habitat: Over reefs, in estuaries and shallow bays down to about 80m/262ft.
Food: Crabs, prawns, molluscs, small fish.
Size: 1.5m/5ft.
Breeding: 4–14 young; livebearer.
Status: Listed as Low Risk by IUCN.

Smooth hammerhead shark
(*Sphyrna zygaena*): 5m/16.5ft
Head bearing an elongated 'hammer' produced by lateral projections, but lacks the notches of other species of hammerheads. Body colour olive or brownish-grey with a whitish underside. Found worldwide in temperate oceans, it prefers depths of less than 20m/65ft deep, but it may be found deeper, and is frequently seen around bays and estuaries, where it feeds primarily on bony fish, small sharks and rays.

Scalloped hammerhead shark (*Sphyrna lewini*): 4.3m/14ft
This species has a centrally located indentation on the front margin of the laterally expanded head. Either side of it are two further indentations, producing a scalloped appearance. Eyes and nostrils are located at the ends of the lateral head projections. Colouration brown-grey to bronze or olive with lighter underside. Females grow larger than males. Found worldwide in coastal temperate and tropical oceans, where it feeds on rays, bony fish and invertebrates, mostly at night. On occasions, several hundred individuals, mainly females, congregate in groups called 'shivers', during which time they perform headshaking, corkscrewing and other movements; this activity is probably linked to mating.

Whitetip reef shark
Triaenodon obesus

As night approaches, schools of whitetip reef sharks leave their daytime resting places among caves and overhangs to fan out over reefs and atolls in search of prey. One of the most common species of shark on reefs, whitetips often appear to hunt and attack as a pack, although this is less of a coordinated activity and more a case of them all going for the same prey and ending up in a feeding frenzy. As with some other sharks, mating involves the male biting the female and grasping her pectoral fins so he can ensure the correct position for sperm transfer. The whitetip reef shark is a curious species and often approaches divers.

Identification: Tapering body. Head with large, blunt nose. Broad pectoral fins. Caudal fin with long upper lobe. First dorsal fin and upper lobe of caudal fin have distinct white tips. Body colour grey-brown, fading to white on underside.

Distribution: Indo-Pacific range from Red Sea and East Africa to Micronesia and south to New South Wales; also eastern Pacific Ocean.
Habitat: Over reefs and in shallow water down to 40m/130ft.
Food: Crabs, lobsters, squid, bony fish.
Size: 2m/6.6ft.
Breeding: 1–5 young; livebearer.
Status: Listed as Near Threatened by IUCN.

Tiger shark
Galeocerdo cuvier

This species gets its common name from the tiger-like body markings. One of the largest and most aggressive of all sharks, the tiger shark is renowned for its varied tastes in food. A powerful and fast swimmer when attacking its prey, it will swallow almost anything that will fit into its mouth, including sea lions, sea snakes, turtles, other sharks and seabirds. It has also been known to swallow items of more dubious nutritional value, such as car licence plates and tyres. It has also been implicated in attacks on human bathers. Tolerant of both marine and brackish conditions, the tiger shark sometimes enters river estuaries and is known to attack land mammals that come to the water to drink.

Identification: Fast-swimming aggressive shark. Body tapers towards tail. First dorsal fin much longer than second dorsal fin. Upper lobe of caudal fin long with subterminal notch. Head with large eyes and a broad, blunt snout. Wide mouth bears rows of large, serrated teeth. Body colour greyish with black spots and vertical bars (reminiscent of a tiger), more prominent in young individuals, pale below.

Distribution: Circumglobal in temperate and tropical oceans and seas. Common around Australian coasts.
Habitat: Coastal waters, including estuaries, and over continental shelf down to about 140m/460ft, but sometimes deeper.
Food: Very varied: scavenger as well as predator of range of creatures including fish, marine reptiles, seabirds, mammals (such as dolphins and sea lions), crustaceans and molluscs.
Size: Up to 6m/20ft.
Breeding: 11–82 young; livebearer.
Status: Listed as Near Threatened by IUCN.

OTHER SHALLOW-WATER SHARKS

The species featured here originate from a number of different shark families. Bottom-dwelling carpet sharks include the giant whale shark – the largest fish in the world – and the well-camouflaged wobbegongs. Saw sharks have long snouts with rows of lateral teeth, while frilled and cow sharks are distinctive for retaining six or seven pairs of gills, whereas most sharks have five.

Nurse shark

Ginglymostoma cirratum

Identification: Body with relatively large fins. Upper lobe of caudal fin held almost level with body. Head with blunt snout (or rostrum) and small eyes. Tiny spiracles (breathing orifices). Mouth bears two distinct sensory barbels. Body colour tan to brown, paler below. Juveniles have spotted markings on their dorsal surface.

This generally docile shark may get its name from the suckling noise it makes when feeding, which is thought by some to be similar to the sounds of a suckling baby. One of just two recorded nurse shark species, the shark rests for much of the day on the sea bottom, sometimes in groups, but at night it hunts for bottom-dwelling invertebrates and fish. It has only a small mouth, but its powerful, bellows-like pharynx (the passage from mouth to stomach) allows it to suck in food with great speed. In summer, nurse sharks migrate to gather in shallow waters in large numbers for several weeks in a frenzy of courtship and mating. Sometimes a single female will be chased by several males before one succeeds in mating with her. The nurse shark is an approachable species that can be touched and hand fed, and it is sometimes even ridden on by young children; however, this practice can be dangerous, for as docile as it is, this shark can deliver a painful, vice-like bite without warning.

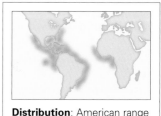

Distribution: American range extends from Rhode Island, US, to Brazil, including Gulf of Mexico and Caribbean. Also south-eastern US Pacific seaboard to Baja California. Eastern Atlantic range extends from Cape Verde to Gabon.
Habitat: Waters from about 1m/3.25ft down to 50m/160ft.
Food: Crabs, octopuses and other invertebrates, fish.
Size: Up to 2.7m/8.8ft.
Breeding: 20–30 young; livebearer.
Status: Not listed by IUCN.

Tasselled wobbegong

Eucrossorhinus dasypogon

Identification: Body flattened. Large pectoral and pelvic fins. Head flattened and bearing many appendages around mouth, thought to act as lures for small prey. Body yellowish-brown in colour and marked with a mosaic of numerous dark spots and lines evolved for camouflage when lying motionless on the sea bed.

With its broad, flat head, its mouth fringed with a mass of outgrowths and flaps and its superb camouflage markings, the tasselled wobbegong, like other wobbegongs, is hard to spot on the seabed. Lying motionless on the bottom for long periods, it has evolved a system of pumping in water through its gill cavity when breathing instead of taking in water through the mouth. Despite its sedentary nature, the wobbegong can react extremely quickly when prey comes within range, snatching it with sharp teeth and gulping it down. The waving appendages around its mouth may even attract small creatures to approach. There are six other species of wobbegongs in the family Orectolobidae, all found in the western Pacific region.

Distribution: South-western Pacific, including eastern Indonesia, Papua New Guinea and northern Australia.
Habitat: Bottom dwelling, on sand and reefs down to about 40m/130ft.
Food: Fish, squid, octopuses, crabs, shrimps.
Size: 1.2m/4ft; sometimes larger.
Breeding: Not known.
Status: Listed as Near Threatened by IUCN.

Longnose saw shark

Pristiophorus cirratus

Distribution: Southern Australia to New South Wales.
Habitat: Sandy and muddy seabeds down to 300m/1,000ft. Sometimes also brackish waters.
Food: Squid, prawns, crabs, small fish.
Size: 1.4m/4.6ft.
Breeding: 6–20 young; livebearer.
Status: Listed as Least Concern by IUCN.

The nine species of saw sharks are identified by their long, blade-like snout, or rostrum, bearing on each side a row of pointed, lateral teeth. In some species, the rostrum can be as long as the rest of the body. The longnose saw shark is a sedentary species, probing the seafloor for invertebrates and bottom-dwelling fish with its sensitive rostrum, aided by long, sensory barbels that extend on either side of the rostrum. When prey is detected, it may be dug out and dispatched by being slashed with the shark's sharp-toothed saw. Saw sharks are not equipped to bite and swallow large prey in the way that many other sharks do, and so their food consists of items such as small fish and invertebrates. Females give birth to live young after a gestation period of about a year. To avoid damaging the mother with their saw teeth, the baby saw sharks are born with the teeth lying flat against the rostrum in a protective sac. Age span is about 15 years.

Identification: Body long and slender. No anal fin. Head with particularly long rostrum bearing conspicuous lateral teeth and two sensory barbels. Large eyes. Body colour generally grey-brown with dark banded markings above, greyish-white on underside.

Northern wobbegong (*Orectolobus wardi*): 60cm/24in
The northern wobbegong has a much less-elaborate colour pattern and less-developed mouth appendages compared with the tasselled wobbegong (*Eucrossorhinus dasypogon*). There are several dark saddles on the head and lightish body, as well as brown blotches. Around the mouth are sensory barbels and flap-like nasal lobes, and there are also lobes on the head. Like other wobbegongs, the northern wobbegong inhabits shallow reefs, where it can lie concealed among overhangs and crevices becoming active at night when it hunts for prey. It is found in waters around northern Australia.

Brown-banded bamboo shark (*Chiloscyllium punctatum*): 1m/3.25ft
These carpet sharks get their common name from the markings seen on juveniles. The alternating dark and light bands resemble the patterning on bamboo stems. However, as the fish becomes adult the body colouring usually assumes a more uniform drab grey or brown. The shark has a long, slender body with well-developed dorsal, pectoral and pelvic fins and a long tail. The head bears short nasal barbels, which help it to locate food hidden on the bottom and among coral reefs. This egg-laying species is found in the Indo-Pacific Ocean. Due to its relatively small size and attractive juvenile markings, the shark is a popular aquarium fish.

Zebra shark

Stegostoma fasciatum

The beautifully patterned zebra shark, also called the leopard shark, is the only member of its family, the Stegostomatidae. It has a body that is scalloped longitudinally, with two ridges running from behind the blunt head to the caudal fin (or tail). Both dorsal fins are low and long, the pectoral fins are broad and well developed, and the caudal fin is long. This shark is often encountered near reefs both inshore and offshore, where it feeds at night on molluscs, crustaceans and fish. With its long, narrow body it can wriggle into caves and crevices using the fleshy sensory barbels to search for prey. It is not known whether the female lays more than one egg at a time. This species is harmless to humans and is regularly taken in inshore fisheries.

Distribution: Indo-West Pacific: Red Sea and East Africa to New Caledonia, north to southern Japan and south to New South Wales.
Habitat: Sandy bottoms of coastal waters to about 60m/200ft.
Food: Molluscs, crabs, shrimps, small fish.
Size: 3.5m/11.5ft.
Breeding: Oviparous; number of eggs unknown.
Status: Listed as Vulnerable by IUCN.

Identification: Body cylindrical with prominent ridges running down, giving a scalloped effect. Head broad with small barbels and a wide, transverse mouth. The spiracles (breathing orifices), situated behind the eyes, are large. The first (anterior) dorsal fin is longer than the second (posterior) dorsal fin. The tail has no ventral lobe and is as long as the body. The body is creamy or yellow with leopard-like dark brown to black spots. Juveniles have zebra-like alternating dark brown and creamy stripes.

SAWFISH AND ELECTRIC RAYS

Sawfish and rays are grouped, along with sharks and chimaeras, in the class Chondrichthyes. The sawfish have elongated rostrums bearing rows of lateral teeth, and resemble the saw sharks described previously in this section. The electric rays have flattened bodies and broad, wing-like pectoral fins. They can produce pulses of electricity to stun prey and ward off predators.

Great-tooth sawfish

Pristis microdon

Identification: Body long and robust; flattish below. Two large dorsal fins. Flattened head with long rostrum bearing 14–22 large teeth on each side. Eyes large. Large spiracle behind each eye. Body colour greenish-grey or brown above with darker fin edges; underside dirty cream.

With its elongated rostrum, or snout, bearing horizontal teeth, and its shark-like fins, this species looks similar to a saw shark. However, the sawfish's gill slits are on the underside of the body. Sawfish also lack sensory barbels. A solitary species, it feeds on bottom-dwelling fish and other creatures. This species often frequents rivers and lakes. Human demand for the sawfish's meat, liver oil and skin, as well as for its rostrum – which is sold as a curio – have all led to a reduction in numbers. This problem is exacerbated by the fact that the fish is a slow breeder and may not breed until it is 20 years old.

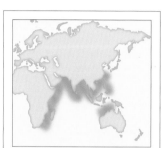

Distribution: Indo-Pacific, including East Africa, India, South-east Asia, Philippines and northern Australia.
Habitat: Near to coasts; also estuaries and in rivers and lakes.
Food: Small bottom-dwelling fish, invertebrates.
Size: 6m/20ft.
Breeding: About 20 young; livebearer.
Status: Listed as Endangered by IUCN.

Small-tooth sawfish

Pristis pectinata

The largest of the six or so species of sawfish, the small-tooth sawfish is found around reefs at depths down to about 10m/33ft, although it often occurs in brackish or even freshwater conditions. It may sometimes venture into deeper water to reach offshore islands. Like other sawfish, the snout is extended to form a long rostrum bearing sharp, horizontal teeth, which it uses to rake up the sea bed, searching for hidden prey, or to ward off predators. Once prey – such as open-water or bottom-living fish – has been found, the sawfish disables it with sideways swipes of its rostrum. Valued not only as a food fish, it is also prized for other parts of its body, such as its oil (used in medicine) and its rostrum. Overfishing and habitat destruction have seen the species eradicated from much of its range.

Identification: Body long and flattened with wing-like pectoral fins. Two large dorsal fins. Flattened head with long rostrum bearing 24–32 teeth on each side. Eyes large. Large spiracle behind each eye. Body colour brownish-grey above, underside white.

Distribution: Western Atlantic: North Carolina, USA, to Brazil; Eastern Atlantic: Gibraltar to Namibia; Indo-Pacific: Red Sea and East Africa to Indonesia, parts of South-east Asia and northern Australia.
Habitat: Near to coasts; enters estuaries and rivers.
Food: Small fish, invertebrates.
Size: 5.5m/18ft; sometimes up to 7.6m/25ft.
Breeding: About 15–20 young; livebearer.
Status: Listed as Threatened by IUCN.

Atlantic torpedo ray

Torpedo nobiliana

Distribution: Subtropical and temperate waters of the Atlantic Ocean.
Habitat: Pelagic but also on sandy seabeds and reefs from 2–800m/6.5–2,600ft.
Food: Mainly small fish.
Size: 1.8m/6ft.
Breeding: About 60 young; livebearer.
Status: Not listed by IUCN.

One of the largest members of the family Torpedinidae, the Atlantic torpedo ray is one of 50 or more species of rays that can produce an electric current using specially modified muscle cells. In some species, including the Atlantic torpedo, the strength of the shock delivered can be up to 220 volts. Electric rays use the electricity both as a form of defence and to capture prey. Fish are the main food of Atlantic torpedos, and prey is usually caught as the ray delivers a stunning shock while wrapping its pectoral fins around it. The ray then manoeuvres the victim into the mouth. Using this method, the ray can catch even fast-moving fish. Juveniles are usually found on the bottom, but adults often swim in open water.

Identification: Most of body flattened and disk-like. Two dorsal fins. Paddle-shaped caudal fin. Snout short. Large spiracle behind each eye. Body colour blackish to chocolate-brown above, white below.

Knife-tooth sawfish (*Anoxypristis cuspidata*): 4.7m/15.5ft
Shark-like in appearance but with slender, elongated snout with lateral teeth. Body greyish above, pale below. Found in marine, brackish and possibly also in freshwater conditions in Indo-Pacific Ocean. Ranges from very shallow water down to about 40m/130ft. Sharp teeth of babies embedded in a protective sheath to avoid damaging the mother during birth. Endangered.

Tasmanian numbfish (*Narcine tasmaniensis*): 47cm/18.5in
Occurring on sandy and muddy bottoms, and sometimes on rocky reefs, the Tasmanian numbfish lives in waters from about 5m/16.4ft down to 640m/2,100ft. It is found in the Pacific including south and southeast Australia. This ray is a fairly uniform chocolate-brown to yellow-brown above, white below. It feeds on worms and crustaceans such as shrimps.

Cortez electric ray (*Narcine entemedor*): 76cm/30in
Found in shallow, sandy places, sometimes close to reefs, along the eastern Pacific from California, USA, to Peru. It has two equally sized dorsal fins and a paddle-shaped caudal fin. It is nocturnal, resting on the bottom by day, often buried in the substrate, before moving into bays to feed on worms and sea squirts. Body greyish-tan.

Spotted torpedo ray

Torpedo marmorata

This ray's common name comes from the mottled appearance of its dorsal surface. Like other members of its family, it has the ability to emit an electric shock that will deter most predators (although large sharks are often not put off) or stun prey, rendering it helpless before being eaten. By day, the spotted torpedo usually lies buried on the seabed with just its eyes visible, but at night it hunts for crustaceans and small fish, which it first overpowers with an electric discharge. The electricity produced by these rays was used from ancient times up until around the 1600s as a form of therapy intended to cure diseases from gout to headaches.

Distribution: Eastern Atlantic Ocean from Britain to southern Africa. Also the Mediterranean Sea.
Habitat: Soft sea bottom around reefs and seagrass meadows.
Food: Small fish and crustaceans.
Size: 1m/3.25ft.
Breeding: About 5–30 young; livebearer.
Status: Not listed by IUCN.

Identification: Most of body flattened and disc-like. Two dorsal fins. Paddle-shaped caudal fin. Snout short. Slightly stalked eyes on top of head. Large spiracle behind each eye. Body colour mottled brown above, underside creamy white.

SKATES, GUITARFISH AND STINGRAYS

There are more than 120 species of skates – flattened cartilaginous fish found in most oceans of the world. In these fish the pectoral fin is fused to the head to give a more or less disc-shaped body. The guitarfish are so called because their body shape resembles the musical instrument. Stingrays have venomous spines at the base of the tail, which are used primarily for defence.

Common skate

Dipturus (Raja) batis

Identification: Body flattened and diamond-shaped. Elongated snout. Eyes on top of head. Conspicuous spiracles behind eyes. Tiny dorsal fins. Thin tail with spiny thorns on upper surface. Body colour grey to brown with white spots on upper surface, white below.

A sought-after and now heavily overfished commercial species, the common or blue skate can grow to 2.9m/9.5ft or more. The snout is elongated and the pectoral fins form broad 'wings', giving the flattened body a more or less diamond shape when viewed from above. Swimming with a typical undulating action of its pectoral fins, the impression of having wings is further enhanced, since the fish seems to be flying through the water. Along the dorsal surface is a series of spiny thorns that may help give some protection from predators. It can also emit a small electric discharge, like the electric rays, but this is insufficient to deter predators and is probably used in courtship. Fertilization is internal, and the leathery eggs are laid in summer. The cases have tendrils to help them attach to weeds and other objects.

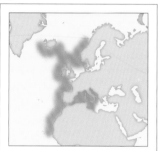

Distribution: Eastern Atlantic Ocean, from Iceland to Senegal, and western Mediterranean.
Habitat: Near seabed, usually down to 100–1,000m/ 330–3,300ft.
Food: Fish, crabs, lobsters.
Size: 2.9m/9.5ft.
Breeding: One or two eggs.
Status: Listed as Endangered by IUCN.

Atlantic guitarfish

Rhinobatos lentiginosus

Somewhat between a ray and a shark in overall shape, the 40 or so species of guitarfish get their common name from their distinctive body shape. The body is long, like that of a typical shark, with well-developed dorsal fins, but it is rounded at the front with broad pectoral fins, and the gill slits are on the underside, like those of a ray. Guitarfish swim by moving their caudal fins from side to side, in the same fashion as sharks. The Atlantic guitarfish is one of the smaller species in the family Rhinobatidae. It often buries itself in the sand or mud and is sometimes found in brackish or even fresh water. The Atlantic guitarfish feeds on bottom-dwelling fish, molluscs and crustaceans. It often uses its snout, or rostrum, to hold the prey down before eating it. Fertilization is internal, with live young being born. This species is of little commercial fishing interest.

Identification: Body flattened and guitar shaped. Two well-developed dorsal fins. Pectoral fins fused to head. Elongated snout. Eyes on top of head. Conspicuous spiracles behind eyes. Paddle-like tail. Body colour brown, grey or olive above, usually with white speckles, yellowish-white below.

Distribution: Western Atlantic range extends from North Carolina, USA, to Yucatan, Mexico.
Habitat: Mainly tropical coastal areas near seabed down to about 30m/100ft; also in estuaries and fresh water.
Food: Fish, molluscs, shrimps, other invertebrates.
Size: 76cm/30in.
Breeding: About six young; livebearer.
Status: Not listed by IUCN.

Spotted eagle ray

Aetobatus narinari

The spotted eagle ray's common name is due to its large size and also because of its swimming movements, which resemble those of a flying eagle. Beautifully marked with white spots on a black, grey or brown background above, and with contrasting white below, the diamond-shaped spotted eagle ray is an active swimmer, often forming into large schools as it migrates across the oceans. This large ray is also found close to the bottom in shallow water, where it digs into the substrate for food such as clams and other molluscs using its curious flat, duck-billed snout. At the base of the long, whip-like tail the eagle ray has a battery of highly potent stinging spines. These are used in defence to deter or injure would-be predators. The spotted eagle ray can also leap out of the water when pursued. This species is no less dangerous if caught and hauled aboard a boat; the lashing fish can deliver painful, occasionally fatal, stings to humans.

Distribution: Wide-ranging in tropical and temperate Atlantic, Pacific, Indian Oceans and Red Sea.
Habitat: Sandy coastal regions and reefs but also found in estuaries and open water.
Food: Clams, oysters, shrimps, octopus, squid, sea urchins, fish.
Size: 2.5m/8.2ft excluding tail; may reach 5m/16ft in total with tail.
Breeding: Up to four pups; livebearer.
Status: Listed as Data Deficient by IUCN.

Identification: Body disc flattened and diamond-shaped. Eyes on side of head. Large spiracles. Broad, bill-shaped snout.

Manta ray

Manta birostris

This impressive fish is the largest of all rays. Despite its size, it eats mainly plankton. The horn-like cephalic fins in front of the head can be rolled up to form a funnel that helps channel water and food into the mouth when feeding. The word 'manta' originates from the resemblance of this ray's wide, flapping fins to a cloak or mantle. The manta ray is a solitary species, but individuals are often accompanied by other fish species, such as cleaner fish, remoras and pilot fish. The lifespan of the manta ray is approximately 20 years.

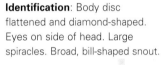

Distribution: Worldwide tropical coastal regions of Atlantic, Pacific and Indian Oceans. Also sometimes in temperate regions.
Habitat: Usually inshore surface waters down to 120m/390ft; occasionally further from shore.
Food: Planktonic crustaceans and small schooling fish.
Size: 5.2m/17ft long; width is approximately 2.2 times greater than length.
Breeding: One young; livebearer.
Status: Listed by IUCN as Data Deficient globally, but Vulnerable in some areas.

Identification: Body flattened. Large, wing-like pectoral fins. Front lobes (cephalic fins) extend on both sides of rectangular mouth. No dorsal or caudal fins. Small teeth, in lower jaw only. Gills on underside of body. Whip-like tail. Body colour variable, but usually brown, grey-blue or black above, white below.

Thornback ray (*Raja clavata*): 1.2m/4ft
This species gets its common name from the dense covering of protective spines that cover the body. The thornback ray is an attractive fish with the typical diamond-shaped body seen in many rays produced by the wide pectoral fins and pointed snout. The tail is narrow and spiny. The upper surface is brown with variously shaded blotches and, sometimes, marbling. Found near coastal seabeds in the eastern Atlantic from Iceland to southwest Africa, it also lives in the Mediterranean and Black seas, and possibly also off South Africa.

Southern ray (*Dasyatis americana*): 1.5m/5ft
Often seen gliding over sandy areas near reefs, the southern ray is common in tropical and subtropical waters in the southern Atlantic Ocean from New Jersey, USA, to Brazil, as well as the Caribbean. It may occur alone, in pairs or in large groups. The southern ray eats a variety of fish, molluscs and crustaceans, which are detected in the substrate by smell, touch and electro-sensitive receptors. Other opportunist fish species often hover nearby to glean morsels disturbed by the feeding ray. The ray's tail can be flicked up to deliver venom from spines to deter potential predators, such as sharks. The broad, diamond-shaped body is grey above and white below. Three to five young are born alive.

SALMON, TROUT AND ALLIES

The Salmoniformes are characterized by having a fatty adipose fin on the back between the dorsal fin and tail. Many species in this group make long-distance migrations between the sea and their breeding grounds in rivers. The related smelts are sardine-like fish, many of which are important commercially. Galaxiids are relatives of the salmon and trout that inhabit the Southern Hemisphere.

Arctic charr

Salvelinus alpinus

Identification: Form typically trout-like, with rounded, streamlined body. Slightly pointed snout and large mouth with teeth in both jaws. Adipose fin present. Caudal fin slightly forked. Colour highly variable according to habitat, size and time of year: often brown or greenish on back, flanks silvery with pinkish or red spots; underside paler. Spawning adults usually have bright orange-red ventral surface and pelvic, pectoral and anal fins.

The arctic charr is found mainly in cold, northern waters. There are both landlocked, freshwater varieties and others that migrate between freshwater habitats – where they spawn – and the sea. The species is an opportunist feeder, taking food from small crustaceans to members of its own species. Spawning takes place between September and October, with the preferred site being shallow, gravelly bottoms. The female builds a nest by turning on her side and using her caudal fin to clear away an area, known as a redd, in which to lay her eggs. After a period of courtship, eggs are laid in the redd and fertilized by the male. Where charr are migratory, the young first venture to the sea after a period of between two and six years.

Distribution: North Atlantic including northern Norway, southern Greenland and Iceland. Also north-western Canada and USA; Beaufort Sea.
Habitat: Deep runs of rivers and lakes, and – in migratory individuals – brackish waters and shallow seas.
Food: Small crustaceans and fish, including other charr.
Size: Usually about 45cm/ 17.7in, but may be bigger.
Breeding: Nest builder; eggs shed in gravel beds of rivers, and fertilized externally.
Status: Listed as Least Concern by IUCN.

Trout

Salmo trutta

Few fish are more variable than the trout. This is partly because many populations are resident in different types of waters, and isolated from each other, but also because some populations migrate downstream to the sea when adult, where they live on a diet of marine fish and invertebrates. The two types are usually known as brown trout (resident form) and sea trout (migratory form). Both are found only in well-oxygenated, clean water. They spawn in winter in gravelly shallows, the sea trout migrating back from the ocean to reach favoured sites. When mature, sea trout then migrate to the ocean, where they feed for one to five years before returning to breed. Brown trout, however, remain in fresh water. Both are prized food and sports fish.

Identification: Streamlined fish with small scales, an adipose fin and a square-cut tail fin. The area of the body in front of the tail fin is relatively deep and flattened. Colour very variable, ranging from brownish with black spots on the back, plus red spots on the sides, often with pale rings, to silvery with fewer spots (especially in migratory fish returning from the sea). The belly is pale coloured, and the fins are dark and only sparsely spotted.

Distribution: Native range mainly Atlantic: Europe and Scandinavia, and east to the Urals. Migratory group introduced to other regions.
Habitat: Cool, clear rivers and lakes, and – in migratory sea trout – mainly shallow seas.
Food: Small crustaceans and insect larvae in fresh water, plus fish; fish and larger crustaceans in the sea.
Size: River trout 40cm/16in; sea trout 1m/3.25ft.
Breeding: Nest builder; eggs shed in gravel beds of rivers, and fertilized externally.
Status: Listed by IUCN as Least Concern. Some decline in migratory groups.

Atlantic salmon

Salmo salar

Distribution: North Atlantic from Canada and Greenland to Iceland, northern Europe and Scandinavia, and Barents Sea. Also adjoining rivers.
Habitat: Rivers when young and when spawning; mainly coastal waters at sea.
Food: Crustaceans, insect larvae when young in fresh water; small fish and shrimps when at sea. Spawning salmon do not feed.
Size: 1.2m/4ft.
Breeding: Nest builder; eggs shed in gravel beds of rivers, and fertilized externally.
Status: Listed as Least Concern by IUCN.

This is one of the most famous of all fish, partly because it is a valuable food species – so much so that it is now raised in fish farms – but also because of its spectacular spawning migrations. After some years feeding in rich ocean waters, adult wild salmon navigate their way back to the rivers where they spent their early lives, and swim upstream to reach spawning sites in shallow, gravelly streams. This involves adapting from salt to fresh water, and up rapids and waterfalls against the current. They use so much energy in the process that many die after spawning, but some migrate back to sea and return to spawn again.

Identification: Large, streamlined fish with a relatively small head, an adipose fin and a shallowly forked tail. Breeding males develop a hooked lower jaw (kype). Adults fresh from the sea are silver-sided with greenish-blue backs, heads and fins; white below. They become darker and browner as spawning nears, with black and red spots. Young salmon in fresh water are dark, with a line of dark blotches and red spots on flanks.

Atlantic rainbow smelt (*Osmerus mordax*): 30cm/12in
This small-sized relation of the salmon has a pale green back and silvery flanks with a purple, blue and pink iridescent sheen. It feeds in North Atlantic coastal waters or in large lakes when it is adult, consuming small planktonic crustaceans and insect larvae, but in spring it migrates up to about 1,000km/620 miles against the current to spawn in rivers draining into the Arctic Ocean.

Jollytail (*Galaxias maculatus*): 15cm/6in
Widespread in the Southern Hemisphere from the southern tip of South America to Australia, including Tasmania, and New Zealand, this slim, scaleless, silvery green fish is one of several related species known as galaxiids. It is found in coastal rivers and lakes and estuaries, and feeds principally on insects, aquatic insect larvae, and on crustaceans.

Rainbow trout (*Oncorhynchus mykiss*): 50cm/20in
Familiar as a farmed food fish, the rainbow trout has been introduced to many freshwater environments worldwide, where it is also valued as a game fish. It can now be found in 45 countries on all continents, apart from Antarctica. The rainbow trout is a native of the eastern Pacific Ocean and rivers from Alaska to northwest Mexico. It resembles a European trout with an iridescent rainbow stripe along each flank, but a large, silvery migratory form, called the steelhead, lacks this characteristic stripe.

Sockeye salmon

Oncorhynchus nerka

The sockeye is one of six species of *Oncorhynchus*, collectively known as Pacific salmon. Like Atlantic salmon, they feed at sea before returning to their home rivers to spawn, running upstream to reach shallow headstreams with gravel beds. Spawning males turn a vivid red, and many are taken by predators such as bald eagles and bears. Those that do spawn die within a few weeks. After hatching, the young fish feed in rivers and lakes for one or two years before migrating out to sea. In some places they remain in fresh water to form landlocked populations. These fish, known as kokanee salmon, are genetically identical to sockeyes but much smaller, owing to a poorer diet.

Identification: A streamlined, laterally compressed fish. A spawning male develops hooked jaws, long teeth and a dorsal hump. Colouration is normally dark steely to greenish-blue on the head and back, with silvery sides and a white to silvery belly; at spawning time the males turn bright red, with greenish heads, paired fins and tails.

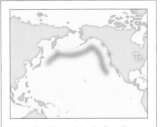

Distribution: North Pacific and adjoining coastal rivers, from northern Japan to Alaska and California. Also landlocked populations (kokanee) in North America, from Alaska to Oregon (US).
Habitat: Fresh water when young, then they migrate to coastal ocean waters. Kokanee are permanently resident in lakes and streams.
Food: Planktonic crustaceans and insect larvae in fresh water; marine crustaceans and fish at sea.
Size: 60cm/24in. Landlocked populations (kokanee) smaller.
Breeding: Nest builder; eggs shed in gravel beds of rivers and streams, and fertilized externally.
Status: Not listed by IUCN.

COD AND RELATIVES

The fish described here are some of the best-known relatives of the Gadiforms, or common codfish. Both the haddock and coalfish are heavily exploited by commercial fishing fleets, causing concern among conservationists. Also fished commercially are hake, which tend to be bottom-dwelling during the day, moving up the water column to feed at night.

Haddock

Melanogrammus aeglefinus

Identification: A large-eyed fish with three dorsal fins – the first triangular with long anterior rays – and two anal fins. It has a very short barbel beneath its short lower jaw. Dark greenish brown on the back, greyish silver on the sides and white below, it has a conspicuous, thumb-print-like black blotch between the pectoral fin and the arched lateral line.

One of the most heavily exploited of food fish, becoming scarce as a result, the haddock is a close relative of the cod (*Gadus morhua*) that feeds on the bottom in the relatively shallow waters of the continental shelves. In the north of its range it feeds inshore in summer, migrating to deeper water in winter, but further south it does the opposite. Although adult fish feed on the bottom, their eggs are buoyant, floating near the surface. The young then feed in the plankton, often swimming with large, drifting jellyfish whose trailing tentacles provide some protection from predators. When they reach about 5cm/2in in length, the young haddock move down to the sea bed in order to feed on worms, crabs, molluscs, brittlestars and small fish.

Distribution: North Atlantic from eastern Canada and New England to southern Greenland, Iceland, northern Europe, Scandinavia and the Barents Sea.
Habitat: Close to the seabed on continental shelf, mainly at depths of 40–300m/ 130–980ft.
Food: Bottom-dwelling invertebrates and small fish such as sandeels.
Size: 75cm/30in.
Breeding: Eggs shed are fertilized externally and hatch into planktonic larvae.
Status: Listed as Vulnerable by IUCN.

Coalfish

Pollachius virens

Also known as the saithe or pollock, and not to be confused with the similar pollack (*Pollachius pollachius*), the coalfish lives in large schools in continental shelf seas. These waters are richer in food resources than the deep oceans, owing to the nutrients scoured up from the relatively shallow sea bed, so even surface-dwelling fish favour them. Mature coalfish feed mainly on smaller schooling fish, frequenting coastal waters in spring and summer, and returning to deeper waters in winter. They spawn from January to April, and their eggs and larvae drift into the coastal shallows where the young fish feed on planktonic crustaceans and small fish for two years before moving into deeper water.

Identification: A typical cod, deep in the belly but tapering towards the tail, with large eyes, a small chin barbel when young that disappears with age, three dorsal fins and two anal fins. Brownish-green back, with silvery sides and belly and a cream-coloured or lighter grey lateral line.

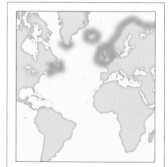

Distribution: North Atlantic from eastern Canada and New England to southern Greenland, Iceland, northern Europe, Scandinavia and the Barents Sea.
Habitat: Schools near the surface and in mid-water to depths of 200m/656ft.
Food: Marine crustaceans and fish.
Size: 1.3m/4.25ft.
Breeding: Eggs shed are fertilized externally; the larvae drift in plankton.
Status: Not listed by IUCN.

Southern hake

Urophycis floridana

Distribution: Western central Atlantic Ocean and Gulf of Mexico.
Habitat: Near seabed in continental shelf seas, to depths of 400m/1,300ft.
Food: Crustaceans, marine worms, fish and squid.
Size: 30cm/12in.
Breeding: Eggs shed into the water are fertilized externally; they are buoyant, and hatched larvae are planktonic.
Status: Not listed by IUCN.

The hakes are closely related to cods and are similar in form, but the second and third dorsal fins present in cod are fused to form a single fin extending all the way down the back to the tail. The single anal fin is similar. This subtropical species occurs in the warm waters of the Gulf of Mexico, and in the western Atlantic as far north as the Carolinas. It is an active predator that travels in schools, generally at depths of less than 300m/980ft, feeding on fish and squid – although younger fish in shallow water also eat a lot of marine worms and small crustaceans. The schools move into shallower coastal waters in cold weather. The southern hake has been the subject of so much overfishing that there are concerns that some populations may not be able to replenish themselves.

Identification: Basically cod-like in form, with a deep belly and tapering tail, it has two dorsal fins instead of three, with the second being very elongated, and one elongated anal fin. It has long barbels beneath the head. Generally brown above and white below, it has dark spots above and behind the eyes and round, white spots at regular intervals along the black lateral line.

Pouting (*Trisopterus luscus*): 45cm/17.7in
This member of the cod family is a rich copper-brown above, and has yellowish-grey flanks with four or five dark bars. It has a single chin barbel and a black spot at the base of each pectoral fin. It occurs in the eastern Atlantic Ocean and the western Mediterranean Sea, and is a common sight on rocky reefs and wrecks. Young pouting often occur in large schools swimming close to the shore.

Poor cod (*Trisopterus minutus*): 40cm/15.75in
Resembling its close relative the pouting (*Trisopterus luscus*) described above, but smaller, the poor cod is a common species in the coastal waters of the eastern Atlantic Ocean and the western Mediterranean Sea. It lives in schools close to sandy or muddy sea beds, and in mid-water, and feeds on crustaceans, marine worms and small fish. In turn, it is preyed on by larger fish and dolphins.

White hake (*Urophycis tenuis*): 1.3m/4.25ft
Ranging from Labrador and Newfoundland to North Carolina, the white hake is a western North Atlantic species that favours soft, muddy areas of the continental shelf, and feeds on small crustaceans, fish and squid.

Atlantic hake

Merluccius merluccius

This moderately deep-water species, also called the European hake, lives near the bottom by day, but makes feeding forays into mid-water at night to find its prey. It feeds mainly on squid and fish, such as anchovies, sardines and herrings, as well as small hake. After spawning in spring and summer, the buoyant eggs and larvae drift into shallower inshore waters where the young hake are less vulnerable to cannibalistic predation, which is a common breeding strategy among fish, and there they feed mainly on planktonic crustaceans. It is an important food species, especially in southern Europe, but has suffered from over-exploitation and is now scarce in many sea areas.

Identification: A slender, large-headed fish with a protruding lower jaw and large, curved teeth, a triangular first dorsal fin and second dorsal and anal fins with elongated bases. Blue-green on the back and silvery on the sides and belly, with a straight, dark lateral line.

Distribution: Eastern Atlantic Ocean from Norway and Iceland to Mauritania; also Mediterranean Sea and southern Black Sea.
Habitat: Near the bottom on the middle and lower continental shelf, usually at depths of 70–370m/ 230–1,200ft but occasionally as deep as 1,000m/3,300ft.
Food: Fish and squid, or crustaceans when young.
Size: 1.4m/4.5ft.
Breeding: Buoyant eggs shed into the water are fertilized externally; the larvae are planktonic.
Status: Not listed by IUCN.

SILVERSIDES, NEEDLEFISH, HALFBEAKS AND KILLIFISH

These fish belong to three closely related orders. Silversides such as grunion are atheriniforms, while the elongated snouts of needlefish and halfbeaked fish are typical of families within the order Beloniformes. Cyprinodontiforms, or killifish, are a diverse group comprising elongate, as well as tubbier, members.

California grunion

Leuresthes tenuis

This small herring-like fish is famous for its spawning behaviour. Instead of shedding its eggs into the water, where they are likely to be eaten, it spawns at night on sandy beaches, just after the higher-than-normal spring tides that occur at the full and new moon. Large numbers of grunion swim in with the waves until they are virtually stranded, and each female works her tail end into the wet sand to deposit her eggs. The male coils around the female to fertilize her eggs, then both fish slip back into the sea. The timing ensures that the eggs remain above water level for about two weeks until they are washed out by the next high spring tide. By this time they are ready to hatch, and the larval grunion emerge within two or three minutes and are swept out to sea.

Identification: A slender, sinuous fish with large eyes, pectoral fins set well forward, two small dorsal fins, an anal fin with an elongated base and a forked tail fin. It has a bluish-green back, silvery sides and belly, and a blue-tinged silvery band bordered with violet along each flank.

Distribution: Coastal eastern Pacific Ocean, from Monterey Bay, California (US) to northern Baja California, Mexico.
Habitat: Coastal waters and bays at depths of no more than 18m/60ft.
Food: Plankton.
Size: 20cm/8in.
Breeding: Eggs are deposited on beaches below the highest tide line, and fertilized externally.
Status: Not listed by IUCN.

Hound needlefish

Tylosurus crocodilus

Widespread in the tropical oceans of the world, this is one of more than 50 similar species of needlefish. It gets its common name from its elongated, cylindrical form and extremely sharp snout, and is notorious for the way that it leaps from the water when agitated or alarmed, perhaps by predators, or when attracted towards lights at night. The fish flies through the air like a spear and people have been impaled by flying needlefish – some being seriously injured or even killed. It also has a habit of skittering across the ocean surface at high speed to escape predators or to move out of the way of boats, using its rapidly vibrating tail rather like an outboard motor – a technique that is reminiscent of the take-off runs of the closely related flying fish. It is a predator of other fish, swimming very rapidly in pursuit of its quarry, although young needlefish feed on plankton.

Identification: A very elongated, cylindrical fish with a sharp, needle-like snout lined with many sharp teeth. This is the only species of needlefish in which the teeth protrude outwards in juveniles, although they are straighter in adult fish. The dorsal and anal fins are set well back on the body, long-rayed at the front and with short-rayed extensions towards the tail fin, which is deeply forked. Body is dark blue above and white below, with silvery sides.

Distribution: Tropical Indo-Pacific Ocean from the Red Sea and South Africa to Polynesia and Japan; also Indonesia and northern Australia; tropical Atlantic range from New Jersey, USA, and Brazil to West Africa.
Habitat: Coral reefs and associated lagoons, to depths of 13m/40ft.
Food: Smaller fish.
Size: 1.5m/5ft.
Breeding: Eggs shed in the water are fertilized externally, and attach to corals and other objects.
Status: Not listed by IUCN.

Sheep's head minnow

Cyprinodon variegatus

Distribution: North and South America, from north-eastern USA to Mexico, the West Indies and Venezuela.
Habitat: Near muddy bottoms in fresh, brackish and saltwaters, including shallow, cloudy, virtually stagnant pools and ditches.
Food: Plant material, insect larvae, smaller fish, algae and detritus.
Size: 5cm/2in.
Breeding: Eggs shed into nest pits are fertilized by the male, which then defends them until they hatch.
Status: Not listed by IUCN.

This small, stumpy fish is one of the killifish, a large and widespread family found mainly in warm climates. It is extremely hardy and adaptable; it can live in muddy puddles that are too shallow for other species, tolerate a wide range of salinities, and survive in warm, virtually deoxygenated water by gulping air at the surface. The sheep's head minnow eats a wide variety of foods, including mosquito larvae, and is eaten in turn by other fish, turtles and wading birds. Its main defence is to travel in schools, but it also burrows into sediments to hide. Before spawning – which can occur at any time of year in warm waters – the males dig nest pits in the bottom mud and entice females to lay their eggs in them. Each female may lay several batches of eggs, each of up to 300, and the male defends the nest until the eggs hatch.

Identification: A short, deep-bodied fish, with a single, tall dorsal fin and a squarish caudal fin. Mainly silvery, with a dark marginal band on the tail, but males glow a bright blue colour when spawning.

Ballyhoo (*Hemiramphus brasiliensis*): 55cm/21.6in
The ballyhoo is a subtropical Atlantic member of the halfbeak family, a group closely related to the needlefish and flying fish. The name refers to the way the upper jaw is very much shorter than the lower; in other respects it resembles a silver-coloured needlefish, with three black stripes extending the length of its back. It lives in schools in shallow inshore waters, where it feeds on seagrasses and small fish.

Hardhead silverside (*Atherinomorus stipes*): 10cm/4in
A relative of the California grunion (*Leuresthes tenuis*), the hardhead silverside is a small, large-eyed, silver-coloured fish that swims in schools and feeds on small crustaceans and other zooplankton. It is an adaptable species that lives on coral reefs and soft seabeds in the tropical and subtropical western Atlantic and Caribbean, and in brackish mangrove creeks and even in freshwater streams.

Sand-smelt (*Atherina presbyter*): 20cm/8in
The slender-bodied sand-smelt has a clear green back and sides, with a broad, bright silver line running along each flank from head to tail. It lives in schools in shallow coastal waters and estuaries in the eastern North Atlantic and western Mediterranean, catching small crustaceans and fish larvae with its strongly protrusile jaws.

Four-eyed fish

Anableps anableps

This bizarre killifish is specialized for life at the water's surface, with eyes that are adapted to see well both above and below the surface. Each eye has a divided retina and two pupils that permit light to pass through the lens in different directions. The lens is ovoid, so light from below the water surface is projected through its longer dimension, while light from above the surface passes through its width. The contrast between the length and width of the lens provides the different optical qualities necessary for seeing well in both water and air. The adaptation allows the fish to target aerial and aquatic prey, and during the day it spends most of its time poised at the surface with its eyes bisected by the water line. It can also survive on mud exposed at low tide in coastal mangrove swamps.

Identification: An elongated, brownish coloured fish with large, rounded pectoral fins, a single dorsal fin set well back on the body, and a rounded tail fin. Each high-set, protruding, frog-like eye is laterally divided into two parts.

Distribution: North-eastern South America, from Trinidad and Venezuela to the Amazon delta in Brazil.
Habitat: Shallow, muddy freshwater streams and brackish mangrove channels and lagoons.
Food: Insects, crustaceans, molluscs and other types of small creature.
Size: 15cm/6in.
Breeding: Males and females mate side-to-side; females bear live young.
Status: Not listed by IUCN.

DORIES, BERYCIFORMS AND SCORPIONFISH

Dories, a well-known commercial food fish, and boarfish, are dominant in the order Zeiformes. They have narrow deep bodies, and large mouths with distensible jaws. Beryciforms include big-eyed members such as the pineconefish and species of squirrelfish, some of which have evolved light organs beneath the eye area. Scorpionfish, such as lionfish and gurnards, are an attractive, though often venomous, family of scorpaeniforms.

John dory

Zeus faber

Identification: Very deep, narrow body; high-set eyes and protrusile jaws. Two dorsal fins, the first with 9–11 strong spines with extended rays; two anal fins. Generally grey with yellow and brown stripes and blotches; yellow-ringed black spot on each flank.

The very distinctive-looking John dory appears to be bulky when viewed from the side, but its body is flattened like a plate. When it turns face-on, it presents an extremely narrow profile, and it may rely on this to make itself seem less threatening and less visible as it slowly approaches its prey, such as herrings, anchovies, sardines and the occasional invertebrate. When it gets close enough, it rapidly shoots out its protrusile jaws to engulf the animal, sucking it in with a current of water. The John dory spawns inshore in spring – or earlier in the year where the waters are warmer; the young take four years to mature.

Distribution: Widespread in shallow temperate seas, including the eastern North Atlantic Ocean, the Mediterranean and Black Seas, western North Pacific Ocean around Japan and Korea, and the western South Pacific Ocean around Australia and New Zealand.
Habitat: Inshore waters close to the seabed, at depths of 5–400m/ 16–1,310ft.
Food: Schooling fish, plus occasional crustaceans, octopus and cuttlefish.
Size: 65cm/25.5in.
Breeding: Eggs are shed into the water where they are fertilized externally.
Status: Not listed by IUCN.

Pinecone fish

Monocentris japonica

This tropical Indo-Pacific fish is heavily defended by an armour of very large, sturdy, ridged plates, and a set of extremely strong dorsal and pelvic spines. It is nocturnal, emerging at night to feed on small planktonic animals. It has big eyes for locating its prey in the dim light, and a pair of small light organs on its lower jaw that may act as lures. The light is produced by symbiotic bacteria within each organ, and the colour of the light varies from orange by day to blue-green at night.

Identification: A rounded, laterally compressed fish with big eyes, covered with ridged, plate-like scales. The first dorsal fin consists of 4–7 very stout spines with no connecting membranes; each pelvic fin has a similarly stout spine that can be erected and locked in place. Body is generally yellow. There is a small light organ on each side of the chin.

Distribution: Tropical Indian and western Pacific Oceans, from the Red Sea and eastern Africa to southern Japan, Australia and northern New Zealand.
Habitat: Rocky reefs below the tide line, in caves and crevices at depths of 10–200m/33–655ft.
Food: Mainly small planktonic crustaceans.
Size: 15cm/6in.
Breeding: Eggs are shed into the water where they are fertilized externally.
Status: Not listed by IUCN.

Red lionfish

Pterois volitans

The red lionfish is one of eight members of the *Pterois* genus native to the coral seas of the Indo-Pacific. Its extravagant dorsal fin is equipped with grooved spines linked to venom glands, making it very dangerous, and its dramatic appearance may act as warning to potential predators. The fish is mostly nocturnal, spending the day almost motionless in a cave or crevice with its head inclined downwards; it counters any threat by advancing with its dorsal spines facing forward. It emerges at night to hunt for smaller fish and shrimps, using its widespread pectoral fins to corner a victim and then striking very rapidly to seize it in its jaws.

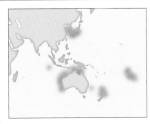

Distribution: Native to the western tropical Pacific Ocean, from southern Japan to northern New Zealand, and west to Sumatra. Also eastern Indian Ocean; introduced to western Atlantic.
Habitat: Mainly coral reefs and lagoons, from 2–50m/ 6.5–165ft.
Food: Small fish, shrimps and crabs.
Size: 38cm/15in.
Breeding: Eggs are shed in buoyant mucous containers; they are fertilized externally and the larvae are planktonic.
Status: Not listed by IUCN.

Identification: Long fin rays on pectoral and dorsal fins, and bold stripes of red to black. Adults often have white spots along the lateral line. There is usually a leaf-like tentacle above each eye.

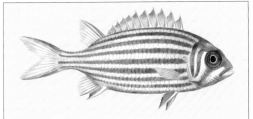

Striped redcoat squirrelfish (*Sargocentron rubrum*): 20cm/8in
Named for the longitudinal red and silver stripes on its deep flanks, this big-eyed subtropical and tropical species (above) has strong spines in its first dorsal fin, on each cheek, and in front of its anal fin. It lives on Indo-Pacific coastal reefs and wrecks, hiding by day and emerging at night to feed on crabs, shrimps and some small fish.

Common boarfish (*Capros aper*): 30cm/12in
Usually deep red with yellowish markings, this deep-bodied fish is equipped with long, stout dorsal and pelvic spines, and shorter anal fin spines. It lives in schools in the shelf seas of the eastern North Atlantic and western Mediterranean, mainly over rocky reefs, and uses its protrusile mouth to capture crustaceans, marine worms and molluscs.

Sable fish (*Anoplopoma fimbria*): 80cm/31in
At first glance, this scorpionfish looks more like a trout, with a long, sleek body and greenish, spotted back. It occurs in the North Pacific, from the Bering Sea to Southern Japan and Mexico, and migrates over long distances. It feeds on crustaceans, marine worms and small fish, and is the basis of a commercial fishery.

Flying gurnard

Dactylopterus volitans

Despite the wing-like proportions of its enlarged pectoral fins, the flying gurnard cannot actually fly. It spends most of its time exploring the seabed, creeping over soft sediments with its pectoral fins expanded so that it resembles a foraging ray. It uses the detached front lobes of these fins like legs, both to propel itself and probe for prey, such as buried bivalve molluscs or small crabs. In the process, it flushes small mobile animals into open water, and the gurnard is often shadowed by opportunist predatory fish that snap up any escapees.

Identification: A large-eyed fish with a big, blunt, armoured head and a long backward-pointing spine on each cheek. Two dorsal fins, the first with two free spines at the front. Greatly enlarged, fan-like pelvic fins, with the front six rays separated to form a mobile lobe. Mainly orange-red with some blue spots on the back; paler below. Pelvic fins mainly brown, with lighter and darker spots.

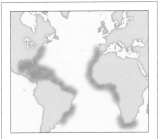

Distribution: Subtropical and tropical Atlantic Ocean, from the US to Argentina, and from France to the Azores. Also found in brackish estuarine waters.
Habitat: Sandy or muddy seabeds, often near reefs, in shallow water to depths of 100m/330ft.
Food: Crabs, shrimps, clams and small bottom-living fish.
Size: 38cm/15in.
Breeding: Eggs are shed into the water where they are fertilized externally.
Status: Not listed by IUCN.

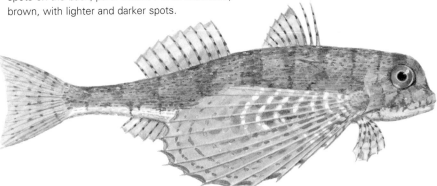

PERCHLIKE FISH

The sheer breadth of this order of ray-finned fish has already been noted. Among the large-bodied, mostly warm-water and tropical perciforms covered on the following pages are representatives from significant food fish families such as the Serranidae, sea bass and groupers, as well as the Letherinidae, made up of bream and emperor species, and many other colourful reef fish and scavengers.

Snook

Centropomus undecimalis

The big, silvery common snook is widespread in the warm waters of the Caribbean region and adjacent Atlantic, and the most abundant species in its family Centropomidae. It occurs in shallow coastal areas of salty and brackish water, usually at depths less than 20m/65ft, where it preys on smaller fish and crustaceans such as shrimps and crabs. It has few predators apart from human sport fishers, for whom it is a prize catch. It spawns in salt water near river estuaries between May and September, and the young larvae then move upriver to live in freshwater tributaries.

Identification: A streamlined, hump-backed fish with a sharp snout, protruding lower jaw and sloping forehead. It has two dorsal fins – the first spiny – a forked tail fin and a prominent black lateral line. It is dull grey in colour above with a yellow or green tinge, and silvery on the sides and belly. In some populations of fish many of the fins are yellow.

Distribution: Western central Atlantic, Gulf of Mexico and Caribbean, from the Carolinas south to Rio de Janeiro, Brazil.
Habitat: Coastal waters, lagoons and mangrove-lined estuaries, penetrating into brackish and fresh water.
Food: Fish and crustaceans, such as shrimps.
Size: 1.4m/5ft.
Breeding: Eggs shed in salt water, where they are fertilized externally. Larvae migrate to brackish and fresh waters.
Status: Not listed by IUCN.

Royal gramma

Gramma loreto

Identification: Small, with a long-based dorsal fin and elongated pectoral fins. It is bluish-purple at the front, fading through pink to yellow at the back. Oblique black stripe through eye; black spot at front of dorsal fin.

This small, brightly coloured, rainbow-patterned reef fish lives in caves and crevices among the coral, often hanging upside down from the roof of a cavity with just its head protruding. Like many reef fish, the royal gramma changes sex as it ages, starting out as a female and becoming a male. It is territorial, and when a territory-holding male dies, a female will change sex in order to take over the role. Breeding males lure females to spawn by preparing nursery sites in small crevices and then lining them with pieces of seaweed and coral. When the eggs are laid, both sexes defend them until hatching, about seven days later.

Distribution: Caribbean and western central Atlantic Ocean from Bermuda to Venezuela.
Habitat: Crevices in coral reefs.
Food: Small planktonic crustaceans, such as copepods; also picks skin parasites off other fish, such as snappers.
Size: 8cm/3in.
Breeding: Eggs shed into a crevice where they are fertilized by the male and tended by both parents.
Status: Not listed by IUCN.

Giant sea bass

Stereolepis gigas

Distribution: Eastern Pacific from California to Mexico.
Habitat: Rocky reefs with kelp beds, in depths of about 5–46m/16–150ft.
Food: Mainly bottom-dwelling fish, squid, octopus, lobsters and crabs.
Size: 2.5m/8.2ft.
Breeding: Eggs are fertilized externally and float to the surface of the water where they hatch within 1–2 days. Larvae are planktonic.
Status: Listed as Critically Endangered by IUCN.

Now extremely scarce throughout its restricted range, the giant sea bass is a bottom-feeding predator that targets slow-moving rays, flatfish, crabs and cephalopods. Cruising through the rocky reefs that are its favoured habitat, it approaches its prey and rapidly opens its huge mouth to create a suction current, drawing the victim in. As an adult, its only natural enemies are large sharks, but it has been intensively exploited as a commercial and sports fish. As a slow-breeding species it has been unable to make good the losses. Its bottom-feeding habits also make it vulnerable to pollution, since the sea bed off California is badly contaminated with toxic chemicals.

Identification: A very large, stout-bodied fish with a big head and a huge mouth, an arched back, and a spiny, long-based first dorsal fin. Bright orange with black spots when juvenile, it turns bronze-purple and then grey or black with age. Adults can change colour rapidly, from jet black to light grey, and hide or display black spots at will.

Orange sea perch (*Anthias squamipinnis*): 15cm/6in
With its lyre-shaped tail, this small, blunt-nosed, spiny-finned, plankton-eating fish from the tropical Indo-Pacific forms large schools on coral reefs. Like many reef fish, it changes sex with age, the orange-yellow female turning into a more reddish male, and develops an elongated spine at the front of the dorsal fin.

Coney (*Cephalopholis fulva*): 40cm/15.75in
Identifiable by the two black spots on its lower lip, the coney is a variably coloured grouper found on coral reefs in the tropical west Atlantic, Gulf of Mexico and Caribbean. It feeds on small fish and crustaceans, favouring water at least 45m/145ft deep.

Florida pompano (*Trachinotus carolinus*): 60cm/23.6in
The Florida pompano is a deep-bodied, laterally compressed fish with a deeply forked tail. It lives in schools in the open coastal waters of the Atlantic and Caribbean from Massachusetts, USA, to Venezuela. Silvery with a yellow throat and belly, it has yellowish pelvic and anal fins. It feeds on molluscs, crustaceans and small fish.

Oriental sweetlips

Plectorhinchus orientalis

Also known as grunts, because of their ability to make sounds by grinding their pharyngeal teeth, the 175 species of sweetlips are bottom-feeding predators that prey mainly on invertebrates buried in the sediments. They use their loose, rubbery lips to suck up the sand – which is ejected through the gills in a cloud – and any animals that it conceals. The oriental sweetlips is one of the biggest and most colourful species, well known for its lack of timidity when approached by divers. It usually feeds by night, often in groups, and shelters in caves during the day.

Identification: A stout-bodied fish with a large, blunt head and a big, low-slung mouth with thick, loose, rubbery lips. The first dorsal fin has up to 15 spines and is joined to the second dorsal fin. The pectoral and pelvic fins are relatively small, and the tail fin is shallowly forked. Very colourfully marked, with longitudinal blue and white stripes on the body, a yellow and black face and eye, and yellow fins spotted and striped with black.

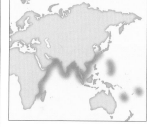

Distribution: Indo-Pacific: East Africa to Samoa, north to Ryukyu Islands, south to New Caledonia; Palau to eastern Caroline and Mariana Islands in Micronesia.
Habitat: Seabed on rocky and coral reefs, to depths of 25m/80ft.
Food: Worms, molluscs, crustaceans, such as crabs and shrimps, and small fish.
Size: 85cm/33.5in.
Breeding: Eggs shed and are fertilized externally.
Status: Not listed by IUCN.

Sweetlip emperor

Lethrinus miniatus

Known by a variety of names, including trumpet emperor, longnosed emperor and red-throat emperor, this bulky species is usually to be found on coral reefs by day, lurking among the coral heads for protection from larger predators, such as sharks. By night, it moves out over the open sand of coral lagoons and similar areas to forage for food, often in small schools. It will take a variety of prey, but favours crabs and sea urchins, which it is able to crack open with its strong jaws. It is regularly caught by both commercial and sport fishers, but if it evades capture, or being eaten by other animals, it may live for 20 years or more.

Identification: A deep-bodied fish with a large head and big mouth, high-set eyes and a moderately long snout. The lips tend to be red in colour, giving this species its common name. Body is silver-grey in colour with about eight indistinct vertical dark bars. The spiny dorsal fin, anal fin and tail are often bright red, and the pelvic and pectoral fin bases and the area around the eye are red-orange.

Distribution: Western Pacific, from northern and western Australia to New Caledonia and Ryukyu Is.
Food: Crustaceans, sea urchins, starfish, molluscs and fish.
Habitat: Favours coral reefs during the day; may move into nearby sandy lagoons at night to feed. Found at depths of about 30m/100ft.
Size: 90cm/35.5in.
Breeding: Eggs are released into the water where they are fertilized externally.
Status: Not listed by IUCN.

Common sea bream

Pagrus pagrus

Usually found on or near rocky reefs and wrecks, the common sea bream is a bottom-feeding fish that preys mainly on crabs, brittlestars, molluscs and small fish. Despite its name, it is now far less common than it once was, having been overexploited by commercial fisheries. Larger, older fish are now rare, and since this is a species that changes sex with age – from female to male – the selective removal of larger fish seriously unbalances the sex ratio. However, like many warm-water fish, the common sea bream tends to accumulate toxins in its body, through eating filter-feeding animals that have themselves ingested mildly toxic microorganisms. The risk of becoming a victim of such poisoning, known as 'ciguatera poisoning', may make humans regard the species less favourably as a food source, and improve its chances of survival.

Identification: A deep-bodied, laterally compressed fish with a large, blunt head, big eyes, a spiny dorsal fin and a forked tail. Silvery red with reddish dorsal, pectoral and tail fins, and faint yellow spots on each scale giving a yellow-striped effect.

Distribution: Eastern Atlantic: Strait of Gibraltar to Madeira and the Canary Is; also Mediterranean and northward to the British Isles. Western Atlantic: New York, USA and northern Gulf of Mexico to Argentina.
Habitat: Rocky or sandy sea beds to a depth of about 250m/820ft.
Food: Crustaceans, echinoderms, molluscs and fish.
Size: 90cm/35in.
Breeding: Eggs are fertilized in the water.
Status: Listed as Endangered by IUCN.

Distribution: Indo-Pacific, including waters off New Zealand, Australia, Indonesia, China, Taiwan and Japan.
Habitat: Rocky and coral reefs, and sandy and muddy brackish estuaries, including seagrass beds.
Food: Bottom-dwelling animals, including crustaceans, marine worms, sea urchins, starfish, molluscs and fish.
Size: 1.3m/4.25ft.
Breeding: Eggs are released into the water where they are fertilized externally.
Status: Not listed by IUCN.

Snapper

Chrysophrys auratus

Widespread in the coastal waters of the western Pacific, but forming several separate populations, the snapper, or squirefish, is a bottom-dwelling species that is most abundant near rocky reef areas on the inner continental shelf. Groups of young snappers are often encountered in shallow inshore areas such seagrass beds, but the older, larger fish tend to stay out on the reefs. It feeds on a variety of hard-shelled animals, such as crabs, sea urchins and topshells, crushing them with its strong teeth, but it will also attack schooling fish and take fish fragments when schools are being targeted by other species. It is a valued food fish, caught in large numbers by commercial fishers.

Identification: Deep-bodied and laterally compressed with a large head, typically with a rounded profile but developing a high forehead with age. It has a fairly small mouth, a spiny dorsal fin and forked tail fin. Pale pink with blue-tinged fins and a scattering of iridescent bright blue spots on back and flanks.

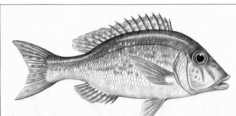

Spangled emperor
(*Lethrinus nebulosus*): 87cm/34.25in
The largest of the emperors, the spangled emperor is very like the sweetlip emperor (see opposite), but yellow-olive with pearly blue spots and streaks, giving a spangled effect. It lives on Indo-Pacific coral reefs and seagrass beds and among mangroves, feeding on sea urchins, molluscs, crustaceans, marine worms and fish.

Jolthead porgy (*Calamus bajonado*): 60cm/24in
Common in the waters of the Caribbean and off southern Florida, USA, as well as the western central Atlantic from South Carolina, USA, to Brazil, this is a deep-bodied, silvery-brown fish with a high, rounded forehead. It has strong, flattened teeth for crushing sea urchins, crabs and molluscs, and its name may refer to its habit of using its head to dislodge shellfish from rocks.

Gilthead bream (*Sparus aurata*): 70cm/27.6in
A shallow-water species that lives in schools over sandy seabeds, it is a deep-bodied fish with a strongly arched, dark grey back, a dark blotch on each gill cover and a golden stripe across its forehead. It preys heavily on mussels and oysters, using the long, pointed teeth in the front of its mouth to prise them from rocks before crushing them with its flattened cheek teeth.

Scat

Scatophagus argus

This very flattened species is common in the brackish waters of the tidal mangrove swamps that fringe estuaries in the tropical Indo-Pacific. It will eat almost anything, including the faeces of other fish – the name *Scatophagus* means 'faeces-eater' – so it has no trouble finding food in the rich, if malodorous, waters of the muddy swamps. The tangled mangrove roots also give it protection from larger predators, so the habitat makes an excellent nursery for the young fish. As they mature, they become less tolerant of brackish water, and move out on to marine coral reefs where they eventually spawn. The larvae then drift back inshore to develop in the relative security of the mangroves.

Identification: A squarish, laterally compressed fish with a small head and mouth, and a steep forehead. The spines in its dorsal, anal and pelvic fins are mildly venomous. Young fish are silvery green or silvery brown with large black spots. As they age, they turn a dull silver, retaining the spots.

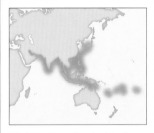

Distribution: Tropical Indian Ocean and western Pacific Ocean, from Kuwait to Fiji and north to Japan.
Habitat: Shallow bays, brackish estuaries and freshwater streams, especially among tidal mangroves.
Food: Worms, crustaceans, insects, plant material and organic detritus.
Size: 35cm/13.75in.
Breeding: Eggs are released and fertilized externally in salt water, and larvae migrate to brackish estuaries.
Status: Not listed by IUCN.

Copperband butterflyfish

Chelmon rostratus

It is not surprising that butterflyfish are valued commercially for their dazzling colouration, which looks conspicuous in an aquarium. In the wild, however, the colour pattern has a greater purpose: against the background of a coral reef it acts as a disruption pattern, breaking up the fish's outline and making it more difficult to see. If a predator does target it, it is likely to be attracted to the prominent eyespot on the dorsal fin rays. This may give the butterflyfish a chance to escape, even if its dorsal fin is shredded in the process. This common species occurs both on coral reefs and in estuaries, singly or in pairs that defend a territory against other fish of the same species.

Identification: A very striking species, which appears taller than it is long because of its compressed, deep-bodied form, long dorsal and anal fins, and vertical yellow stripes on a white background. The snout is long and slender, and the dark eye is less conspicuous than the dark eye-spot on the dorsal fin. There is also a dark band at the base of the tail. Similar in shape to its relative *Chelmon marginalis*, the margined coralfish, although the latter has just one prominent copper-coloured stripe and fewer dorsal rays.

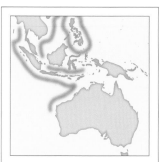

Distribution: Western tropical Pacific Ocean, from the Andaman Sea to the Philippines and Australia.
Habitat: Rocky shores, coral reefs and estuaries, to a depth of 25m/80ft.
Food: Small marine crustaceans and encrusting animals.
Size: 15cm/6in.
Breeding: Eggs are shed in the water where they are fertilized externally; the larvae are planktonic. Pairs usually mate for life.
Status: Not listed by IUCN.

Royal empress angelfish

Pygoplites diacanthus

Identification: A deep-bodied, compressed fish with a short snout. Basically yellow – or orange when young – with black-edged vertical white bars on the body and front part of the dorsal fin. The rear of the dorsal fin is deep blue, and the anal fin has yellow and blue stripes. Juvenile fish have an eye-like dark spot of colour at the base of the dorsal fin, which fades as they mature.

Closely allied to the butterflyfish, and equally spectacular in appearance, angelfish are more bulky creatures with shorter snouts and a heavy spine at the base of each gill cover. The royal empress angelfish is a particularly colourful species, but the visually disruptive effect of its vertical stripes may make it harder for a potential predator to pick it out clearly in its natural habitat. It feeds on the encrusting animals that live among the corals, and it is usually seen singly or in pairs near caves and overhanging ledges, which the animal uses as refuges. As with butterflyfish fish, the royal empress is often exported as an aquarium species, but will rarely achieve long life under these conditions.

Distribution: Tropical Indo-Pacific Ocean, from Red Sea and East Africa to the Tuamoto Islands, north to the Ryukyu Islands, and south to the Great Barrier Reef.
Habitat: Coral reefs and associated coral-rich lagoons; may seek refuge in underwater caves if threatened by predators.
Food: Sponges, sea squirts and similar animals.
Size: 25cm/10in.
Breeding: Eggs are shed in the water and fertilized externally, developing into planktonic larvae.

Orange clownfish

Amphiprion percula

Distribution: Western South Pacific, New Guinea and Solomon Islands.
Habitat: Coral reefs.
Food: Small planktonic crustaceans and similar animals, and algae.
Size: 8cm/3in.
Breeding: Eggs are laid in a nest site prepared by the male, which he then fertilizes and defends.
Status: Not listed by IUCN.

One of five species with similar habits, this tropical reef fish lives in association with large sea anemones, sheltering within their stinging tentacles as a defence against other fish. It is apparently immune to the stings, being protected by a coating of mucus that it secretes in response to its first contact with the tentacles. It always chooses one of three species of anemone, suggesting that it may not be immune to the stings of other species. It lives in small groups consisting of a breeding pair and up to four non-breeding males. The breeding female is the largest; if she dies, the male of the pair changes sex to take over as egg-layer, and one of the younger fish is promoted to the role of breeding male.

Identification: A plump, blunt-nosed fish, nearly always found sheltering among the tentacles of an anemone. It is orange with three irregular black-bordered vertical white bands. The rounded fins are orange and edged in black. Often confused with the clown anemone fish, *A. ocellaris*, although the latter lacks the black borders between coloured stripes.

Four-eye butterflyfish (*Chaetodon capistratus*): 6cm/2.3in
Named for the large, white-ringed black eyespot on the rear end of its disc-shaped, dove-grey and pale yellow body, this elegant little fish lives on shallow reefs in the Caribbean, Gulf of Mexico and nearby western Atlantic. Its real eye is normally masked by a dark stripe. Their common name of 'butterflyfish' refers to the flitting action of these fish as they feed delicately on the reef.

Forceps butterflyfish (*Forcipiger longirostris*): 15cm/6in
Widespread but generally uncommon on the coral reefs of the tropical Indo-Pacific Ocean, this butterflyfish has a highly elongated snout with a very small mouth at the tip. It uses this to pick tiny invertebrates from among the spines of sea urchin and in coral crevices. It is mainly bright yellow, but its head is black above and off-white below, and it has a grey-green tail.

Sergeant major (*Abudefduf saxatilis*): 15cm/6in
One of the most widespread damselfish, the sergeant major is a tropical Atlantic and Caribbean species with black vertical bars on its deep, yellowish-green body. It lives mainly on reefs, where it forms large schools that feed on algae, small crustaceans, invertebrate larvae and small fish. Some populations also scavenge floating offal, and juveniles may pick parasites from the skin of larger animals, most notably green turtles.

Striped mullet

Mugil cephalus

This sleek fish is one of about 80 species of mullets found mainly in salty and brackish water. Typical of its family, it has a muscular, gizzard-like stomach and a long intestine for processing vegetable foods as well as more easily digested animals. It can also ingest detritus and absorb the nutrients that it contains, making it flexible in its eating habits. In addition, it can tolerate variations in salinity that enable it to range upstream in rivers and return to the sea. Young fish exploit this by spending their early years in estuaries, where they are less vulnerable to predators. However, this makes the striped mullet easy to raise in fish farms, and it is widely cultivated in Southeast Asia.

Identification: A streamlined, round-bodied fish with an upturned mouth, two small triangular dorsal fins, the first with spines, and a large, shallowly forked tail. Bluish grey or greenish above, with silver sides and a white belly.

Distribution: Widespread in tropical and subtropical oceans and seas.
Habitat: Coastal and shallow waters to depths of 120m/390ft, favouring muddy areas; also estuaries and rivers.
Food: Small planktonic animals, bottom-living worms and microorganisms, small algae and detritus.
Size: 1.2m/4ft.
Breeding: Females typically spawn between 5 and 7 million eggs. Eggs shed and externally fertilized offshore; larvae then move inshore to develop in estuaries.
Status: Not listed by IUCN.

Giant kelpfish

Heterostichus rostratus

The giant kelpfish is the largest of the blennies. Like all true blennies, it has a continuous dorsal fin of which the first part is spiny and the remainder is soft, and a pelvic fin which is situated under the throat. The giant kelpfish spends its life among the submerged 'forests' of giant kelp – a type of large seaweed – that grow along the Pacific coasts of North America. The giant kelpfish's body colour varies to match that of the local kelp, and its elongated form blends in well with the strap-like kelp fronds. The bottom-feeding adults prey on a variety of shellfish and small fish. As adults they are solitary by habit, but the young occur in schools.

Identification: A large blenny with a long head and body, long dorsal and anal fins with prominent rays and a small tail fin. Often found among rocks often associated with giant kelp. Usually brownish or greenish in colour, mottled with silvery white, and often with darker vertical bars along the flanks. Adults solitary, young swim in schools.

Distribution: Coastal eastern Pacific from central California, USA, to southern Baja California, Mexico.
Habitat: Among rocks in coastal kelp forests, to depths of 40m/130ft.
Food: Crustaceans, molluscs and small fish.
Size: 60cm/24in.
Breeding: Released eggs attach to coral-like seaweeds, where they are fertilized and guarded by the male.
Status: Not listed by IUCN.

Moorish idol

Zanclus cornutus

This is one of the most spectacular of all reef fish, thanks to its bold, striped colour scheme and its elongated, sickle-shaped dorsal fin. Sometimes the extended tip of the fin is cut short, presumably when in conflict with predators or prey. It lives mainly on tropical coral reefs, where it uses its long snout to probe cracks and crevices for coralline seaweeds and encrusting animals such as sponges to eat. It occurs in a variety of reef habitats, from cloudy lagoons and sheltered reef flats to exposed reef faces, and down to considerable depths. Usually found in small groups, it occasionally swims in large schools of a hundred or more individuals. Young exist as free-swimming larvae for a considerable period after hatching, and may cover great distances, accounting for the lack of variation seen in this species over its widespread geographical distribution.

Identification: A deep-bodied, laterally compressed fish with an extended, tube-like snout, a short projection over each eye, and a backswept dorsal fin extended into a very long filament. It has two broad, vertical black bars on its yellow and white body, another black bar on its small tail, and an orange or yellow saddle-like patch on top of its tubular snout. The small mouth is lined with elongate teeth which act as bristles.

Distribution: Subtropical and tropical Indo-Pacific from East Africa to Polynesia, Hawaii and Japan, and coastal eastern Pacific from Gulf of California to Peru.
Habitat: Coral reefs, from shallow water to depths of more than 180m/590ft. Also favours the slightly turgid waters of inland lagoons.
Food: Small encrusting animals and coralline algae.
Size: 20cm/8in.
Breeding: Eggs are released into the water where they are fertilized externally. The larvae drift for a considerable period before settling.
Status: Not listed by IUCN.

Golden damselfish

Amblyglyphidodon aureus

Usually found at depths of 12–24m/40–80ft on the steep outer coral reef slopes and in deep channels, this delicate-looking fish favours waters with strong currents where there are plenty of sea fans and gorgonian sea whips growing. The fish lays its eggs on the stems of these organisms, and then the male guards them against egg predators until they have hatched. Adults feed on the small animals of the zooplankton, typically alone or in small groups, quite close to the bottom or the reef face. The young have a similar diet to the adults, but they live in schools close to the feeding polyps of soft corals for defence.

Identification: A small, deep-bodied, laterally compressed fish with long-based, backswept dorsal and anal fins. Body colour is golden yellow with small bluish to purplish spots on its face and belly, and often blue-tinged fins.

Distribution: Tropical eastern Indian Ocean and western Pacific Ocean.
Habitat: Coral reefs, in deeper zones with gorgonian corals and strong currents, at depths of 3–45m/10–150ft.
Food: Small planktonic crustaceans.
Size: 10cm/4in.
Breeding: Lays eggs on coral-like sea whips and sea fans, where they are fertilized and guarded by the male.
Status: Not listed by IUCN.

Achilles tang (*Acanthurus achilles*): 30cm/12in
A striking coral reef fish from the tropical west Pacific, the Achilles tang is a deep-bodied, laterally flattened species with a largely black body outlined with white, a bright orange tail and orange patch towards the rear of each flank. It is common on Hawaiian reefs, where it favours rocky areas with large cracks, caves and crevices in the shallower, well-oxygenated surge zones.

Rainbow parrotfish (*Scarus guacamaia*): 1m/3.25ft
This is one of at least 80 species of parrotfish, named for the strong beak-like jaws they use to scrape algae from stony corals. The rainbow parrotfish is one of the largest, and lives on reefs in the tropical west Atlantic and Caribbean. The multicoloured adults are very variable, but typically greenish blue with orange fins. The young live among mangroves. The species is under threat because of habitat destruction.

Unicorn fish (*Naso lituratus*): 50cm/20in
Also known as the lipstick tang because of its prominent yellow lips, this greenish grey, Indo-Pacific reef fish has a black and grey dorsal fin, a yellow anal fin, a crescent-shaped tail with a black band, and a prominent 'unicorn' bump on its steep forehead. Two yellow patches on each side of the tail base mark the positions of sharp spines.

Blue tang

Acanthurus coeruleus

The beautifully coloured blue tang is one of the surgeonfish, named for the sharp, scalpel-like spine on each side of the caudal peduncle, or tail base. These spines fit into horizontal grooves, but can be extended to make effective defensive weapons, capable of inflicting slash wounds. Juveniles are yellow rather than blue. In the intermediate phase before reaching maturity, they are blue anteriorly with a bright yellow tail (as shown). In addition to grazing algae, juveniles pick dead skin and skin parasites from green turtles, often forming 'cleaning stations' with other reef species such as sergeant major fish.

Distribution: Tropical western Atlantic Ocean, Gulf of Mexico and Caribbean. Also near Ascension Island in southeastern Atlantic.
Habitat: Coral and rocky reefs, and seagrass beds from 2–40m/6.5–130ft.
Food: Mainly small marine algae from rocks and reefs.
Size: 30cm/12in.
Breeding: Eggs are shed into the water where they are fertilized externally.
Status: Not listed by IUCN.

Identification: Laterally compressed body, large head with protruding mouth, and long-based dorsal and anal fins. Adults deep blue with narrow stripes of paler blue on body, and a pale yellow spine on each side of tail base. Juveniles yellow, may retain yellow tail until fully mature.

FLATFISH

Flatfish (Pleuronectiformes) are flattened laterally and, as adults, they swim and rest on their sides, one eye migrating around the head during their metamorphosis from the larval form. It is interesting to note that some species have both their eyes on the right side, others on the left side. Another feature of flatfish is that their eyes are protrusive – an adaptation to living partially buried on the sea bed.

Turbot

Psetta maxima

Identification: An almost circular flatfish, with a large head and both eyes on the left side. The dorsal and anal fins form a fringe around the scaleless body. Usually dull sandy brown.

The thickset, powerful turbot is an active hunter that preys mainly on other fish – particularly bottom-dwelling species such as sand eels and small members of the cod family – although it also takes a few invertebrates. It is also a prime target for commercial fisheries. Like most other flatfish, it lives mainly on the bottom, but its young swim in midwater with the aid of a buoyant swimbladder that they lose as they mature. This feature helps the young fish disperse from the spawning grounds. When they settle on the bottom they live in shallower water than the breeding adults – a fact that helps prevent them being eaten by their own species.

Distribution: North-east Atlantic Ocean from Arctic Circle to North Africa, plus Mediterranean and Black seas, and most of Baltic Sea.
Habitat: Sandy or rocky seabeds, including brackish waters, in depths from 20–70m/65–230ft.
Food: Smaller fish, such as sand eels, herring, whiting and gobies, plus large crustaceans and bivalve molluscs.
Size: 1m/3.25ft.
Breeding: Eggs are shed in the water and are fertilized externally.
Status: Not listed by IUCN.

European plaice

Pleuronectes platessa

Identification: A medium-sized flatfish with an approximately diamond-shaped body and a small head, with both eyes on the right-hand (upper) side, and a row of bony knobs between the eyes and the upper gill opening. Upper side of fish is brown with red or orange spots; lower side is white.

The plaice is one of the most familiar of the flatfish, because it is widely caught and sold whole for food. It is also one of the commonest species to be seen alive by recreational divers in northern Europe, and young plaice may even be disturbed by people paddling on holiday beaches. This is because it favours sandy shores, where it swims in with the rising tide to prey on buried molluscs and worms as they emerge to feed. It often nips off the siphon tubes of burrowing clams and other bivalves, and grazes the tentacles of fanworms, using the well-developed teeth on the left-hand, lower side, of its mouth. It is most active at night, typically spending the day lying on the sea bed partially buried by sediment.

Distribution: North Atlantic coastal waters from southern Greenland and Iceland to Scandinavia and southern Europe, Barents Sea, western Baltic, Mediterranean and southern Black Sea.
Habitat: Sandy or muddy seabeds at depths of 10–50m/30–165ft.
Food: Bottom-dwelling molluscs, crustaceans, worms and small fish.
Size: 50cm/20in.
Breeding: Eggs released into the water are buoyant; they develop into larvae living near the surface.
Status: Not listed by IUCN.

Panther flounder

Bothus pantherinus

Distribution: Tropical Indo-Pacific Ocean, from Red Sea to Tahiti and southern Japan.
Habitat: Sandy and silty areas associated with coral reefs.
Food: Bottom-dwelling invertebrates and small fish.
Size: 25cm/10in.
Breeding: Eggs are shed in the water and are fertilized externally.
Status: Not listed by IUCN.

Named for its spots – and also known as the leopard sole – the tropical panther flounder spends most of its time on shallow sandy sea beds among coral, half hidden by sediment that it flicks over its camouflaged body until only its rather protuberant eyes are visible. This helps it avoid the attentions of most of the large predators that patrol the reef, although hunters such as sharks may detect it. It feeds on the small animals that live in the sand, such as crustaceans, molluscs and worms, and also preys on the larval fish. This may explain why its own young are often found in intertidal pools, where the adults are unlikely to encounter them.

Identification: A small flatfish with an oval profile and protruding eyes on the left (upper) side. The rays of its very long-based dorsal and anal fins are elongated to form a spiny fringe, and the male's pectoral fin rays are extended into long filaments. Its colouration is highly variable, but generally mottled brown with a pattern of dark spots surrounded by pale spots, and a dark blotch on the lateral line.

Starry flounder (*Platichthys stellatus*): 80cm/31in
This North Pacific flatfish lives in cold coastal waters from the Bering Sea south to Korea and California, USA. It gets its name from the bold pattern of yellow or orange bars on its blackish dorsal, anal and tail fins; these seem to radiate from the point in the middle of its roughly diamond-shaped body, like rays. Otherwise it is dark brown with darker, blotches. It lives in a wide range of salinities from salty to fresh water, feeding on bottom-dwelling invertebrates.

Small-headed sole (*Soleichthys microcephalus*): 20cm/8in
Known only from the Pacific waters off New South Wales, Australia, the small-headed sole is a subtropical species of estuaries and shallow bays, where it partly buries itself in sandy or muddy sediments. It is vividly coloured for a flatfish, being orange-brown with a series of darker bars and a bright blue fringe formed from the dorsal, anal and tail fins.

Atlantic halibut (*Hippoglossus hippoglossus*): 2m/6.5ft
This big, elongated, dull green-brown flatfish lives in North Atlantic and Arctic waters, where it preys on other fish such as cod, haddock and skate. There are records of it reaching 4m/13ft. This large fish is now rare due to overfishing, and the species has been classified as Endangered.

Dover sole

Solea solea

The Dover sole is distinguished by the way its small, curved mouth is set to one side of its extremely rounded snout. It is largely nocturnal, but may be active on dark days or in cloudy water. It usually spends the day partly buried in the sediment, emerging at night to feed largely on small bottom-dwelling invertebrates. It sometimes swims well clear of the bottom to take small fish. As with all flatfish it begins life looking like a normal fish, and lives near the surface, but its eyes move to one side as it metamorphoses into a small flatfish. It is an important food-fish and is often sold whole like the plaice.

Identification: An elongated flatfish with both eyes on the right-hand (upper) side of its head, a very blunt snout, a small mouth and a small pectoral fin. Medium to dark brown with irregular, indistinct dark patches on its upper side, and a dark spot on the upper pectoral fin; white below.

Distribution: Coastal north-eastern Atlantic Ocean from Norway to Senegal and Cape Verde Islands, western Baltic, Mediterranean and southwestern Black Seas.
Habitat: Sandy and muddy seabeds at depths of 10–100m/33–330ft, moving to deeper waters in winter.
Food: Mainly bottom-dwelling worms, molluscs and crustaceans, plus small fish.
Size: 70cm/27.5in.
Breeding: Eggs are released into the water and fertilized externally.
Status: Not listed by IUCN.

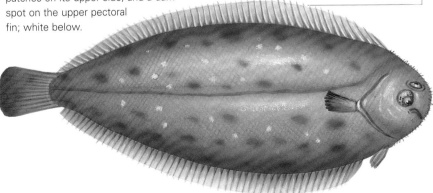

TRIGGERFISH, BOXFISH AND PUFFERFISH

The fish on the following pages belong to the order Tetradontiformes – a term which is derived from the Greek for 'bearing four teeth'. Members have two pairs of sharp teeth set at the front of the jaw, which may be visible even when the mouth is closed. These fish also lack pelvic fins. Puffers and porcupine fish can rapidly inflate their bodies to deter predators, and many are also venomous.

Clown triggerfish

Balistoides conspicillum

Identification: An oval-bodied fish with high-set eyes and two dorsal fins. Basically black, it has white spots on its belly, flanks and caudal peduncle, a yellowish, reticulated pattern on its back, pale bluish-white dorsal and anal fins with black tips, a yellow band on its caudal fin, and bright orange lips.

This reef fish owes its name to the 'clown' effect of its broad orange lips set off by the flamboyant, spotted, black and white pattern on its belly. Like all triggerfish, the first dorsal fin has three strong spines. The first, especially strong, spine can be erected at will and locked in place with the second dorsal spine, which acts as a trigger, engaging the locking mechanism. The spines cannot be lowered while the mechanism is locked. The fish uses this adaptation to wedge itself in a reef crevice when it is not feeding, and thus make itself safer from predators. When the danger has passed, the mechanism is 'unlocked' and the spines lowered. The skin also has a protective covering of tough scales.

Distribution: Tropical Indo-Pacific Ocean from Africa to Samoa, and north to Japan.
Habitat: Coral reefs, on the deep seaward reef slopes. May also venture into clear coastal waters.
Food: Sea urchins, crustaceans, molluscs and sea squirts.
Size: 50cm/6in.
Breeding: Eggs are released into the water and fertilized externally.
Status: Not listed by IUCN.

Scrawled file fish

Aluterus scriptus

The file fish are close relatives of the triggerfish. Each species has a single, long dorsal spine that is typically saw-toothed on its rear edge, like a file. This is the largest species in its family, found in warm seas where it lives mainly on coral reefs and in their associated lagoons. It uses its small mouth to graze algae and plant-like animals from hard corals and rocks, and is often seen at a variety of angles using its pointed snout to probe into crevices. It can also be found sheltering beneath floating objects in open oceans well away from reefs, having been swept from its usual range by the current.

Identification: A moderately deep-bodied fish with a large head, long snout and large, high-set eyes. It has two dorsal fins, the first of which is reduced to a single spine, and its long caudal fin – about one-third the length of its body – is often folded so it seems to be pointed. Its second dorsal and anal fins are yellow, and its greenish brown or tan body is covered with numerous black or blue spots and lines.

Distribution: Tropical and subtropical oceans worldwide.
Habitat: Coral and rocky reefs to depths of 120m/395ft.
Food: Algae, seagrasses, corals and encrusting animals such as colonial anemones and sea squirts.
Size: 40cm/15.75in.
Breeding: Eggs are released into the water and fertilized externally.
Status: Not listed by IUCN.

Longhorn cowfish

Lactoria cornuta

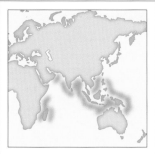

Distribution: Tropical Indian Ocean and Red Sea, north to southern Japan and south to the north-eastern tropics of Australia.
Habitat: Sandy areas with algae (seaweeds) near coral reefs.
Food: Bottom-dwelling invertebrates.
Size: 30cm/12in.
Breeding: Eggs are released into the water and are fertilized externally.
Status: Not listed by IUCN.

The boxfish, or trunkfish, have bodies that are encased in an angular, box-like defensive armour formed from thick, fused scales. This protective armour acts like a shell, preventing all body movement, so the fish have to move themselves laboriously through the water with just their small fins. The longhorn cowfish has the additional feature of very long fleshy horns above its eyes. It feeds by swimming head-down over sandy seabeds among coral, and blowing jets of water into the sand to disperse it. This exposes any small buried animals, which it then sucks into its mouth.

Identification: Very distinctive-looking fish, with cuboid body armour made of fused scales and long 'horns' above the large, high-set eyes. It has a small, low-slung mouth and a relatively long tail. Body colouration varies – from green or yellow to orange with blue spots – depending on habitat.

Blotched porcupine fish (*Diodon liturosus*): 40cm/15.75in
The porcupine fish are similar to pufferfish, but are covered with spines that bristle out when the fish is inflated. This Indo-Pacific reef species forages at night for crustaceans and molluscs, hiding away by day in crevices and caves. It is named for the large black blotches on its yellowish body.

Queen triggerfish (*Balistes vetula*): 30cm/12in
Found in the waters of the west Atlantic and Caribbean, the queen triggerfish (below) is a deep-bodied, large-headed tetradontiform, and has particularly sharp teeth for feeding on invertebrates such as starfish and sea urchins. Its colour varies with its habitat, but it always has iridescent bluish-purple stripes around its mouth, and fringing its dorsal, anal and caudal fins.

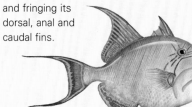

Blue-spotted boxfish (*Ostracion tuberculatus*): 30cm/12in
A relative of the longhorn cowfish (see above), this Indo-Pacific reef species has the same body form. Young fish are a clear, bright yellow with black spots, but as they get older the yellow turns bluish. It feeds on seaweeds and small animals taken from the water and sand.

Fugu pufferfish

Takifugu niphobles

Pufferfish are famous for two features: the way they can inflate their bodies with water or air to discourage enemies and make themselves hard to swallow, and the fact that their internal organs contain poisons called tetrodotoxins that can be fatal if eaten by humans. Despite this, some species are considered delicacies in Japan, where they are known as *fugu*. They are normally prepared by chefs trained to remove the toxic organs, but fish prepared incompetently cause several deaths every year. This is one of the smaller species, found in shallow waters where it uses its strong beak to crack the shells of the crabs, clams and other shellfish that form most of its diet.

Identification: Plump-bodied with a tough 'beak', high-set eyes and small fins. Greyish or brown above with paler spots, and a black blotch on its flank just above the pectoral and another just below the dorsal fins. When inflated, the body becomes rounded.

Distribution: North-western Pacific Ocean, from Vietnam to Japan.
Habitat: Sandy seabeds.
Food: Hard-shelled molluscs and crustaceans.
Size: 10cm/4in.
Breeding: Eggs are released into intertidal water and fertilized externally.
Status: Listed as Data Deficient by IUCN.

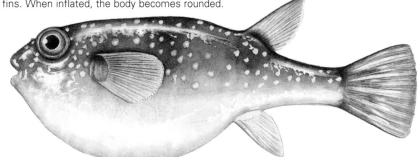

LIZARDS, SNAKES, CROCODILIANS AND AMPHIBIANS

As well as the turtles, many other species of reptiles also live in the world's oceans. Some are adapted to a life spent entirely at sea, whereas others live part of their life on the land. The marine toad is an example of an amphibian that lays its eggs in brackish water.

Marine iguana

Amblyrhynchus cristatus

Identification: Large lizard with a spiny dorsal crest running from the back of the head to the tip of its flattened tail. Squarish head with blunt snout; covered with horny protuberances around the eyes and nose. Feet are long and clawed. Colour dark greyish-brown to black; sometimes featuring a greenish crest and reddish flanks.

The marine iguana is the only living lizard to use the sea as its main habitat. This reptile is a strange sight basking on the wave-swept rocks of its Galapagos home, but to see it dive and swim in the cold sea is even more unexpected. But it is perfectly adapted for its lifestyle; it has a powerful, flattened tail for swimming – at which time it normally holds its limbs close to its body to aid streamlining. It cannot breathe under water, but during diving its heart rate slows, reducing blood flow and conserving oxygen. Special nasal glands remove excess salt from the body ingested with its food, which consists of marine algae. Highly territorial, males fight to defend small areas of the shore and attract females, often indulging in head butting fights to ward off rival males.

Distribution: Seas around the Galapagos Islands.
Habitat: Coastal rocks and waters.
Food: Marine algae.
Size: 1.5m/5ft.
Breeding: Two to three eggs laid in a sandy area, where they incubate for more than 100 days.
Status: Listed as Vulnerable by IUCN.

Saltwater crocodile

Crocodylus porosus

Identification: Large head with powerful jaws and large, conical teeth. Rows of bony plates run from behind the neck to the tip of the tail. Juveniles tan with black stripes and spots on the body and tail. Adults are darker, with tan or grey areas on back and flanks, creamy white or yellow.

Also known by several other common names including the estuarine crocodile, this is the largest species of living crocodile. Once widely hunted for its hide and because of its large size, this species has been the subject of extensive conservation programmes since the early 1970s, and numbers have now dramatically recovered. As its common name suggests, it frequents marine environments, although it is also encountered in freshwater rivers and swamps. The saltwater crocodile spends little time on land, and is a long-distance traveller with a wide distribution, swimming with the aid of its flattened tail. Prey varies according to the size of an individual – full-grown specimens can take prey as large as buffalo. Breeding territories are formed in freshwater sites and eggs are laid in a mound constructed from mud and vegetation. The female guards the nest until the eggs hatch. Then, alerted by their calls, she releases them from the nest.

Distribution: Indo-Pacific: South-east Asia to New Guinea and Australia.
Habitat: Brackish and coastal waters; also rivers and swamps.
Food: Invertebrates, such as crustaceans, and vertebrates, including fish, amphibians, seabirds and large mammals.
Size: Up to maximum of 6.3m/20.7ft; males more often reaching 5m/16.4ft; females about 3m/10 ft.
Breeding: 40–60 eggs laid in mound during the November–March wet season, hatching about 90 days later.
Status: Listed as Low Risk by IUCN.

Broad-snouted caiman

Caiman latirostris

This highly aquatic crocodilian frequents a range of habitats including swamps, marshes and mangroves, in addition to freshwater river systems. It also occurs around the mangrove regions of small coastal islands in southern Brazil. It is a medium-sized species, characterized by its exceptionally broad snout. It has a preference for eating aquatic snails, although it also takes other invertebrates and vertebrates, such as frogs and fish. By the time the broad-snouted caiman is adult, its jaws are strong and wide enough to crush turtle shells, so these also figure on the menu. In the breeding season, nests are often constructed on remote river islands. The young hatch after about 70 days and may be assisted in leaving the nest and reaching the water by their mother. It is estimated that there are about 250,000 to 500,000 individuals alive in the wild today.

Distribution: Argentina, Bolivia, Brazil, Paraguay and Uruguay.
Habitat: Brackish and coastal waters; also rivers and swamps.
Food: Snails and other invertebrates; also turtles, fish and amphibians.
Size: Up to maximum of 3.5m/11.5ft; usually about 2m/6.6ft.
Breeding: 20–60 eggs laid in mound during the wet season, hatching about 70 days later.
Status: Low Risk.

Identification: Head very broad and relatively short with a central ridge. Jaws lined with conical teeth. Body and legs scaly. Adults are often pale olive-green in colour.

Turtle-headed sea snake (*Emydocephalus annulatus*): 80cm/31in
Most species of sea snake are highly venomous, but the turtle-headed sea snake is an exception and its venom is mild. A shallow coral-reef species, it has evolved to feed on the eggs of fish, using its hard, pointed snout to dislodge the eggs from crevices before swallowing them. Found from Indonesia to the Philippines and northern Australia.

Olive sea snake (*Aipysurus laevis*): 1.8m/6ft
This large, short-headed, highly venomous sea snake inhabits the waters of coastal coral reefs, and is common in the seas around northern Australia and southern New Guinea. It belongs to the group of hydrophiid sea snakes, which evolved from venomous terrestrial Australian snakes about 30 million years ago. Unlike the kraits, which lay their eggs on land, hydrophiid snakes spend their entire lives in the sea, and even give birth to live young in the water.

Marine toad (*Bufo marinus*): up to 24cm/9.5in
Also called the cane toad, this is one of the largest of all amphibians. Although it often lays its eggs in brackish water, its natural habitat is tropical swampy forest. It ranges from Texas, USA, to Peru, although it has been introduced to other parts of the USA and Australia to control pests. Its skin glands contain a powerful toxin, although it is often preyed on by snakes.

Banded Sea Snake

Laticauda colubrina

Like other sea snakes, the banded sea snake, or sea krait, is a highly venomous reptile adapted to a life at sea. Many species of sea snakes never leave the water, but the banded sea snake comes ashore to mate and lay its eggs. Although it is an extremely capable swimmer and diver, it breathes surface air, and special valves on its nostrils close when it submerges, preventing water entering the nasal cavity. The banded sea snake also has a laterally flattened, oar-like tail, which it uses to propel itself through the water. Sea snakes shed their skin frequently – about every two to six weeks – and this helps rid them of aquatic parasites. Not generally aggressive to humans, the banded sea snake can nevertheless deliver a highly toxic venom in its bite – unwary divers and people fishing are the most common victims. However, the venom is usually used to subdue quickly its natural prey of invertebrates and fish, which it most often hunts at night.

Distribution: Oceanic waters of Australia, New Guinea, Pacific Islands, the Philippines, Southeast Asia, Sri Lanka and Japan.
Habitat: Coastal waters and coral reefs.
Food: Crabs, cuttlefish, squid, fish and fish eggs.
Size: 2m/6.6ft.
Breeding: Viviparous; up to 14 young.
Status: Not listed.

Identification: This is a long, narrow-bodied snake. The head is small and its eyelids have been replaced by modified scales. The tail is laterally flattened and terminates in a rounded tip. The body colour is pale blue with rings of black bands running the length of the body.

WHALES, DOLPHINS AND PORPOISES

The whales, dolphins and porpoises are air-breathing mammals totally adapted to a life spent entirely in an aquatic environment – even the young are born in the water. These animals swim by using powerful up-and-down movements of their horizontal tail flukes. These are most often social animals living in groups from a few individuals up to many hundreds.

Beluga

Delphinapterus leucas

Often known as the white whale because of its gleaming white skin when adult, the beluga is a northern species favouring coastal waters and, in winter, the edge of the floating pack ice. It is gregarious, normally travelling in groups of ten or more. Groups are either all males or all females and their darker-skinned young. All-male herds of more than 100 are known. Belugas feed mainly on fish, such as herring, cod and salmon, but also dive to the seabed for crabs and molluscs. They communicate with whistles, squeaks and belching sounds, and have an echo-location system that is probably used when feeding. Like many whales they are threatened by hunting and, in some areas, pollution.

Identification: A relatively small whale with a stocky frame, a bulbous forehead and a mobile face. It has gleaming white skin when mature, but is darker skinned when young. The dorsal fin has been replaced by a dorsal ridge, which is more prominent in males. The males are some 50 per cent heavier than the females.

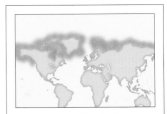

Distribution: Arctic Ocean and adjoining seas, including the Sea of Okhotsk, Bering Sea, Gulf of Alaska and Hudson Bay, plus a small population in the Gulf of St Lawrence, Canada.
Habitat: Fjords, estuaries, and shallows in summer; near ice edge in winter.
Food: Fish and squid, plus crabs, octopus and other bottom-living invertebrates.
Size: 4m/13ft.
Breeding: One calf born after a 12-month gestation; birth interval 2–3 years.
Status: Listed as Vulnerable by IUCN.

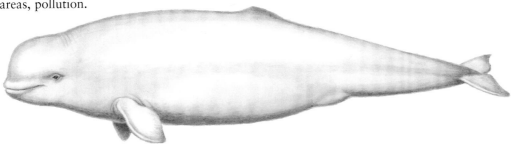

Narwhal

Monodon monoceros

Related to the beluga (*Delphinapterus leucas*) described above, the narwhal is famous for the single, long 'unicorn' tusk of the adult male. This is a modified tooth, which grows to a length of 2m/6.5ft or more, and has a pronounced left-hand spiral. The function of the tusk is not certain: it is extremely well supplied with nerve endings that make it sensitive to water temperature and pressure, but it is not clear why this sensitivity is not shared by females. Since narwhals are social animals, usually seen in small groups that sometimes associate in larger herds, the tusk may act as an indicator of male status – like the antlers of deer. Both sexes take the same prey, often feeding at depth on bottom-living invertebrates as well as fish taken in open water.

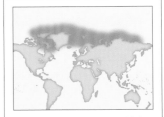

Distribution: Ranges widely throughout the Arctic Ocean, from north-eastern Canada and Greenland to northwestern Siberia.
Habitat: Mainly deep water near pack ice, following the ice edge as it advances and retreats with the seasons.
Food: Mainly fish, squid and shrimps.
Size: 4.5m/14.75ft.
Breeding: A single calf (rarely twins) born after a 15-month gestation; birth interval 2–3 years.
Status: Listed as Data Deficient by IUCN.

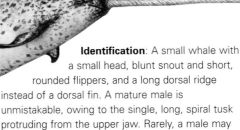

Identification: A small whale with a small head, blunt snout and short, rounded flippers, and a long dorsal ridge instead of a dorsal fin. A mature male is unmistakable, owing to the single, long, spiral tusk protruding from the upper jaw. Rarely, a male may have two tusks, and tusked females are known. Body colour is light grey mottled with darker patches, becoming paler with age.

Humpback whale

Megaptera novaeangliae

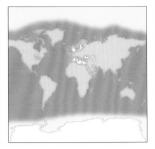

Distribution: All oceans, but seasonally resident in cold polar waters in summer, and warm subtropical or tropical waters in winter.
Habitat: Feeds and breeds in relatively shallow waters, but crosses deep oceans on migration.
Food: Schooling fish and krill.
Size: 14m/46ft.
Breeding: Single calf born every 2 years or so, in warm-water wintering areas.
Status: Listed as Vulnerable by IUCN.

This is probably the most familiar of the big rorqual or baleen whales, thanks to its spectacular acrobatic displays. Despite its immense weight, it may leap right out of the water, falling back with a huge splash: a behaviour known as breaching. Both sexes also slap their tail flukes and flippers on the water, and males communicate with a complex repertoire of whale 'songs'. They are social animals, travelling and feeding in small groups that often form part of larger aggregations. They have a cooperative feeding technique that involves swimming around and below fish or krill while releasing a rising curtain of bubbles to concentrate the school. Each whale then lunges upwards to scoop up a vast volume of prey and water. It expels the water through the sieve-like baleen plates lining its mouth.

Identification: A large whale with a pronounced hump in front of its dorsal fin, a stout body and very long flippers – the longest of any whale. There are rounded knobs on top of the large head, beneath the jaw, and on the front edges of the flippers. These are often encrusted with barnacles. Some 12–36 grooves extend from the chin to the belly. Body colour is basically black, with a variable pattern of white patches below and on the flippers and tail flukes.

Southern right whale (*Eubalaena australis*): 17m/56ft
Found only in the waters around Antarctica, between 30 and 50 degrees south, this large whale was considered the 'right' whale to catch by whalers. It has a very big head, no dorsal fin, and no throat grooves, and is basically brown to black in colour with white horny growths on its head. It feeds on planktonic crustaceans such as copepods and krill.

Grey whale (*Eschrichtius robustus*): 14m/46ft
This north Pacific Ocean whale has a very coastal distribution, since it feeds by sieving small animals from the bottom sediments, usually in water that is less than 50m/164ft in depth. The whale feeds in Arctic waters during the summer months, migrating to the subtropics for the winter season. It has a relatively small head, and its grey skin is encrusted with variable paler patches of barnacles.

Bryde's whale (*Balaenoptera edeni*): 12m/39ft
Identifiable by the three ridges located on top of its head, prominent sickle-shaped dorsal fin, dark-grey back and pale-coloured throat, Bryde's whale occurs worldwide in warm tropical or subtropical oceans. It is an opportunistic feeder, taking mainly schooling fish and crustaceans by straining water through the baleen plates lining its mouth.

Long-finned pilot whale

Globicephala melas

The pilot whales are basically big dolphins, and this species has the same habit of living in large groups, or 'pods', of between 10 and 50, and occasionally 100 or more. It is essentially oceanic, roaming nomadically in search of schools of squid or, failing that, fish. Its preference for the deep ocean means that it is poorly adapted for shallow coastal waters, and it is prone to becoming stranded on tidal shores. Its social bonds are so strong that one disoriented whale is followed by others, and mass strandings are common. The long-finned pilot whale also has a long history of exploitation in the North Atlantic, particularly in the Faeroes where a traditional hunting practice involves driving whole pods ashore to be killed. Some 1,200 pilot whales are killed in this way each year.

Identification: A medium-sized whale with a very bulbous head, especially in males. It has long, backswept flippers and a round, slightly hooked dorsal fin. It is black or dark grey with a white diagonal stripe behind the eye, and greyish areas on the belly and chin.

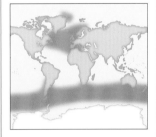

Distribution: Temperate to sub-polar waters of the North Atlantic Ocean, entering the western Mediterranean Sea, and the southern Pacific, Atlantic and Indian Oceans.
Habitat: Mainly the deep oceans, but may stray into shallower coastal waters in search of food.
Food: Mainly squid, plus schooling fish.
Size: 5m/16.4ft.
Breeding: A single calf is born after a gestation of 15–16 months. Birth interval 3–4 years.
Status: Not listed by IUCN.

OPEN OCEAN AND DEEP WATER

Despite its enormity, the open ocean supports surprisingly few species. Life in the 'big blue' tends to be concentrated in small areas, with one species attracting another to create small and often ephemeral communities – for example, a drifting object, or organism, will attract zooplankton, plankton feeders and spawning fish, which in turn attract filter-feeding fish and larger predators.

At the edge of the continental shelves, the sea floor slopes steeply away and a strange, alien world begins. The residents of this still largely unexplored environment continue to amaze scientists, with new species and novel ways of life discovered on almost every journey to the depths.

Amazingly enough, there are representatives of almost all major marine groups living in deep water – bony fish and sharks, crustaceans, echinoderms, molluscs and various worm phyla are all present and all have found ways to cope with the low light and low energy conditions. Even mammals, such as the sperm whale, although tied to the surface by the imperative to breathe air, make it to extraordinary depths.

Above, left to right: Deep water peaked shrimp (Acanthephyra curtirostris); Atlantic menhaden (Brevoortia tyrannus); slender snipe eel (Nemichthys scolopaceus).

Right: Freckled driftfish (Psenes cyanophrys) shelter under an abandoned plastic oil can in the open ocean.

SPONGES AND CORALS

The organisms on these pages are among the simplest forms of multicellular animal life. Both sponges and corals exhibit extraordinary diversity and demonstrate that evolutionary success can be achieved without a complex body plan. Many can form colonial reefs and sizes given below reflect this. Sponges once surpassed corals as the dominant reef-builders on earth.

Venus' flower basket

Euplectella aspergillum

This exquisite glass sponge is the best known of its class. The others live in even deeper water and are rarely seen. Venus' flower basket takes the form of a tall vase, with a deep internal chamber, the spongocoel. The external structure consists of a brittle framework of fused six-rayed silicaceous spicules. The tissues around this delicate skeleton consist of fibrous proteins and wandering cells called amoebocytes, which perform a wide variety of functions, not least the repair of damaged tissues. The glassy skeleton often persists after the sponge has died and has been valued as an ornament or gift in societies as diverse as Victorian England and traditional Asian cultures. The spongocoel is often home to a pair of commensal shrimps of the genus *Spongicola*, which enter when small and then grow too large to leave. For this reason the sponge is sometimes given as a gift at weddings, to symbolize lifelong partnership.

Identification: A tall, cylindrical, sessile organism that is supported by a delicate lacy scaffold of pale silicaceous spicules. It is attached to the substratum by a cluster of long glassy threads, which protrude from its base like a tuft.

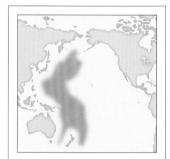

Distribution: Western Pacific Ocean.
Habitat: Benthic, on rocky sea bed from 100–1,000m/ 330–3,280ft.
Food: Microplankton and particles of organic debris.
Size: 1.3m/4.25ft.
Breeding: Not known.
Status: Harvested for gift and souvenir market, apparently common; not listed by IUCN.

Glass coral

Lophelia pertusa

Identification: Soft tissues are a variably intense shade of yellow or pink. Each individual polyp has about 50 small tentacles surrounding a central mouth collecting food particles in the water.

This reef-building species grows in medium-to-deep water off the continental shelves. Polyps are about 1–1.5cm/0.4–0.6in across and grow within a calcareous skeleton. The skeletons of neighbouring polyps are attached to the rocky substratum or to one another. In the Gulf of Mexico and the North Sea off Norway especially, these clusters may grow large, and the skeletons of successive generations accumulate to form substantial reefs. The species is generally associated with areas of sea bed where moderate-to-strong currents bring a good supply of food – mainly particles of organic matter. Living in deep, dark waters, these corals cannot rely on photosynthetic zooxanthellae to sustain them. Breeding appears to be seasonal, with populations in different part of the world spawning at different times of year.

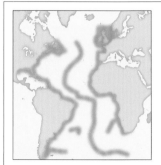

Distribution: Tropical and temperate Atlantic.
Habitat: Benthic, reef forming from 40–1,000m/ 130–3,280ft deep.
Food: Organic particles and deep-water plankton.
Size: Polyps about 1.2cm/0.5in across.
Breeding: Seasonal spawning consists of external fertilization and development via planula larvae.
Status: Not listed by IUCN, but may face threats from trawling and oil-exploration.

Bamboo coral

Acanella arbusca

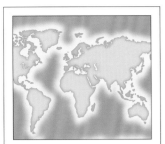

Distribution: All oceans.
Habitat: Benthic, from around 30m/97.5ft down to 1,300m/4,265ft or more.
Food: Organic particles suspended in the water.
Size: Individual polyps rarely exceed more than a few millimetres in diameter.
Breeding: Not known.
Status: Not listed by IUCN; is sometimes used in jewellery manufacture.

There are more than 100 documented species of bamboo coral, all of which are similar. Their classification into species is the subject of much debate among experts. A key physical characteristic of the group is bony, finger-like structures interspersed with bands or nodes of dark-coloured protein material a bit like horn. In *Acanella* and its close relatives, the 'fingers' branch in whorls, forming a relatively complex three-dimensional bushy structure. Other animals seek shelter among the branches, so *Acanella* colonies may play an important role in benthic ecosystems. The tiny polyps sprouting from the fingers each have eight tentacles.

Identification: With this species of bamboo coral, branching always occurs in the bony white part of the 'fingers' (internodes). Other bamboo corals are unbranched or they branch at the nodes.

Ivory tree coral (*Oculina varicosa*): Colonies 10–150cm/4in–5ft tall
Known from shallow waters of the South Atlantic, this bony, branching species also occurs in a single, documented deep-water location called the Oculina Bank, off Florida, USA. The colony is thought to be more than 1,500 years old and forms a reef about 165km/100 miles long.

Pink precious coral (*Corallium secundum*): Colonies rarely exceed 60cm/2ft across
A highly valued Pacific Ocean sea fan, it has been collected intensively in the past for making into jewellery, but is now protected. It grows at depths of 400m/1,300ft or more.

Black coral (*Antipathes grandis*): Colonies rarely exceed 2m/6.7ft in diameter
With about 150 species, the black coral group is named for the dark brown to black skeleton, which typically develops thorny outgrowths. The living soft tissues may be brightly coloured. Black corals typically live in deep water, though shallow-water species are also known.

Glass sponge (*Heterochone calyx*): Colonies grow up to 150cm/5ft tall
This knobbly vase-shaped sponge is the dominant species in recently discovered sponge reefs off British Columbia, Canada. These reefs may be more than 9,000 year old and were previously thought to be long extinct.

Mushroom coral

Anthomastus ritteri

This small, slow-growing, colonial soft coral is nicknamed the dog-toy coral. This is because when its tentacled feeding polyps are withdrawn it has the look of a rubber ball or mushroom attached to the sea floor by mean of a rubbery base. It occurs in moderately deep water where it feeds on particles of organic matter and small plankton-dwelling organisms that float past on the current. The tentacles are sticky and armed with stinging cells for paralyzing small prey. But they are also the most vulnerable part of the coral, hence their ability to withdraw rapidly into the tough base. Mushroom coral are dioecious (meaning sexes are separate). Males release sperm into the water and eggs are fertilized while still inside the female polyp. The embryos are brooded internally until they reach the free-swimming stage, when they are released and disperse.

Identification: Stout, mushroom-shaped base is usually pale and bears numerous pink polyps.

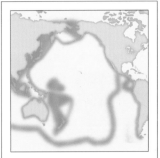

Distribution: Pacific Ocean.
Habitat: Benthic on rocky sea floor between 200 and 1,300m/656 and 4,265ft.
Food: Particles of organic matter and zooplantkton.
Size: Colony 15cm/6in across; stalk 30cm/12in.
Breeding: Internal fertilization, larvae released at free-swimming stage.
Status: Relatively common; not listed by IUCN.

HYDROZOANS, JELLYFISH AND COMB JELLIES

The free-swimming members of the phylum Cnidaria include some of the most admired and feared animals in the sea. All are armed with stinging cells, some of which are lethal to humans. The mysterious comb jellies of the phylum Ctenophora look rather similar, but do not sting.

Portuguese man-o-war

Physalia physalis

The Portuguese man-o-war is a floating cluster of individual hydrozoan animals that work together so closely they appear to be a single organism. The colony drifts at the water surface supported by a large medusa, or swimming bell, which is modified into a gas-filled float. Dangling from the float is a stem bearing clusters of polyps specialized for performing different tasks, such as feeding, reproduction or defence. Feeding polyps are armed with fine, stinging tentacles that trail in the water to snare and paralyze prey, such as small fish or shrimp. Any food that is caught is shared with other non-feeding polyps – all are connected by a common central cavity that serves as a gut. Reproductive polyps bud off new individuals, which usually remain part of the colony. The polyps with the largest stinging tentacles are concerned exclusively with defence of the colony. Hundreds of thousands of people swimming in the sea receive unpleasant stings from man-o-war tentacles every year, although a few marine animals are able to tolerate them.

Identification: The large float bears a tall sail and supports a cluster of tentacled feeding polyps, small reproductive polyps and defensive polyps with very long tentacles. Polyps may be pink, lilac or bright blue in colour.

Distribution: Tropical and temperate waters of Atlantic, Pacific and Indian Oceans and adjoining seas.
Habitat: Surface.
Food: Small fish and larvae, shrimps and other plankton.
Size: 30cm/12in; tentacles 50m/164ft in length.
Breeding: Colonies grow by asexual budding of member polyps. Hermaphrodite reproductive zooids release eggs and sperm into the water, fertilized eggs develop into planula larvae that may found new colonies.
Status: Common; not listed by IUCN.

Purple jellyfish

Pelagia noctiluca

Also known as the mauve stinger, this dainty jellyfish has fine tentacles that grow up to 3m/10ft long. There are eight tentacles in all, growing from the rim of a mushroom-shaped swimming bell. Beneath the bell, four large, frilly arms surround the central mouth, creating a funnel-like opening called the manubrium. Both the swimming bell and tentacles are well-endowed with stinging cells, though to humans the sting is more a nuisance than a serious hazard. The scientific name *noctiluca* means 'night light'. Purple jellyfish may produce a bioluminescent glow when disturbed and secrete a glowing mucus when handled. Larvae of the purple jelly develop directly into miniature jellyfish, called ephyrae. There is no sessile polyp stage. The species occasionally occurs in great numbers – these 'jellyfish plagues' can pose a major nuisance to fishermen and on tourist beaches.

Identification: Mushroom-shaped swimming bell is covered in pink or purple warts. The bell has eight lobes, with a single, long tentacle and sense organ growing from the notches in between. The four oral arms are well developed and have elaborate frills.

Distribution: Warm-temperate waters of the North Atlantic and North Pacific and adjoining seas.
Habitat: Warm surface waters in coastal areas and over deep water.
Food: Small fish and plankton-dwelling invertebrates.
Size: 60cm/24in in diameter.
Breeding: External fertilization; fertilized eggs develop via ephrya larvae to juvenile medusae with no polyp phase.
Status: Common; not listed by IUCN.

Lion's mane jelly

Cyanea capillata

Distribution: Arctic, Atlantic and Pacific Oceans, north of 42°, and adjoining seas.
Habitat: Cold and cool waters.
Food: Mainly other jellyfish.
Size: Occasionally 2m/6.6ft across; tentacles 30m/100ft.
Breeding: Little is known about reproductive behaviour, but individuals mature within a few months.
Status: Not listed by IUCN.

The lion's mane jelly is named for the dramatic tangle of brownish-orange frills associated with the four food-gathering arms surrounding the mouth in the underside of the bell. The bell is divided into eight lobes, and there is a cluster of between 60 and 150 thread-like tentacles associated with each lobe. The tentacles are sticky and easily snare smaller jellies – the species' main prey. In humans, the tentacles usually cause a moderately painful sting similar to that of a severe nettle rash, which in very extreme cases can be life-threatening. Lion's mane medusae live only a single year. In the summer they reproduce sexually, with fertilized eggs that develop into tiny larvae. These sink to the sea floor where they develop into over-wintering polyps, which begin budding off tiny new medusae in the spring of the following year. The largest specimens are found in the far north in the autumn.

Identification: Yellow or orange saucer-shaped bell with deeply scalloped edges; four short, very frilly arms and eight clusters of very long, fine, sticky tentacles.

By the wind sailor (*Velella velella*): 6cm/2.4in in diameter
This is another surface-dwelling oceanic colony, like the Portuguese man-o-war. Also known as the bluebottle on account of striking indigo pigmentation of the large float and associated tissues. The float bears a fin-like sail, allowing the colony to be carried long distances aided by wind and current. It is found in tropical and temperate Atlantic, Pacific and Indian waters.

Hula skirt jelly (*Physophora hydrostatica*): 40cm/15.75in in diameter
This colony floats in mid-water to depths of 1,000m/3,280ft or more, controlling its buoyancy by secreting gas into a float. The float supports an elongated stem, which bears polyps specialized to the tasks of feeding and breeding. As with the by the wind sailor, it is found in tropical and temperate zones of the Atlantic, Pacific and Indian oceans.

Venus' girdle (*Cestum veneris*): 1.5m/5ft long
A highly unusual comb jelly that grows widthways to form a delicate, belt-like body, with the mouth in the middle of the leading edge. The animal normally swims with the long leading edge forwards, but can perform worm-like undulation that propels it quickly sideways. It occurs widely throughout the temperate and tropical waters of the Atlantic, Pacific and Indian oceans, and adjoining seas.

Giant comb jelly

Beroe forskalii

Like most other comb jellies, *Beroe* species are slightly elongate jellyfish-like animals with eight rows of comb-like structures running the length of the body. Unlike their relatives the sea gooseberries, they lack tentacles of any sort. The 'body' comprises a sac with a large cavity with a single, large opening – the mouth. For such delicate-looking animals, they are surprisingly voracious predators. The jelly relies on luck to encounter prey, mainly other jellies, which are engulfed whole by the particularly sizable mouth. Comb jellies drift about in open water, propelled weakly by the rhythmic, wave-like beating of the cilia (hair-like structures) lining their comb-rows. Under certain illumination, the rows refract white light to create spectacular displays of shimmering rainbow colours. This is not bioluminescence, although some related animals are able to produce light, usually a pale blue glow.

Distribution: Warm-temperate north Atlantic and Mediterranean waters.
Habitat: Open water.
Food: Other comb jellies.
Size: 15cm/6in.
Breeding: Hermaphroditic; eggs and sperm released into the water develop into cydippid larvae and then into adult jellies.
Status: Not listed by IUCN.

Identification: Elongate body with eight parallel rows of light-splitting comb-rows. The mouth is particularly large, opening directly into the digestive cavity, which, in turn, branches into eight interconnected canals that run alongside the comb-rows.

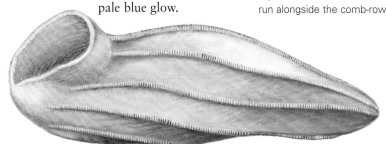

WORMS

Worms are rare in open water because few have mastered the art of swimming. On the deep-sea floor, however, they are among the dominant forms of invertebrate life and many have evolved extraordinary methods of adapting to the challenges of the abyss. The species described in detail below are annelids grouped within sub-categories of this phylum: the classes Polychaeta and Pogonophora.

Giant beardworm

Riftia pachyptila

The giant beardworm is the largest of an obscure group of worm-like invertebrates discovered growing alongside hydrothermal vents. Each worm lives inside a protein tube. At the top of each tube, a bright-red beard projects into the water. Beardworms have no gut, mouth or anus, and so rely on unconventional means of obtaining nutriment. Some organic matter appears to be absorbed from the water, but most comes from millions of symbiotic bacteria that live inside the worm's body and account for up to 15 per cent of its body weight. The beard acts as a sort of gill, taking in carbon dioxide and sulphides needed by the bacteria. The bacteria then convert the carbon dioxide and sulphides into sugars, a proportion of which is absorbed by the worm.

Identification: White tube grows attached to sea floor. The plume, or beard, is bright red due to the high concentration of the blood pigment haemoglobin in the tissues.

Distribution: Full distribution not known, but two distinct habitat zones exist around vents of the eastern Pacific Ocean and Galapagos trench.
Habitat: Benthic in very deep water, adjacent to hydrothermal vents.
Food: Organic compounds produced by millions of symbiotic bacteria.
Size: Up to 1.5m/5ft.
Breeding: Male and female worms release eggs and sperm into the water; larvae develop from fertilized eggs and settle nearby.
Status: Appear to be common in suitable habitat, not listed by IUCN.

Pelagic worm

Tomopteris pacifica

Identification: Body is transparent, dorsoventrally flattened and clearly segmented. Segmental appendages (parapodia) bear paddle-like structures, but bristly chaetae are absent. Long, trailing antennae are characteristic of the family.

This pelagic polychaete is a graceful swimmer. It propels itself through the water using paddle-shaped appendages called parapodia. There are no bristly chaetae, like those seen in most bottom-dwelling polychaetes. It is an active predator of much smaller pelagic invertebrates. The body is colourless, but *Tomopteris* is able to produce yellow bioluminescence from light organs at the tips of the parapodia. The light appears as a shower of little sparks when the worm is disturbed. Yellow bioluminescence is very unusual – most other light-producing animals glow blue-green or red. *Tomopteris* worms are hermaphrodites. Eggs are carried on the parapodia and released into the water when fertilized.

Distribution: Pacific Ocean, including coastal areas.
Habitat: Mid-water.
Food: Other zooplankton.
Size: Up to 5cm/2in.
Breeding: Hermaphroditic; fertilized eggs released into water and develop into planktonic larvae.
Status: Common; not listed by IUCN.

Pompeii worm

Alvinella pomejana

The scientific name commemorates the remote-controlled submarine *Alvin*, with which the first specimens of this amazing animal were observed in deep water off the Galapagos Islands. The common name comes from the ancient city destroyed by a volcanic eruption. Pompeii worms appear to thrive on heat and toxic chemicals – they live right on the walls of so-called 'black smokers', underwater chimneys belching clouds of black superheated water containing dissolved chemicals that would cook or poison more conventional organisms. They tolerate a range of temperatures from 20–80°C/68–176°F. They feed on micro-organisms tough enough to survive the extreme conditions and, like the superficially similar but only distantly related beardworms, they also have a symbiotic relationship with bacteria, which live in the gut and produce an excess of organic 'fuel' to feed the worm.

Distribution: Full distribution not known, but two distinct habitat zones exist around vents of the eastern Pacific Ocean and Galapagos trench.
Habitat: Hydrothermal vents.
Food: Detritus, heat tolerant micro-organisms and organic matter produced by symbiotic bacteria.
Size: 13cm/5in.
Breeding: Males release sperm into water; females may brood fertilized eggs within body.
Status: Apparently common, not listed by ICUN.

Identification: Body can be fully retracted into a tube made of papery material secreted by the animal. Mucous secretion on the worm's back encourages the growth of dense fleece-like colonies of bacteria, which help deflect some heat.

Deep-sea roundworms

(Phylum Nematoda) Nematode worms are among the very few organisms that can tolerate life in the thick oxygen-deprived anaerobic ooze that covers much of the ocean floor. Also known as threadworms, these tiny creatures range from a fraction of a millimetre in length to about 1cm/0.4in long (see individual, below-right). They feed mainly on bacteria and live in colonies (above-left). As many as 15,000 nematode species are in existence.

Whale bone worm (*Osedax rubiplumus*): Males usually under 1mm; females up to 2cm/0.8in
A highly specialized cousin of the beardworms with an equally bizarre way of life, this species lacks a functional mouth and gut and lives embedded within the decaying bones of dead whales, where symbiotic bacteria help it to absorb oils and other nutrients. Males are very tiny and live as parasites within the body of the larger females. This species and its relatives are also known as zombie worms.

Ribbon worms (Phylum Nemertea)
Nemerteans have a long, unsegmented body, cylindrical at the front end but becoming flat and ribbon-like further along. They have large, piercing mouthparts. Typically, adult nemerteans may grow to 8–9cm/3.2–3.6in in length.

Pelagic polychaete

Poeobius meseres

Poeobius is an unusual and little understood polychaete – a marine worm possessing both sexes and with bristly paired parapodia (appendages) – the only known member of its family. A single specimen of what might be a related species, appropriately named *Enigma*, was found in 2001, but then lost. The largely transparent body of *P. meseres* comprises 11 rather indistinct segments within a jelly-like sheath. At the front end are two retractable green tentacle-like palps and a circle of long whiskers, or branchiae, surrounding the mouth. *Poeobius* catches food by spinning a net of sticky mucus in which drifting particles and small plankton-dwelling organisms become trapped.

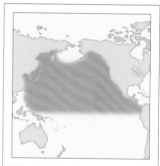

Distribution: Sub-Antarctic waters of the North Pacific Ocean, including coasts.
Habitat: Mid-water below 300–1,300m/985–4,265ft.
Food: Plankton-dwelling organisms and detritus.
Size: Up to 2.7cm/1in.
Breeding: Not known.
Status: Not known.

Identification: The body is largely obscured by a gelatinous mucous sheath. Pale green tentacles are retractable.

SNAILS, SLUGS AND BIVALVES

A few extraordinary members of the molluscan classes Nudibranchia, Gastropoda and Bivalvia live at the surface of the ocean and in its most inhospitable depths. As larvae, the young of a great many more species spend the first weeks or months drifting as part of great swarms of plankton. The unusual mollusc Neopilina galathea, *a recent marine discovery, continues to thrill and baffle scientists.*

Neopilina galathea

Identification: Apex of asymmetric conical shell droops to the front of the body. Broad muscular foot (see view of underside, below-right) provides means of attachment and locomotion. Foot surrounded by peripheral groove containing feeding and respiratory organs.

Dredged from a deep-sea bed in 1952, this mollusc was the first of its kind to be discovered alive. Its anatomy differs considerably from that of other molluscs, and its only known relatives are 400-million-year-old fossils. *Neopilina* has a thin shell, broadly similar to that a limpet, except that the apex tilts towards the front of the animal. There is a large foot around which lies a groove containing five or six gills, mouth and anus. Several important organs, including the nervous system and gills, are arranged in a repeating pattern, like that seen in the segmented bodies of annelid worms and arthropods (insects and crustaceans). At first this was seen as evidence of an ancestral link between the molluscs and other invertebrate groups, but it now seems likely that the segmented features of *Neopilina* evolved long after these groups had split.

Distribution: Full extent not yet known; probably exists in deep oceans around the world.
Habitat: Sea floor at great depths – 2,000–6,000m/ 6,560–19,685ft.
Food: Deep-sea sponges, diatoms and foraminifera.
Size: 3.5cm/1.4in.
Breeding: Not known.
Status: Not listed by IUCN.

Violet sea snail/Purple bubble raft snail

Janthina janthina

Identification: Air chambers at the apex of the spiral shell impart positive buoyancy. In life, the body of the snail occupies the last two whorls of the shell.

This sea snail has a delicate, purple shell similar to that of land snails. It lives in open water, drifting with the current while floating upside down beneath a raft of tough, gluey bubbles secreted by its fleshy foot, or attached to the body of jellyfish-like siphonophores, which it also eats. Somehow, the snail manages to avoid being killed or paralyzed by the stinging tentacles of animals such as the Portuguese man-o-war and the by-the-wind sailor. Instead, it scrapes away at the tentacles with its rasping *radula* (tongue), thus getting a meal as well as a ride. If disturbed, it often ejects a squirt of purple ink. This substance is produced by a gland in the mantle (the fleshy part of the body attached to the inside of the shell). The function of this intriguing behaviour is not known for sure, but it is assumed to be some kind of diversionary tactic to deter predators. The young are brooded by the parent and eventually released as fully formed miniature snails. They all start life as males, only turning into females when sufficiently large to produce eggs efficiently.

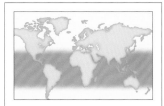

Distribution: Tropical and sub-tropical oceans and seas worldwide, including coasts.
Habitat: Open water, at the surface.
Food: Mostly hydrozoans, such as the Portuguese man-o-war and by-the-wind sailor.
Size: 3cm/1.2in.
Breeding: Hermaphrodite: eggs develop in clusters attached to adult, which are then released as miniature snails with no larval phase.
Status: Common; not listed by IUCN.

Molluscan larvae as plankton

Of the 50,000 or so species of living mollusc known to science, only very few live in the challenging environment of the open ocean – except, that is, as larvae. While most adult marine molluscs live in relatively shallow, coastal habitats, their young make extensive, albeit helpless, excursions into the unknown – drifting at the whim of prevailing currents as part of the plankton community. The larval stage can last anything from a few days to several months, depending on species, during which time a larva may travel many hundreds, even thousands of kilometres. This dispersal is an important strategy and the means by which species with a relatively sedentary adult stage manage to colonize far-flung habitats. Of course, from the perspective of individual larvae, it's highly risky, as the vast majority never reach a suitable place to settle and most are eaten by other animals.

Below: Molluscan larvae spawned by a member of the Tridacnid family of bivalves; possibly a species of giant clam.

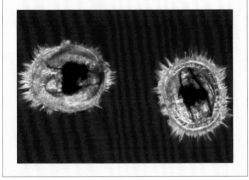

Blue sea slug

Glaucus atlanticus

Like the violet sea snail (see opposite), the blue sea slug spends its adult life upside-down at the water's surface, usually attached to the body of a drifting siphonophore such as *Physalia* (bluebottle or Portuguese man-o-war) or *Velella* (by-the-wind sailor). To hide it from predators, the parts of the body that face upwards are vibrant blue, while the back, which habitually faces down into the water, is pale silvery grey. This mollusc is not only immune to the stings of the jellies' tentacles, it appears to select those with most stinging cells to eat. The stinging cells are not digested; instead they are stored within the tips of its feathery appendages (*cerata*). Here they retain their stinging potential and protect the slug from other predators.

Distribution: Tropical and temperate oceans worldwide, including coasts.
Habitat: Surface water, associated with floating siphonophores.
Food: Tentacles of jellyfish-like siphonophores.
Size: 0.5–30cm/0.2–12in
Breeding: Hermaphroditic: eggs are laid in sticky strips attached to host, and develop directly into tiny slugs with no larval phase.
Status: Common; not listed by IUCN.

Identification: Body comprises a long muscular foot; ventral surface has inky blue stripes. Clusters of radiating, lobe-like appendages serve as defensive weapons, but may also be used in swimming.

Giant vent clam

Calyptogena magnifica

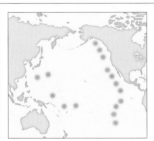

Distribution: Thermal vents located on Pacific ocean floor; likely to extend to other oceans.
Habitat: Thermal vents of deep-ocean volcanoes, several thousand metres deep.
Food: Nutriment obtained from bacteria living in the gills.
Size: 30cm/12in long.
Breeding: Unknown
Status: Probably common; not listed by IUCN.

This deep-sea clam lives clustered around hot vents, water from which is superheated to 350°C/662°F or more – only the enormous pressure prevents it instantly vaporizing. The outflow is rich in sulphides and other chemicals that would be toxic to marine life from most other habitats. Deep-sea clams not only tolerate these conditions, they thrive in them. There is little in the way of conventional food here, but the clam has no gut anyway – it gains nutriment from symbiotic bacteria living inside its gills. These bacteria use chemical oxidation to convert sulphides into organic matter, in much the same way that conventional plants use sunlight to make sugars from carbon dioxide and water. The bacteria reproduce inside the clams' tissues, and are passed on from parent clam to offspring within the cytoplasm of its eggs. Adult clams can crawl around on the sea floor using their muscular foot, which also anchors the animal securely into a crevice when it finds a home.

Identification: Twin shells are made of calcium carbonate and protein. Living tissues dark red due to haemoglobin pigment that transports oxygen to the tissues and bacteria living within.

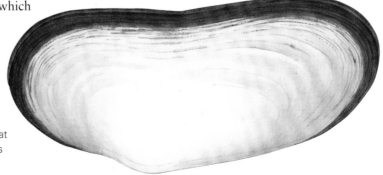

CEPHALOPOD MOLLUSCS

The cephalopods rank among the most highly evolved and intelligent invertebrates. Several species of octopus and squid have adapted to life in the open ocean, and some live at extreme depths. Biologists are only just beginning to learn the secrets of these mysterious deep-sea molluscs, some of which have famously evaded human observation for decades, existing only in legend.

Nautilus

Nautilus pompilius

Identification: The shell is an expanding spiral, with brown bands above, but pure white below. The opening of the shell is shielded by a tough hood. Two prominent eyes and a cluster of small tentacles protrude from the large living chamber.

The genus *Nautilus* is all that remains of a once great order of molluscs. They are the closest living relatives of another vast but wholly extinct group, the ammonites. Nautili are considered very primitive – they have retained a large external shell and their movements are slow – more like that of snails than of other cephalopods. The shell contains a series of sealed chambers – the body of the animal occupies the largest of these, which is also the most recently made. The others contain gas for buoyancy, as well as the gas-producing organ. The nautilus propels itself by weak jet propulsion or crawls over the sea floor using its tentacles. It spends the day in deep water but rises to shallower areas at night. Food is collected by the tentacles around the mouth. Nautili are long-lived by cephalopod standards, but breed slowly – females produce a dozen or so large eggs in a year, which hatch into nautili 2cm/0.75in across.

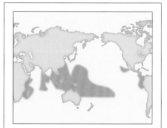

Distribution: Tropical areas of Indian and Pacific Oceans.
Habitat: Deep water close to reefs down to 800m/2,600ft.
Food: Small fish, crustaceans and dead animals.
Size: Up to 25cm/10in.
Breeding: Internal fertilization; large eggs develop directly into miniature versions of the adult, reaching maturity in 5–10 years.
Status: Feared to be in decline; not listed by IUCN.

Giant squid

Architeuthis dux

The giant squid has all the hallmarks of a mythical sea monster – enormous size, fearsome weapons in the form of powerful arms and tentacles and a beak that could bite though steel cable. Until recently, it was known only from dead specimens washed up on beaches, but in 2005 Japanese scientists published video footage of a giant squid taken from a research submersible. Their observations showed the squid to be an active and aggressive predator. Giant squid have few enemies – sperm whales and sleeper sharks eat smaller specimens, but it is quite possible for larger individuals to fight back successfully. Little is known about the life history of giant squid. The larvae were once thought to belong to an entirely different genus, *Rhynchoteuthis*.

Identification: Front of the animal's body bears eight arms with rows of powerful serrated suckers and two long tentacles with suckers at their clubbed ends. The fins, positioned at the end of the body, are small. The eyes are the largest in the animal kingdom at up to 30cm/12in across. Two large gills are located inside the mantle cavity.

Distribution: Temperate and deep waters of tropical oceans worldwide.
Habitat: Deep water, often associated with continental and island slopes of 200–1,000m/650–3,300ft in depth.
Food: Mostly deep-sea fishes and smaller squid species.
Size: Up to 18m/59ft in length
Breeding: Little known; fertilization is internal; larvae and juveniles sometimes found in shallower water.
Status: Unknown. Strandings may be result of changing ocean currents. Not listed by IUCN.

Football octopus (Pelagic tuberculate octopus)

Ocythoe tuberculata

Distribution: Temperate and deep waters of tropical oceans worldwide.
Habitat: Surface waters of open oceans.
Food: Smaller pelagic animals.
Size: Up to 1m/3.25ft.
Breeding: Ovoviviparous.
Status: Thought to be rare but not listed by IUCN.

Female football octopus rise to feed in surface waters at night. By day, it seems they sink to deeper water. They are strong swimmers. A unique feature is the presence of a gas bladder, like that seen in many bony fish, which helps the animal control its buoyancy. Males are tiny, about one-tenth the size of females. Males and juvenile females sometimes seek shelter inside the gelatinous body of salps (pelagic tunicates). The species is the only living cephalopod known to give birth to live young, which hatch from their eggs while still inside the mother. It is not yet known quite how the tiny males manage to fertilize the females' eggs, but the process probably involves passing a packet of sperm (a spermatophore) to the female. Football octopus are eaten by many large fish and marine mammals.

Identification: Upper and lower pairs of arms longer than those that spread to the sides. The body and arms are highly muscular and the skin of the upper surface of the mantle is covered in small bumps, or tubercles.

Colossal squid (*Mesonychoteuthis hamiltoni*): may exceed 30m/100ft
Potentially far exceeding even the giant squid in size, the colossal squid is a relatively recent discovery. Known only from abyssal depths of the icy seas around Antarctica, it must rank among the greatest living predators. Its tentacles are armed with saw-edged suckers and hooks capable of tearing through flesh and hide.

Firefly squid (*Watasenia scintillans*): 10cm/4in
A pelagic species so far only known from the sea around eastern China and Japan where it is commercially fished. Photophores on the mantle and arms emit a bright blue luminescence.

Deep-sea finned octopus (*Staurotheuthis syrtensis*): 15cm/6in
A delicate-finned octopus from the deep Atlantic, with arms linked by a web of skin forming a bell or balloon shape, depending on the posture of the arms. Two rounded fins give the impression of large, flapping ears. The small suckers are modified into luminescent organs.

Bigfin squid (*Magnapinna pacifica*): Adult size unknown
Known from just three young individuals, the Pacific bigfin squid has a small body, eight small arms and two slightly larger tentacles. The back of the body bears two enormous membranous fins, several times longer than the body itself.

Vampire squid

Vampyroteuthis infernalis

The scientific name of this species is rather unflattering. It means 'Vampire squid from hell' – a little melodramatic considering the animal is no larger than a human hand. The vampire squid is a small, nimble swimming deep-water squid. The eyes are large – relative to the animal's size, perhaps the largest in the animal kingdom. The arms bear rows of sharp spines with which the squid grasps its prey. The arms are connected by an extensive web. The second pair of arms are retractile, and can be extended to several times the length of the body. There are numerous light-producing organs all along the arms and the tips. It can secrete clouds of glowing fluid, which may be used to confuse predators in much the same way as other squids use ink.

Distribution: Tropical and temperate oceans worldwide.
Habitat: Typically found at depths of 600–1,200m/ 2,000–4,000ft.
Food: Copepods, prawns and cnidarians.
Size: 13cm/5in.
Breeding: Internally fertilized eggs, up to 4mm across, are released into the water, where they drift within small, free-floating masses.
Status: Threatened, becoming endangered.

Identification: Gelatinous body with spiny arms connected by a web and two oval fins resembling flapping ears. Has very large eyes.

OSTRACODS, COPEPODS, ISOPODS AND AMPHIPODS

The taxa on these pages are representatives of the most abundant group of animals in the ocean – the crustaceans. Many members of these groups are small and cryptic, but they occur in stunning variety and in such numbers that without them, the entire marine food web would collapse.

Mussel shrimps (Subclass Ostracoda)

Ostracods are also known as pea shrimps or mussel shrimps on account of their hinged carapace, which forms a delicate spherical case into which the entire body can be withdrawn. The body plan is amazingly successful and more than 8,000 species of ostracod have been described. Most, however are less than 2mm in diameter, with *Gigantocypris* the giant of its kind. Ostracods swim in mid-water using rowing actions of the large antennae. The other appendages remain tucked inside the carapace. Movement of the antennae generates a feeding current, drawing tiny prey, such as algae or copepods, close enough to snare on the bristly appendages.

Right: The giant ostracod Gigantocypris agassizii *grows up to 3cm/1.2in across and lives inside a near spherical translucent carapace.*

Identification: Ostracods live within a pair of hemispherical carapace valves. These open slightly to allow antennae and other appendages to emerge to allow feeding and locomotion.

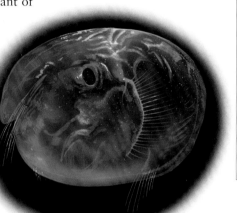

Distribution: All oceans.
Habitat: Pelagic and benthic from coasts and surface to depths; also fresh water.
Food: Algae, bacteria, other small invertebrates and fish larvae.
Size: Up to 3cm/1.2in.
Breeding: Female ostracods brood young inside carapace; many species reproduce by parthenogenesis (virgin birth).
Status: Abundant; not listed by IUCN.

Copepods (Subclass Copepoda)

Above: The deep-water copepod Euaugaptilus hyperboreus *is a tiny, colourless copepod that lives in the deep, cold waters beneath the Arctic pack ice.*

Copepods are tiny crustaceans and are among the most numerous animal on Earth. They are on the menu for hundreds of species of plankton feeders, from jellyfish whales, which filter them from the sea at a rate of trillions per day. However, copepods are not wholly helpless. With reaction times among the fastest of any aquatic animals, these tiny animals can respond to changes in water pressure that might signal an approaching predator. They react by making sudden darting movements generated by powerful flicks of the antennae. When threatened, many deep-water species emit puffs of bioluminescent dye to divert possible predators. The risk of being eaten is also reduced by avoiding sunlit surface waters during the day – copepods are among the multitude of vertical commuters that rise from deeper water to feed at night. The group includes a number of larger parasitic species that live attached to the bodies of larger species.

Identification: Tiny crustaceans with a single eye in the middle of the head, or cephalosome.

Left: The pelagic copepod Undinula vulgaris. *This common species of tropical waters worldwide forms a large part of the diet of many filter-feeding animals.*

Distribution: All oceans and seas worldwide.
Habitat: Mostly pelagic from coasts and surface to depths.
Food: Algae and particles of organic matter; some are parasitic.
Size: 1mm–1cm/0.04–0.4in.
Breeding: Females carry fertilized eggs in one or two large clusters attached to the abdomen.
Status: Abundant; not listed by IUCN.

Left: The deep-sea Pleuromamma xiphias *is one of the species known to produce bioluminescence in response to the threat of predation.*

Sea lice (Order Isopoda)

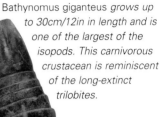

The isopods are one of the largest and most diverse groups of crustaceans, with more than 10,000 species. Of these, the majority live in deep water and are rarely seen. Each segment of the body is covered with a curved plate, or tergum. Many species can roll into a ball like a woodlouse (a terrestrial member of the same group). There are eight pairs of thoracic legs, the first of which (the maxillipeds) assist the mouthparts, while the others are used for crawling. The abdominal appendages are used for swimming and also serve as gills. Isopods are good parents. Females brood their young in a pouch called the marsupium (similar in function to the pouches of marsupial mammals). The brooding phase can last several months, during which time the female is often especially cautious, sometimes remaining hidden in a burrow or lair where she and her young are relatively safe.

Above: The deep-sea louse Bathynomus giganteus *grows up to 30cm/12in in length and is one of the largest of the isopods. This carnivorous crustacean is reminiscent of the long-extinct trilobites.*

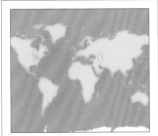

Distribution: All oceans and seas worldwide.
Habitat: Mainly benthic, some live associated with flotsam (there are also freshwater and terrestrial species).
Food: Small fish and a wide range of invertebrates.
Size: 5mm–40cm/0.2–15.75in.
Breeding: Mating occurs after a partial moult; females brood eggs and larvae; young are released at late larval stage or as miniature adults.
Status: Common; not listed by IUCN.

Identification: As a general rule, isopods are flattened animals, with a segmented body lacking a carapace.

Right: The pelagic sea slater Idotea metallica *is a common species of sea louse from tropical and warm-temperate waters.*

Whale parasites and commensals

Commensalism refers to a particular type of parasitism, where one organism benefits, and the other is neither aided nor afflicted.

Whale barnacles

Many species of whale barnacle are highly specialized and will only grow on certain species of whale. Mature larvae settle on the skin of a whale and attach themselves with a special cement. They use the whale as transportation while filtering plankton as food.

Whale lice

Whale lice are amphipods belonging to the genus *Cyamus*. They are about 1–2cm/0.4–0.8in long. Superficially spider-like, they live nestled in among the clusters of barnacles on the heads of great whales. Like other amphipods, they eat a mixture of plankton and detritus, including flakes of dead skin shed by their huge hosts. They do not appear to do the whales any harm, and are passed from whale to whale, most often from mother to calf, by physical contact.

Copepods

Whales are among the list of vertebrates targeted by parasitic copepods. These animals are equipped with a long mouth tube and a set of serrated jaws, which they use to burrow through the host's skin. They remain attached there, the ribbon-like body trailing alongside the host, while feeding directly on its blood.

Amphipods (Subclass Amphipoda)

Amphipods are a diverse group of animals. Most of the 8,000 or so species bear seven pairs of thoracic appendages and, on the abdomen, three pairs of swimming legs and three pairs of stiff appendages. However, one group, known as skeleton shrimps, is very spindly, with body and appendages of more or less equal thickness. The lifestyles of amphipods are extremely diverse, with pelagic, bottom-dwelling, burrowing, tube-building and parasitic examples (there are also many freshwater and even some terrestrial species). They move by walking on the thoracic legs or swimming using the abdominal appendages or the antennae.

Identification: Diverse, though usually shrimp-like, with a laterally compressed body.

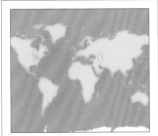

Distribution: All oceans and seas worldwide.
Habitat: All marine habitats (also in fresh water and on land).
Food: Particles of organic material, algae, smaller invertebrates; some species are parasitic.
Size: 1mm–30cm/0.04–12in.
Breeding: After mating, the female carries fertilized eggs in a brood pouch under body; the young emerge as miniature versions of their parents.
Status: Abundant; not listed by IUCN.

Above: The deep-sea amphipod Eurythnes gryllus *is a cosmopolitan scavenger found in water as deep as 6,500m/21,325ft.*

Right: The pram bug Phronima sedentaria *is a pelagic amphipod that seeks shelter inside the body of pelagic salps. It is allegedly the inspiration for the monster in the science-fiction film* Alien.

KRILL AND SHRIMPS

*The class Malacostraca includes some of the world's most abundant species, and some of the most
exploited. Apart from being a great natural spectacle, swarms of krill and shrimp are a vital resource for
larger animals and increasingly a target of commercial fisheries. Research is underway in various oceanic
locations to verify the impact of over-fishing on numbers and breeding.*

Deep water opossum shrimp

Gnathophausia ingens

The order Mysidacea includes
about 800 small shrimp-
like crustaceans
named for the pouch-like
marsupium in which females
brood their larvae – which is a little
like the pouch of marsupial mammals
such as opossums. By the time the young
emerge from the pouch they have developed
into miniature versions of their parents. The group
also includes the extremely delicate-looking fairy shrimps.
Opossum shrimps live in large swarms, usually close to the
sea floor. They are eaten by many kinds of fish, and many
species seek sanctuary among stinging anemones, moving
carefully between the stinging tentacles. Deep-sea species such
as *Gnathophausia* produce bioluminescence when disturbed,
presumably in an attempt to confuse potential predators.
They feed mainly on plankton and other organic material
filtered from the water using their bristly thoracic legs.

Identification: Usually
distinguished by its large size
and bright red colour,
Gnathophausia is a primitive
opossum shrimp, in which only
the first pair of appendages on
the thorax are modified into
mouthparts. The other thoracic
legs and abdominal appendages
are used for swimming.

Distribution: Likely to be
present in all oceans.
Habitat: Benthic, from near
surface to deep water.
Food: Mainly algae and
detritus drifting down through
the water.
Size: 0.1–35cm/0.04–13.75in.
Breeding: Eggs fertilized and
develop into larvae within the
female's brood pouch.
Status: Common; not listed
by IUCN.

Antarctic krill

Euphausia superba

Identification: Elongate, translucent, segmented body,
with a head dominated by large, round eyes. Of eight
thoracic appendage, two are modified into
mouthparts, six are long, bristly legs
used for catching food.
Abdomen has five pairs
of appendages.

Dense swarms of this
phenomenally abundant
shrimp-like crustacean may
stretch over several square
kilometres of ocean to a
depth of 5m/16ft or
more. These vast
aggregations contain
billions, even trillions
of small, shrimp-like
animals with a segmented
body, two pairs of long
antennae, and six to eight pairs of thoracic appendages, five
pairs of abdominal swimming legs and two pairs of tail
appendages either side of long tail segment. Antarctic krill are eaten
by all kinds of other animals, most notably the world's largest animal, the
blue whale, which in the Southern Hemisphere feeds almost exclusively on this
species at a rate of up to 4,000kg/4 tons a day during the summer. Krill are filter
feeders, and use long bristles on their thoracic appendages to form a basket under the
body that sieves plankton and organic matter from the water or sediment.

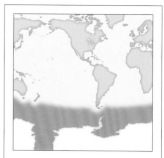

Distribution: Southern
Ocean.
Habitat: Surface waters of
open ocean down to about
100m/330ft.
Food: Algae and small
zooplankton.
Size: 5cm/2in.
Breeding: Spawns several
times over the summer
period; fertilization is external;
no parental care.
Status: Abundant but
declining under increasing
pressure from commercial
fishing interest. Not listed
by IUCN.

Deep water peaked shrimp

Acanthephyra curtirostris

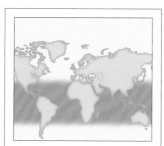

Distribution: Tropical and subtropical oceans worldwide.
Habitat: Deep mid-water, from 200–2,200m/660–7,200ft.
Food: Small pelagic animals.
Size: Up to 8cm/3in.
Breeding: External fertilization; larvae develop in mid-water without any parental care.
Status: Common; not listed by IUCN.

This bright-red shrimp spends its entire life in the mid-water zone, never once touching the bottom or reaching the surface. The striking red colour helps it to remain invisible, even in the upper reaches of its depth range where a small amount of blue and green light from the surface penetrates, but no red light. Under these conditions the body appears to be entirely black. It swims using broad, paddle-like appendages on its abdomen known as pleopods. The thoracic legs, which benthic shrimps use for walking, also assist with swimming, but are used mainly for catching food. The species is carnivorous, and preys on smaller members of the mid-water community – principally other small crustaceans – in which it lives.

Identification: Scarlet body, carapace forms a peak over the head; two pairs of antennae – one short, one very long; thoracic legs are delicate, abdominal appendages much more robust, and biramous (branching in two).

Northern shrimp (*Pandalus borealis*): up to 12cm/4.75in
This predatory shrimp is among the most heavily exploited of all the crustaceans and is a familiar food item. It is present in cold parts of the Atlantic and Pacific oceans, and has a variety of common names, some of which refer to its reddish-pink colour. In far northern waters, most individuals start off as males, becoming females when they have grown large enough to produce eggs.

Deep-water krill (*Bentheuphausia amblyops*): up to 5cm/2in
This North Atlantic bottom-dwelling species lives in water more than 1,000m/3,300ft deep and, unlike all its close relatives, lacks bioluminescent body markings. It also has much smaller eyes, suggesting that it depends more heavily on other senses to find food and mates and to detect predators.

Icelandic boxer shrimp (*Spongicoloides profundus*): size unknown
This shrimp lives at depths of up to 1,500m/4,900ft in the North Atlantic and is often associated with glass sponges, in which it may live. Boxer shrimps are named for their greatly enlarged walking legs, which are often carried in front of the head, in the manner of a boxer taking guard. New species of the *Spongicoloides* genus are now being discovered in the Pacific.

Pelagic red crab

Pleuroncodes planipes

The red crab belongs to a group of crustaceans know as squat lobsters. The body appear short because of the small carapace and a characteristic posture in which the abdomen and tail are tucked up under the body. Of the five pairs of walking legs, the first are very large and bears robust claws. There are no specialized swimming appendages, but red crabs still swim, using powerful flicks of the abdomen. For most of the year, they live and feed on the sea bed, but in spring they swim to the surface to moult and breed. They form aggregations numbering millions or even billions of animals, and provide a food resource for both grey and blue whales, loggerhead turtles and predatory fish such as tuna. From time to time – especially in El Niño years – red crab swarms are washed ashore.

Distribution: Pacific Ocean.
Habitat: Benthic most of the year, rising to surface waters of open ocean to breed.
Food: Plankton.
Size: 2–8cm/0.75–3in.
Breeding: Females brood developing eggs attached to their abdomen; larvae develop though several moult stages.
Status: Common; not listed by IUCN.

Identification: Small lobster-like crustacean with bright-red body. First pair of walking legs bear long claws. All legs have bristles to help gather small food items from the water.

CRABS, LOBSTERS AND SEA SPIDERS

Despite appearing to slot into a rather natural-looking group, the similarities between these bottom-dwelling marine scuttlers are limited. Crabs and lobsters are decapod crustaceans, while sea spiders belong to a small and entirely separate branch of the arthropod tree, the class Pycnogonida. Despite the Pycnogonids' superficial resemblance to land spiders, their anatomy is quite different.

Alaskan king crab

Paralithodes camtschaticus

The king crab is a species of stone crab – a group related to hermit crabs. Their recent ancestors had an abdomen adapted to fit into the abandoned shell of a gastropod mollusc, which served as a protective 'house'. Modern stone crabs carry their abdomen tucked up under the body, like true crabs. But, like hermit crabs, the fifth pair of legs is reduced in size and the abdomen is lopsided, with appendages growing only on one side – those on the other side were lost by the hermit ancestors when they adapted to wearing a shell. King crabs gather in shallow water to breed, with pairs forming a close embrace while spawning. Juvenile crabs often gather together in dense clusters.

Identification: Carapace is red or purple, covered in nodules and spines. Of the five pairs of thoracic legs, only the middle three are used for walking. The first are claw-bearing chelipeds; the fifth are small and tucked away.

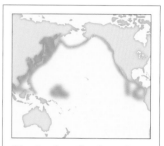

Distribution: Continental shelves in the North Pacific Ocean.
Habitat: Benthic, on sea floor 200–300m/650–1,000ft down.
Food: Echinoderms, molluscs and other bottom-dwelling invertebrates.
Size: Legspan 1m/3.25ft; carapace 25cm/10in across.
Breeding: Spawns in spring.
Status: Highly commercial; not listed by IUCN.

Vent crab

Bythograea thermydron

Identification: Unremarkable-looking crab with adults having an all-white body. Delicate carapace, five pairs of slightly bristly walking legs, of which first pair bear robust pincers that are used for tearing up food.

Vent crabs live at enormous depths, typically favouring the waters around hydrothermal vents – places where scalding hot water from deep inside the Earth is expelled into the sea along with dissolved chemicals that most marine life would find toxic. The crabs live among the clusters of tube worms that grow alongside the vents, in water temperatures that vary widely depending on proximity to the vent itself. Vent crabs move about by crawling or swimming. They are carnivorous – feeding on other specialized animals with which they share their extreme habitat, mainly tubeworms, shrimps and mussels. Juvenile vent crabs are bright orange – but their colour fades with successive moults until they attain the white colour of adults.

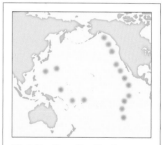

Distribution: Pacific Ocean, restricted to thermal vents.
Habitat: Close to thermal vents at an average depth of 2,700m/8,850ft.
Food: Other vent invertebrates.
Size: Up to 13cm/4.75in.
Breeding: Little known – planktonic larvae probably provide means of dispersal from vent to vent.
Status: Thought to be common; not listed by IUCN.

Japanese spider crab

Macrocheira kaempferi

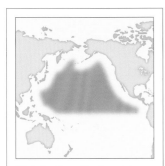

Distribution: Continental shelves of North Pacific.
Habitat: Benthic, at depths of 150–200m/480–650ft.
Food: Bottom-dwelling molluscs, other crustaceans and dead animals.
Size: Legspan as much as 4m/13ft.
Breeding: Ventures into shallower water to spawn.
Status: Common; not listed by IUCN.

The world's largest living arthropod, the Japanese spider crab is a deep-water giant, with a carapace measuring up to 37cm/14.6in across. Its longest appendages, the great pincer legs, or chelipeds, are up to 2m/6.6ft long. An individual of this size will weigh up to 20kg/44lb. They are able to attain such proportions only with the aid of water to help support the weight of their legs. The length of the legs is an adaptation to moving about on soft marine sediments – by spreading its weight over a wide area the crab avoids sinking into the choking silt. On land, they are all but helpless. They can live up to 100 years.

Identification: Carapace is teardrop-shaped, with the narrow end at the front, usually orange or red, with short spines. Legs are enormously long – fifth pair noticeably smaller; first pair modified into super-long claw-bearing chelipeds.

Crustacean larvae as plankton

For the most part, crustacean larvae look nothing like their parents. In the course of their development from fertilized egg through to juvenile, they pass through a number of larval stages, or 'instars' – a term that is perhaps more often associated with insect development. The names vary between the different groups, but in most taxa the earliest larval form is a microscopic but rotund little creature known as the nauplius. Nauplii have two pairs of large antennae, a set of mandibles (jaw-like mouth parts) and a single eye positioned in the middle of the head. From these humble beginnings, the larva passes through several more instars, acquiring more body segments and appendages at each new stage, and growing to look more and more like the adult parent. Like insects, crustaceans must shed their rigid exoskeleton in order to grow larger, and so each instar is separated from the next by at least one moult.

Below: A nauplius larva of the goose barnacle group.

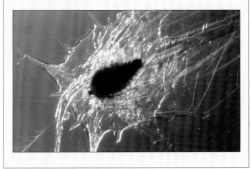

Giant deep sea spider

Colossendeis colossus

This bizarre-looking animal is not a true spider, but belongs to a sister group of the chelicerates (spiders and scorpions) called the Pycnogonida. Sea spiders appear to be all legs – the body is reduced to a small trunk, the head is virtually nonexistent and the abdomen is a tiny stump, like a short tail. The animal's body is so small that most of the vital organs are located in the leg bases. Sea spiders feed on soft-bodied prey, mainly 'grazing' on organisms such as hydras and bryozoans (sea mosses), which encrust rocks and firm surfaces on the sea bed. Food is sucked up through the proboscis at the front. The giant sea spider is the largest species known: usually 30–40cm/ 12–15.75in long; occasionally 70cm/27.5in.

Identification Tiny trunk section bears four pairs of walking legs. A fifth pair grows from the head section of females, and in males there is a sixth pair of legs used for carrying eggs.

Distribution: Likely to be present in all oceans.
Habitat: Benthic in deep water down to 3,000m/ 9,750ft.
Food: Mainly benthic sessile invertebrates.
Size: Up to 70cm/27.5in.
Breeding: Males carry fertilized eggs in clusters on specialized legs.
Status: Unknown; not listed by IUCN.

ECHINODERMS

*The echinoderms are a diverse and mysterious group, and are only ever found in marine environments –
they could not tolerate life in freshwater habitats. The majority of echinoderm species live in shallow
water, but the ones that have adapted to life at greater depths are often among the dominant
benthic fauna in those less hospitable parts of the ocean.*

Tall urchin

Dermechinus horridus

Like most sea urchins, *Dermechinus* has a rigid, brittle
shell, the test, made up of a closely fitting jigsaw of
mineralized plates. Its test is unusual in that it is
taller than it is wide – almost egg shaped. Small
holes in the plates allow delicate, hydraulically
operated tube feet to reach out into the
surrounding sediment and seawater. The fitted
plates also bear rounded papillae, which act
as smooth ball-joints for several tiny mobile
spines. *Dermechinus* is gregarious, typically
occurring in groups, known as herds, of up
to several hundred animals. It is often the
dominant form of animal life on the deep
sea bed, where it feeds on whatever organic
matter happens to be available.

Identification: The test can be up to three times
taller than it is wide. Five radial grooves extend from
the mouth at the base to the anus at the top. Rows of
knobbly papillae support short, mobile spines.

Distribution: Patchy
distribution in temperate
waters of southern
Pacific Ocean.
Habitat: Benthic in deep
water from 180–560m/
600–1,850ft.
Food: Other benthic
invertebrates and detritus.
Size: Up to 13cm/5in tall.
Breeding: External
fertilization; the young
develop via plankton-
dwelling larval phase.
Status: Apparently common;
not listed by IUCN.

Deep water sea cucumber

Irpa abyssicola

This small species of sea cucumber was first described from a single rather battered
specimen dredged from the North Atlantic in 1878. It was not seen again until 1999 when
scientists using a remote-controlled submarine were able to collect several more from the
cold, dark waters of the Hayes Deep, off the Arctic archipelago of Svalbard. It may seem
an obscure, rather insignificant animal, but worldwide, at 4,000m/13,000ft, this species
and its relatives in the order Elasipodia account for about 50 per cent of all living metazoan
organisms (animals other than single-celled protozoa). At double this depth, this figure rises
to a staggering 90 per cent. The key to their success in these impoverished waters is a low-
energy lifestyle. They eat sediment, digesting out organic material in much the same way
as earthworms process soil.

Identification: Body an
elongated gelatinous oval,
lacking pigment. The
mouth is surrounded
by ten tentacles and is
on the underside at the
front end; the anus is on
top at the back. The
animal crawls with the
aid of hydraulically
operated feet.

Distribution: Temperate
northern Atlantic.
Habitat: Benthic, found
at depths of around
5,000m/16,400ft.
Food: Organic matter
digested from sediment.
Size: Up to 6cm/2.4in.
Breeding: Not
known.
Status:
Uncertain; not
listed by IUCN.

Scarlet sea star

Pseudarchaster parelii

Distribution: Atlantic and Pacific Oceans.
Habitat: Benthic from 150–2,800m/500–9,200ft.
Food: Benthic invertebrates.
Size: 12cm/4.75in.
Breeding: External fertilization; pelagic larval stages.
Status: Probably common; not listed by IUCN.

This sea star lives on soft sediments beneath deep, temperate waters. It has a firm body that holds its shape due to a well-developed skeleton of bony plates, called ossicles, that fit together in a more flexible version of the brittle test seen in sea urchins. The starfish has a system of internal water canals, which opens into rows of hydraulically operated tube feet on the underside of each arm. The mouth is on the underside, in the middle of the central disc. This species is an active predator and scavenger, feeding on sessile or slow-moving invertebrate prey and other organic material. During spawning, eggs and sperm are released from small pores in the top of the central disc.

Identification: Scarlet or orange body is covered on the upper surface with small bumps, called tubercles. On the underside, a groove, called the ambulacrum, runs along the middle of each arm, leading to the mouth.

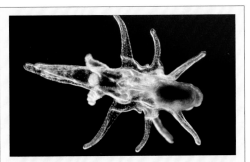

This well-evolved larva of a starfish shows the darker-coloured mass that will become the adult starfish at metamorphosis.

Echinoderm larvae

The larvae of echinoderms form an important and interesting component of marine zooplankton. Unlike their parents, they are bilaterally symmetrical. This difference has been the subject of much debate and research because it helps to bridge the gap between the radially symmetrical echinoderms and the majority of other advanced life forms, which, like humans, are bilaterian. These larvae mean that we can more readily group the echinoderms with other phyla. In fact, the early stages of echinoderm embryo development are not so very different from those of vertebrates, including humans. Although most fully mature echinoderms can move about to some extent, it is their larvae that make the long-distance journeys – dispersing in ocean currents and populating far-flung waters. Very few actually survive, however – like all zooplankton, they run a high risk of being eaten. But the sheer number spawned compensates for this bleak reality.

Common basket star

Gorgonocehpalus eucnemis

The basket star belongs to the same group as the brittlestars. The body is brittle but flexible and the animal moves with surprising agility. Basket stars feed at night, usually in elevated or exposed positions on the tops of reefs or rocks, where they can take a advantage of food arriving on the current. Each animal has five arms radiating out from a central disc. Each arm branches several times to produce a basket-like structure, whose large surface area maximizes the chances of food capture. The basket can be tilted to face in any direction, and is usually orientated into the current.

Distribution: Temperate waters of oceans worldwide, and deep water in the tropics.
Habitat: Benthic, from coastal shallows to depths of 20–2,000m/65–6,500ft.
Food: Small shrimps, plankton and organic debris
Size: Up to 50cm/20in.
Breeding: External fertilization follows coordinated spawning; young pass though planktonic larval phase before settling and metamorphosing into tiny stars.
Status: Common; not listed by IUCN.

Identification: Arms are pale in colour, or even ghostly white; central disc may be pink, purple or brown, with radial markings. Arm tips often tightly coiled, like the gnarled branches of a tree.

TUNICATES

The soft-bodied tunicates of deep and open water are among the simplest of the chordates. Like the vertebrates, with whom they are descended from the parent taxon Chordata, they possess a stiffening rod, the notochord, for part of their life history, during which stage they resemble tadpoles. Once mature, they live as solitary animals or in colonies of cloned individuals.

Oikopleura

Oikoplura dioica

Identification: Tadpole-like body is usually entirely surrounded by a translucent, disposable mucous case, which traps food particles.

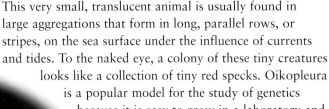

This very small, translucent animal is usually found in large aggregations that form in long, parallel rows, or stripes, on the sea surface under the influence of currents and tides. To the naked eye, a colony of these tiny creatures looks like a collection of tiny red specks. Oikopleura is a popular model for the study of genetics because it is easy to grow in a laboratory and it also has the smallest genome of any chordate (about 15,000 genes). Each individual spins a tiny pea-sized 'house' of mucus, to which other small, planktonic organisms adhere and are then ingested. Each house is abandoned after an hour or two and a new one is produced – up to ten a day. The abandoned houses gradually sink, forming descending clouds of 'marine snow' and thus providing an important source of food for detriviores (organisms that live on detritus) lower in the water column.

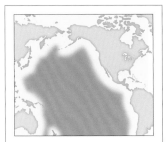

Distribution: Tropical and temperate Pacific Ocean.
Habitat: Surface water.
Food: Algae.
Size: Up to 5mm/0.2in.
Breeding: Sexual reproduction; very rapid development; fertilized eggs develop into feeding juveniles in just 7 hours; total lifespan 2–5 days.
Status: Abundant; not listed by IUCN.

Thalia salp

Thalia democratica

Identification: The body is translucent with a thick, gelatinous test and five bands of visible muscle surrounding the large pharynx. In solitary individuals, there are two projections at the rear end and the gut is opaque. The colonial zooids lack these rear projections.

Salps such as *Thalia* forage extremely efficiently, and when food – mainly planktonic algae – is plentiful they take full advantage of it. In ideal conditions, their growth rate is spectacular – solitary and colonial forms of *Thalia democratica* can increase their body length by 10 per cent every hour, and the number of individual zooids in a colony can increase by two and a half times in the same time frame. Known as vegetative reproduction or cloning, this is the fastest reproduction rate for any metazoan animal, and, during periods where algae is extremely abundant, populations can expand so rapidly that aggregations cover several thousand square kilometres of ocean. The colonies drift passively, close to the surface. *Thalia* feeds by using a net of mucus emitted by glands in the pharynx to trap plankton.

Distribution: All temperate and tropical oceans and seas.
Habitat: Surface waters.
Food: Plankton, mainly algae.
Size: Individuals 2cm/0.8in; colonies up to several metres across.
Breeding: Alternating sexually and asexually (cloning) reproducing generations.
Status: Not listed.

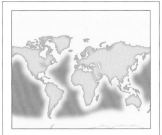

Distribution: Tropical and temperate Atlantic, Pacific and Indian Oceans.
Habitat: Surface waters of open ocean and coastal waters.
Food: Single-celled algae and zooplankton.
Size: Colonies up to 60cm/24in long.
Breeding: Alternating sexually and asexually (cloning) reproducing generations.
Status: Common; not listed by IUCN.

Common pyrosome

Pyrosoma atlantica

Colonies of these small tunicates form elongated, largely transparent tubes up to about 60cm/24in in length. A colony hovers in mid-water – rising closer to the surface at night and sinking again during the day to a depth of 800m/2,600ft, where there are few predators to concern them. *Pyrosoma atlantica* is thought to be an important element in the leatherback turtle's diet. The whole colony behaves rather like a single organism, swimming by means of the beating of hundreds of tiny hair-like cilia, which pulse in a coordinated fashion. Colonies produce a startlingly bright blue-green bioluminescence when they are disturbed – the name comes from the Greek *pryas* meaning 'fire' and *soma* meaning 'body'. Individual zooids within a colony produce eggs and sperm. Fertilized eggs develop into solitary individuals, which have the capacity to become the founders of new colonies by budding off a series of clones (genetically identical copies of themselves).

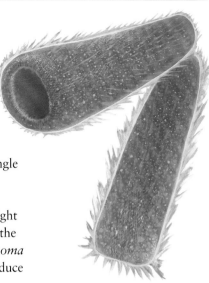

Identification: The colony forms a tapering tube, closed at one end. The overall colour can be pink or green.

Colonial salp (*Cyclosalpa affinis*): 8cm/3in
Lives in solitary and aggregate phases. During the latter, the original animal buds off a series of clones. Each clone remains attached to the parent, forming whorls of a dozen or so individuals.

Common salp (*Salpa fusiformis*): 5cm/2in
A torpedo-shaped salp that forms long chain-like aggregations in tropical and temperate regions of all major oceans. The aggregations swim actively by the muscular pulsing of each body. Onshore currents can bring swarms close to shore and sometimes they wash up on beaches.

Pelagic salp (*Thetys vagina*): 30cm/12in
An unusually large pelagic salp, of which solitary individuals have up to 20 muscle bands inside a rigid but translucent spiny tunic. Rear projections and gut contain black pigment.

Graptolites: *Subphylum hemichordata*:
Pterobranchs are a group best known as fossils called graptolites (below). These fossils are from rocks up to 400 million years old. The name comes from the Greek for 'writing' and 'rock', because the fossils often resemble hieroglyphics. The known living forms are small, colonial organisms. Mature individuals have a simple, sac-like body with a fringe of tentacles around the mouth. They reproduce by budding copies of themselves from the base or occasionally by producing eggs and sperm.

Big mouth tunicate

Megalodicopia hians

This ghostly, entirely soft-bodied invertebrate lives anchored firmly to the wall of deep-sea canyons or to the rocky sea floor. The body comprises a gelatinous stem and a voluminous hood with a large slit-like opening. The big mouth tunicate is thought to be a close relative of shallow-water sea squirts such as *Ciona intestinalis*. The enormous oral hood is an adaptation for trapping food, including small invertebrates, such as copepod crustaceans, and various single-celled organisms. The species also feeds on dead material drifting down from the ocean above. Touch-sensitive cells on the inside of the hood trigger a rapid contraction of muscles that close the 'mouth', trapping food items inside. This matter is carried into the gut by strands of sticky mucus.

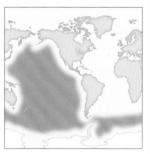

Distribution: Pacific and Southern Oceans.
Habitat: 200–1,000m/ 650–3,300ft.
Food: Plankton.
Size: Up to 13cm/4.75in.
Breeding: Hermaphrodites – mature individuals produce eggs and sperm. Free-swimming larvae settle and develop into adults.
Status: Not listed by IUCN.

Identification: A stout, usually colourless stem enclosed in a tough translucent tunic. The pharyngeal (throat) region is swollen into an almost spherical hood with a slit-like opening that gapes when the animal is feeding, as seen left.

CHIMERAS AND RAYS

*The species described here are deep water and oceanic cartilaginous fish. Modern chimeras
(of the order Chimaeriformes) are a small group consisting of just a few dozen species. Rays and skates
(Rajiformes), on the other hand, exhibit a wide variety of physical forms and lifestyles, from
sluggish bottom-dwellers to graceful predators of mid-water habitats.*

Chimera/Rabbit fish

Chimaera monstrosa

The common chimera is one of about 40 species belonging
to the subclass Holocephali. Of these, many are deep-water
specialists about which little is known. The common Atlantic
species, however, is familiar to the local fishing industry.
It is most active at night, when it migrates to shallower
waters to feed. Chimeras, like the agnathans, have a
persistent notochord – a flexible supporting rod running the
length of the body. Males have a clasping structure on the
forehead which may help to hold the female
while mating.

Identification: Elongate, ventrally
flattened body tapering to a very
fine tail, with large pectoral fins
held at right angles to the sides
of the body. Dorsal fin has
prominent spine; eyes large; body
patterned with irregular
longitudinal brown and
white stripes and spots.

Distribution: Eastern Atlantic
range, from tropical waters
to northern temperate zone;
also Mediterranean Sea; may
be present in western Pacific,
but not widely confirmed.
Habitat: Deep water of
the continental slope
descending to sea floor, at
depths of 1,000m/3,300ft.
Food: Benthic invertebrates.
Size: Up to 1.5m/5ft.
Breeding: Oviparous, with
internal fertilization; young
hatch fully formed; no
parental care.
Status: Common; not listed
by IUCN.

Blind electric ray

Typhlonarke aysoni

Identification: A small, drab-
looking ray with a rather floppy
disc and poorly developed tail.
The pelvic fins, not shown here,
are modified into limb-like
appendages.

Electric rays are also known as numbfishes because of their
ability to deliver electric shocks large enough to stun prey or
leave a potential predator with an unpleasantly tingling
sensation. The shock is the result of electric discharge from
specialized muscle cells, called electrocytes, situated mainly
in the animal's 'wings'. This small species is known
only from New Zealand waters, where it is
considered rare. It turns up occasionally as
bycatch, and there are concerns that it may
be threatened by fisheries using bottom-
trawling techniques. Little is known of
its ecology, but
anatomical
studies suggest
that it is a poor
swimmer, and
usually moves by 'walking' along the sea
floor using its modified pelvic fins. It feeds
mainly on polychaete worms collected from the
sea bed. Its lifespan is not known.

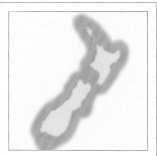

Distribution: Endemic to
New Zealand. Distribution is
likely to extend to south-
western Pacific, but range
and extent is not certain due
to confusion with a similar
species, *T. tarakea*.
Habitat: Sea floor in water
that is as deep as 900m/
3,000ft.
Food: Benthic invertebrates,
mainly worms.
Size: Up to 38cm/15in.
Breeding: Probably
ovoviviparous.
Status: Listed as Data
Deficient on IUCN.

Pelagic stingray

Pteroplatytrygon violacea

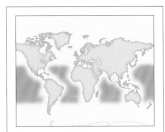

Distribution: Tropical and subtropical oceans and seas worldwide.
Habitat: Open water down to 240m/800ft.
Food: Fish and pelagic invertebrates.
Size: Up to 1.6m/5.25ft.
Breeding: Ovoviviparous, litters of 4–9 pups born after gestation of 2–4 months, with probably 2 litters a year.
Status: Common; not listed by IUCN.

Identification: Pectoral fins give the body a diamond-shaped outline; tail almost twice as long as the body with one or two large spines. Eyes are slightly sunken. Colour varies from brown to bluish green on dorsal surface and purplish below, but there are no markings. Dorsal area bears numerous spines.

The only ray adapted to truly open-water existence, the pelagic ray is a large, graceful swimmer able to swim upside down when attacking prey from below. It eats pelagic cephalopods, crustaceans and jellyfish, sometimes using its pectoral fins to help manipulate them to the mouth on the underside or the head. The sting is a defensive weapon, capable of inflicting a painful wound – not life-threatening to humans, but sufficient to deter most fish. Young of the species hatch from eggs while still inside the uterus and continue to grow here, nourished by a secretion from the uterine walls.

Spotted ratfish
(*Hydrolagus colliei*): 97cm/38in
A native of the eastern Pacific Ocean this relatively common species has a venomous spine at the front of the dorsal fin. Sometimes taken as bycatch, it has limited economic value and the risk of injury from the sting and its powerful bite mean it is not targeted by fishing.

Long-nosed chimera (*Harriotta raleighana*): 1.2m/4ft
Found in deep tropical and temperate waters around the world, the long- or narrow-nosed chimera has a long, flattened upturned snout and a tail tapering to a long thread.

Deep sea skate (*Bathyraja abyssicola*): 1.4m/4.6ft
Like so many deep-sea species, very little is known about the ecology of this large ray. It is a predator feeding mostly on deep-water shrimp, amphipods and squid. It turns up in bottom trawls off Japan, Canada and the USA.

Sandpaper skate (*Bathyraja interrupta*): 86cm/34in
Also known as the Bering skate, this species feeds mainly from the sea floor – burrowing invertebrates, such as polychaete worms and amphipods, make up most of its diet. It may be at risk from bottom-trawling fisheries.

Alaska skate

Bathyraja parmifera

Very little is known about the ecology of this deep-sea ray. It is a predator feeding mostly on deep-water shrimp, amphipods and squid. The same bottom-trawling techniques that bring up individual Alaska skate off the coasts of Japan and North America also sometimes bring up eggs. These are tough, leathery pouches with horns projecting from the corners that help anchor them in the sand or sediment of the sea floor. This type of egg is fairly typical of the skate family and is known colloquially as 'mermaid's purse'.

Distribution: Temperate northern Pacific Ocean.
Habitat: Sea floor in deep water down to 3,000m/9,842ft.
Food: Deep-water shrimp, amphipods and squid.
Size: Up to 91cm/36in.
Breeding: Oviparous.
Status: May be at risk from deep-water trawling, but not currently listed by IUCN.

Identification: Body wider than it is long. Snout pointed, body outline follows convex then concave curve from mouth to pectoral fin tip. Upper surface is brown with variable spots and blotches. Pelvic fins of male modified into very large claspers. Two small dorsal fins on tail.

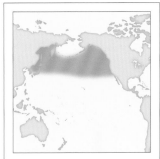

SIX-GILLED AND DOGFISH SHARKS

*These primitive-looking sharks belong to the orders Hexanchiformes and Squaliformes. They lack the
sleek lines and athleticism of their more documented relatives, the requiem sharks. Hexanchiforms
include the six- and seven-gilled sharks: fossils suggest that the latter may bear a striking resemblance to
Jurassic ancestors. 'Dogfish sharks' is a colloquial term for a small group that live in northerly oceans.*

Six-gilled shark

Hexanchus griseus

This large shark is usually found swimming in water as deep
as 1,800m/5,900ft and is therefore rarely seen. However,
between July and November the blunt-nosed six-gilled shark
migrates into some shallow water locations, allowing divers
a rare glimpse of it. A robust, elongate shark with a long
caudal fin and a single dorsal fin, it gets its common name
because it has six gill openings on each side of the head;
most sharks have five pairs of gill openings. This species is a
member of the order Hexanchiformes, known as the frilled
sharks and cow sharks – all of the sharks in this order have
six or even seven pairs of gill openings. Although a predator
of small sea creatures, it will also scavenge on
the carcasses of larger marine animals.

Identification: Body robust with
a single dorsal fin set well back,
close to the caudal fin. Caudal fin
has a long upper lobe and a short
lower lobe. Pectoral fins broadly
triangular in shape. Head with
blunt snout and large eyes set
far forward on the head. Has
six gill slits. Teeth in upper jaw
are saw-like, those in the lower
jaw are more pointed in shape.

Distribution: Widespread in
tropical and temperate seas.
Habitat: From the intertidal
zone (occasionally) down to
1,875m/6,150 ft but usually
about 90m/300ft.
Food: Varied diet includes
crustaceans, other fish,
whale carcasses and seals.
Size: Up to 4.8m/15.8 ft.
Breeding: Ovoviviparous,
with litters of over 100 pups;
gestation may take up to
2 years or more.
Status: Listed as Lower Risk
by IUCN.

Frilled shark

Chlamydoselachus anguineus

This deep-water species looks more like an eel than a shark.
The frilled shark is the only surviving member of its family
and is something of an evolutionary relic. Frill sharks live
mostly in deep water and were only discovered in the late
1800s. The name refers to the first of the six pairs of gill
slits, which forms a continuous, frilly edged opening that
runs right around the throat from one side of the head to
the other. Each of the hundreds of teeth that develop and
are shed in a lifetime is shaped like a trident, with three
sharp points – other species with teeth like this are known
only from the fossil record. The teeth are suitable for
gripping prey but not for slicing or tearing, so victims are
swallowed whole. The jaw opens very wide to allow this.

Identification: Body is long and
slender with six pairs of frilly gill
slits, the first of which extends
right around the throat. The
mouth opens at the front of the
head – it is not underslung as in
most other sharks. The eyes are
large, the skin is pale brown. The
tail fin is asymmetrical, lacking
a lower lobe.

Distribution: Eastern Atlantic
populations off north-eastern
Europe and southern Africa;
in Pacific
it inhabits
waters off
Japan and
New Zealand.
Habitat: Cold waters
of the continental shelf
and slope down to
1,600m/5,250ft.
Food: Smaller fish, including
sharks and rays.
Size: Up to 2m/6.6ft.
Breeding: Ovoviviparous;
young hatch from eggs inside
female and are born as
independent sharks.
Status: Not listed by IUCN.

Sleeper shark (Greenland shark)

Somniosus microcephalus

Distribution: Northern Atlantic and Arctic Ocean, occasional records from the Southern Hemisphere.
Habitat: Cold, deep water of the continental shelf down to 1,200m/3,950ft.
Food: Varied diet includes other fish, smaller marine mammals, squid, octopus and carrion.
Size: Up to 7.3m/24ft.
Breeding: Ovoviviparous, with litters of a dozen or more pups.
Status: Probably common, but not listed by IUCN.

These huge members of the dogfish order are so named because of their somewhat sluggish movement, despite which they are effective predators and scavengers, occupying the top of the deep-sea food chain. Recent research suggests that sleeper sharks are one of very few predators capable of tackling giant squid. Sleeper sharks are not fished commercially but they turn up regularly as bycatch and are targeted by Inuit subsistence fisheries. The flesh contains high levels of urea and trimethylamine oxide. If eaten fresh it is toxic, inducing a condition similar to drunkenness, but it can be dried or carefully cooked to make it fit for human consumption. Sleeper sharks develop and grow slowly and females give birth to live young that hatch from eggs inside the uterus.

Identification: A very large, heavy-set shark with five pairs of gill slits that are small in relation to the animal's size. The dorsal and pectoral fins are also small, and the tail fin is asymmetrical with a notch in the upper lobe. They are generally brown, black or grey in colour, with some having dark lines or white spots along the flanks.

Bramble shark (*Echinorhinus brucus*): up to 2.75m/9ft
A large, deep-water shark with dark grey-brown metallic-looking skin and a scattering of spiky scales. The tail fin is highly asymmetrical. The species is best known from the Mediterranean region and the continental shelves of the north-eastern Atlantic, but has been recorded in all oceans, with the possible exception of the Indian Ocean.

Spined pygmy shark (*Squaliolus laticaudus*): up to 21cm/8.25in
This is a miniature deep-water shark that migrates to shallower depths at night to prey on small fish, squid and crustaceans. There is a characteristic spine – common to most of the 130 or so species of squaliform shark – in front of the first dorsal fin, and it has a bioluminescent patch on the belly.

Goblin shark (*Mitsukurina owstoni*): up to 5m/16.4ft
This is a bottom-dwelling species found in tropical oceans. Its exaggerated facial features account for the shark's common name, and it is characterized by having a particularly long, pointed snout that overhangs the mouth, looking like a huge nose. It swims relatively slowly, but is able to project its jaws rapidly forward in order to snap up prey, such as cephalopods and crabs.

Cookiecutter shark

Isistius brasiliensis

This is a small shark, with a long, narrow, cylindrical body and a short, blunt snout. The lips can be formed into a sucker with which the shark attaches itself to much larger prey. The shark then bites into the flesh with saw-like rows of lower teeth and rotates its entire body to remove a neat circular chunk of meat. Cookiecutter scars are commonly seen on a variety of species of larger fish and marine mammals. The scientific name *Isistius* refers to Isis, the ancient Egyptian goddess of light. This is appropriate, as cookiecutters are bioluminescent, and the skin of the belly contains a great many photophores. These are cells containing chemicals that react with enzymes to produce an eerie, green glow. The arrangement of photophores enhances the counter-shading effect, making the fish extremely difficult to see from below. Cookiecutters lurk in deep water during the day, and migrate to shallower depths to feed at night.

Distribution: Tropical and temperate Atlantic, Indian and Pacific Oceans.
Habitat: Open ocean and deep water down to 3,500m/11,500ft.
Food: Eats small fish and crustaceans whole; parasitic on larger fish and marine mammals.
Size: Up to 56cm/22in.
Breeding: Ovoviviparous with litters of up to 12 young.
Status: Not listed by IUCN.

Identification: Long, narrow body with an even brown colouring, except for dark collar. Dorsal and anal fins are small. Snout is short and conical; mouth has flexible, muscular lips for creating suction.

WHALE, REQUIEM AND MEGAMOUTH SHARKS

The gentle whale shark spends most of its time in the open ocean, along with several much smaller and more aggressive sharks, which make a living through speed, ferocity and superbly acute senses. The rarely-sighted megamouth is neither especially large, fast or fierce – but it is exceptional in other ways.

Whale shark

Rhincodon typus

This, the world's largest living fish, is only just beginning to be understood. Until recently it was known mainly from shallow seas, as a seasonal visitor to reefs and coasts. But for several months a year it disappeared. Studies have revealed it to be migratory and able to descend to great depths in search of food. Like other large marine organisms, it is a filter feeder, specializing in plankton and small fish. Where food is plentiful, whale sharks may temporarily gather in groups of up to 100 or more. They are hunted mainly for their fins. Left undisturbed, they can live to more than 100 years.

Identification: Vast, bulbous-bodied shark with square snout and large mouth. The body has several longitudinal ridges, is dark grey to brown above, white below, marked with a pattern of white spots and horizontal stripes on back and flanks. Of its two dorsal fins, the second is very small; the pectoral fins are triangular, the pelvic and anal fins small. Its tail is large with a longer upper lobe.

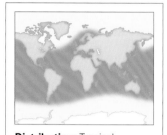

Distribution: Tropical and warm temperate oceans worldwide.
Habitat: From coastal reefs to deep open ocean, down to 1,000m/3,300ft or more.
Food: Plankton and small fish.
Size: Up to 20m/66ft.
Breeding: Ovoviviparous, with large litters of up to 300 pups.
Status: Listed as vulnerable by IUCN.

Blue shark

Prionace glauca

Identification: Long, narrow body with asymmetrical caudal fin. Dorsal fin is not particularly large, but pectoral fins are very long. Eyes appear large on conical, flattened head. Body is strikingly counter-shaded – dark blue on the back, bright blue on the flanks and paler in colour underneath.

Also known as the blue whaler because of its frequent association with dead whales, the blue shark is a species whose future may be under threat due to increased commercial exploitation – more than 10 million are killed annually for food. Blue sharks are curious and opportunistic and readily investigate any possible source of food, including divers and shipwreck victims, thus earning a reputation as one of the more dangerous shark species. However, more usual food sources include squids and small fish, such as herrings – schooling species are especially favoured in the open ocean, where feeding opportunities can be few and far between. Female blue sharks can produce a great many young. One female was recorded carrying 134 embryos, though it is unlikely all would have survived to birth.

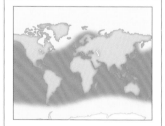

Distribution: Tropical and temperate oceans and seas worldwide.
Habitat: Open water to 350m/1,150ft deep.
Food: Smaller fish and invertebrates, including octopus and squid; may also scavenge carcasses of larger animals.
Size: Up to 4m/13ft. There have been unconfirmed reports of larger individuals being sighted.
Breeding: Ovoviviparous, 4–80 pups born per litter; there is no parental care.
Status: Listed as Near Threatened by IUCN.

Oceanic white tip shark

Carcharhinus longimanus

The oceanic white tip is a solitary wanderer and an opportunistic feeder. It spends most its time cruising the warm surface waters of open oceans, with its acute senses alert to the possibility of food. Temporary aggregations may form around plentiful food resources, and the species is often involved in feeding frenzies. It is intensely curious and will eat almost anything, including medium to large fish, especially tuna and dorados, as well as other sharks, rays, squid, turtles, sea birds and even human garbage. It will also eat humans, and it is often among the first of the large scavengers to gather at the scene of a disaster at sea. However, attacks close to shore are less likely. It is often accompanied by remoras, a species of fish that it seems not to eat.

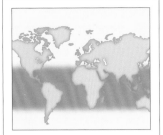

Distribution: Tropical and subtropical waters of all oceans.
Habitat: Surface waters of open ocean down to about 150m/500ft.
Food: Mainly bony fish, but this opportunistic feeder will eat virtually anything.
Size: Up to 4m/13ft.
Breeding: Ovoviviparous; litters of 1–15 pups.
Status: Abundant at present, but suffering from exploitation for its fins and as bycatch. Listed as Near Threatened by IUCN.

Identification: A stout shark with a very large dorsal fin. The rest of the body is brownish grey above and pale coloured below. Pectoral fins are long and tapering; tail fin lobes are asymmetric. All but the smallest fins are tipped with white. Often seen in association with remoras, which may hitch a ride by attaching themselves to the shark's body.

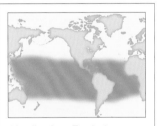

Silky shark (*Carcharhinus falcifomis*): up to 3.5m/11.5ft
This is a long, slender, deep-water specialist found in subtropical and tropical waters as deep as 4,000m/13,100ft, but equally at home in surface waters, where it is regarded as dangerous to humans. In fact, the reverse is much more often the case, as this is one of the most intensively fished shark species, and is exploited for meat, hide, fins and liver oil.

Night shark (*Carcharhinus signatus*): up to 2.8m/9ft
A slender brown shark with a long pointed snout. Night sharks lurk in waters off Atlantic continental shelves, often in schools. They are nocturnal and eat small fish and squid. They pose no threat to humans.

Spinner shark (*Carcharhinus brevipinna*): up to 3m/10ft
This grey-coloured shark of the tropical and subtropical Atlantic, Indian and Indo-Pacific has a very pointed snout and a highly asymmetric tail with a greatly elongated upper lobe. It is named for its feeding behaviour, which involves a spectacular open-mouthed vertical ascent – complete with rapid spinning motion – through schools of fish. This is conducted at such speed that the shark may leap clear of the water.

Megamouth shark

Megachasma pelagios

This bizarre-looking species is known only from 27 confirmed sightings and just six landed specimens, the first of which was taken off Hawaii in 1976. Named for its enormous jaws, which can be protruded forwards, the megamouth sounds intimidating, but the jaws are lined with very tiny hooked teeth and the species is at least a partial filter feeder, taking nothing larger than shrimps, jellyfish and small pelagic fish. It migrates vertically on a daily basis, rising to surface waters at dusk along with the planktonic animals it feeds on. When the jaws are protruded, a bright-white band of tissue is exposed between the upper lip and jaw. This is highly conspicuous, even in gloomy water, and may play some role in feeding or in individual recognition.

Distribution: Tropical waters of Pacific and Atlantic Oceans.
Habitat: Pelagic in open ocean, from surface waters possibly down to 1,000m/3,300ft.
Food: Larger planktonic animals, small fish and jellyfish.
Size: Up to 5.5m/18ft.
Breeding: Ovoviviparous.
Status: Listed as Data Deficient by IUCN.

Identification: Large rounded head and large mouth. Dark bluish-grey above, paler below. One large and one small dorsal fin; pectoral fins very large, as is the asymmetrical tail, fins usually tipped with white.

LOBE FINS AND EELS

The cumbersome coelacanth is an iconic reminder of our own origins – fish like this are believed to have given rise to all terrestrial vertebrates. Their modern distribution is limited to part of the Indian Ocean, while that of eels and their relatives is enormous. Several species of eel spend part of their lives in both freshwater and marine environments.

Coelacanth

Latimeria chalumnae

Coelacanths are perhaps the world's most famous 'living fossil'. Before a specimen turned up in 1938 as bycatch of a trawler from the Indian Ocean port of East London, South Africa, scientists thought fish like this had been extinct since the time of the dinosaurs. A second species, from Sulawesi, was discovered in 1999. The structure and action of the flexible lobe-like pectoral and pelvic fins suggest a likely means by which four-legged land animals might have evolved from a fish ancestor. The fish appears to use them for propelling itself slowly over the sea floor. The fins support no weight, but their movement is similar to walking in quadrupeds. The second dorsal and anal fins are also lobate and are used for swimming, performing slow sculling movements. Coelacanths invest heavily in their young. The eggs are among the largest known for ovoviviparous fish, at up to 10cm/4in across.

Distribution: Western Indian Ocean off South Africa, Mozambique, Madagascar and the Comoros Islands.
Habitat: Rocky sea bed at depths of 150–700m/ 500–2,300ft
Food: Deep-sea fish and invertebrates.
Size: Up to 2.5m/8.2ft.
Breeding: Ovoviviparous; up to 20 young – over 30cm/12in long – born after a 13-month gestation period. Life span of individuals up to 50 years.
Status: Critically Endangered. Species is of enormous scientific significance.

Identification: Chunky fish with dark bluish-brown heavy scales. The fins are fleshy lobes with hollow rays. The eyes and mouth are large, and the tail is a symmetrical, muscular paddle, with a continuous fringing fin.

Slender snipe eel

Nemichthys scolopaceus

The snipe eel's elongated, outwardly curving jaws are lined with tiny backward-pointing teeth. The fish cannot really bite, or even properly close its mouth. It hunts by swimming with its mouth open, sweeping the water. Once snagged by the teeth, small prey finds itself in a position it can only move in one direction – down the eel's throat. The eel is particularly efficient at catching shrimp, whose long antennae are easily snagged. The tactic can backfire and snipe eels have been found clinging to the tails of fish too large to swallow from which they are unable to disengage. The body is thin, ending in a thread-like tail. A dorsal fin runs halfway along the body, and is replaced by a row of short spines running to the tail. The anal fin is a little taller than the dorsal and soft rayed all the way to the tail.

Distribution: Tropical and temperate seas and oceans worldwide.
Habitat: Deep mid-water down to 2,000m/ 6,560ft.
Food: Pelagic crustaceans and small fish.
Size: Up to 1.3m/4.25ft.
Breeding: Oviparous, with planktonic leptocephali larvae typical of eels; no parental care; spawns only once in its lifetime.
Status: Not listed by IUCN.

Identification: The strange, almost bird-like head is by far the thickest park of the body, with large eyes and long, slender outwardly curving jaws. The skin is dark brown above, almost black on the belly.

American eel

Anguilla rostrata

The American eel is a long, snakelike predatory fish. Immature individuals are yellow to green and live in freshwater rivers. Mature adults develop a metallic silvery colour when ready to breed. Eels are catadromous, meaning that they migrate from freshwater rivers to the ocean to spawn. The American eel and the European eel (*Anguilla anguilla*) are extremely similar. The few subtle physical differences between them may be caused by nothing more than differences in water temperature as the eggs develop. As adults, both species migrate from their home rivers to the mid Atlantic Ocean to breed. Eel larvae are then carried back to their destination rivers by ocean currents. It takes young American eels several years to reach the eastern seaboard of North America, by which time they have developed into juvenile elvers.

Distribution: Eastern Atlantic Ocean and Caribbean and from rivers of eastern North and Central America and West Indies to mid-Atlantic.
Habitat: Freshwater and marine, from estuaries to open ocean.
Food: Smaller fish and invertebrates
Size: Up to 1.5m/5ft; females slightly smaller
Breeding: Oviparous; no parental care; adults complete single spawning migration to the Sargasso Sea and then die.
Status: Common; commercially fished; not listed by IUCN.

Identification: Long, snake-like body with a small, pointed head. The skin of the eel appears to be scaleless, but there are minute scales in the adult. The skin produces a slimy mucilage in response to stress, such as being handled. Pelvic fins absent, dorsal and anal fins form a continuous fringe around the rear two-thirds of the body.

Gulper eel (pelican eel)

Eurypharynx pelicanoides

It is not difficult to see why the gulper eel is so named – this fish has a huge, gulping mouth. The jaws are greatly extended and the soft tissues of the mouth are highly elastic, giving the fish a truly gargantuan gape and allowing it to take in enormous quantities of water from which prey is filtered out and then swallowed whole. Not surprisingly, the gulper is not a particularly fussy eater and will take anything unlucky enough, and small enough, to come within range – in practice this means mostly deep-water shrimps and other crustaceans, small fish and squid. There is no tail fin as such – the body tapers into a long whip-like tail with a swollen tip containing light-producing cells. Adult gulper eels appear to enter a rapid decline and die shortly after spawning. Fertilized eggs develop into planktonic larvae, like those of other eels, known as leptocephali.

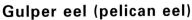

Spiny eel
(*Notacanthus chemnitzii*):
up to 1.2m/4ft
Spiny eels are large, elongate fish distinguished by a row of spines along the back and another row on the belly in front of the anal fin. They live in deep, temperate waters of all oceans and feed mainly on bottom-dwelling invertebrates, especially sea anemones.

Bobtail eel (*Cyema atrum*): up to 15cm/6in
A rather obscure relative of the snipe eel, found in very deep mid-water of all oceans. The bobtail has a moderately elongated body and long, narrow, outwardly curving jaws.

Longneck eek (*Derichthys serpentinus*):
up to 40cm/15.75in
A cosmopolitan, deep-dwelling eel with a long, snake-like black body. The head is separated from the body by a narrow neck, behind which the dorsal and anal fins form a continuous fringe running the entire length of the body and around the tail. Longneck eels eat small fish and planktonic crustaceans.

Japanese eel (*Anguilla japonica*): up to 1.5m/5ft
A highly valuable food fish and close relative of the American and European eels. Like these eels, it develops in freshwater rivers and migrates to the open ocean to spawn. Japanese eels are thought to spawn near the Marianas Islands of the Pacific Ocean.

Distribution: Temperate and tropical oceans and seas worldwide.
Habitat: Very deep water down to 7,500m/24,600ft.
Food: Small fish and invertebrates.
Size: Up to 1m/3.25ft.
Breeding: Oviparous; no parental care; spawns only once in lifetime.
Status: Not listed by IUCN.

Identification: Gulper eels lack scales. The skin is smooth and slippery and that of the huge mouth is very stretchy. There is a single long dorsal fin running the length of the body and tail and a long anal fin. The long, narrow tail has terminal light organ.

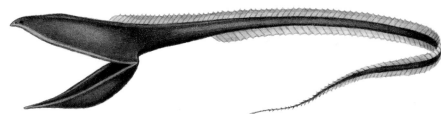

HERRINGS, ANCHOVIES AND RELATIVES

Clupeids are narrow-bodied, soft-finned, bony fish with oily flesh and a forked tail. Herrings, sardines, anchovies and shad are all clupeids. The two main families, herrings and anchovies, contain some 320 species, most of which are marine. They rely on the principle of safety in numbers, and form some of the most spectacular schooling formations in the oceans.

Atlantic herring

Clupea harengus

Herrings are adapted for long periods of rapid swimming and have a body plan that has not changed for million of years. Atlantic herrings live in large schools, mainly feeding by night either on individual items or on planktonic copepods strained from the water with specialized gill rakers. They retreat to deeper water by day. Vast schools of herring attract the attentions of predators, whose approach triggers a behaviour known as 'bait balling', in which every fish tries to hide in the middle of the crowd, creating a dense, swirling mass. This schooling behaviour is also exploited by trawlers, with almost certainly unsustainable numbers taken each year.

Identification: Slender fish with a triangular, pointed head and large mouth angled slightly upwards. There is a small dorsal fin halfway along the back, roughly level with pelvic fins; tail is large and forked. The body is covered in thin, silvery scales, with a row of thicker ones forming a keel along the underside.

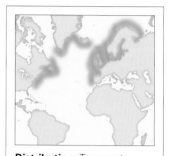

Distribution: Temperate waters of North Atlantic Ocean.
Habitat: Mainly coastal waters, down to about 200m/650ft.
Food: Plankton.
Size: Up to 45cm/17.75in.
Breeding: Oviparous; spawns annually (timing varies), eggs sink and adhere to weed or the substratum.
Status: Almost certainly threatened by fishing on an industrial scale. Not listed by IUCN.

European pilchard

Sardina pilchardus

Identification: A small, spindle-shaped fish with a single, small, delicate dorsal fin and inconspicuous pectoral, pelvic and anal fins. The tail is deeply forked. The body is counter-shaded – steely grey above and bright silver below. Some fish display a series of dark spots on the flanks. Has typically oily skin which can give off a beautiful shimmer of colour when seen underwater.

A small cousin of the herring, the pilchard is intensively exploited by commercial fishing interests, and is eaten either fresh or canned as 'sardine'. Strictly speaking, a sardine is a young pilchard. As well as by humans, the species is also exploited by a large number of marine predators, including dolphins, sharks and larger bony fish such as tuna and mackerel. Pilchards feed close to the surface at night and retreat to deeper water by day. Different populations spawn at different times of year, with the main peaks in spring and summer. Females produce tens of thousands of small, floating eggs at a time, which hatch into larvae within 2 to 4 days. Like other schooling clupeids, pilchards spend their entire life in a school of similar aged and sized fish.

Distribution: Temperate waters of north-eastern Atlantic Ocean.
Habitat: Pelagic; in open oceans as well as close to shore, occasionally entering estuaries, from 10–100m/33–330ft.
Food: Plankton.
Size: Up to 25cm/10in.
Breeding: Oviparous; no parental care.
Status: Common, highly commercial; not listed by IUCN.

Wolf herring

Chirocentrus dorab

Distribution: Tropical and sub-tropical in-shore waters of the Indian and western Pacific Oceans.
Habitat: Pelagic, surface waters down to 120m/400ft.
Food: Other fish.
Size: 3.5m/11.5ft.
Breeding: Oviparous, but other details not known.
Status: Appears common; not listed by IUCN.

Named for their reputation for attacking anything that moves, wolf herrings are fast-swimming predators capable of leaping from the water, and 'porpoising' before the bow wave of boats. They swim in schools, searching out schools of smaller fish, in particular herrings and anchovies. Wolf herrings have rows of needle-like teeth at the front of the mouth, and smaller ones covering the roof of the mouth – once prey is snatched there is virtually no chance of escape. In addition to their teeth, wolf herrings also have gill rakers, which they can use to strain smaller prey from the water. Wolf herrings are sometimes used in Asian cooking, but tend not to be specifically targeted by fisheries – they fight hard and bite readily, and present a substantial risk of injury.

Identification: Long, narrow body with triangular head and large mouth armed with very sharp teeth; dorsal, anal, pectoral and pelvic fins are all small, caudal fins form large, deeply forked tail. The body is covered in small, silvery scales.

Anchoveta (*Engraulis ringens*): up to 20cm/8in
A diminutive fish that supports a vast fishing industry and provides the dietary mainstay of hundreds of predatory fish, birds and mammals. It lives in the south-east Pacific Ocean, where populations fluctuate alarmingly – crashes are usually associated with El Niño years.

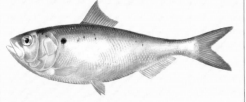

Atlantic menhaden (*Brevoortia tyrannus*): up to 50cm/20in
A schooling, pelagic fish, deeper-bodied than other herrings but ecologically similar. Schools are generally restricted to warm surface waters where they provide an important food resource for larger fish and cetaceans.

Pacific herring (*Clupea pallasii*): up to 46cm/18in
A temperate species, less oceanic than its Atlantic equivalent and most common in waters of the continental shelves of the north Pacific. Adults venture into coastal waters to breed, sometimes entering estuaries.

Landlocked clupeids: The herring family includes a number of species found in coastal waters, some of which enter estuaries and can survive in brackish and fresh water. The American alewife (*Alosa pseudoharengus*), for example, thrives in the Great Lakes and in a number of other landlocked, freshwater habitats.

Pacific anchovy

Engraulis mordax

Anchovies spend their lives in huge schools, within which individuals move and react in unison. They use good eyesight and the lateral line organ to sense movement in their companions, and their reactions are so quick that the school appears to move as one. As with herrings, anchovies obtain most other food by filtering small animals, mainly copepods, from the water with their gill rakers, but they will also nibble at larger items. Spawning peaks in summer, but females continue to produce eggs in batches of a few hundred all year around. The eggs are unusual in being slightly oval rather than round. They hatch very quickly in warm water, in just a few days. This is just one of several anchovy species supporting large commercial fisheries.

Identification: Slender-bodied fish, almost circular in cross section; with small dorsal, anal and paired fins and deeply forked tail. The head appears chinless due to large snout and small lower jaw. Mouth is large, eye large and located well forward on head. Body bears silver scales on flanks that fade with age.

Distribution: Sub-tropical waters of north-eastern Pacific Ocean.
Habitat: Pelagic, surface waters of continental shelf down to 300m/1,000ft.
Food: Plankton.
Size: Up to 25cm/10in.
Breeding: Oviparous; spawns several times a year at the surface.
Status: Highly commercial; not listed by IUCN.

LIGHTFISH, HATCHETFISH AND RELATIVES

Members of the order Stomiiformes live in deep water, and they include some of the most bizarre-looking fish in the sea. Many species are bioluminescent, with colourful photophores arranged in a variety of striking patterns over the head and body.

Black dragonfish

Idiacanthus atlanticus

The species has marked sexual dimorphism – only females grow large, while males rarely exceed 5cm/2in long. Females are black in colour and are armed with large, fang-like teeth. They also have a single long, fleshy barbel, which dangles from the chin and serves as a fishing lure. The body and the lure bear a number of light-producing photophores that glow both blue and red. Female dragonfish migrate from the depths to shallower water to hunt at night. The tiny males are a paler shade of brown than females and lack impressive teeth, a barbel or pelvic fins. They rarely, if ever, venture above 1,000m/3,300ft and are apparently unable to feed, lacking a functional gut. They probably only live long enough to reproduce. Larval black dragonfish are even more peculiar than their parents. They are long, thin, and almost transparent, with eyes set on very long, thread-like stalks that can be almost half as long as the rest of the body.

Distribution: Sub-tropical and temperate waters of south Atlantic, south Pacific, southern Indian Ocean and Southern Ocean.
Habitat: Deep water to 2,000m/6,600ft.
Food: Females prey on smaller fish and invertebrates.
Size: Up to 40cm/15.75in.
Breeding: External fertilization results in unusual, glassy larvae.
Status: Not listed by IUCN.

Identification: Females of the species have a long, eel-like body with long, delicate dorsal and anal fins and a pair of feathery pelvic fins. The teeth are recurved and needle-sharp. There are bioluminescent cells along the flanks and concentrated in the tip of the long chin barbel, which probably acts as a lure.

Viperfish

Chauliodus sloani

Identification: Body long and gently tapering, covered with thin, iridescent scales that allow dark brownish-blue colouration to show through. First dorsal fin is soft but tall with a very long first ray. Paired pectoral and anal fins are long and narrow. Head relatively large, with large eye and mouth full of long, pointed teeth.

The viperfish has teeth so large that it cannot fully close its mouth. The teeth are adapted for impaling prey rather than for cutting or tearing flesh. Once the prey is caught, the teeth tilt inwards on slightly flexible roots to aid the swallowing process. The jaws can be dislocated and the stomach expanded in order to accommodate prey that is very nearly as large as the viperfish itself. A circular, light-emitting photophore situated under the eye serves to lure potential prey close to the animal's deadly fangs. Smaller light-emitting cells are arranged in rows along the belly and scattered over the body. The viperfish migrates from the depths to shallower water on a regular basis, rising at dusk from a daytime depth of about 2,000m/6,600ft or more to night-time hunting grounds at about 600m/2,000ft.

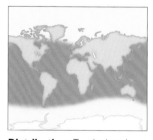

Distribution: Tropical and temperate waters of all oceans, and some adjoining seas.
Habitat: Deep water down to 2,500m/8,200ft.
Food: Smaller fish and pelagic crustaceans.
Size: Up to 35cm/13.75in.
Breeding: Oviparous, with external fertilization and no parental care.
Status: Not listed by IUCN.

Stoplight loosejaw

Malacosteus niger

Another deep-sea oddity, the stoplight loosejaw is named for the photophores under and behind the eyes, which glow red and green respectively. The lights probably serve to attract prey and to illuminate it so the loosejaw can aim its attack. Like other members of its family, the species has enormous jaws – far longer than the skull. When the fish open its mouth, the lower jaw dislocates and extends forward – a row of sharp, backward-pointing teeth hook into prey, which is then dragged back into the mouth. Rather than being enclosed within a sheath of flesh and skin, the skeleton of the lower law is exposed. This reduces drag and allows the lower jaw to shoot quickly forward without creating a pressure wave that might alert the prey.

Identification: The elongate body tapers to a tiny, laterally flattened tail fin. The paired fins are very narrow, the median fins are larger but very delicate. The fish is not a powerful swimmer and its jaws are longer than its skull. It has a red comma-like photophore under the eye and a green circular one behind the eye. Its head and body are black. The fish is shown here with mouth open, the exposed skeleton of the lower jaw swinging forward to its full extent and revealing the enormous gape between upper and lower jaws.

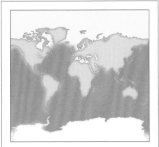

Distribution: Tropical and temperate zones of the Atlantic, Indian and Pacific Oceans.
Habitat: Deep water down to 2,500m/8,200ft.
Food: Bony fish and crustaceans, including deep-water shrimps and copepods.
Size: Up to 24cm/9.5in.
Breeding: Presumed to be oviparous, but details of its breeding are unknown.
Status: Not listed by IUCN.

upper jaw

lower jaw

Jellynose (*Guentherus altivela*): up to 2m/6.6ft
The jellynose lives close to the sea floor of the continental slopes of the eastern Atlantic and eastern Pacific Oceans. It has a plump body that tapers to a pointed tail and feeds on other smaller fish. The second dorsal and anal fins form an almost continuous fringe around the tail.

Snaggletooth (*Astronesthes gemmifer*): up to about 20cm/8in
A long, black, scaleless fish found in all the world's oceans. It produces violet light from rows of light-producing organs on its flanks and two more close to each eye. The large mouth contains the intimidating array of very long, sharp teeth for which the species is named.

Pearlsides (*Maurolicus muelleri*): up to 8cm/3in
This small but striking fish lives in the Atlantic and Pacific at intermediate oceanic depths of about 1,500m/4,900ft, migrating vertically to shallower waters at night to feed on plankton-dwelling invertebrates, such as copepods. Its flanks are covered with gleaming silvery scales.

Lightfish (*Icthyococcus ovatus*): up to 5cm/2in
A deep-bodied fish, generally brownish-yellow with silvery flanks. The body tapers sharply to the tail and the caudal fin is small. Dorsal and anal fins are small, soft rayed and delicate. Photophores in two rows along underside. Found in all oceans, except northern Pacific.

Silver hatchetfish

Argyropelecus aculeatus

Hatchetfish are named for their body shape – they are flattened laterally, with a narrow tail and very deep front end, resembling the handle and blade of a hatchet. The species is able to hide even in open water thanks to a combination of shape, reflective scales and blue-emitting photophores that make its silhouette disappear when viewed from below. Hatchetfish lurk in the deeper part of their range during the day, rising at dusk to 100–300m/330–1,000ft to feed on a variety of small planktonic animals – copepods and the larvae of other crustaceans and fish are all taken, but best of all are ostracods.

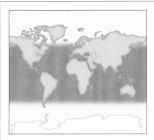

Distribution: Tropical, sub-tropical and warm-temperate areas of the Atlantic, Indian and Pacific Oceans.
Habitat: Pelagic in open ocean at depths 100–600m/330–2,000ft.
Food: Zooplankton.
Size: Up to 8cm/3in.
Breeding: Fertilization is external; there is no parental care.
Status: Common; not listed by IUCN.

Identification: The body is flattened laterally and is deeper in the front half. Its fins vary greatly in size and shape. The eye is very large and the mouth so steeply oblique as to be almost vertical.

GRINNERS

Members of the order Aulopiformes are commonly known as 'grinners' on account of their exceptionally wide mouth and sharp, prominent teeth. The order consists of 13 living families of ray-finned marine fish, a number that includes a large number of deep-water specialists, many of which spend at least part of their lives as potentially self-fertilizing hermaphrodites.

Tripodfish

Bathypterois grallator

Among the deepest dwelling of all fishes, the tripodfish spends most of its time 'standing' on the sea floor, propped up on three elongated stiffened rays from the pelvic and caudal fins. Food is scarce at such great depths, and this characteristic posture, facing into the current, offers a low-energy alternative to swimming. The tripodfish can swim, and when it does so, the fin rays trail behind. The eyes are greatly reduced in size. Adult tripodfish live solitary lives in a habitat where it can be difficult to find a mate. As a result, they have evolved to be simultaneous hermaphrodites – both male and female reproductive organs mature in the same body at the same time, making it possible, if necessary, for a single individual to fertilize its own eggs.

Identification: Body has a diamond pattern of dark scales. The first ray of each pelvic fin and the last ray of the tail serve as tripod supports. The pectoral fins form streamers while the dorsal fin stabilizes the body.

Distribution: Tropical and temperate Atlantic, Indian and Pacific Oceans and deep adjoining seas.
Habitat: Deep-ocean floor to 3,500m/11,500ft.
Food: Nekton (deep-water plankton), mostly copepods.
Size: 40cm/15.75in.
Breeding: Simultaneous hermaphrodism.
Status: Not listed by IUCN.

Greeneye

Chlorophthalmus acutifrons

Identification: Has a tapering body which is at its widest at the head, dominated by large, green-coloured eyes. The fins are elongate, but soft rayed and delicate; the tail fin has a deep cleft. Body colour is green overall with patches of brilliant iridescence. The belly is paler in colour.

This is one of about 20 closely related species and the greeneye family has an almost global distribution. This particular species is commercially fished in Japan and the Philippines. Greeneyes live close to the sea floor, where they hunt smaller fish and invertebrates. They are named for their unusual eyes, which are very large and strikingly iridescent. There are further iridescent patches elsewhere on the head, while the rest of the body is drab by comparison. Like most members of this order, greeneyes appear to be hermaphrodites. They are thought to form schools for spawning. Greeneye larvae live in mid-water, sinking deeper and adopting a bottom-dwelling lifestyle as they reach adulthood.

Distribution: Western Pacific Ocean.
Habitat: Demersal (living close to the sea bed) in water down to 950m/3,100ft.
Food: Fish and invertebrates.
Size: Up to 30cm/12in.
Breeding: Hermaphroditic; oviparous; external fertilization; no parental care.
Status: Not listed by IUCN.

Telescope fish (*Gigantura chuni*):
up to 16cm/6.3in
A small relative of the larger grinner species, this tropical fish has a long, cylindrical body with large, rounded, soft-rayed pectoral, dorsal and anal fins and a deeply cleft, lopsided and ragged-looking tail fin with several overlong fin rays. It hunts smaller pelagic fish in deep water.

Daggertooth (*Anotopterus vorax*):
up to 1.05m/3.4ft
Adults of this long-bodied predatory fish live in deep mid-water in the chilly Southern Ocean. Having reached maturity, they make a one-way trip to warm temperate waters of the southern Atlantic, Pacific and Indian Oceans to spawn, after which they die. Two closely related species, *A. pharao* and *A. nikparini*, breed in the north Atlantic and Pacific, respectively.

White barracudina (*Arctozenus risso*):
up to 30cm/12in
Also known as the ribbon barracudina, this fast-swimming, silvery grinner favours the cold waters of the North Atlantic. It hunts alone or in large schools, using speed to ambush pelagic shrimps and smaller fish.

Grideye fish (*Ipnops agassizii*): up to 15cm/6in
This long, narrow-bodied relative of the tripod fish has large, short-based fins with soft rays. It, too, lives close to the sea floor at abyssal depths of 1,500–4,000m/5,000–13,000ft down.

Bombay duck (Bummalo)

Harpodon nehereus

The confusingly named and etymologically uncertain Bombay duck is an aggressive predator of smaller fish. The teeth are very sharp and curve slightly backwards. They also flex slightly so that prey, once caught, can easily be swallowed but much less easily released. Bombay duck are normally inhabitants of deep water, but at certain times of year (monsoon) they venture much closer to shore and may even enter estuaries in large schools. Adults spawn several times a year, releasing eggs and sperm that mingle in the water. There is no parental care and the larval fish are left to fend for themselves. They reach sexual maturity when they are about 13cm/5in long. Few ever reach the maximum size of 40cm/15.75in because the species is a highly commercial food fish. The fish is often dried and salted, and once processed like this, the odour is so strong that it has to be transported in air-tight containers.

Distribution: Indian Ocean and adjoining seas, including Indo-Pacific.
Habitat: Benthic in deeper waters of the continental shelf, down to 50m/160ft.
Food: Smaller fish.
Size: Up to 40cm/15.75in.
Breeding: Oviparous; external fertilization; no parental care.
Status: Not listed by IUCN.

Identification: Body is slightly flattened laterally. Has a very large first dorsal fin. Pale colour gives impression of tranlucency. An obvious lateral line of scales runs from the pectoral fins on each flank into a pointed middle lobe of the tail.

Longnose lancetfish

Alepisaurus ferox

Distribution: Atlantic and Pacific Oceans and the adjoining seas.
Habitat: Deep mid-water down to 2,000m/6,600ft or more.
Food: Fish and invertebrates.
Size: Up to 2.15m/7ft.
Breeding: Oviparous; possibly asynchronous hermaphrodism; external fertilization; no parental care.
Status: Not listed by IUCN.

Identification: The body appears silvery, but all the fins are either black or dark brown. The first dorsal fin is very large, and the third, fourth and fifth dorsal fin rays may extend to form long, distinctive streamers. Second dorsal fin very small. The tail fin deeply forked, with an elongated first ray.

With its super-streamlined body and tall dorsal fin, the lancetfish is built for acceleration. Two or three fin rays in from the front, there are several over-long rays that form streamers. The mouth is armed with sharp teeth and two prominent fangs used for snatching prey – mostly smaller fish, but also invertebrates, from mid-water. Feeding adults may venture into sub-arctic waters, where prey can be abundant during the short summer, but they return to the tropics and sub-tropics to breed. Juveniles have undifferentiated gonads that may have the potential to develop into functional male or female sex organs, or perhaps both, although not at the same time.

LANTERNFISH, OPAH AND RIBBONFISH

The small order Myctophiformes contains about 250 species of lanternfish and blackchins, most of which are small, deep-dwelling and thus relatively little is known about them. The other species shown here all belong to the more diverse order Lampridiformes, which includes some of the most remarkable looking, and elusive, fish in the seas.

Blue lanternfish

Tarletonbeania crenularis

Identification: The mouth of the blue lanternfish is large, extending back past the eye. The body is counter-shaded – dark metallic blue on the back fading to silvery white on the underside. Even when not emitting light, the light organs on the belly and flanks can be seen as small, round spots (pimples).

Adult blue lanternfish spend their daylight hours at depth, rising much closer to the surface at night when they feed on plankton-dwelling crustaceans. Large eyes help the lanternfish to see in the gloom of deep water and in the dim light of moonlit surface waters. They, in turn, are eaten by larger predatory fish, such as albacore. Different species of lanternfish are distinguished largely by the pattern of the light-producing photophores found on their lower body. In the blue lanternfish, these photophores are arranged in sparse clusters and rows. Unlike their parents, larval lanternfish cannot afford to expend the energy required to retreat to deep water and so remain in surface waters for several weeks, feeding on smaller plankton, such as algae and fish and invertebrate larvae.

Distribution: Temperate and sub-arctic areas of the northern and eastern Pacific Ocean – off the coasts of North America, Russia and Japan.
Habitat: Deep mid-water down to 700m/2,300ft.
Food: Crustaceans.
Size: Up to 13cm/5in.
Breeding: Oviparous; external fertilization; spawning occurs in winter and spring; no parental care.
Status: Not listed by IUCN.

Opah

Lampris guttatus

Identification The opah is counter-shaded dark blue on the back to silvery on the belly, with many white spots. All the fins are a dramatic deep red. The first dorsal, pectoral and pelvic fins are pointed and curved slightly backwards; the second dorsal and anal fins form a fringe above and below the tail.

Also known as the spotted moonfish, the opah is a resident of open water with a laterally flattened body that appears almost round when seen in profile. Opahs grow very large – the heaviest individual on record weighed in at 270kg/595lb. Opahs are generally solitary but are often seen in the company of fast-swimming mackerel or tuna. Despite their ungainly proportions, opahs can produce a good turn of speed using a rigid flapping of their sharply tapering pectoral fins. They eat mainly small fish, crustaceans and small squid, which they swallow whole or tear into small pieces – the mouth is small and lacks teeth. Opahs are not targeted by fisheries, but they are considered a valuable bycatch, which may ultimately put them at risk.

Distribution: Tropical and temperate Atlantic, Pacific and Indian Oceans, and some adjoining seas.
Habitat: Mid-water at 50–500m/150–1,600ft.
Food: Smaller fish, crustaceans and squid.
Size: Up to 2m/6.6ft.
Breeding: Oviparous; spawning occurs in spring.
Status: Not listed by IUCN, but may face exploitation in the future.

Blackchin (*Scopelengys tristis*): up to 20cm/8in
A small, drab-looking relative of the lanternfish, lacking light organs or metallic colouring. Blackchins are plankton eaters found throughout the tropics, and appear to spend their entire adult lives in water more than 400m/1,300ft deep.

Dealfish (*Trachipterus arctica*): up to 3m/10ft
One of several deep-sea ribbonfish species, the dealfish has a long, laterally flattened body that tapers steadily from head to tail. Confined to Arctic and north Atlantic waters, it eats smaller fish and squid and has a very slow reproductive cycle – taking 14 years to reach sexual maturity.

Scalloped ribbonfish (*Zu cristatus*): up to 1.2m/4ft
This tropical ribbonfish has an abruptly tapering body, is laterally flattened but it is less plank-like than its larger relatives, the dealfish and oarfish. Juveniles have an undulating, scalloped edge to the belly. The first rays of the dorsal fin and the pelvic fins form long streamers.

Sailfin (*Velifer hypselopterus*): up to 40cm/15.75in
A disc-shaped, laterally flattened fish with large, ragged-looking dorsal and anal fins. Thought to be rather rare, the species is restricted to tropical waters of the Indo-Pacific Ocean.

Oarfish

Regalecus glesne

The oarfish may well be the longest species of fish – specimens up to 17m/55.8ft long have been reported, though the largest reliable record is of a specimen 11m/36ft long. This extraordinary creature is thought to be the inspiration for many myths of sea monsters – even the Loch Ness monster. Oarfish are most often encountered washed up on land – sightings of live individuals are rare. Two recent accounts suggest that the fish maintains a vertical position in the water, propelling itself slowly with rippling movements of the dorsal fin, which runs the entire length of the body. The long, ribbon-like pelvic fins, meanwhile, are held out to the sides as stabilizers. Oarfish have no teeth and instead of scales their skin is covered with a fine coating of guanine, the material that gives all fish their silvery colour.

Distribution: Recorded in Atlantic Ocean and Mediterranean Sea, also in Indo-Pacific waters and eastern Pacific Ocean.
Habitat: Mid-water of open oceans from 20–1,000m/ 60–3,300ft.
Food: Pelagic crustaceans, small fish and squid.
Size: May exceed 11m/36ft in length.
Breeding: Oviparous; larvae known from surface waters.
Status: Not listed by IUCN.

Identification: Enormously long body is laterally flattened, silvery in colour with dark bluish-grey markings. The fins are crimson. The first dozen or so rays of the long fringing dorsal fin form a spectacular crest. Each of the pelvic fins comprises a single soft ray.

Tube-eye

Stylephorus chordatus

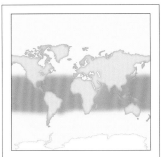

Distribution: All tropical oceans worldwide.
Habitat: Deep water.
Food: Small planktonic animals, mainly copepods.
Size: 30cm/12in.
Breeding: Not known.
Status: Not listed by IUCN.

A fish of deep tropical oceans, the tube-eye has upward-pointing goggle-eyes and a long, silver body that tapers to the tail. The lower lobe of the tail fin is elongated to form a whip-like extension. Like the oarfish (above), the species has a dorsal fin running the length of the body, and it swims vertically in the water. It migrates from the deep ocean to surface waters in order to feed each evening and it uses powerful suction to draw small crustaceans, such as copepods, into its small mouth. The buccal cavity (mouth chamber) can expand like a balloon to 40 times its resting volume to generate the necessary suction. Plankton is filtered from the water as it drains out through the gill slits. The details of its life history and breeding are virtually unknown.

Identification: Long, tapering body ends in very long, whip-like tail fin, the rays of which are up to twice as long as the rest of the body. Large eyes are telescopic. The snout is tubular and the mouth is small.

BROTULAS, GRENADIERS AND COD RELATIVES

The large order Gadiformes includes many well-known species related to the familiar cods and hakes. Several of these live at great depths. The brotulas belong to a loosely related order, the Ophidiiformes, and they include the deepest living of all known fish species.

Abyssal brotula

Abyssobrotula galatheae

The abyssal brotula, discovered in the mid 1970s, is the deepest-living species of fish known to science. The record-breaking specimen was collected at 8,372m/27,467ft by a remotely controlled submersible in the deepest part of the Atlantic Ocean, the Puerto Rico trench. Unsurprisingly, very little is known of the species' behaviour or ecology – live specimens have been observed only on a handful of occasions. However, it is thought to be rather uncommon and its reproductive anatomy suggests that it is oviparous, although nothing is known of breeding ecology or larvae.

Identification: A short, rounded head is inclined slightly downward; body tapers steadily from pectoral region to tail. The dorsal and anal fins form a continuous fringe around the tail, and there is no caudal fin. Teeth are long and fang-like, and there is a short spur attached to the base of the lower jaw.

Distribution: Tropical seas and oceans worldwide.
Habitat: Deep and abyssal zones at 3,000–8,400m/ 10,000–27,500ft.
Food: Not known.
Size: Up to 17cm/6.7in.
Breeding: Not known.
Status: Not listed by IUCN.

Abyssal grenadier

Coryphaenoides armatus

Also known as rattails because of the way the body tapers to a long, narrow, pointed tail, grenadiers are among the most abundant fish of the deep oceans, with a collective biomass estimated at several million tonnes. Their abundance is a consequence of being very long-lived (60 years), as the rate of reproduction is actually very low. Grenadiers grow slowly – the rate of maturation depends on the availability of food. If necessary, a grenadier can go several months without feeding, but this inhibits development. It seems likely that the species is semelparous, meaning individuals have only one chance at reproduction – adults die soon after spawning for the first and only time. The sex ratio in some populations weighs heavily in favour of males. There is a small light-emitting organ on the animal's belly.

Distribution: Deep areas of all tropical and temperate oceans worldwide.
Habitat: Deep mid-water to 4,700m/15,400ft.
Food: Deep-sea crustaceans, sea cucumbers, squids and other fish.
Size: 1m/3.25ft.
Breeding: Oviparous; probably breeds only once in its lifetime.
Status: Very common; not listed by IUCN.

Identification: Large conical head with small chin barbel. Body tapers from pectoral region to very narrow tail. Dorsal fin has two long spines, followed by a short fringe of soft rays running the length of the body. Most of body is silvery brown or pink, becoming bluish on the belly.

Silver hake
Merluccius capensis

Distribution: Temperate waters of the south-eastern Atlantic.
Habitat: Close to the sea bed in water from 50–1,000m/ 150–3,300ft.
Food: Wide variety of smaller fish and invertebrate prey.
Size: 1.4m/4.6ft.
Breeding: Oviparous; spawns throughout the year.
Status: Some commercial harvesting; not listed by IUCN.

Identification: Elongate body, with tiny silver scales and conspicuous, wavy lateral line. All fins are large. First dorsal fin is triangular, second and third are fused to form a tall median fin with a dip in the middle – the anal fins form a mirror image. Tail fin is large with a slightly concave trailing edge.

Like other hakes and codfish, silver hakes are efficient predators. Their eyes and mouth are both large, reflecting indiscriminate, visual hunting habits. They will eat just about anything of manageable size, including smaller members of its own species. Breeding activity peaks in early spring (August and September), but continues to a lesser extent all year around. Given the species' cannibalistic tendencies, schools tend of contain fish of similar age and size. Adults perform an annual migration, heading south in the spring to take advantage of the abundant prey available in sub-Antarctic waters during the summer, returning to temperate waters in the autumn. The species is of minor commercial importance to fisheries based in southern Africa.

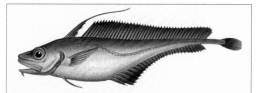

North Atlantic Codling (*Lepidion eques*): up to 45cm/17.75in
A medium-sized cod relative of temperate waters, with a large head and large, bulging eyes. The body tapers to a narrow tail with a small caudal fin. Codlings are predatory, feeding mainly on crustaceans and polychaete worms.

Bullseye grenadier (*Bathygadus macrops*): 50cm/20in
A moderately deep-dwelling fish of the tropical and subtropical north Atlantic. Occasionally caught and eaten, but not in large numbers.

Deep sea cusk eel (*Barathrites iris*): up to 65cm/25.6in
A deep-sea (5,300m/17,500ft) relative of the commercially important cusk eels, *Barathrites* has much the same shape – a small head and long, tapering body with a continuous dorsal-caudal-anal fin fringing the tail. Known Atlantic distribution; also present Indian and Pacific.

Gelatinous blindfish (*Aphyonus gelatinosus*): up to 15cm/6in
A relative of cusk eels and brotulas, specimens have turned up in bottom trawls of very deep water from tropical zones, but never in large numbers. The species has a pale body without scales or functional eyes, and bears live young.

Luminous hake
Steindachneria argentea

The luminous hake is a little-known relative of the cod, but unlike this more familiar species it is too small to attract the attentions of commercial fisheries. It lives at moderate depths, where very little daylight penetrates, and uses bioluminescence to help disguise its outline. There are light-emitting organs arranged in rows along the underside and on the head, and when these are glowing with their bluish light they make the fish very difficult to see from below. In addition, dark shading on its back helps to hide it from above. Luminous hake prey on smaller fish and invertebrates and are in turn targeted by larger species of hake, as well as by sharks. Juvenile fish tend to feed on crustaceans and small, deep-dwelling fish such as lanternfish.

Distribution: Tropical western Atlantic waters, from Florida, USA, and northern Gulf of Mexico through Central America to Venezuela.
Habitat: Close to sea floor in water 200–400m/ 650–1,300ft deep.
Food: Smaller fish and invertebrates.
Size: 30cm/12in.
Breeding: Ovoviviparous; details not known.
Status: Common; not listed by IUCN.

Identification: Body tapers from the head, which has large eyes and mouth, to a narrow tail. The first dorsal fin has an elongated first ray, posterior and anal fins form a continuous fringe. Body is silvery, tinged with brown above, purple on the belly.

ANGLERS AND TETRAODONTIFORMS

The grotesque-looking angler fish, many of which have evolved dorsal apparatus to 'lure' bait, are often used to illustrate the weird and wonderful life of the deep oceans, though many species actually live in shallow water. The order Tetraodontiformes is famous for another reason – it includes the world's largest bony fish, the magnificent ocean sunfish.

Sargassum fish

Histrio histrio

Identification: The body is in variable shades of brown with various flaps and frills to mimic the fronds of weed among which it usually lives. The dorsal fin ray is modified into a stout fishing lure to tempt prey close enough to ambush.

This unusual angler fish is a shallow-water, open-ocean specialist. It is usually associated with the floating seaweed *Sargassum*, but will also make use of other flotsam. The pelvic fins are specialized and able to grasp, rather like hands. The Sargassum fish is a relatively weak swimmer, but uses its fins to hold on to fronds of weed to avoid being swept away. Its camouflage makes it difficult to see among the weed. Breeding starts with courtship, with the male closely following the female. She then makes abrupt darts to the surface to spawn. The eggs are embedded in a jelly that expands on contact with seawater, creating a floating raft. The eggs may drift far from shelter and young fish are vulnerable.

Distribution: Ranges widely in Indian Ocean and Indo-Pacific; also found Western and Southern Pacific and Atlantic.
Habitat: Surface waters in drifts of *Sargassum* seaweed.
Food: Smaller fish and crustaceans (shrimps).
Size: 20cm/8in.
Breeding: Eggs fertilized externally, develop in floating mass with no parental care.
Status: Occasionally caught for food and aquarium trade; not listed in IUCN.

Giant sea devil

Ceratias holboelli

This is the original sea devil – the first and largest deep-sea angler to be described. Prey, in the form of smaller fish, is attracted by the sea devil twitching a fishing lure (the esca), formed from the modified first spine of the dorsal fin (the ilicium), and is then engulfed by the angler's huge mouth. Needle-like teeth ensure there is no escape. The other dorsal fin rays form distinctive knobbly protuberances, called 'caruncles', along the back. These fish are slow swimmers. Female sea devils produce eggs that float in rafts of jelly and hatch into tiny larvae that live as plankton. Males remain very small, and when mature seek out the larger mature females, which release chemical signals to guide suitors in the dark water. On finding a female, the male latches on to her body with sharp teeth and over time becomes permanently fused. He extracts what little nourishment he needs directly from her blood supply, through a placenta-like intermeshing of blood vessels, and produces sperm to fertilize her eggs.

Identification: Adult female has a bulbous body that tapers to the tail. Mouth is huge and opens upwards. Dorsal fin is modified into a fishing lure and caruncles.

Distribution: Tropical, sub-tropical and temperate oceans worldwide.
Habitat: Mostly deep water to 2,000m/6,562ft.
Food: Smaller fish.
Size: Females up to 1.2m/4ft long; males from 1–16cm/ 0.4–6.3in.
Breeding: Males form parasitic attachments to females. Eggs fertilized externally, develop in floating mass with no parental care.
Status: Not listed by IUCN.

Toothy sea devil (*Neoceratias spinifer*)
6–7cm/2.4–2.8in
This mini-monster of the western central Pacific
is the only known member of its family. Unusual
among anglers in lacking a lure, it relies on a
nightmarish array of moveable teeth mounted on
the outer jaws.

Deep sea angler (*Linophryne macrodon*):
females 9cm/3.5in; males 2cm/0.8in
Females of this eastern central Pacific species
have the most elaborate appendages of any
angler species. They also bear a large barbel
dangling from the lower jaw. Both lure and
barbel are bioluminescent.

Whipnose (*Gigantactis elsmani*): females
38cm/15in
The fly fishermen of deep-sea anglers, the large
upper jaw bears a highly elongated ilicium, or
fishing rod, with a fleshy, tentacled lure at the
tip. Recorded in various deep-water Pacific
habitats, but full range still unknown.

Deep sea coffinfish (*Bathychaunax
melanostomus*): up to 10cm/4in
This Indian Ocean species belongs to a family of
anglers know as sea toads. Its bulbous body and
narrow tail are covered with small spines. Lure
rests in a groove on the head when not in use.

Spotted oceanic triggerfish

Canthidermis maculatus

Triggerfish are named for the shape of the
first dorsal fin, which can be locked in
an upright position, presumably as an
anti-predation measure that makes the
fish difficult to swallow. This species is
characterized by a mainly blue or purple
body, with some counter-shading. Unlike
most other trigger fish, which are associated
with reefs and coastal waters, the oceanic
trigger is something of a nomad. It relies on
the shelter of floating debris, such as
detached fronds of weed, logs or pieces of
floating wreckage and debris. This cover is
essential – without it the trigger is exposed
to predation. It eats other, smaller fish it
finds there, but is especially
intolerant of other triggers.
It will dash at intruders
aggressively, driving them
away from its
territory.

Identification:
Body is stout, with
symmetrical tail fin and
large, pointed, roughly equal
second dorsal and anal fins.
Marked with white or blue spots.

Distribution: Tropical
and sub-tropical
oceans worldwide.
Habitat: Surface dweller
down to about 100m/330ft,
associated with flotsam.
Food: Smaller fish and
pelagic invertebrates.
Size: 50cm/20in.
Breeding: External
fertilization, no parental care.
Status: Common, not listed
by IUCN.

Giant oceanic sunfish

Mola mola

This is the world's largest bony fish, weighing in at anything
up to 2,300kg/5,070lb. The vast, disc-shaped body is
laterally compressed and stabilized by tall dorsal and anal
fins. The name refers not to the fish's shape, but to
its habit of 'sunbathing' while floating on its
side near the surface. There is no tail;
instead the body ends with a rounded
rudder (the clavus) formed from the
last few rays of the dorsal and anal
fins. The skin is scaleless and tough.
The sunfish has well-developed teeth,
which are fused to form a sort of beak.
The jaws are powerful enough to bite
through shell and bone, but the mouth is small
and the sunfish is not a fast swimmer, so it
preys mostly on slow-moving or drifting
animals. Mature females produce an
astonishing number of tiny eggs, which drift
the oceans – the chances of any one being
fertilized and surviving infancy are small.

Distribution: Tropical to
temperate waters of Pacific,
Atlantic and Indian Oceans.
Habitat: Open ocean, close
to surface, but may dive to
500m/1,600ft or more.
Food: Jellyfish, fish,
molluscs, crustaceans
and echinoderms.
Size: 3.3m/11ft long.
Breeding: Produces
hundreds of millions of tiny
eggs which are fertilized
externally; these drift in the
oceans with no parental care.
Status: Not listed by IUCN.
Occasionally fished for meat
and body parts used in
Chinese medicine.

Identification: Very large
truncated body, lacks tail. Caudal
and pelvic fins are absent, dorsal and
anal fins are tall, providing some
stability and steering when swimming.

FLYING FISH AND SAWBELLIES

The 180 or so species of the order Beloniformes are mostly fast-swimming surface-dwellers, several of which can launch themselves out of the water to perform long glides. Members of the order Beryciformes, on the other hand, are far from streamlined – many have deep bodies with large heads, and spend their lives in moderate to deep water.

Cosmopolitan flying fish

Exocoetus volitans

This is the most common and widespread species of flying fish in the suborder Exocoetoidei. In preparation for take-off, it swims close to the surface and beats its tail up to 50 times a second. This causes the front of the body to lift from the water like an over-revved speedboat. Then, with a final flick of the tail, the fish leaves the water, accelerating rapidly as it breaks free of the surface tension.

The pectoral fins spread wide to provide lift and it glides for 50m/164ft or more. This is a strategy for escaping predators, such as tuna and swordfish. These fast-swimming hunters can be left trailing once the flying fish leaves the water and speeds off through the air.

Identification: Slender body, dark above and silvery below. Eyes are large. Pectoral fins greatly enlarged and can be opened out to the sides when gliding. Tail fin deeply notched and asymmetrical, with an enlarged lower lobe.

Distribution: Tropical and sub-tropical oceans and adjoining seas worldwide.
Habitat: Surface waters of open ocean, down to about 20m/66ft.
Food: Range of planktonic animals, mainly crustaceans.
Size: 30cm/12in.
Breeding: Oviparous; planktonic larvae; no parental care.
Status: Common; not listed by IUCN.

Needlefish

Belone belone

This is a fish of many common names – it is informally known as the garpike, sea pike, sea needle, greenbone and mackerel guide. This highly distinctive species is fished commercially as well as for sport – when hooked it fights hard, leaping clear of the water. It feeds mainly on schooling pelagic fish, such as smaller herrings and mackerel, and migrates along with these species – summering in the northern Atlantic and Baltic and retreating to warmer waters during the winter months. Female needlefish produce eggs that float at the water's surface, often becoming attached to floating weed or other debris by long tendrils. Needlefish of all sizes are eaten by a variety of fast-moving predators, including tuna, swordfish and seals.

Identification: Athletic fish with a greatly elongated, cylindrical body shaped by well-developed swimming muscles. Long, narrow snout and large eyes. Lower jaw is longer than upper jaw. Dorsal and anal fins set well back on body, close to the tail with a forked caudal fin. Silvery body. Sometimes confused with similiar species *Belone svetovidovi*.

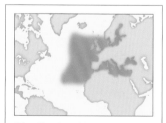

Distribution: North-eastern Atlantic Ocean, also Mediterranean and Black seas.
Habitat: Open water close to surface; may occasionally enter estuaries.
Food: Smaller fish, especially sardines and anchovies.
Size: 95cm/37.5in.
Breeding: Oviparous; no parental care.
Status: Commercial game fish; not listed by IUCN.

Hairyfish (*Mirapinna esau*): up to 6cm/2.4in
Thought to be a relative of the tapetail, this strange-looking fish is known from only one specimen, which was collected near the Azores in the mid Atlantic.

Four-winged flying fish (*Cheilopogon furcatus*): up to 35cm/13.75in
This fish and its relatives have greatly enlarged pectoral and pelvic fins, well suited to 'flying'. They can glide for distances of up to 200m/660ft at speeds in excess of 80kmph/50mph. Found in tropical and sub-tropical oceans.

Alfonsino (*Beryx decadactylus*): up to 60cm/23.6in
A laterally flattened, deep-bodied, pelagic fish of tropical and temperate oceans. Has large eyes and a forked tail. The body is covered with small, comb-like scales, and is bright pink or red.

Tapetail (*Eutaeniophorus festivus*): up to 5cm/2in
A bizarre little fish belonging to the small order Cetomimiformes. Occurs in all tropical and temperate oceans but is not common in any of them. Body is elongate, with large fins. The pelvic fins are situated forward of the pectorals, at the throat. The tail ends in a long streamer.

Fangtooth

Anoplogaster cornuta

The common fangtooth, also know as the ogrefish, is named for its unpleasant gape full of needle-like teeth. It is a prickly customer in other ways, too – the body is covered in scales bearing short spines, giving it the feel of coarse sandpaper. The dorsal, anal, pectoral, pelvic and caudal fins all have conspicuously unwebbed fin rays. The lower fangs fit neatly into cavities in the palate when the mouth is closed. These cavities extend up inside the head, either side of the brain. The teeth are used for snagging smaller fish and invertebrates, but despite its fearsome appearance, it frequently falls victim to larger predators, especially tuna and albacore.

Identification: Head and mouth large, body short and deep with conspicuous lateral line lying within a groove that sweeps along the flank in a curve from eye level to the midline of the tail. Colour uniform dark brown to black.

Distribution: Tropical and temperate oceans worldwide.
Habitat: Close to sea floor in deep areas, from 500–5,000m/ 1,600–16,500ft.
Food: Smaller fish and invertebrates.
Size: 15cm/6in.
Breeding: Oviparous; larvae develop in surface waters; no parental care.
Status: Not listed by IUCN.

Orange roughy

Hoplostethus atlanticus

The orange roughy grows exceptionally slowly, taking two or three decades to reach maturity. Examination of growth rings in otoliths (ear boxes) suggests that this species may live for up to 150 years – making it the longest-living fish species known to science. Orange roughy breed once a year, coming together in large schools to spawn near the surface. This behaviour is easily exploited by fishermen.

The species' slow growth rates and sedentary nature are cause for great concern to conservationists. Populations have been greatly diminished by overfishing in recent times and numbers are very slow to recover.

Identification: A large head takes up about one-third of body length. Body is deep, laterally flattened and covered with small scales. In life, body is brick red, fading to orange when dead. Well-developed dorsal and anal fins, deeply notched tail fin. Pelvic fins set almost as far forward as pectoral fins.

Distribution: Western Atlantic off Namibia and Pharoes, Pacific and Indian Oceans off Australia, New Zealand, Madagascar and southern Chile.
Habitat: Deep water from 200–2,000m/656–6,560ft.
Food: Crustaceans and smaller fish.
Size: 75cm/30in.
Breeding: Oviparous; no parental care.
Status: Protected by strict quotas in Australia and New Zealand, but not listed by IUCN.

JACKS, REMORAS AND RELATIVES

These members of the large order Percifomes reflect just some of the diversity within this vast group. They all possess spiny fin rays, pelvic fins located well forward at the throat and thin, bone-like scales with a serrated edge. Most are fast-swimming predators, but a few are positively sluggish and some even resort to hitching rides on other fish.

Yellowtail amberjack

Seriola lalandi

Yellowtail amberjacks are a familiar sight on reefs and in coastal waters, but they also live in open ocean – juveniles, in particular, often live in schools far out to sea, having been carried with ocean currents as larvae. Large adults are more often solitary. All jacks are efficient swimmers – the carangiform mode of swimming, where the head stays still and the tail sweeps from side to side, is named after this family. The tall, forked tail fin offers powerful thrust without excessive turbulence. Amberjacks are predators of smaller fish species and invertebrates, which are ambushed and caught with a burst of speed.

Identification: Long, torpedo-shaped body with large, forked tail. Body is dark blue above and white below; tail fin is yellow or dark with yellow trailing edge. Single dorsal and anal fins are small with a triangular leading portion and an elongate fin base reaching nearly to the tail.

Distribution: Tropical and warm-temperate waters worldwide.
Habitat: Coasts, reefs and open ocean, usually close to sea floor, from shallows to 825m/2,700ft.
Food: Small fish, cephalopods and crustaceans.
Size: 2.5m/8.2ft.
Breeding: Oviparous; no parental care.
Status: Minor commercial importance, a popular gamefish; not listed by IUCN.

Man-o-war fish

Nomeus gronovii

Identification: Small fish with silvery body and out-sized pelvic fins. The body is marked with large dark-blue to black spots. It has two similar-sized, darkly pigmented dorsal fins, small pectoral fins and a large, deeply forked tail.

As its name suggests, this species specializes in feeding on colonies of Portuguese man-o-war. By hiding in the trailing tentacles, it receives protection from potential predators wary of the stings. The relationship may also benefit the man-o-war, for as long as the fish does not eat polyps faster than they can be replaced, its presence may attract other fish that are not immune to the siphonophore's stings. The man-o-war fish alternative name, 'driftfish', equally describes its lifestyle – it is not a powerful swimmer and apparently spends most of its life seeking or sheltering beneath its prey, drifting wherever ocean currents take it. This is certainly the case for juveniles, although it is thought that adults may descend into much deep waters later in life. Its absence from the eastern Atlantic Ocean and Mediterranean Sea has not been fully explained.

Distribution: Tropical and sub-tropical waters of Indian, Pacific and western Atlantic Oceans.
Habitat: Juveniles and sub-adults, surface waters from coastal areas to far offshore; adults may live near sea bed.
Food: Jellyfish and siphonophores.
Size: 39cm/15.4in.
Breeding: Oviparous; details not known.
Status: Not listed by IUCN.

Pilotfish (*Naucrates ductor*): up to 70cm/28in
The pilotfish (above) is a boldly patterned relative of the jacks. Its body is a dark-blue colour or black with seven or eight broad, evenly spaces white vertical bands. It lives in the surface waters of tropical and subtropical seas worldwide, and it is associated with floating objects, such as seaweed and jellyfish.

Halfmoon fish (*Medialuna californiensis*): up to 48cm/19in
A Pacific chub, from the perciform family Kyphosidae, the halfmoon is found around coasts and rocky reefs. Further out to sea, it habitually associates with floating kelp or sargassum weed or other flotsam. It is a popular food fish and is caught both commercially and for sport.

Horse mackerel (*Trachurus trachurus*): up to 70cm/28in
A widespread pelagic (a fish favouring the open ocean) carangid, the horse mackerel is a medium-sized, schooling fish of the Atlantic and western Pacific Oceans. The body is a greenish-grey colour above and silvery below, and it has large keeled (ridged) scales on the flanks. It is fished commercially in the eastern Atlantic Ocean and the North Sea.

Remora

Remora remora

Remoras can live a free-swimming existence, but their particular speciality is hitching a ride by attaching themselves to the body of larger fish, especially sharks and rays. They will also travel attached to turtles, cetaceans and even inanimate objects, such as ship hulls or diving gear. The attachment is made by a modification of the dorsal fin, which forms a large suction disc just behind the head. The disc is made up of stout, flexible membranes that can be raised and lowered to generate suction. The remora 'pays its fare' by picking off any parasites clinging to the host's skin – mainly copepods. It may also detach from the host in order to pursue free-living prey. Remoras are not parasites and appear to be tolerated by their hosts.

Identification: Elongate body, large, slightly forked tail fin. Pectoral fins are rounded, second dorsal fin is a low triangle. First dorsal fin is modified into an oval-shaped suction disc on head. Colour variable from dark grey or brown to off-white.

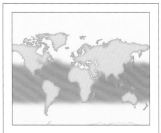

Distribution: Tropical, sub-tropical and warm-temperate oceans and seas worldwide.
Habitat: Reef and pelagic zones as passengers of larger animals.
Food: Parasitic crustaceans and small, free-living planktonic invertebrates.
Size: 85cm/33.5in.
Breeding: Details not known.
Status: Common; not listed by IUCN.

Dorado/dolphinfish

Coryphaena hippurus

This large, boldly coloured fish is known from coastal and open oceans. It lives in schools and frequently shelters under pieces of flotsam. Dorados are a prized food fish, often sold simply as 'dolphin', to the confusion and consternation of non-locals. Dorados are themselves active predators – as larvae and juveniles, they feed mainly on small crustaceans, graduating on to fish as they grow larger. As adults, they will tackle almost anything of suitable size. They are quick swimmers, able to make darting pursuits of even other swift species, such as flying fish. They themselves fall prey to other speed specialist, such as tuna and billfish.

Distribution: Tropical and sub-tropical waters of Atlantic, Indian and Pacific Oceans.
Habitat: Open ocean, and coastal areas, occasionally brackish water; surface waters down to 85m/280ft.
Food: Small fish and zooplankton.
Size: 2m/6.6ft.
Breeding: Oviparous; breeds several times a year in its 5-year lifespan, associating in pairs to spawn.
Status: Commercially fished; not listed by IUCN.

Identification: Body tapers from a large head and upper body to a large forked tail. Down-turned mouth. A single dorsal fin runs the length of the body, pectorals and pelvics large, anal fin long and low. Males have conspicuous bony head crest. Body is vibrantly coloured: green, blue and yellow on back and flanks, white and yellow underside. Fins are blue and green.

TUNAS, MACKEREL AND BARRACUDAS

With their torpedo-shaped muscle-packed bodies, these perciforms are built for speed and endurance. They are among the most voracious hunters in the seas, but also among the most hunted – their meaty, oily flesh makes them enormously popular, and they support large fishing industries. Over-fishing, plus the increasing levels of pollutants being accumulated in the flesh – are arousing serious concern.

Northern bluefin tuna

Thunnus thynnus

This is probably the largest of all the tuna species. The largest known individual was 4.58m/15ft in length and weighed 684kg/1,508lb. This size is achieved through an insatiable appetite for smaller fish and invertebrates, which the bluefin hunts day and night outside the breeding season. Bluefins live in schools often containing a mix of species, but all members of the school will be of similar size to avoid accidental cannibalism. These 'warm-blooded' fish migrate north in summer and spend winter in the tropics, where they breed. Their huge swimming muscles make them exceptionally meaty. There is real concern that the species is being over-fished.

Identification: Large, torpedo-shaped fish, two dorsal fins followed by series of finlets on tailstock. Pectoral and pelvic fins short, anal and second dorsal fin highly falcate (sickle-like), caudal fin a stiff, symmetrical crescent with darkly pigmented lobes. Body counter-shaded – bluish-grey above, silvery below.

Distribution: Northern Atlantic, Mediterranean and Black Sea. Sub-population off coast of South Africa. American range extends from Canada to Brazil.
Habitat: Oceanic, usually in surface waters, occasionally down to 3,000m/9,800ft; visits coastal waters.
Food: Smaller fish and pelagic invertebrates; will also take benthic animals and kelp close to shore.
Size: 4.5m/14.7ft.
Breeding: Oviparous, spawning up to 10 million floating eggs a year.
Status: Listed as Data Deficient by IUCN.

Albacore

Thunnus alalunga

Identification: Body rotund but highly streamlined with pointed snout and tapering tailstock. Eye is large. Two dorsal fins and dorsal and ventral rows of finlets. Pectoral and anal fins are small; dark-blue caudal fins form a shallow crescent-shaped tail with pointed tips. Pectoral fins are very long. Body steely blue above, silvery white below.

These fish move around their distributional range in schools, performing extensive migrations in search of food or to spawn in tropical waters in summer. They often congregate at thermoclines – depths where the water changes temperature, where upwelling currents bring nutrients up from below and prey is more abundant. Large albacore tend to live deeper than small ones. Albacore have a strong schooling instinct and often form mixed schools with other types of tuna. As with other tunas, over-fishing is a concern. The flesh is considered to be excellent and is sold as high-quality canned tuna. Also worrying from a consumer's perspective is the tendency of the species to accumulate high levels of mercury in the flesh.

Distribution: All tropical and temperate oceans and seas including Mediterranean. Very common off Australian coast.
Habitat: Pelagic in open ocean, mainly in surface waters to 600m/1,968ft.
Food: Smaller fish.
Size: 1.4m/4.6ft.
Breeding: Oviparous; spawn in tropical waters during the summer.
Status: Commercially fished; listed as Data Deficient by IUCN.

Wahoo (*Acanthocybium solandri*):
up to 2.5m/8.2ft
A close relative of tunas and mackerel, the wahoo (above) is a long, narrow-bodied predatory fish known from the surface waters of warm, tropical and sub-tropical oceans and seas worldwide. It can be solitary or schooling, and is fished commercially and for sport.

Skipjack tuna (*Katsuwonus pelamis*):
up to 1.08m/3.5ft
A small, cosmopolitan species of tuna. Skipjacks live in schools, and hunt smaller fish and pelagic invertebrates. In turn, they are important prey for larger tunas and sharks. Skipjack tuna account for the majority of tuna consumed by humans.

Bonito (*Sarda chiliensis*): up to 1m/3.25ft
A pelagic schooling tunafish of tropical and temperate oceans, the bonito is also an important commercial and game species.

Spanish mackerel (*Scomberomorus maculata*):
up to 90cm/36in
A streamlined, silvery mackerel of Atlantic and Pacific surface waters. Spanish mackerel form huge schools that are targeted by highly commercial fisheries. Like other scombrids, they are fast swimmers and prey on smaller fish and zooplankton.

Atlantic mackerel

Scomber scombrus

Schools of this species tend to remain in deep water in winter, but in summer feed close to the surface, travelling in search of suitable prey. Plankton, crustaceans and fish larvae make up the bulk of the diet, but the mackerel is also well adapted for pursuing small fish such as sand eels. Mackerel lack a swimbladder, and rely on lightweight oily musculature as well as continual, fast swimming to stop them from sinking. Their gills are ventilated by the force of water passing into the open mouth rather than by any kind of pump, so if they stop swimming they die. The species is highly commercial and supports large fishing industries.

Identification: Slender, near cylindrical body with pointed snout and tapering tailstock. Tiny scales; body is silvery green to white on belly, marked with vertical or slightly oblique black bands on back and flanks. All fins are small, tailstock bears tiny finlets, caudal fin forms a pointed crescent.

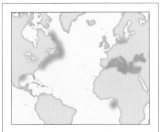

Distribution: Parts of northern Atlantic, also Mediterranean and Black Sea. Western Atlantic range is from Labrador to Cape Lookout, Oregon.
Habitat: Oceanic, in surface waters to 200m/650ft.
Food: Zooplankton and small fish.
Size: 60cm/23.6in.
Breeding: Oviparous; larvae feed actively and attain lengths of 25cm/10in in first year.
Status: Common and widespread but heavy exploitation may lead to declines; not listed by IUCN.

Great barracuda

Sphyraena barracuda

Unlike most tunas and mackerel, the great barracuda is a largely solitary species, though juveniles may form small schools and adults will gather at rich food resources. Barracudas are opportunistic or ambush predators of other fish, capable of short bursts of rapid acceleration. Their sharp teeth easily snag prey, and the jaws are powerful enough to bite fish in half that are too large to be swallowed whole. They are curious of divers and swimmers, but despite a bad reputation pose little serious danger. Attacks on humans do occur, but these usually consist of a single lunge, and although painful, a barracuda bite is unlike to be fatal. The species is fished for sport and sometimes for eating, although it is frequently contaminated with dangerous levels of toxins.

Identification: A long, slender, cylindrical body with a long, pointed head and large eyes. Very sharp teeth. Lower jaw extends further than upper jaw. Body is silvery green, marked on upper flanks with dark bands and also black blotches of variable size and shape. Dorsal and anal fins can be raised and lowered to aid steering.

Distribution: Tropical and sub-tropical waters of oceans and seas worldwide.
Habitat: Surface waters down to 100m/330ft; most often recorded near shore, but performs extensive migrations into open ocean.
Food: Fish.
Size: 2m/6.6ft.
Breeding: Oviparous; spawns offshore in deep water during spring.
Status: Not listed by IUCN.

BILLFISH

*These spectacular members of the order Perciformes rank among the most glamorous of marine fish –
their speed and athleticism is legendary and their dramatic fins and colouration make them the
ultimate trophy for many game fishermen. All billfish possess a bony, sword-like extension of
the upper jaw, which is used to strike down prey.*

Blue marlin

Makaira nigricans

The largest and most spectacular of the billfish, the blue marlin is well adapted for
sustained, high-speed swimming. Its extremely muscular body is superbly streamlined, and
its powerful tail generates enormous thrust, allowing it to swim fast and tirelessly. The pelvic
and pectoral fins fold into grooves in the body to enhance streamlining. The species is also
highly acrobatic, sometimes leaping a metre or more clear of the water surface. These
qualities make is a very popular gamefish. It also makes good eating and is heavily fished in
many parts of its range. Marlin are generally solitary and hunt by day in surface waters.
Certain populations appear to show a marked preference for open, deep water. Swipes of the
bill are used to stun prey. Marlin sometimes
work cooperatively when hunting and in the
excitement some of the colours on the body
appear to 'light up' as the pigment cells glow
under nervous stimulation.

Identification: Cylindrical body tapers from
the back of the head to the tail. First dorsal
fin is long and tall, second much smaller;
pelvic and pectoral fins are small. Tail fins
form a slender crescent; bill is less than a
quarter of body length and stout. Dark
blue or black dorsal area; below
lateral line
is silvery-
white with
15 vertical stripes on
each flank, each bearing pale-blue spots.

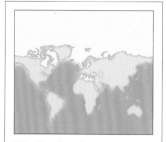

Distribution: Range shown
here is pantropical in Atlantic,
Indian and Pacific. However,
there is some debate as to
whether Pacific and Indian
dwellers constitute a
separate species, *M. mazara*.
Habitat: Pelagic; open ocean
down to 200m/660ft.
Food: Smaller fish,
cephalopods.
Size: 5m/16.4ft.
Breeding: Oviparous; no
parental care.
Status: Highly commercial;
not listed by IUCN.

Black marlin

Makaira indica

A slightly smaller and less decoratively marked relative of the blue marlin, this species is
only slightly less athletic and occupies a wider ecological niche. Its use of deeper water
enables it to take a greater diversity of prey than blue marlin, and it is fast enough to
specialize in hunting small tunas. The bills of all marlins are rounded in cross-section and
thus make crude weapons compared with the blade-like bill of the swordfish, but they are,
nevertheless, sometimes used to slash at prey. Black marlin have been recorded in the
Atlantic Ocean, but these are thought to be vagrant individuals and there is no evidence that
they breed there. Female marlin spawn anything up to 40 million eggs, which hatch as
larvae that develop in mid-water. The maximum lifespan
of this species is not yet known. Heavy commercial
and sport fishing exert serious pressure, and
monitoring is needed to ensure it does
not become threatened.

Identification: Body shape much
as blue marlin, but usually lacks
obvious stripes; pectoral fins
stick out from sides of body
and cannot be folded away
(unlike blue marlin).

Distribution: Tropical,
sub-tropical and warm-
temperate waters of
Indo-Pacific Ocean.
Habitat: Pelagic, surface
waters of open ocean,
occasionally down to
900m/2,950ft; frequently
visits near-shore habitat.
Food: Fish, cephalopods,
crustaceans.
Size: 4.65m/15.25ft.
Breeding: Oviparous; spawns
in warm water.
Status: Highly commercial,
possible risk of over-
exploitation, but not listed
by IUCN.

The need for speed

The species illustrated on these pages include some of the fastest swimmers in the sea. They are highly streamlined, with cylindrical bodies comprising large blocks of very solid muscle. These muscles contain both red (or fast) fibres and white (or slow) fibres, providing an unrivalled combination of speed and stamina. The crescent-shaped tail fins characteristic of the billfish generate maximum power while minimizing drag. In achieving great speed, the billfish sacrifice some manoeuvrability, but the sailfish, the fastest of them all, uses its enormous dorsal fin to help it make surprisingly rapid turns. At cruising speed, the fin is held half erect; when going for a sudden sprint, the fin is lowered completely to maximize streamlining. When a sudden change in direction is required, it is flicked fully open and used to bring the fish quickly about.

Below: The sailfish uses its dorsal fin to swim at speed and turn sharply.

Pacific sailfish

Istiophorus platypterus

This is the world's fastest swimming fish and can attain speeds of 100kmph/62mph plus. It is distinguished by a long, slender but muscular body and a sail-like first dorsal fin that is taller than the body is deep, and runs three-quarters the length of the back. Like the marlin, the sailfish lights up with bright blue vertical stripes when it becomes agitated. Sailfish migrate long distances on an annual basis to spawn in the tropics, sometimes in schools with similar-sized individuals, but they may also cruise the oceans alone in search of aggregations of prey.

Identification: Long, slender body, dark blue above, pale silver-white below, with faint vertical bars on upper flanks made up of blue spots; clearly visible lateral line. Huge, dark dorsal fin. Caudal fins form a large, slender crescent; pectoral fins large; pelvic fins each modified to a single spine.

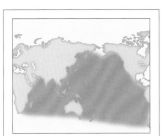

Distribution: Tropical and temperate waters of Indian and Pacific Oceans.
Habitat: Pelagic, warm surface waters of open ocean to 200m/660ft.
Food: Fish, pelagic crustaceans and cephalopods.
Size: 3.5m/11.5ft.
Breeding: Oviparous; spawns in summer; juveniles grow rapidly, reaching 3kg/6.6lb in 6 months.
Status: Not listed by IUCN.

Swordfish

Xiphias gladius

The scientific names *gladias* means 'sword', as in gladiator. The bill of the swordfish is flat with sharp edges, and is used as a deadly weapon, to kill and slice prey into pieces small enough to swallow. Swordfish tackle a wide variety of prey, mostly other fish, but also pelagic invertebrates. They travel long distances, overwintering and spawning in warm waters in spring, then heading for cooler waters to take advantage of seasonally abundant prey over the summer. Juveniles have a fully developed sword by the time that are 1cm/0.4in long, and begin hunting immediately.

Females grow slightly faster than males and reach a larger size. Swordfish is a tasty food fish; however, the species' position at the top of the food chain means it has a tendency

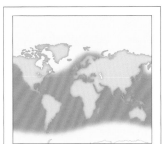

Distribution: Tropical and temperate oceans and seas worldwide.
Habitat: Pelagic in mid-water from 200–800m/650–2,600ft.
Food: Fish, cephalopods, crustaceans.
Size: 4.55m/15ft.
Breeding: Oviparous; spawns in spring; larvae grow rapidly.
Status: Listed as Data Deficient by IUCN.

to accumulate dangerously high levels of certain marine pollutants, especially mercury, so frequent consumption is not recommended.

Identification: Body tapers from head to tail, which bears long caudal fins forming a crescent. Pelvic fins are absent, pectorals are long and low slung. Single dorsal fin is tall and single anal fin is small – both are falcate. Head is large with large eyes and the upper jaw is modified into a long, blade-like bill.

REPTILES OF THE OPEN OCEAN

The relatively few reptiles adapted to life at sea include some of the world's great ocean nomads. Marine turtles, including the enormous leatherback, may travel thousands of miles a year in search of food, but must return to land to breed. The pelagic sea snake, however, is wholly aquatic and unusual among marine serpents for its open water distribution – even its young are born at sea.

Yellow bellied sea snake

Pelamis platurus

This is the only sea snake that ventures into truly open waters and it is often found hundreds of miles offshore. It is also known as the pelagic sea snake, and its wide-roaming habits have earned it the distinction of being the world's most widespread snake species. It can actively swim by wiggling its body – much as a terrestrial snake would move on land – but spends much of its time drifting idly near the surface, usually with head hanging slightly down. The sea snake feeds mainly on small pelagic fish and invertebrates, such as shrimp, which it catches with sudden, darting movements. Highly potent venom is injected into the prey on the first bite, and once immobilized the meal is swallowed whole, head first. The venom is sufficiently potent to kill a human, but the snakes are not aggressive and will not normally bite unless they are provoked.

Identification: Long narrow head and slender body with smooth scales; striking yellow and black colouration serves as a warning to potential predators that this species is toxic.

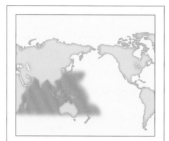

Distribution: Tropical and sub-tropical waters of Indian and Pacific Oceans.
Habitat: Surface waters of open ocean, also in coastal waters and reefs.
Food: Small fish.
Size: 90cm/35in.
Breeding: Mating occurs at the surface; live young born in water.
Status: Common; not listed by IUCN.

Leatherback turtle

Dermochelys coriacea

The world's largest marine turtle, the leatherback is unique in having a rubbery carapace, or shell, instead of a hard, brittle one. The largest individuals are true giants, weighing more than 900kg/1,984lb – as much as 12 average men. Their large size helps them retain some of the heat generated by their metabolism so that, while they remain cold-blooded, their core temperature is usually a few degrees above that of the water, allowing them to exploit higher latitudes than other marine reptiles. They make extensive migration into temperate zones, returning to the tropics to breed. Mating takes place at sea, and the females come ashore to bury their leathery eggs on beaches. This species has undergone a steep decline and is at risk from pollution and disturbance of nesting sites. They feed exclusively on jelly animals and tunicates such as salps and pyrosomes.

Identification: Carapace is rubbery, with prominent longitudinal ridges Very large foreflippers are characteristic. Dorsal surfaces are black, while the underside is mottled pale pink and black.

Distribution: Tropical to cool-temperate waters of oceans worldwide.
Habitat: Surface waters from coasts to open ocean, sometimes diving to more than 500m/1,640ft.
Food: Jelly animals.
Size: 2.8m/9ft.
Breeding: Mates offshore; eggs laid in batches of 60–100 on sandy beaches; no parental care after laying, although nesting sites are selected with great care.
Status: Listed as Critically Endangered by IUCN.

Olive ridley turtle

Lepidochelys olivacea

Distribution: Tropical waters of the Atlantic, Pacific and Indian Oceans.
Habitat: Surface waters from coasts to open ocean.
Food: Fish and marine invertebrates.
Size: 75cm/30in.
Breeding: Females breed every few years, mating offshore and crawling up beaches in order to lay 2–3 clutches of up to 120 eggs over the course of a breeding season.
Status: Listed as Endangered by IUCN.

Adults of this species spend much of their time in open sea, feeding on fish and squid. They return to the coasts to breed. The mass arrival (or *arribada*) of females at breeding beaches and the subsequent mass hatching of offspring are one of the world's great natural history spectacles. Up to 150,000 females may arrive simultaneously, climbing over one another in an effort to find a patch of sand in which to lay their eggs, and often digging up those of other females as they excavate a nest. Mass egg laying leads to the synchronous hatching of hundreds of thousands of young and a feeding frenzy for terrestrial and marine predators. But force of sheer numbers works in the turtles' favour – by making the dash for the sea together the youngsters gain at least some degree of protection.

Identification These diminutive marine turtles have an olive-coloured, heart-shaped carapace. The carapace is distinct in that there are more than five scutes, or plates, down each side.

Loggerhead turtle

Caretta caretta

Considered the most migratory of all sea turtles, loggerheads have been known to make crossings of both the Atlantic and Pacific Oceans. Even young animals spend long periods far out to sea, drifting along with clumps of sargassum weed or other flotsam. The heavy, powerful jaws and associated muscles that earn the species its name are able to demolish the shells of large crabs and molluscs. Thousands of loggerheads are killed annually when accidentally entangled in fishing nets, and since they develop and mature slowly, populations are slow to recover from these losses. Most damaging of all, however, is the effect of human disturbance at nesting beaches.

Hawksbill turtle
(*Eretomchelys imbricata*): up to 1.12m/3.7ft
A relatively small sea turtle of tropical and sub-tropical waters, with a carapace made up of overlapping scutes, and a beak-like mouth. Feed mainly on sponges, jelly animals and seaweed. Listed as Critically Endangered by the IUCN.

Green turtle (*Chelonia mydas*): up to 1.5m/5ft
Endangered turtle named for the colour of its flesh. The populations of the Atlantic and Pacific Oceans are regarded as separate subspecies. Green turtles may travel thousands of kilometres a year at sea but return to their natal beaches to breed. As adults, they are strictly herbivorous, feeding on algae and seagrasses.

Kemp's ridley turtle (*Lepidochelys kempii*): up to 80cm/31.5in
This is a close relative of the olive ridley turtle. It is the world's most threatened marine turtle, with a breeding population estimated at just two or three thousand individuals. It nests only in Mexico.

Distribution: Tropical to warm-temperate waters of oceans worldwide and adjoining seas.
Habitat: Surface waters, from coasts to open oceans.
Food: Marine invertebrates.
Size: 1.2m/4ft.
Breeding: Females breed every 2–3 years, and may produce several clutches of eggs, up to 100 at a time, in a single breeding season.
Status: Listed as Endangered by IUCN.

Identification: Carapace is reddish brown; scales on front flippers reddish fringed with yellow; ventral surface (plastron) is yellow.

OCEANIC DOLPHINS

The cetacean family Delphinidae includes several species that are equally at home in coastal waters or far out to sea. Most are highly social and athletic and they have a natural curiosity that means they often approach boats, providing a welcome spectacle to break the tedium of long sea voyages.

Spinner dolphin

Stenella longirostris

Spinners are among the most conspicuous ocean-going dolphins. They are social, and groups sometimes converge to create schools several thousand strong. The species is named for its unique aerial displays, which involve leaping up to 3m/10ft clear of the water and rotating the body three or four times along the long axis. Spinners are closely associated with schools of tuna and they were the species most severely affected by careless fishing techniques during the second half of the 20th century, when tens of thousands were drowned in nets. Four subspecies are recognized, each with very distinct physical characteristics. Spinners hunt mainly at night in offshore waters, but may visit shallow waters around tropical islands by day. Males are larger in size than females.

Identification: Head tapers to a characteristically long and narrow beak and melon (or domed forehead) has low profile. Body is slender with erect falcate (sickle-shaped) or triangular dorsal fin set half way back. Tail often has a pronounced ventral bulge. Body is predominantly grey, but the belly is pale in some subspecies.

Distribution: Tropical and subtropical waters of oceans worldwide.
Habitat: Open ocean.
Food: Small fish, squid and crustaceans.
Size: 2.35m/7.7ft long.
Breeding: A single calf is born approximately every 3 years, after a 10–11-month period of gestation; calves weaned at 1–2 years of age.
Status: Not listed by IUCN.

Risso's dolphin

Grampus griseus

Risso's dolphins are gregarious, typically living in groups of 20 or so individuals, but occasionally coming together in large schools of several hundred. They are often seen from ships, and occasionally from the shore, and appear curious and playful – apt to leap and breach in a very acrobatic manner. At other times, whole schools seem to disappear completely – presumably migrating in search of food, but the details of these movements and many other aspects of the species' behaviour remain a mystery. Mass strandings occasionally happen. The scars that make the species particularly distinctive are thought to be the result of tussles with other dolphins and with large squid. In older individuals, the scarring may be so dense that the body appears to be almost completely white.

Distribution: Patchy distribution in tropical, sub-tropical and temperate waters in oceans worldwide and many adjoining seas.
Habitat: Open oceans, typically above steeply sloping continental slope.
Food: Mainly squid and other cephalopods.
Size: 3.8m/12.5ft long.
Breeding: Virtually unknown.
Status: Not listed by IUCN.

Identification: Blunt head with a square profile and no beak. Body is stout and robust, with long, falcate pectoral fins, a tall falcate dorsal fin and a slender tail. Skin is a variable shade of grey to brown dorsally, pale on the belly.

Atlantic white-sided dolphin

Lagenorhynchus acutus

Distribution: Temperate and sub-polar North Atlantic and Arctic Oceans.
Habitat: Open waters over deep slopes, canyons and steep ocean-floor topography.
Food: Fish, especially herring, hake and mackerel, squid and other invertebrates.
Size: 2.8m/9.2ft long.
Breeding: Single calf born every other year after an 11-month gestation period; weaned at about 18 months.
Status: Common; not listed by IUCN.

This distinctive species is easily recognized by its consistent flank markings. It is very gregarious, forming schools of anything from a handful of individuals to several hundred. Large numbers form around abundant food sources or when migrating in search of food. Members of a group work together to round up schools of prey fish, especially Atlantic herrings, forcing them into a tight ball, which is then attacked. White-sides often associate with other species, in particular white-beaked dolphins and larger cetaceans, such as fin and humpback whales. They are athletic and playful, and are commonly seen riding the bow waves of ships.

Identification: A stout, torpedo-shaped body; a tall, sharply pointed, falcate dorsal fin; broad, falcate pectoral fins; and a thick tailstock. The head is short with a short, thick beak and a low, tapering profile. The back, fins and flukes are black, while the flanks are grey with a white flash and broad stripe that is creamy-yellow in colour. The belly is white.

Pantropical spotted dolphin (*Stenella attenuata*): up to 2.4m/7.9ft
The pantropical spotted dolphin is probably the most abundant dolphin species, with a population numbering several million worldwide in most tropical and temperate oceans. It is highly gregarious and athletic, and huge schools have been seen performing spectacular displays of leaping and riding the bow waves of boats.

Striped dolphin (*Stenella coeruleoalba*): up to 2.65m/8.7ft
This is a familiar species of dolphin, common in tropical and temperate waters worldwide. It is a highly gregarious species and individuals are usually to be found in large schools of several dozen animals up to several hundred. They prey on small, schooling fish.

Rough-toothed dolphin (*Steno bredanensis*): up to 2.65m/8.7ft
An off-shore specialist of tropical and sub-tropical oceans with a long beak and tapering head profile. The teeth are finely grooved. Members of the species typically live in small groups of 10–20 individuals, and they appear to be highly intelligent and cooperative. Animals perform deep dives, lasting up to 15 minutes, in the search for squid and fish. Large prey, when caught, may be shared out among the group.

Common bottlenose dolphin

Tursiops truncatus

The bottlenose dolphin is known from a wide variety of marine habitats. There are distinct coastal and offshore forms. Popular with people because of their playful nature and apparent 'smile', bottlenoses are also considered to be among the most intelligent of mammals. The species has recently been separated from its close relative the Indo-Pacific bottlenose. Groups may number up to several hundred animals. Aggression is relatively common, especially towards other similar-sized cetaceans. Bottlenoses act cooperatively when hunting or in defence, and they communicate using a highly refined repertoire of body postures and sounds. Prey is detected by echo-location using pulses of sound focused through the melon.

Identification: Long, slender body with tall falcate dorsal fin and short falcate pectorals. Head has pronounced melon and short cylindrical beak. Mouth is slightly curved in what appears to be an appealing smile. Skin is fairly uniformly grey, slightly darker on the dorsal surface.

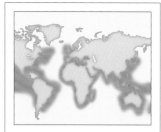

Distribution: Tropical and temperate oceans and adjoining seas worldwide, except High Arctic.
Habitat: Open and coastal waters.
Food: Pelagic and bottom-dwelling fish and invertebrates.
Size: 3.8m/12.5ft long.
Breeding: Single calves are born at intervals of 3 years or more; the young are weaned at 18–20 months, but they may then remain with their mothers for several more years.
Status: Some populations are thought to be in decline, but not listed by IUCN.

TOOTHED AND BEAKED WHALES

Larger members of the Delpinidae are commonly referred to as whales rather than dolphins. The beaked whales of the family Ziphiidae include many of the least known cetacean species. Adult males of the latter group often have just a single pair of teeth which erupt from the lower jaw outside the mouth. It appears these may be used for fighting. Adult female and juvenile beaked whales lack any functional teeth.

Pygmy killer whale

Feresa attenuata

Pygmy killer whales, also known as slender blackfish, earn their common name through their similarities to orcas – both species have black and white colouration and a large dorsal fin. They are, however, much longer-bodied than true killer whales and are closer in appearance to pilot whales. They are reported to be unusually aggressive when cornered, but in open water they are apparently gregarious and live in groups of up to 50 individuals. While they are certainly capable of killing large animals, including other small cetaceans, there is no evidence they actively hunt them. Examinations of stomach contents suggest that they eat mainly squid. They are relatively slow moving, only rarely performing the athletic leaps associated with other dolphin species. They appear to be rather rare animals, and they may be at risk from accidental entanglement in fishing nets.

Identification: Stout torpedo-shaped body and rounded head with pronounced melon and no beak. There is a large falcate dorsal fin half way along the back and moderately long pectorals. The skin is dark grey to black, with white markings on the belly and throat and around the mouth.

Distribution: Tropical and sub-tropical waters of oceans worldwide.
Habitat: Open ocean.
Food: Squid and fish.
Size: 2.6m/8.5ft.
Breeding: Virtually unknown.
Status: Appears to be relatively rare and there are some conservation concerns. Listed as Data Deficient on IUCN.

Cuvier's beaked whale

Ziphius cavirostris

Despite being among the best-studied of all ziphiids, detailed knowledge of Cuvier's beaked whale is still lacking. This deep-diving species may go 30 minutes or more without surfacing for air, and when it does it keeps a low profile – breaching is rare. Hence, sightings are relatively few and far between. The species is either recorded alone or in small groups. Cuvier's beaked whales hunt a variety of deep-water prey, mostly soft-bodied squid, which are sucked into the mouth and swallowed whole as the whale has no functional teeth. Mass strandings of these whales are a concern, since they seem to be related to military exercises involving underwater explosions and other loud noises. It seems likely that these disturbances affect their ability to navigate.

Identification: A large, cylindrical body, with a small falcate dorsal fin set well back, and small rounded pectorals. The head is large and tapers steeply but smoothly to a short beak. Skin is dark grey to black, sometimes flushed with pink around the face and marked with white spots and scars. In adult males, two small teeth protrude from the tip of the lower jaw.

Distribution: Tropical and temperate oceans and adjoining seas worldwide.
Habitat: Offshore specialist favouring deep water.
Food: Mainly squid, some pelagic fish and shrimp.
Size: 2.7m/8.8ft.
Breeding: Details unknown.
Status: May be in decline but listed as Data Deficient by IUCN.

Blainville's beaked whale
Mesoplodon densirostris

This medium-sized toothed whale occupies a very large distributional range, but reliable sightings are relatively infrequent outside three main areas close to the Bahamas in the Atlantic and Hawaii and the Society Islands in the central and South Pacific, where most research has been conducted. Dives are prolonged, up to 20 minutes or more, and probably take the animal into deep water in search of its prey – squid. On surfacing, Blainville's beaked whale breaks the surface beak first, takes a breath, then rolls forward with very little splashing, and is therefore difficult to spot. The bones of this species are among the densest of any mammal and the teeth are bizarre – they erupt from the side of a strangely stepped jaw, and are usually encrusted with tufts of barnacles.

Identification: Spindle-shaped body with small falcate dorsal fin and short pectorals. Head has a long, narrow beak and a strongly arched lower jaw with a large emergent tooth on each side. The skin is dark above and paler on the belly and usually covered with pale scratches and circular scars, the result of attacks by cookiecutter sharks, squid and other whales.

Distribution: Patchy distribution in tropical and warm temperate waters of oceans worldwide and some adjoining seas.
Habitat: Open waters, particularly those above continental slopes.
Food: Squid and small pelagic fish; possibly also bottom-dwelling crustaceans.
Size: 4.4m/14.4ft and perhaps longer.
Breeding: Details not known.
Status: Listed as Data Deficient by IUCN.

Northern bottlenose whale
Hyperoodon ampullatus

Among the largest-beaked whales, the northern bottlenose was previously subject to intensive hunting, but is now protected. Resident populations appear to inhabit deep water off Nova Scotia and off the Bay of Biscay, while other populations appear to be more nomadic or migratory. They live in small groups of fewer than 10 individuals, usually about four. Feeding dives are typically quite short, around 10 minutes, but they can perform extended dives of an hour or more, especially when frightened, and may reach depths of 1,500m/5,000ft. They appear to favour one species of squid (*Gonatus fabricii*) above all other food, but they may also opportunistically take fish and other invertebrates. Despite a history of hunting, they remain curious animals and will sometimes approach boats.

Identification: Cylindrical body with small pectoral fins and a dorsal fin set two-thirds of the way back. Has a prominent, rounded melon and pronounced beak. Skin is dark grey. The melon and beak are white (grey in females).

Distribution: North Atlantic Ocean and into Arctic Ocean.
Habitat: Deep water, often close to pack ice. Dives to depths of 1,500m/4,920ft.
Food: Mostly deep-water squid.
Size: 9.8m/32ft.
Breeding: Calves born singly in spring after a gestation lasting at least 12 months.
Status: Species is protected internationally and listed as Lower Risk, Conservation Dependent by IUCN.

Baird's beaked whale (*Berardius bairdii*): up to 12.8m/42ft
The largest member of the Ziphiidae, also known as the giant bottlenose whale. Females are slightly larger than males. The species is restricted to deep waters of the northern Pacific Ocean. Little is known of its ecology and behaviour, though detailed anatomical studies have been made as a result of Japanese whalers using International Whaling Commission regulations that allow them to take whales for 'scientific purposes'.

Sowerby's beaked whale (*Mesoplodon bidens*): up to 5.5m/18ft
A little-known species found in the North Atlantic, Sowerby's beaked whales live in small schools of fewer than 10 individuals. Males have two tusk-like teeth erupting from halfway along the lower jaw. They are thought to eat mostly squid and perhaps certain groundfish, such as Atlantic cod.

Strap-toothed whale (*Mesoplodon layardii*): up to 6.2m/20ft
A medium-sized beaked whale restricted to the cool-temperate waters of the Southern Hemisphere. Both sexes are black with extensive white markings at the front of the body and a dark facial mask. Males have long, laterally flattened tusks protruding from either side of the lower jaw.

SPERM AND OCEANIC BALEEN WHALES

These giant whales include the largest members of the animal kingdom. Most undertake vast migratory journeys in a lifetime, and some may live for more than 100 years. They may communicate with others of their species over hundreds of miles via 'songs'. The slow reproduction rate means that populations are unable to recover rapidly from the impact of past commercial exploitation.

Sperm whale

Physeter macrocephalus

The largest of the toothed whales and the largest predatory animal on Earth, sperm whales tackle prey up to 10m/33ft long. They are also the deepest-diving mammals, able to descend an estimated 3,000m/10,000ft. Sperm whales mature slowly – calves begin taking solid food at 2 years, but may continue to supplement this with milk for 10 years or so. This slow reproductive rate makes them vulnerable to over-exploitation, and they suffered heavy losses before hunting was banned in the 1980s. The oil inside the head, known as spermaceti, was used as a high-quality lubricant. In life, the spermaceti is thought to control buoyancy and focus sound. Also of value are the teeth, used in scrimshaw, and ambergris – a grey substance voided from the gut and used in perfume making.

Identification: Massive head, which contains spermaceti organ, is one-third body length. Teeth present only on lower jaw, which is very narrow. Skin of body is often wrinkled. Dorsal fin is very small and set well back, followed by several small bumps. Pectoral fins are short and broad; tail flukes are very wide.

Distribution: All oceans except ice-bound polar waters, although may be seen close to pack ice.
Habitat: Deep water; dives to 3,000m/10,000ft.
Food: Giant squid and other deep-water cephalopods.
Size: Up to 18.3m/60ft.
Breeding: Single calf born every 4–6 years after a gestation period of 15–18 months; calf weaned at 2 years. May live for more than 70 years.
Status: Protected by IWC ban on hunting. Listed as Vulnerable by IUCN.

Bowhead whale

Balaena mysticetus

Identification: Very large, deep-bodied whale with a massive head, and enormous, highly arching jaws which support 600 or more strips or plates of baleen up to 4m/13ft in length. There is a ridge on top of the head, in front of the blowholes. Dorsal fin is absent, pectorals are broad and triangular and tail flukes form a notched triangle. Males vocalize a haunting and highly varied song in the spring, in order to attract females.

This giant of Arctic waters spends its life close to the edge of the sea ice. It can travel considerable distances under ice and, if necessary, can ram air holes in ice almost 2m/6.6ft thick. There is some evidence that this species uses echo location to help them navigate around ice floes and bergs. Vocalizations, or 'songs', are common. The massive head and bowed jaw support hundreds of strips, or plates, of a horny material known as baleen. These plates act as strainers, filtering planktonic life from the water as the whale swims. The discovery of 19th-century harpoon tips in individuals alive at the end of the 20th century suggests the species is long-lived.

Distribution: Circumpolar waters of the North Atlantic, North Pacific and Arctic Oceans.
Habitat: Deep water, close to pack ice.
Food: Mainly krill and copepods, as well as other planktonic invertebrates.
Size: Up to 19.8m/65ft.
Breeding: Single calf born every 3–4 years; weaned from about 12 months, but may stay with mother several more years. May live for over 200 years.
Status: Listed as Low Risk, Conservation Dependent by IUCN.

Blue whale

Balaenoptera musculus

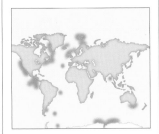

Distribution: All oceans, with three major populations in North Pacific, North Atlantic and Southern Hemisphere.
Habitat: Open ocean, may also visit coastal waters.
Food: Krill.
Size: 33m/108ft.
Breeding: Single calf born every 2–3 years after a gestation period of 11 months; development is rapid, young are weaned and independent within 8 months. May live for up to 70 years.
Status: Listed as Endangered by IUCN.

Identification: The largest of the the baleen whales. Head broad and flattened. Mouth contains up to 800 baleen plates. Throat folds into about 60 pleated furrows. Dorsal fin is tiny and set well back; pectorals are long and tapering; tail flukes are large and triangular. The skin is mottled grey, appearing blue in water. The underside is often coated in a sulphur-yellow growth of diatoms (single-celled algae).

The blue whale is the largest animal ever to have lived on Earth. Even a newborn calf is over 7m (23ft) long. It is difficult to assess to what extent these giants might be social – they are usually seen apparently alone or in small groups that disperse rapidly, but for animals of such size, with calls that carry vast distances, several whales spread out over, say, 200 miles or several hundred kilometres might still constitute a cohesive group. There appears to be a southerly migration in the austral summer, when travelling whales may consume up to 4 tonnes of krill per day. The species suffered severely from commercial whaling until it was protected in the mid 20th century and doubts remain over its ability to recover.

Fin whale (*Balenoptera physalus*):
up to 27m/89ft
Second only to the blue whale in size, this species has strange, asymmetrical colouring on the sides of the head – black on the left and white on the right. Cosmopolitan in all oceans, it can swim at speeds of up to 47kmph/29mph. Feeds on krill and schooling fish such as herring.

Southern minke (*Balaenoptera bonaerensis*):
up to 10.5m/35ft
Southern relative of the 'common' and dwarf minkes, but actually more closely related to the large, fast-swimming sei whale. Distinctive for their flat head, pointed snout, very curved dorsal fin and pale grey pectoral fins.

Northern right whale (*Eubalaena glacialis*):
up to 17m/56ft
The northern right whale and its southern counterpart (*E. australis*) are closely related, but live at opposite ends of the Earth, with no apparent overlap. They look very similar, with a massive head and arched jaw. However, the northern species has white belly patch and facial calluses often encrusted with barnacles.

Minke whale

Balaenoptera acutorostrata

Distinguished by its pointed snout, the minke is the smallest and most common of the great whales. These whales are apparently migratory, but movements are difficult to follow. It seems that pregnant females travel to the tropics in winter to give birth, and the young are independent in time for the return journey. Minkes were intensively hunted in the mid 20th century and are still taken by Norway and Japan in defiance of an international ban on whaling. The so-called dwarf minke, regarded as a subspecies of *B. acutorostrata*, lives only in the Southern Hemisphere but should not be confused with the southern minke (see left).

Identification: Streamlined with a pointed snout and a ridge along the midline. There are 500–700 short pale plates of baleen and 50–70 pleated furrows on the throat. The skin is black dorsally with a grey chevron on its back; white on the throat and belly, with a white patch on the pectoral fins.

Distribution: Tropical, temperate and polar waters of North Atlantic and North Pacific Oceans (dwarf subspecies occurs in Southern Hemisphere).
Habitat: Open ocean, often over continental shelves and sometimes coastal waters.
Food: Mainly small fish, such as herring, sandlance and capelin, as well as some swarming planktonic crustaceans.
Size: 10.5m/35ft.
Breeding: Single calf born every 1 or 2 years after a gestation period of 10 months, weaned at about 6 months and independent soon after. May live for up to 50 years.
Status: Listed as Low Risk by IUCN.

GLOSSARY

Acanthocephala Phylum of parasitic 'spiny-headed' worms, found in the gut of some vertebrates including bony fish

Acanthopterygii The largest superorder of bony fish within the class Actinopterygii

Actinopterygii Class of bony fish, which accounts for about half of all vertebrates and approximately 96% of all fish. Around 60% of actinops live in the marine environment. Distinguishing features include fins supported by rays (spiny fins) and the presence of a single dorsal fin

Agnatha Superclass of jawless primitive freshwater and marine fish, of which only the lamprey and hagfish exist in the present day

Amoebocyte A cell capable of amoeboid movement; found in vertebrate body fluids such as blood

Amphibian A cold-blooded vertebrate which usually spends part of its life on land and part in water; includes frogs, toads and salamanders

Amphipod Member of the order Amphipoda (small crustaceans, including sand hoppers and ghost shrimps)

Ampullae Membranous anatomy usually associated with the semi-circular canals of the inner ear

Ampullae of Lorenzini Sensory organs forming a network of jelly-filled canals within the anterior part of sharks and rays, penetrating the surface of the skin as pores and usually visible as dark spots

Annelida Phylum containing wormlike creatures (annelids) with segmented bodies

Anterior At, or towards, the front

Anthozoa Class of cnidarians including hard and soft corals, sea pens and sea anemones

Aperture An opening, as for example, in a gastropod mollusc's shell

Aplacophora Worm-shaped marine molluscs lacking a shell

Appendage Broadly used for an external, protruding body part, ranging from (for example) the limbs of a vertebrate, or the antennae or mandibles of an invertebrate

Appendicularia Class within the phylum Urochordata or Tunicata

Arthropoda Phylum consisting of invertebrates with an exoskeleton and segmented bodies, to which

are attached pairs of jointed legs. Includes the insects, arachnids and crustaceans

Ascidiacea Class within the phylum Urochordata or Tunicata. Adults may be solitary, sessile zooids, or form colonies by budding

Asteroidea Class of echinoderms containing the sea stars

Atoll A circular or ring-like coral island enclosing a lagoon

Baleen Horny plates growing from the upper jaw of baleen whales and used in feeding by straining tiny food items, such as krill, from the water

Barbel A sensory, tentacle-like structure found around the mouth of certain types of fish

Barrier reef A long, narrow, coral reef usually found in shallow water and running close to the shore

Benthic Bottom dwelling

Bilateral symmetry Describes an organism in which one half is a mirror image of the other half if an imaginary line is drawn along its longest axis; insects, fish and mammals are among animals that show bilateral symmetry

Bioluminescence The emission of light by a living organism that occurs as the product of a chemical reaction

Bivalve Describes a shell consisting of two halves, or valves. Animals with bivalve shells belong to the mollusc class Bivalvia

Brachiopoda Small phylum of ancient molluscoidal creatures, with a long, often spiral bivalve shell. Includes the lampshells (Lingula)

Branchiopoda Class or subclass of primitive crustaceans, predominantly freshwater but with a few marine representatives

Bryozoa Small phylum of coral-like moss animals that form colonies by budding

Bycatch The unintentional harvest of commercial fisheries

Calcarea Class within the phylum Porifera, containing sponges with calcareous skeletons

Calcareous Chalky; term used to describe the shells of crabs, for example

Carapace The shield-like, dorsal part of the exoskeleton of various crustaceans; also used to describe the domed part of the shell of tortoises and turtles

Catadromous Describes a species which migrates from fresh water to the sea to breed

Cephalaspidomorphi Class of primitive jawless fish, most of which are now extinct, but which may include the living lamprey

Cephalocarida Class or subclass of primitive crustaceans. Living members usually exhibit paddle-like

appendages on the thorax

Cephalopoda Class of often highly-evolved molluscs including octopii and squid. Typical features include a large head, large eyes and, in some cases, an ink sac

Chaetognatha Phylum of small, almost transparent wormlike creatures with bristles around the mouth. Commonly known as arrow worms

Chela A pincer-bearing leg of a crustacean

Chelicera (pl. chelicerae) One of the pair of pincer-like mouthparts in front of the mouth opening in chelicerates (animals such as the horseshoe crab)

Chelicerata A subphylum of arthropods, members of which are known as chelicerates

Choanocyte A type of ciliated cell found in sponges

Chondrichthyes Class of cartilaginous, jawed fish whose members include sharks, skates and rays

Chordate An anima belonging to the phylum Chordata, having a single, hollow dorsal nerve cord, a notochord, gill slits, and a postanal tail at least during some part of its development; chordates include the vertebrate animals

Chromatophore A pigment-containing cell which can change its size or colour

Chrondrocyte A specialized cell in chimeras, sharks and rays that produces the gel-like substance chrondromucoprotein, which forms the basis of cartilage

Cilium (pl. cilia) A tiny, hair-like structure growing out from some cells; its whip-like beating action produces movement

Circumglobal Distributed around the world within a fairly specific latitudinal range

Cirripedia Class of marine crustaceans including barnacles

CITES The Convention on International Trade in Species; an agreement between nations that restricts international trade

Class A taxonomic level between phylum and order

Clupeid Member of the order Clupeiformes; includes herrings and anchovies

Cnidarian Member of the phylum Cnidaria (the hydroids, jellyfish, anemones and corals)

Cnidocyte One of the stinging cells found in most cnidarians

Comb-row, or **ctene** Part of the sensory equipment of comb jellies, which is lined with cilia

Commensalism A relationship between different organisms where at least one benefits from the association but neither is harmed

Copepoda Class or subclass of crustacean. Members typically have six pairs of appendages on the thorax; many exist as parasites and plankton

Coral reef A reef formed from coral (the protective limestone skeletons secreted by certain species of cnidarians)

Cosmopolitan (Of species) found ranging widely

Costal Concerned with the ribs

Crenulated (Of shells, especially bivalves) indented or scalloped effect at edges of shell

Crinoidea Class of echinoderms containing the sea lilies and feather stars

Crustacea Subphylum of arthropods including lobsters, crabs, shrimps and barnacles

Ctenoid A fish scale with a toothed posterior edge; found in perciform (perchlike) fish, for example

Ctenophora Phylum of invertebrates commonly known as comb jellies

Cubozoa Class of cnidarians with a cube-shaped medusa and a highly venomous sting. Also known as sea wasps

Cydippid Larval phase associated with ctenophores

Delta An often triangular, low-lying deposit of sediment at the mouth of a river

Demospongiae The largest class of sponges within the phylum Porifera, which have typically soft, spongy bodies

Detritivore An organism that feeds on detritus, or decomposing organic material

Deuterostome A member of a group of multicellular animals in which the mouth is formed as a secondary opening, and the original embryonic opening (blastophore) becomes the anus

Dimorphism Having two distinct forms (for example, different colours or sizes) within a species; sexual dimorphism refers to a marked difference in physical characteristics between males and females of the species

Dioecious Having separate sexes

Ecdysozoa One of the major groups of protostome animals, including the phylum Arthropoda

Echinoderm Members of the phylum Echinodermata

Echinodermata Phylum of exclusively marine creatures with radially symmetrical bodies formed around a central disk, in which the mouth is located. May be star-shaped, cylindrical or spherical

Echinoidea Class of echinoderms containing the sea urchins and sand dollars

Echiura Phylum of wormlike

creatures, commonly known as spoonworms. Have various features in common with the annelids, but lack a segmented body

Elver A young eel

Emarginate Having a notched margin

Ephyra Larval phase associated with medusoid animals

Epidermis The outermost layer of cells of an animal or plant

Errant Describes a species that actively hunts for food, for example, some kinds of marine worms

Esca The lure, or bait, at the end of the angling apparatus (see ilicium) of anglerfish and frogfish (order Lophiiformes)

Eukaryote A cell which has genetic material contained within the nuclear membrane

Eumetazoa Subkingdom of multicellular organisms, members of which are called Metazoans

Eversible Describes a structure which can be everted, for example, the pharynx of some marine worms

Exoskeleton Hard, external, shell-like structure that supports and protects the body of some invertebrates, including the Arthropods

Falcate Sickle-shaped; as found in the dorsal fin of some sharks and dolphins, for example

Flagellate Refers to the whip-like portion (flagellum) of cells connected with feeding or reproduction, within simple multicellular organisms such as sponges

Flotsam Floating refuse or debris, usually the result of a wreck at sea

Fringing reef A coral reef occurring in the shallow water just off-shore

Gastropoda The largest class of molluscs, with representatives in terrestrial, freshwater and marine habitats. Members include slugs, snails, limpets and cowries

Gill An organ found in fish and many aquatic invertebrates, such as molluscs, which is used to absorb oxygen from water and to remove carbon dioxide

Gnathostomata Superclass of vertebrates with jaws and paired appendages, in contrast to the more primitive agnathans

Gnathostomulida Small phylum of microscopic marine worms

Hermaphrodite Organism possessing functioning male and female sex organs

Heterocercal Describes a tail fin in which the upper lobe contains some of the vertebrae of the backbone and is usually longer than the lower lobe

Hexactinellida Class within the phylum Porifera containing sponges with siliceous, or glassy, skeletons

Holothuroidea Class of echinoderms containing sea cucumbers

Homocercal Describes a tail fin in which both lobes are of equal length

Hyaline Clear or transparent; in animals it is a glassy substance usually associated with cartilage and skin

Hydrozoa Class of cnidarians where generations typically alternate between a colonial polyp (hydroid) phase and a medusoid phase. Medusae may form from individuals budded off by the colony. Includes the Portuguese Man-o-war

Ilicium The extensible part of the angling apparatus of anglerfish and frogfish (order Lophiiformes) formed from modified tissue on the first dorsal fin ray, which terminates in a 'lure' (see lure), used to attract prey close to the mouth

Invertebrate An animal lacking a backbone

Instar A larval stage in the life cycle of some invertebrates

Intertidal Between the tides

IUCN The International Union for the Conservation of Nature; responsible for assigning organisms to agreed categories or rarity

IWC International Whaling Commission

Jetsam Traditionally referred to cargo and objects from a ship that was washed ashore; now largely used in the same way as flotsam

Kingdom A major grouping within the living world; for example, the animal kingdom

Krill Shrimp-like crustacea that form part of the plankton and are an important food source for many animals, from fish to whales

Lamella A thin, membranous plate-like structure; also part of the delicate, blood-rich tissue in a gill

Laminarian One of several types of large brown seaweed or kelp

Lophotrochozoa One of the major groups of protostome animals, including the phyla Mollusca and Annelida

Lower shore The part of the shore that is only normally fully uncovered (exposed) by the lowest level of the spring tides. See also sublittoral

Malacostraca Class of crustaceans that includes krill, mantis shrimps, sand-hoppers and sea slaters

Mammal A warm-blooded vertebrate animal which suckles its young

Mammalia Class of jawed vertebrates whose members are mammals

Mandible One of the pair of jaw-like mouthparts found in some in crustaceans and insects

Mantle The folded tissue covering the body of molluscs; its outer layer secretes the shell

Marsupium The 'pouch' developed by some animals to brood their young – and which gives marsupial mammals their name; however, may also be present in creatures as tiny as sea lice

Maxillopoda Class of crustaceans including barnacles, copepods and ostracods

Medusa (pl. medusae) Free-swimming, bell-shaped cnidarians with a fringe of tentacles; may be a phase of sexual development in some jelly animals

Medusoid Relating to the medusa form or phase

Melon The lump of fatty tissue that forms the characteristic 'domed forehead' of many dolphins and whales

Metazoan A multicellular animal, i.e. one with cells differentiated into tissues and organs

Microtubule A very small protein filament found in cells

Middle shore The part of the shore that is covered and uncovered every 12 hours or so

Mollusca Phylum of bilateral invertebrates with unsegmented bodies and a mantle. Includes terrestrial and aquatic snails and slugs; also octopii, squids, clams, mussels and oysters

Molluscoid Of, or resembling, the molluscs

Monoplacophora Ancient class of molluscs whose few living members include the species *Neopilina galathea*

Morphology The study of the physical structure of an organism

Mucous Bearing mucus

Mucus The slimy, viscous fluid produced in the body of certain animals; used variously for lubrication and protection

Myxini Class of primitive jawless fish (agnathans) including the hagfish

Negative buoyancy Where an inanimate object or living creature is more dense per unit volume than water and will sink

Nematocyst A type of cell found in cnidarians which discharges a thread in order to sting or snare prey

Nematoda Phylum of simple, unsegmented worms found in terrestrial, freshwater and marine habitats

Nematomorpha Phylum of simple-bodied, parasitic worms with physical similarities to the nematodes. Commonly known as horsehair worms

Nemertea Phylum of unsegmented marine worms including ribbonworms, or proboscis worms

Neutral buoyancy Where an inanimate object of living animal is equal in density to the same volume of water and will therefore suspend in the water

Nictitating membrane Transparent 'third eyelid' in some species of cartilaginous fish

North Atlantic Drift A warm sea current

Notochord A rod of cells running along the back in the early stages of development in chordates; in most chordates it is later replaced by the spinal column, but in primitive forms it is retained in adult life

Nuda Class of ctenophores lacking tentacles

Nudibranch A gastropod mollusc of the order Nudibranchia that lacks a shell and often has a beautifully coloured body

Operculum The gill cover found in many bony fish; also the lid that closes the shell of some invertebrates

Ophiuroidea Class of echinoderms containing the brittle stars

Organelle A specialized structure found in a living cell, for example, the ribosomes and nucleus

Ossicle A small bone in the ear of vertebrates; also the plate-like structures in the skin of many echinoderms

Ostracoda Extensive crustacean group of generally small members, whose shape has given rise to common name 'mussel shrimps'

Otolith A small calcium carbonate granule found in the vertebrate inner ear; vital for balance

Over-winter To survive over the winter period, often in a state of dormancy

Ovigerous (Of legs) bearing eggs

Oviparous Reproducing by eggs which hatch outside the mother's body

Ovoviviparous Reproducing by eggs which are retained inside the mother's body until they hatch

Palp One of the sensory structures found around the mouth of various invertebrates

Pantropical Distributed throughout the tropics

Parapodium One of the many paired, paddle-like structures found on the side of polychate worms; used for locomotion in free-living types

Parasite An organism that lives in, or on, another organism at its expense, and depends on it for food

Parazoa Subkingdom of multicellular organisms, including sponges (Porifera), with less specialized cell arrangement that metazoans

Parthenogenesis The growth and development of an embryo without fertilization by the male; essentially virgin birth

Pedicellariae The tiny, pincer-like grooming and defensive structures on the bodies of starfish and urchins

Pelagic Living in the surface waters of the ocean

Peristome The area around the mouth in some invertebrate animals; the edge of the aperture of a spiral shell

Phoronida Small phylum of hermaphrodite marine worms that live in the substratum

Photophore A light-emitting organ often evolved by creatures living in habitats where little or no light penetrates; mainly used to attract partners for mating or prey

Phylogeny The evolutionary history of a group of organisms

Phylum (pl. phyla) One of the major subdivisions of a kingdom, consisting of one or more classes

Pinna The external ear flap of a mammal such as a sea lion

Plankton Microscopic plants and animals, including algae, protozoans and larvae, that drift in marine or fresh water

Planula A larval stage in the life cycle of some marine organisms such as cnidarians

Plastron Ventral, flat part of a turtle's shell, made up (as more visible parts of shell) of bony material with a layer of scutes (plates)

Platyhelminthes Phylum of creatures commonly known as flatworms; also includes parasitic tapeworms and flukes

Pleopod One of the paired abdominal appendages found in crustaceans modified for swimming and, in females, for carrying eggs

Podia The rows of suckerlike appendages on the underside of the arms of echinoderms, associated with gas and water exchange; also movement and manipulation of prey

Pogonophora Tubelike, benthic creatures that usually dwell in deep-sea habitats. Also known as beardworms

Poikilothermic Describes an animal whose body temperature fluctuates with the temperature of the surrounding environment

Polychaete A type of marine worm characterized by bristle-like appendages (chaetae) along its body; includes ragworm. Belong to the class Polychaeta

Polyplacophora Class of molluscs bearing a shell composed of overlapping calcareous plates. Includes the chitons

Porifera Phylum of invertebrate animals including the sponges

Positive buoyancy Where an inanimate object or living creature is less dense per unit volume than water and will rise

Posterior At, or towards, the rear

Proboscis A feeding tube

Prokaryote A cell which has genetic material lying free in the cell cytoplasm instead of contained within the nuclear membrane

Protostome A member of a group of multicellular animals in which the original embryonic opening (blastophore) becomes the mouth. Major protostome phyla include molluscs, annelids and arthropods

Pycnogonida Class of marine arthropod within the subphylum Chelicerata, consisting of sea spiders

Pyloric Referring to the pylorus, the part of the digestive system situated between the stomach and the intestine

Radial symmetry Of anatomy repeated around a central axis, like the arms of a starfish

Ray A small spine that supports the fin membrane in a fish

Reef A ridge of rock, sand or coral, usually in shallow water

Remipedia Class of cave-dwelling, free-swimming crustacean lacking pigmentation and eyes

Reptile A cold-blooded, vertebrate animal with a dry, scaly skin; most reptiles lay eggs with waterproof shells

Reptilia Class of jawed vertebrates whose members are reptiles

Rete mirabilis A network of blood vessels found in some animals, such as certain species of shark, that enables them to maintain their body temperature at a higher level than the surrounding water

Rorqual A type of baleen whale of the genus Balaenoptera, such as the blue whale

Rotifera Small phylum of minute worms with whiplike cilia on the head, giving the appearance of revolving wheels. Predominant in freshwater habitats

Sarcopterygii Class of primitive fish with rounded (lobed) fins, including lungfish and coelacanths

Scaphopoda Class of mollusc also known as tusk shells, with cylindrical shells open at both ends

Sclerospongiae Extinct class of fossil marine sponges

Scrimshaw Name given to the craft of fashioning by-products from whaling into ornaments; often involves the engraving of bones and teeth

Scutes Plates on a turtles shell; may be costal (on the side) or vertebral (across the back)

Scyphozoa Class of cnidarians that usually alternate between sessile polyp and free-swimming medusae forms, although some retain only one of these forms throughout their existence

Semelparous Of an organism that reproduces just once in its lifetime

Sequential hermaphrodite Organisms born as one sex but which later transform into the other, in contrast to Simultaneous hermaphrodites

Sessile Attached in one place; non-moving

Simultaneous hermaphrodite A species which has male and female reproductive organs that mature at the same time, making self-fertilization a possibility. May also be referred to as a synchronous hermaphrodite

Siphon Tubular organ in various invertebrates, usually connected with the sucking in and/or expulsion of water

Sipuncula Phylum of unsegmented wormlike creatures. Commonly known as peanut worms due to their tendency to retract into the anterior part of the body when disturbed

Sister group Closely related taxa; usually those appearing adjacent to each other in a typical family tree style classificatory diagram

Spermatophore Essentially a 'packet' of sperm

Spicule Minute crystalline fragment used as a skeletal support in sponges, for example

Spine The backbone, often used to describe the dorsal surface of an organism; also a long, narrow tapering structure – often venomous – such as the spine of a stingray or a weever fish

Spongin Interlocking, collagen-like fibrous material found in sponges such as the bath sponge

Spongocoel Central cavity of a sponge

Subadult Stage of growth where an organism possesses many of the physical attributes of an adult, but is not yet fully sexually mature

Subkingdom A major subgrouping of living things within a kingdom

Sublittoral Area below the littoral, or tidal, zone. Equivalent to lower shore

Subphylum A major subgrouping within a phylum

Substratum, or **substrate** The place where an organism is attached or situated, such as the seabed

Subtidal Below the tide level

Superclass A grouping between a phylum and a class

Suture Spiral seam or joint marking the junction of whorls of a gastropod shell

Symbiosis A relationship between different organisms in which each benefits from the association

Symbiont An organism taking part in a symbiotic relationship, for example, the photosynthesizing algae found in the cells of giant clams

Symbiotic Describes a relationship in which symbiosis occurs

Taxon (pl. taxa) Any grouping within the system of classification, such as a phylum, class or species

Teleost A member of the Teleostomi, the largest group of bony fish; includes most living species of fish except for primitive types such as sharks, rays, lampreys, sturgeons and lungfish

Tentacle One of the tactile or prehensile appendages found around the mouth in various invertebrates, such as in octopuses and squid

Tentaculata Class of ctenophores with retractable or reduced feathery tentacles

Test The 'shell' of a sea urchin or sand dollar

Thaliacea A small class of pelagic tunicates

Thorax The section of an animal's body situated between the head and abdomen

Tube foot A hydraulic appendage found in echinoderms, used in locomotion; part of the water vascular system

Tunicate A member of the phylum Tunicata, such as a sea squirt

Umbo (pl. umbones) One of the 'hinges' of a bivalve shell

Univalve Describes a shell consisting of one valve

Upper shore The part of the shore that is only normally covered by the highest level of the spring tides

Varix (pl. varices) One of the prominent ridges or ribs traversing the whorls of a univalve shell

Urochordata Phylum also known as Tunicata, containing the tunicates

Vertebrate An animal with a backbone

Water vascular system The hydraulic system found in echinoderms comprised of structures such as tube feet, and used for functions such as locomotion

Zooid An individual animal within a colony; usually used to describe cnidarians and ectoprocts (bryozoans)

Zooplankton Small invertebrate animals that feed on other plankton; zooplankton also includes the eggs and larvae of larger animals

INDEX

PICTURE ANCKNOWLEDGEMENTS

Note: t= top; m=middle; b=bottom; l=left; r=right

Illustrations
The illustrations appearing on the jacket, and on pages 1–7, 54–65 and 68–256 of this book, were supplied by the following artists: Mike Atkinson, Peter Barrett, Penny Brown, Jim Channell, Felicity Rose Cole, Julius Csotonyi, Stuart Jackson Carter and Denys Ovenden.
In addition, Anthony Duke created all maps appearing on pages 53br and 72–256; Peter Bull drew the artworks appearing on: 16bl, 17 (panel: denticles), 18b, 19tr, 19 (panel), 20b, 22t (panel), 24bl, 27t, 31tl, 31tr (panel), 37tl (Crustacean larval stages), 39b (panel), 44bl (panel), 45bl, 52b ('the moving continents'); Peter Barrett drew the mosaic moray appearing on 22b; Felicity Rose Cole drew the tube-eye appearing on 25tl; Penny Brown drew the four gastropod artworks appearing 34bl; Stuart Jackson Carter drew the large habitat artworks appearing on pages 54–65.

Photographs
The following photographs were taken by Rowan Byrne, www.marinecreatures.com
All jacket photographs except dolphin.
Inside pages: 6tr, 6bl, 7b, 10t, 11tl, 14t, 14bl, 15br, 17tr, 17 (panel: shark teeth), 18t, 20 (all), 23tl, 23tr, 23ml, 23mr, 24tr, 25tr, 27tl, 27tr, 29 (panel), 30tl, 30bl, 30bm, 31br, 32tl, 33 (panel), 34tl, 35tl, 35tr, 35mr, 36tr, 36ml, 36bl, 36br, 37

(panel), 38tl, 38tr, 38bl, 38br, 39tl, 40bm, 42 (all), 43tl, 43tr, 44ml, 44mr, 45t, 47 (all), 48 (all), 49 (all).
The following photographs were taken by Amy-Jane Beer and supplied courtesy of Origin Natural Science: 10b, 35 (panel: chiton photographs), 46t, 46bl.
The following photographs were supplied by photographers (as credited), courtesy of www.imagequestmarine.com:
2: Roger Steene; 16t: Kike Calvo/V&W; 17 (panel: far-left): Jez Tryner; 19tl: James D Watt; 19br: Valdimar Butterworth; 22mr: Masha Ushioda; 23bl: Carlos Villoch; 24tl: Roger Steene; 24 (panel): James D. Watt; 25br: Jez Tryner; 26 (panel): Hal Beral/V&W; 27bl: Carlos Villoch; 27br: Peter Herring; 28t: Jez Tryner; 28bl: James D. Watt; 28br: Peter Parks; 29tr: Roger Steene; 29br: Peter Parks; 30tr: Jim Greenfield; 30br: Peter Batson; 32tr: Masha Ushioda; 32bl: Roger Steene; 32br: Peter Parks; 33tr: Jim Greenfield; 33bl: Kåre Telnes; 39tr: Scott Tuason; 40t: Peter Parks; 41tl: Alexander Haas; 41tr: Valdimar Butterworth; 41br: Peter Batson; 43bl: Fritz Poelking/V&W; 43br: Scott Tuason; 66–7: Carlos Villoch; 131: Carlos Villoch; 90 (inset): Kåre Telnes; 92 (inset): Kåre Telnes; 191: Masha Ushioda; 207: Peter Parks; 209: Peter Parks; 199: Peter Parks; 239 (panel): Johnny Jensen.
The parasitic barnacle appearing in the panel on page 93 was taken by Andy Horton and supplied courtesy of www.glaucus.org.uk.
The sea lion photograph on 71 was taken by Patrick Fagot, courtesy of NHPA (www.nhpa.co.uk).